Moments of
Despair

Moments of

Despair

SUICIDE, DIVORCE,

& DEBT IN CIVIL WAR ERA

NORTH CAROLINA

David Silkenat

The University of North Carolina Press Chapel Hill

All rights reserved. Designed by Courtney Leigh Baker and set in
Minion Pro and American Scribe by Tseng Information Systems, Inc.
Manufactured in the United States of America. The paper in this book
meets the guidelines for permanence and durability of the Committee
on Production Guidelines for Book Longevity of the Council on Library Resources. The University of North Carolina Press has been
a member of the Green Press Initiative since 2003.

Library of Congress Cataloging-in-Publication Data
Silkenat, David.
Moments of despair : suicide, divorce, and debt in Civil War era
North Carolina / David Silkenat. — 1st ed.
p. cm.
Includes bibliographical references and index.
ISBN 978-0-8078-3460-2 (cloth : alk. paper)
1. Suicide—North Carolina—History—19th century.
2. Divorce—North Carolina—History—19th century.
3. Debt—North Carolina—History—19th century.
4. United States—Politics and government—1861–1865.
I. Title.
HV6548.U52N87 2011
362.975609′034—dc22
2010036102

15 14 13 12 11   5 4 3 2 1

Contents

Figures

Acknowledgments

B OOK ACKNOWLEDGMENTS OFTEN employ the rhetoric of debt to describe the help that the author has received. Given that this particular book is in part about changing conceptions of debt, I have thought long and hard about the ways and words I would use to thank those who have helped me along the way. I have, to be sure, accrued many debts in researching and writing it: financial, professional, and personal. I hope that my words here can start to repay these debts, though I doubt that I could ever hope to attain solvency through words alone.

I would like to thank the faculty, staff, and graduate students of UNC's Department of History. I have grown tremendously from their tutelage and friendship. In particular, I would like to thank William Barney for his constant support and whose extraordinary command of the Civil War era has inspired me, Heather Williams for some excellent reading suggestions, and Jim Leloudis, under whom this project had its origins. I would also like to thank Harry Watson and Kathleen DuVal for their assistance at a critical juncture. Many of my graduate school classmates also deserve thanks for their friendship during this process. I would particularly like to thank Tim Williams, Hilary Green, and Matt Harper for the aid they have given me. I would also be remiss if I did not offer thanks to Duke University's Peter Wood, whose undergraduate classes and continuing friendship have spurred me to think about history in new ways. Finally, I cannot thank Fitz Brundage enough for his guidance, generosity, and friendship throughout this process. He has read many chapter drafts with alacrity, attention to detail, and thoughtfulness. His insightful comments have forced me to reflect on the broader conclusions of my work and write with greater clarity and purpose. I am a better scholar because of him.

Research for this book has taken me to archives across North Carolina, and the final product would not have been possible without the aid of many librarians and archivists. I would like to thank the staffs of the Southern Historical Collection (particularly Laura Clark Brown) and the North Carolina Collection. The hours I have spent in Wilson Library perusing manuscripts and microfilm will never leave me. I have also benefited tremendously from the aid of librarians at the North Carolina State Archives, Duke University, East Carolina University, Appalachian State University, and Livingstone College. I would also like to thank the staffs of Dorothea Dix and Cherry hospitals for allowing me to study their records. These research trips were funded in part by the North Caroliniana Society's Archie K. Davis Fellowship, and I am very thankful for its generous aid.

The process of revising this work for publication was made considerably easier because of the support I've received from my colleagues in the Department of History, Philosophy, and Religious Studies and in the School of Education at North Dakota State University. The staff of UNC Press has been invaluable in helping me usher the manuscript toward publication, and the book has benefited significantly from the readers who reviewed drafts of the manuscript for UNC Press.

My deepest debts are to my family. I would like to thank my father for encouraging me to pursue a graduate degree and supporting me throughout the endeavor and my mother for providing an excellent retreat from North Carolina's August heat. My parents-in-law, Willis and Leona Whichard, deserve special praise for being there whenever I needed them and for opening doors for me that would otherwise have remained closed. My children, Chamberlain, Dawson, and Thessaly, have endured many hours away from their father as he buried himself in his books and papers, and they provided him with an excellent reason to put his work aside. My wife, Ida, has been my best friend and greatest inspiration. I dedicate this book to her.

Moments of Despair

Introduction

REFLECTING ON TRANSFORMATIONS in North Carolina society since the Civil War, Rev. Frank L. Reid, pastor of Raleigh's Edenton Street Methodist Church and editor of the *Christian Advocate*, observed in 1887, "There is a spirit of unrest, disquietude and discontent, which seems to foreshadow some great change. Public feeling is about to cut loose from its old fastenings. . . . Ties that have bound men together heretofore are weakening. . . . The foundations of our social fabric are being shaken."[1] Born in 1851, Reid had seen firsthand how the Civil War had transformed North Carolina's political, economic, and social order. Yet the most significant changes he had witnessed were intangible. An 1881 editorial in the *Raleigh Farmer and Mechanic* expressed a similar opinion: "We are tempted to add some regrets which occur to us whenever called upon to chronicle the decrease of any of our old citizens. These be the links, whose gradual dropping away, one by one, lessen the ties between the Old South and the New; the Old Time South, with her Hospitality, Chivalry, Integrity, and High Personal Honor; the New South with her Money Getting, Wire Working, Energetic, Scheming, Go-a-head, Free-and-Easy Social and Personal 'ideas'!"[2] At the root of both sentiments was a deep unease about how the Civil War had transformed the moral framework through which North Carolinians interpreted their world.

Generations of historians have explored the myriad ways in which the Civil War left a lasting imprint on the South. They have outlined in great detail how Confederate defeat and emancipation transformed the region's political, economic, and social landscape.[3] Yet, as the quotations above indicate, many North Carolinians understood that behind or beneath these visible changes, there had also been a significant shift in moral sentiments.

This study explores a few of these changing moral sentiments in Civil War era North Carolina. Specifically, it examines black and white North Carolinians' mutable views of suicide, divorce, and debt. As social constructs, suicide, divorce, and debt functioned as barometers of change reflecting the relationship between the individual and society.

This work argues that the Civil War forced North Carolinians to reevaluate the meaning of suicide, divorce, and debt and that the nature of this reinterpretation was predicated on race. The Civil War transformed how both white and black North Carolinians understood their place in society and the claims that society had upon them. For whites, this transformation entailed a shift from a world in which individuals were tightly bound to their local community to one in which they were increasingly untethered from social ties. For black North Carolinians, however, these trends headed in the opposite direction, as emancipation laid the groundwork for new bonds of community.

Albert Camus observed in *The Myth of Sisyphus* that suicide presents the "one truly serious philosophical problem": whether life in a given social context is worth living.[4] Committing suicide, Camus argued, answered that question in the negative, rejecting social ties in favor of an unknown fate. Divorce and debt, in their own ways, ask similar questions about the value of social relationships. When someone commits suicide, he or she is making a claim about the capacity for a particular individual to live in his or her society. When someone files for divorce, he or she is making a claim about marriage and the social and cultural institutions that sanctioned it. When someone participates in credit relationships, he or she is also making claims about the nature of social obligations. In turn, the ways in which others respond to another's decision to commit suicide, file for divorce, or declare bankruptcy reflect not only their own attitudes toward these practices but also what such actions say about social order, community values, and deviancy.

These moral barometers did not exist in isolation but developed in a complex interplay with individual behavior. Individuals evaluate the merits of a particular course of action based in part on prevailing cultural attitudes. Their decision either to conform to or deviate from cultural norms can itself exert some small force on the cultural attitude, strengthening or weakening it. Usually, ideas and actions reinforce each other in a period of stasis. At other times, however, small changes in behavior or attitudes can institute an autocatalytic process that can quickly transform old moral sentiments and create new ones.[5] To draw a biological metaphor, the Civil War started a cascade of change in this punctuated equilibrium of moral sentiments.

Some of the cultural changes documented in this study reflect broader patterns that transformed American society. Suicide, divorce, and debt all became pressing social questions during the nineteenth century, manifestations of what social critics considered the degradation of traditional society and the perils of modernity.[6] I argue, however, that in two significant respects, the ways in which North Carolinians understood suicide, divorce, and debt differed from broader patterns of cultural change. First, attitudes toward these cultural practices changed more abruptly and rapidly in the South than in American society as a whole. As historian James Roark has noted, slavery was "a kind of log jam behind which forces of social and cultural change had stacked up, and with emancipation, the South moved toward the mainstream of American development." The loss of the Civil War resulted in "torrents of change" that transformed not only the southern political and economic order but also the ways in which southerners understood themselves and their place in society. "In their mental habits and social relations," Roark argues, "change was subtle and intangible but even more fundamental."[7] Second, North Carolinians understood suicide, divorce, and debt through the prism of race, a characteristic not present in the national discourse on these subjects. At a fundamental level, questions of race shaped how North Carolinians interpreted suicide, divorce, and debt, encoding these cultural practices with racial meanings.

The significance of suicide, divorce, and debt as barometers of moral change in nineteenth-century North Carolina extends beyond their unique regional characteristics. They represent a sea change in the ways in which black and white North Carolinians understood their relationship to their communities and the varying importance of social stigma for enforcing certain patterns of behavior. Although treated separately, they are part of broad social transformation. While only a few hundred North Carolinians committed suicide, a few thousand filed for divorce, and hundreds of thousands coped with debt, white and black North Carolinians used a common vocabulary to describe these phenomena, differing in intensity and frequency but retaining a familiar rhetoric. Further, the radical changes in how black and white North Carolinians understood suicide, divorce, and debt parallel each other too closely to be mere coincidence. Instead, they provide the clearest example of how white and black North Carolinians' moral frameworks were transformed by the Civil War and emancipation. They reveal that the Civil War had a lasting significance in North Carolina's social order that extended well beyond 1865. These social reverberations continued for decades afterward, often not reaching their apex until the end of the nineteenth century.

The rough chronological boundaries of this study extend from 1820 to 1905, stretching forty years before the start of the Civil War to an equal period after the end of hostilities. Some scholars might dispute whether such a long period of time properly falls under the banner of the "Civil War era." Although more restrictive parameters might be appropriate for purely political or economic questions, I argue that certain types of social and cultural questions require a longer view in order to see the full articulation of change. The Civil War effected significant transformations in almost every aspect of southern life. Some of these changes, such as the end of chattel slavery, were readily apparent in 1865; others took decades to become fully evident.[8]

This work is organized into three parts, each of which is divided into several chapters. Part I, entitled "By His Own Hand," explores the changing meaning of suicide. Chapter 1 examines how antebellum white and black North Carolinians adopted very different attitudes toward suicide. The trauma of war and the elation of emancipation shook these attitudes at their foundation. Chapter 2 assesses how in the postwar period black and white North Carolinians constructed new interpretations about the meaning of suicide in the midst of what some commentators referred to as the "suicide mania" and how the postbellum medical community, particularly doctors associated with the state's mental hospitals, understood suicide and treated suicidal patients. Chapter 3 presents some hypotheses using recent research in suicidology to understand the Civil War's role in changing the frequency and meaning of suicide in North Carolina, and it investigates the sensational trial in 1889 of Dr. Eugene Grissom, the superintendent of the North Carolina State Insane Asylum, which focused on the proper treatment of suicidal patients.

Part II, entitled "To Loosen the Bands of Society," examines changing conceptions of divorce. Chapter 4 contrasts antebellum white North Carolinians' abhorrence of divorce (because it threatened social order) with enslaved black North Carolinians' more nuanced conception of marriage termination. Denied the legal right to sanction their unions and often forcibly separated from their partners, black North Carolinian slaves developed an alternative understanding of marriage's permanency. Chapter 5 investigates how the Civil War undermined many white marriages, leading to a dramatic increase in divorce in the postbellum period, while newly emancipated black North Carolinians sought to construct new cultural paradigms about divorce to reflect their new legal and social status. Chapter 6 examines how religious leaders, led by Bishop Joseph Blount Cheshire, sought to reform North Carolina's divorce laws so as to prevent what they thought was imminent social breakdown.

Part III, entitled "Enslaved by Debt," considers the evolving culture of credit and debt in nineteenth-century North Carolina. Chapter 7 explores how antebellum white North Carolinians constructed complex webs of credit and debt that served as both financial and social bonds of solidarity. Chapter 8 examines how economic conditions during and immediately after the Civil War completely decimated the antebellum credit system. Chapter 9 looks at the new ways in which North Carolinians coped with debt, including the development of new credit practices in general stores, pawnshops, and boardinghouses. Chapter 10 scrutinizes how agrarian reformers at the end of the nineteenth century sought to reform North Carolina's credit culture.

Ultimately, this book intends to complicate our understanding of the lasting consequences of the Civil War in the American South. To attribute white and black North Carolinians' changing views of suicide, divorce, and debt to the Civil War is not to resort to what Robert Penn Warren referred to as the "Great Alibi"—that all social ills in the South could be attributed (and thereby excused) by tying them to Confederate defeat.[9] Rather, by using ideas about suicide, divorce, and debt as barometers of moral change, we can develop a deeper understanding of the Civil War's lasting personal and psychological impact.

PART I

By His Own Hand

Suicide

I N JULY 1862, heavy fighting around Richmond and Petersburg overwhelmed the cities' hospitals with wounded Confederate soldiers. A
series of battles, known as the Seven Days, had left, according to one
North Carolina soldier, "the dead and dying actually stink[ing] upon the
hills."[1] In converted tobacco warehouses, banks, schools, and private homes,
doctors tended men from throughout the South. By early June, according
to a conservative estimate, the twenty-five military hospitals in the Confederate capital housed at least 5,000 soldiers; other observers placed the
figure at twice that number. Petersburg fared even worse, as more than 2,500
wounded soldiers overwhelmed the city's rudimentary hospital facilities.
Torrential rains at the end of May had turned the roads into mud, slowing
the arrival of mule-drawn carts carrying wounded soldiers, some arriving
weeks after receiving their injuries.

Of the wounded, thirty-one-year-old Captain Eugene Grissom of Granville County, North Carolina, considered himself lucky. Shot in the upper
leg on 23 June in the lead-up to the Battle of Mechanicsville, Grissom was
admitted to Moore Hospital in Richmond a week later, on 30 June. He was
transferred later that month to the Second North Carolina Hospital in
Petersburg, a converted Baptist church, evidence perhaps that his wounds
were healing. A graduate of the University of Pennsylvania's medical school,
Grissom was unable to walk without a limp and probably spent his initial
weeks in Petersburg in bed or hobbling around on crutches, providing whatever aid he could to the overburdened hospital staff. He could look around
the makeshift hospital to see the bodies of two dozen other soldiers from
his native state. As a trained doctor, Grissom knew that he probably would
recover from his injuries, assuming that his wound did not become infected.

He could see that many of the other patients in his ward would not share his fate. In the years that Grissom had practiced medicine, he had never seen such traumatic physical wounds. Several of his fellow patients had had limbs amputated. Indeed, during the past two months, Confederate doctors in Virginia had performed amputations on more than five hundred soldiers, almost half of whom did not survive the procedure. Other patients had abdominal wounds so severe that Dr. Edward Warren, the hospital's supervising physician, doubted they would live the night.[2]

Both Grissom and Warren recognized that the effects of combat on soldiers extended beyond their physical wounds. Many patients displayed deep psychological scars. Some believed that they were still on the battlefield, reliving their combat experiences over and over in their mind. Others cried all night. Some made no sound at all. Many patients appeared entirely rational one minute, only to explode the next. For both Grissom and Warren, their most memorable experience at the Second North Carolina Hospital came on the morning of 25 August 1862 while Warren made his usual early rounds and Grissom gingerly tested his weight on his wounded leg.

Admitted the previous night, nineteen-year-old John Roland had, like Grissom, fought in the Seven Days. Hospital attendants later recalled that he had slept well and had acted normally that morning. As Dr. Warren passed his cot, however, in a "sudden fit of desperation," Roland attacked him with a large knife, wounding him in the hand and neck, narrowly missing the jugular vein. As hospital attendants rushed to Warren's side, Roland assaulted them as well, stabbing one of them three times and nearly cutting three fingers off another. With blood splattered over the floor and hospital blankets, Roland stabbed himself in the chest and then cut his own throat twice, severing the windpipe. He then jumped out a nearby window, expiring some twenty minutes later on the sidewalk outside.[3]

The sight of Roland's suicide stayed with Eugene Grissom for the rest of his life. When he had recovered sufficiently, Grissom joined Dr. Warren's staff, replacing one of the attendants Roland had injured. After serving one term in the North Carolina legislature and as a delegate in the 1865 Constitutional Convention, Grissom was appointed by Governor William W. Holden to head the North Carolina Insane Asylum in Raleigh. During his twenty-one-year tenure at the Insane Asylum, from 1868 to 1889, Dr. Grissom treated hundreds of suicidal patients: indeed, more than a third of the patients at the hospital had either threatened or attempted to take their own lives. Suicidal insanity, Grissom wrote in his annual report to the state legislature in 1872, "from information in my possession . . . in this State, is largely on the increase." Grissom was struck by the extent to which suicide preyed upon the state's elite. Although the asylum was intended for those who could not afford private treatment, its halls were filled with college professors, merchants, and the children of planters. "Look through the Register of the Asylum of the Insane of North Carolina," Grissom wrote in the 1877 annual report, "and you will be appalled at seeing the names of so many of the good and great, who have been distinguished in the colleges, schools, legislatures and learned professions."[4]

Grissom was not alone in observing how common suicides had become among white North Carolinians in the three decades after the Civil War. Newspaper editors from across the state regularly remarked on how common suicide had become. Reporting on the death of Silas Steele in 1892, the *Winston-Salem People's Press* noted that "the suicide mania has struck Germantown."[5] Likewise, in describing the hanging suicide of Jane Teague in 1883, it noted that "this makes five suicides which have occurred in the Abbott's Creek neighborhood within our recollection."[6] The *Raleigh Farmer and Mechanic*, a weekly newspaper, provided the fullest coverage of the increase in suicides. In January 1880 it reported that "in our exchanges by Friday's mail were reports of eighteen cases of self-destruction"; ten months later it revealed that "suicides by the hundred every week are reported in our exchanges."[7] After running a half dozen suicide notices in recent weeks, the *Farmer and Mechanic* began its article about the death of the editor of the *Claredon Press* by exclaiming, "More suicides!"[8] The *Farmer and Mechanic* declared that suicide had become a "Self-Slaying Epidemic," claiming that "the year 1881 will be famous in history on many accounts, but its record for suicides will be without a parallel."[9] A year later, the paper was reporting on "suicides by dozens, by scores, by hundreds! Not a day passes without from five to ten cases." It seemed that many had become "tired of waiting for Death" and had succumbed to the "Suicide Mania."[10] The next year the paper concluded: "Suicides—It is enough to make one wonder at human nature, to read the daily accounts of *felo de se* [suicide] occurring all over the land. It is the legacy of the war we suppose. North Carolina now averages one suicide every other day!"[11]

Generations of historians have recognized the central role that violence has played in southern history. Slave revolts, lynchings, dueling, and feuds have dominated both the academic and popular conceptions of southern violence, while recent scholarship has explored rape, domestic violence, and slave-on-slave violence, among other forms of belligerence.[12] Despite this robust corpus on violence in southern history, very little scholarly attention has been given to the social role and cultural meaning of suicide, violence against the self.[13] As with other forms of violence, southerners imbued suicide with layers of meaning. This study of suicide borrows two concepts from this broader scholarship on southern violence. First, as a social construct, the meaning of suicide evolved over time, reflecting the changing social conditions in North Carolina over the course of the nineteenth century. Second, North Carolinians saw suicide, as they saw other forms of violence, primarily, but not exclusively, through the prism of race.

The Civil War and emancipation fundamentally reoriented how North Carolinians understood suicide in its social and cultural contexts. Many white North Carolinians believed that suicides had increased dramatically in the years after the Civil War. Further, the Civil War brought about a revolution in cultural attitudes toward suicide. Widely condemned by the white community in social, moral, and religious terms before the Civil War, suicides became a tolerable, albeit regrettable, choice by the end of the nineteenth century. Although suicide never lost its stigma as a deviant behavior, white North Carolinians came to sympathize with the plight of suicide victims in ways unthinkable to their antebellum forebearers. Suicidal Confederate veterans played a critical role in this postbellum reorientation. The deaths of these veterans, who were revered social figures, helped to moderate how white North Carolinians understood suicide.

While white North Carolinians became more tolerant of suicide after the Civil War, the state's African American population demonstrated the opposite propensity. Compared with whites, antebellum black North Carolinians demonstrated a comparatively permissive attitude toward suicide. This tolerance was particularly apparent in the 90 percent of the state's black population held in bondage. Prominent in a wide variety of accounts of slave life, suicide functioned as a one of the socially permissible responses to the injustices of bondage. After emancipation, however, this tolerant attitude toward suicide disappeared. In its place, black North Carolinians constructed a new ethos that abhorred suicide regardless of the circumstances.

CHAPTER ONE

Most Horrible of Crimes

Suicide in the Old South

I N 1798, the Philanthropic Society, one of the University of North Carolina's two debating societies, considered whether suicide was ever justifiable. Although vigorous debate ensued on both sides of the issue, the final resolution was unanimous: suicide was never justifiable. Even in the case of the legendary Roman matron Lucretia, whose suicide after being raped inspired the Roman Republic and countless Renaissance artists, the students concluded that her act was unwarranted.[1] This absolute condemnation of suicide typified the attitude of antebellum white North Carolinians. In their public and private discourse, they damned suicide as one of the most deplorable acts that an individual could commit. Their rhetoric affirmed a deeply held belief that suicide violated divine, social, and natural order.

Antebellum newspaper accounts routinely condemned white suicide victims for their action. Describing the death of John Domler, a German immigrant living in Salisbury, the *Winston-Salem People's Press* claimed that he "put a period to his life by committing that most horrible of crimes, suicide, with a pistol."[2] In 1843, the *Highland Messenger* adopted a similar tone to describe the shooting suicide of Francis M. Peeples, the eighteen-year-old son of a prominent lawyer. Declaring that the suicide was "horrible to relate," the paper explained that it printed an account of "the horrid affair" in the hope that it would "deter others from pursuing the same course. What a solemn warning to the youth of our country!"[3] Likewise, the *People's Press* reported in 1857 on the suicide of James Henry Robinson, a student at the University of North Carolina, observing that "we have not learned what cause led him to commit the terrible deed."[4] Newspapers repeatedly described suicides in such terms, "horrible" and "terrible" the most common labels.

Newspaper accounts reported the physical minutiae of suicides in graphic detail. For example, the *Raleigh Register* described Henry Picard's 1851 suicide at length, reporting that he "first attempted to cut his throat, and inflicted upon himself a frightful wound; failing in this, he took down a gun, put the muzzle in his mouth, and attempted to blow out his brains—but it would not go off. He finally seized a canister of powder, to which he applied a torch, and a terrible explosion followed, tearing open the windows and shattering everything in its way. The unfortunate victim of his own rashness was found in a shockingly mutilated condition, but not yet dead! He lingered until the next day, when he was released from his agonizing pains by death."[5] Likewise, the *Highland Messenger* described the suicide of Henry Johnson in bloody detail, noting that "the head was half disengaged from the body, his clothes and the ground around him were dyed in blood, and by his side lay a dull pocket knife with which no doubt the desperate deed was perpetrated."[6] The inclusion of these ghastly descriptions ostensibly condemned suicide victims.

The private discourse about suicide revealed similar sentiments. Burdened by failing business prospects, Enoch Faw, a lawyer and recent graduate of Trinity College in Randolph County, wrote in his diary in 1858, "Doing nothing will kill me. It makes me tired of life. It leads to no good result. If life don't amount to something noble I don't want to live longer. The sooner I get off the stage the better. Suicide would be a temptation. Lest I could commit suicide rather than live an inglorious life." Fearing the social stigma associated with killing himself, however, Faw could not bring himself to act upon his impulses. In his next diary entry, dated less than seven months later, he noted, "I feel peculiarly well this morning—comfortable, cheerful, just-right."[7] Business had improved.

While Faw feared the social condemnation that suicide would bring, H. T. Brown, a student at the University of North Carolina, could not bring himself to end his own life because of what he thought might happen to his soul after death. Emotionally and physically abused by his father and plagued by his own sense of inadequacy, Brown wrote in his diary in December 1857, "I sometimes have a high and vaulting ambition, and think I will someday make a grand man, but then I have too much common sense to delude myself with that dream for any length of time." A month later, his depression led him to the brink of suicide. However, fear that suicide would sentence him to eternal damnation stopped Brown from following through with the action. "I often feel weary of the long monotonous road before me," he wrote in his diary, "and I have often felt an inclination to voluntarily abandon it but there every one who reflects on such a subject must know that it is base and cowardly to do so and then if there is any truth in the Bible, what comes of such a death is a weighty consideration."[8]

In both public and private discussions, antebellum white North Carolinians couched their condemnation of suicide in religious terms. Reporting on the suicide of Robert Hamilton in 1840, the *Highland Messenger* claimed that he "rush[ed] unbidden into the presence of his Maker"; five years later, it used the same phrase to describe the suicide of John Tyson's teenage daughter.[9] Writing to his girlfriend in 1861, John Wesley Halliburton, a student at the University of North Carolina, described the suicide of a classmate as "a self murder . . . which sentences him to eternal death."[10] An 1852 letter from J. Edward Horton of Lenoir, North Carolina, to his Aunt Octavia expressed a remarkably similar attitude toward suicide. Describing the death of family friend Robert Pruit, he wrote, "Poor fellow who can tell where he is now; but the omnipresent, omnipotent, and all wise god. But from what I have heard and know he committed suicide, worst of all."[11] Horton was not alone in classifying suicide as the "worst of all." In 1859 Woodbury Wheeler of Murfreesboro, North Carolina, wrote to his sister describing a college classmate's suicide. He claimed that "all of course, censure him, but he has a harder master than the world to deal with."[12] In each of these cases, suicide's social stigma rested upon a religious presumption that those who committed suicide would suffer divine punishment. Rev. John Todd Brame offered probably the most damning religious condemnation of suicide in a sermon entitled "The Folly and Danger of Making a Covenant with Death and an Agreement with Hell" before his congregation in Washington, North Carolina, in 1849. Trying to reinforce the notion that eternal punishment awaits unrepentant sinners, he claimed that "in the case of suicides," the person is "dying at the moment of the commission of the crime" and therefore cannot atone for the sin and can never enter the kingdom of heaven.[13]

There is no evidence that the religious prejudice against suicide extended to burial practices. The custom of burying suicide victims at crossroads or outside consecrated ground, while common in medieval and early modern England, appears to have died out in the colonies before the American Revolution.[14] The grave markers from nearly fifty antebellum white suicides that I have been able to locate offer no indication that the deceased had taken their own lives and are indistinguishable from neighboring grave markers. There is some evidence, however, that suicide's stigma led suicide victims' families to bury their relatives privately and discreetly. When compared with their postbellum counterparts, descriptions of antebellum suicides noticeably omit any mention of the deceased's funeral, indicating perhaps that if funeral rites were held, they were inconspicuous affairs. One Baptist minister remarked that an antebellum suicide's sparsely attended funeral was "a solemn and instructive scene."[15]

White North Carolinians, then, held unequivocally negative attitudes toward suicide. Assessing how black North Carolinians understood suicide proves to be more challenging. Suicide regularly appears in the sources that social historians have traditionally used to understand the private lives of slaves: fugitive slave narratives, newspaper accounts in the northern black press, and Works Progress Administration interviews of former slaves in the 1930s. Indeed, taken at face value, these sources appear to support the claim that suicide was endemic among enslaved North Carolinians. At the same time, the use of slave suicide in abolitionist literature should be recognized as serving two roles. On the one hand, these accounts of slave suicide represent the real experiences of enslaved North Carolinians, as told by close friends and family members. For fugitive and former slaves, tales of loved ones taking their own lives were among their most palpable memories of bondage. These accounts allow us to understand how black North Carolinians understood suicide.

On the other hand, these accounts of slave suicide served a polemical function. The representation of suicide in abolitionist literature was intended to highlight the deep injustices of the institution. Written primarily for a northern audience, these accounts of slave suicide reflect both the former slave's attitude toward suicide and an effective rhetorical device for spurring an apathetic northern populace to support the abolitionist cause. Although the latter probably helped to shape the final presentation of suicide in the narrative, at their core these accounts of slave suicide reveal much of the raw emotional response of the narrator.[16]

The narratives of two fugitive slaves from North Carolina, Moses Roper and Moses Grandy, provide a meaningful starting point for a discussion of suicide in North Carolina slave culture. Both Roper and Grandy struggled with suicidal thoughts and repeatedly attempted to take their own lives. Examining how they characterized these tendencies and how other slaves and whites responded to their suicidal behavior provides insight into how antebellum black North Carolinians understood suicide.

Forced exile drove Moses Roper to contemplate suicide. Born in 1815 in Caswell County, Roper was sold or transferred at least a dozen times in the decade after his first owner died. These repeated dislocations tore Roper from friends and family, exacting a deep psychological cost. In his account, these bouts of melancholy became suicidal at the age of nineteen, when he was sold to a plantation owner known for his cruelty. On board a ship taking him to his new owner, "I procured a quart bottle of whiskey, for the purpose of so intoxicating myself that I might be able either to plunge myself into the river, or so enrage my master that he should dispatch me forthwith." On this occasion, Roper was prevented from ending his own life "by a kind Providence" of an elderly slave who, "knowing my intention, secretly took the bottle from me."[17]

The actions of both Roper and the old slave who prevented his suicide are indicative of the role that suicide played in the context of a slave society. Deeply committed to his own freedom from bondage, Roper sought to extract himself from a situation that he found unbearable. By listing suicide as one of two possible outcomes of his intoxication, Roper's account reveals that he saw suicide as a means of controlling his own enslavement. His personal experience to that point had confirmed that he had only limited means to dictate the terms of his life. Roper came to believe that suicide was among those options available to him. Like running away or physically resisting the dictates of an owner, suicide was an extreme response to the oppressive conditions of bondage but at the same time one that a significant number of slaves exercised or at least contemplated. The speed with which the elderly slave intervened to prevent Roper's suicide also indicates how common suicidal tendencies were among slaves. The old slave quickly recognized that Roper's intentions were not to drown his sorrows in a bottle of whiskey, presumably a common phenomenon, but to end his own life, implying that the old slave had seen enough during his life to distinguish between normal depression and suicidal tendencies.

Roper's suicidal inclinations did not abate after this first abortive attempt. Less than two months later, he again contemplated taking his own life by drowning. Running away from his new owner shortly after arriving on his plantation, Roper made a lengthy and hazardous trek through swamps, woods, and alligator-infested rivers to reach Savannah. Boarding a ship bound for Rhode Island, he anticipated that his freedom was only days away. However, when the captain discovered that Roper was of African descent and not Native American as he had claimed, the captain sent him back on the tugboat that had escorted them out of the harbor. Fearing that returning to the waterfront would mean returning to bondage, Roper again felt a "strong temptation to throw myself into the river."[18] Luckily for Roper, when the tugboat returned to Savannah harbor, he found another vessel willing to take him, and two days later he was a free man in New York.

The threat of sale and aborted attempts at freedom also drove Moses Grandy to contemplate suicide. Born in Camden County, North Carolina, around 1786, Grandy had suffered repeated forced estrangements from friends and family, including involuntary separation from two wives. Like Roper, Moses Grandy responded to these isolating events with both a deep depression and a commitment to securing his own freedom. When one of his owners threatened to sell him and thus separate him from his new wife, he responded, "I would cut my throat from ear to ear rather than go with him."[19] Instead of suffering through another traumatic separation, Grandy threatened to end his own life. As a form of resistance, he found this particular threat effective, as his owner immediately desisted from efforts to sell him. To threaten suicide, Grandy discovered, was more than a desperate response to a traumatic situation; it was a challenge to his owner's authority.[20]

Like Moses Roper, Grandy experienced a second episode of suicidal thoughts on a ship bound for freedom. After buying his own freedom and moving to Boston, Grandy returned via cargo vessel to the South to purchase the freedom of his son. Although he stayed on board ship for the duration of his trip, he feared that white authorities would attempt to return him to slavery. Witnessing a boatload of white men approaching his vessel, he "thought they were officers coming to take me; and such was my horror of slavery, that I twice ran to the ship's waist, to jump overboard into the strong ebb-tide then running, to drown myself." About to hurl himself to his death, Grandy hesitated, as "a strong impression on my mind restrained me each time."[21] Luckily for Grandy, the men did not attempt to return him to slavery, and he was able to return to the North unhindered, though he was unable to take his son with him.[22]

While Moses Roper and Moses Grandy recounted their own suicidal tendencies, other black North Carolinians remembered how the cruelties of slavery drove some to take their own lives. One slave from Franklin County recalled: "I helped to get a man's body out of the river who had drowned. He drew his wagon and team right in the river and drowned himself, almost drowned his master's team. His master was such a mean man and worked his slaves so hard that most of them either ran off or killed themselves."[23] The suicide of family members evoked the most vivid recollections. According to Annie Tate, her grandmother was driven to suicide after her owner beat and then sold her husband to a slaveholder in Mississippi. When she discovered that her husband was gone, "pore gran'maw am nigh 'bout crazy so she walks off'en de plantation. Down on de aidge of de plantation runs de Neuse [River] so gran'maw gits dar, an' jumps in."[24] Similarly, Elizabeth

Keckley, a slave in Hillsborough, recalled her uncle killing himself to avoid a beating. After losing a set of plow lines, he "hung himself rather than meet the displeasure of his master. My mother went to the spring in the morning for a pail of water, and on looking up into the willow tree which shaded the bubbling crystal stream, she discovered the lifeless form of her brother suspended beneath one of the strong branches. Rather than be punished the way Colonel Burwell punished his servants, he took his own life. Slavery had its dark side."[25]

Charles Ball's narrative presents perhaps the most thorough assessment of the role of suicide in slave society. Born in Maryland around 1780, Ball labored in slavery in several southern states, including a brief stint in North Carolina. Everywhere he went, he witnessed his fellow slaves taking their own lives. "I do not marvel," he wrote, "that the slaves who are driven to the south often destroy themselves. Self-destruction is much more frequent among the slaves in the cotton region than is generally supposed."[26] Like Moses Roper and Moses Grandy, Charles Ball felt suicidal at times. When sold and separated from his wife and children, Ball descended into a depression so severe that "I had at times serious thoughts of suicide so great was my anguish. If I could have got a rope I should have hanged myself."[27]

We have no reliable measure of how many slaves took their own lives. However, suicide's prominence in fugitive slave accounts and abolitionist newspapers indicates that many African Americans saw suicide as a fundamental aspect of slave life. The *National Era*, a black abolitionist newspaper based in Washington, D.C., claimed in 1850 that anyone who was "a reader of the newspapers . . . must know that suicide among slaves is not infrequent."[28] Frederick Douglass's *North Star* estimated that "thousands of American slaves" had taken their own lives.[29] As Mark Schantz has recently observed, black newspapers tended to interpret slave suicides sympathetically, viewing them as acts of defiance and bravery.[30]

Many North Carolina slaves saw suicide, at least in part, as a form of resistance to an owner's authority.[31] To be sure, the forces that drove an individual slave to suicide were complex, and accurately delineating the conscious and unconscious motivations in each case is beyond historical analysis. Nevertheless, when examining the behavior of slaves and slave owners in the context of slave suicides, one observes many of the familiar patterns of negotiation present in other forms of resistance. Slaves sought to maximize their autonomy and material condition, while slave owners sought to minimize these factors.

The ways in which slave owners responded to and attempted to prevent suicide among their slaves support the argument that suicide functioned as an extreme form of resistance. "Suicide amongst the slaves is regarded as a matter of dangerous example," wrote Charles Ball, "and one which it is the business and the interest of all proprietors to discountenance and prevent. All the arguments which can be devised against it are used to deter the negroes from the perpetration of it; and such as take this dreadful means of freeing themselves from their miseries, are always branded in reputation after death, as the worst of criminals; and their bodies are not allowed the small portion of Christian rites which are awarded to the corpses of other slaves."[32] Like a runaway slave, a slave who killed him- or herself meant two forms of loss to his or her owner. First, the owner lost the slave's labor and the money invested in purchasing and maintaining him or her. Second, and probably more troubling to the owner, was the example that an individual suicide could provide to other slaves. Unlike with a runaway slave, however, the owner had no hope of recapturing a suicidal slave. Instead, he attempted to use the suicide's body as a tool for preventing suicide by other slaves.

While, as Charles Ball indicates, North Carolina slave owners attempted to defame the victim of suicide, outside North Carolina, slave owners were known to take even more extreme measures to dissuade their slaves from killing themselves. In the Caribbean, owners often mutilated the body of slave suicides and forced their other slaves to witness the disfigured corpse. At times, owners forced their slaves to actively participate in this corpse mutilation.[33] As a deterrent, this public spectacle resembled the punishments meted out by slave owners against other forms of slave resistance. Just as slave owners routinely used public whipping of runaway or recalcitrant slaves to intimidate and control other slaves, they used the physical mutilation of suicide bodies to frighten and prevent others from following the same path.

Slave owners worried that a slave's suicide would reflect poorly on their reputation. According to Charles Ball, "When a negro kills himself, the master is unwilling to let it be known, lest the deed should be attributed to his own cruelty. A certain degree of disgrace falls upon the master whose slave has committed suicide—and the same man, who would stand by, and see his overseer give his slave a hundred lashes, with the long whip, on his bare back, without manifesting the least pity for the sufferings of the poor tortured wretch, will express very profound regret if the same slave terminates his own life, to avoid a repetition of the horrid flogging."[34] Therefore, the suicide of a slave presented an owner with something of a dilemma. He needed to publicly display the body of the suicide victim to dissuade other slaves from killing themselves; at the same time, he wanted to prevent knowledge of the suicide from spreading beyond the bounds of his plantation.

Although most whites' blanket disapproval of suicide extended to the actions of slaves, the determination of some slaves to end their lives could lead to a degree of begrudging respect. When a runaway slave held in a county jail in Rutherford County hanged herself, the local newspaper observed, "We have never known an instance where so much firmness was exhibited by any person as was by this negro. The place from which she suspended herself was not high enough to prevent her feet from touching the floor; and it was only by drawing her legs up and remaining in that position that she succeeded in her determined purpose."[35] In this case, the newspaper applied, perhaps ironically, the positive virtues of firmness and determination, virtues usually reserved for white men, to an enslaved black woman for committing an act that usually received severe condemnation.

If the suicide of an individual slave can be seen as a form of resistance akin to running away, slave group suicide presented a challenge to owners' authority in much the same way that a slave revolt did. Like slave rebellions, group suicides were an extreme response to the injustices of slavery. Also like slave rebellions, group suicides were comparatively rare events, though group suicides have been documented in South Carolina, Georgia, Brazil, Cuba, and throughout the West Indies.[36]

Only one account of group suicide survives from North Carolina. Around 1805, a group of slaves newly imported from Africa were assigned to dig a drainage canal on a plantation near Lake Phelps in Washington County. After hours of backbreaking labor, "they would grasp their bundles of personal effects, swing them on their shoulders, and setting their faces towards Africa, would march down into the water singing as they marched till recalled to their senses only by the drowning of some of the party."[37]

Several factors help to explain the prominence and comparative tolerance of suicide among North Carolina slaves. First, slaves took their own lives because of the devastating effects that slavery inflicted upon their psyches.[38] Although slavery in North Carolina was not a "total institution" as claimed by some historians, the demands of slavery took a significant emotional and psychological toll on those in bondage.[39] Even if the vast majority of North Carolina slaves were able to adjust and accommodate to the injustices regularly inflicted upon them in ways that fell short of taking their own lives, they understood the emotional distress that would prompt suicide in another. When they saw another slave take his or her life after being forcibly separated from a loved one or having hopes for freedom dashed, they could sympathize with the anguish and torment that such an experience would engender. "Surely if any thing can justify a man in taking his life into his own hands, and terminating his existence, no one can attach blame to the slaves on many of the cotton plantations of the south, when they cut short their breath, and the agonies of the present being, by a single stroke," argued Charles Ball. "What is life worth, amidst hunger, nakedness and excessive toil, under the continually uplifted lash?"[40]

A second explanation for the role of suicide among North Carolina's slaves can be traced to African beliefs that survived the Middle Passage. While white antebellum North Carolinians inherited centuries of Christian tradition that condemned suicide, black oral tradition included African ideas about suicide that were at odds with Christian tradition. Although most of North Carolina's African American population can be nominally described as Christian by the eve of the Civil War, a variety of African religious and moral traditions remained, even if subsumed under a veil of Christian practice.[41]

The West African cultures that generated most of North Carolina's slave population displayed an array of attitudes toward suicide, ranging from absolute condemnation to widespread acceptance. Most fell somewhere in the middle of this spectrum, condoning suicide under certain specific conditions. In Yoruba and Ashanti cultures, for instance, suicide could be "acclaimed as praiseworthy," and those who took their lives because they found "life burdensome, disgraceful, and perilous" could receive "great credit and honour."[42] Among slave traders, some West African cultures developed reputations for being particularly prone to suicide. For example, Igbo slaves from the Calabar region of the Niger Delta were stereotyped as suicidal, while the Fantee were believed to rarely commit suicide.[43]

One of the inherited African religious traditions retained by some North Carolina slaves included the belief that after death they would return to an earthly paradise in Africa and that suicide provided the quickest route to this paradise. According to Charles Ball, "They are universally of opinion, and this opinion is founded in their religion, that after death they shall return to their own country, and rejoin their former companions and friends, in some happy region, in which they will be provided with plenty of food, and beautiful women, from the lovely daughters of their own native land."[44]

Antebellum North Carolina, then, had two distinct traditions for understanding suicide. White North Carolinians saw suicide as a fundamental threat to divine and social order, reeking of anarchy and atheism. They condemned the act whenever the opportunity presented itself. Alternatively, black North Carolinians saw suicide as an understandable response to traumatic situations and even, at times, as a form of resistance to slavery. Inherited in part from West African cultural traditions, this tolerant attitude toward suicide recognized the deep emotional toll of slavery on the individual psyche.

These distinct conceptions of suicide reflect broader assumptions about the relationship between the individual and society in antebellum North Carolina. White North Carolinians espoused an organic conception of society in which each individual had his or her place, a position ordained by God and ratified by community consensus. Suicide threatened this order by giving individuals the opportunity to reject their position and thereby upset the social order by taking their own lives. Black North Carolinians, however, tended toward a more atomized conception of society. Their experience in slavery taught them that social relationships could be easily fractured by circumstances beyond their control. As black North Carolinians sought to retain some semblance of individual autonomy within social, institutional, and legal constructs that denied their humanity, some turned to suicide as an ultimate declaration of independence, protest, and despair.

These contrasting and deeply entrenched attitudes did not survive the Civil War. The traumatic experience of fighting and losing the Civil War forced white North Carolinians to reconsider and reformulate how they understood suicide. As Confederate veterans and community leaders apparently committed suicides in record numbers, the white community in North Carolina came to believe that suicide did not necessarily warrant outright social condemnation. Instead, white North Carolinians developed a more nuanced understanding of the meaning of suicide, predicated on the individual actor's situation and motivation for ending his or her own life. For black North Carolinians, emancipation also forced a reassessment of the role and meaning of suicide. Once they were freed from the bonds of slavery, suicide could no longer serve as a symbol of resistance. Instead, postbellum black North Carolinians claimed that suicide affected only whites and that their abstinence from the suicide mania demonstrated their social virtue. What had once been acceptable, even laudable, now stood at odds with new standards of personal and community responsibility.

CHAPTER TWO

The Self-Slaying Epidemic
Suicide after the Civil War

P ROFESSOR RALPH GRAVES'S suicide in 1889 sent the community at the University of North Carolina into mourning. Born in 1851, Graves had grown up on campus, where his father had taught and where his great-grandfather had served as the school's first steward. Graves himself attended the university until 1868, when he transferred to the University of Virginia, receiving a master's degree in mathematics, chemistry, and physics.[1] Graves returned to the University of North Carolina in 1875 to teach, attaining the title of professor of mathematics in 1881. In 1877, he married Julia Charlotte Hooper, the daughter of fellow faculty member J. De Berniere Hooper.

Though widely respected by both students and faculty, Graves struck many observers as removed from the realities of everyday life. He buried himself in the remote world of pure mathematics, taking little interest in politics or community affairs. Absorbed in his work, Graves succumbed to a deep depression in February 1889. Although the exact nature of his depression remains unclear, one former student remarked that he believed that "Prof. Graves' sickness was brought about by his continued and deep concentration of mind in propounding these original [mathematical] problems."[2] Shortly after his death, his neighbor Cornelia Phillips Spencer observed:

> He was an omnivorous reader—perhaps the best read man in the faculty—he was a born mathematician, taking great delight in the problem of the higher walks of science. He erred probably in this direction, preferring to seclude himself with book and pencil, rather than attend to the claims of social life, or the imperative demands

of hygiene. Men of letters in these days cannot afford to neglect their health. The nervous system is more irritable and more frail than it was a generation ago, and breaks down with a crash under the work which would not have touched our fathers.[3]

Unable to continue teaching, Graves first sought treatment at a private sanitarium in Baltimore. Believing himself sufficiently recovered by the late spring of 1889, Graves returned to North Carolina only to find his depression returning almost immediately. After one particularly frightening incident, Julia Graves took her husband to the North Carolina State Insane Asylum in Raleigh, where he was admitted on 30 June 1889. Less than two weeks later, there at the asylum, Graves cut his own throat.

Hearing of Graves's death, members of the university's Philanthropic Society, the same organization that had concluded a generation earlier that suicide was never justifiable, decreed a period of mourning, declaring that the walls of its meeting hall would be draped in black for thirty days. Professor George Winston, Graves's faculty colleague and one of his closest friends, eulogized him in a lengthy speech on University Day in the autumn after his death. Graves, he declared, was man of "usefulness and honor." Winston also noted how Graves had been buried in a place of honor in the university cemetery, among "the graves of his friends, preceptors, and predecessors."[4] William M. Little, one of Graves's former students, assessed the mood surrounding his death most clearly: "If Prof. Graves' life had been prolonged he would have continued to bring great honor to the University and to North Carolina. His memory cannot be too much honored by the people of the State. Perhaps, North Carolina is not inclined to honor as much as she should, her leading thinkers and actors. . . . Although only thirty-eight at the time of his death, he may justly be considered one of the great men in the history of the State."[5] *Raleigh News and Observer* editor Josephus Daniels, who had studied under Graves when he attended the University of North Carolina, declared that Graves had been one of the smartest men he had ever encountered.[6] The repeated references to Ralph Graves's scholarly and personal virtue, despite the way in which he ended his life, indicate the extent to which white North Carolinians' assessment of suicide had changed.

In the aftermath of her husband's suicide, Julia Graves received dozens of letters offering solace. Francis Venable wrote that "in his death the whole state has sustained a great loss; this however is not comparable to your loss and affliction." Perhaps most comforting was the letter of Dr. A. W. Mangum, the university's professor of mental and moral science:

As to the distressful history of the last few weeks, let me, as a Minister, say that as you have striven to be and to do all that a devoted wife could; and as you have doubtless made your supplications to a loving Father in Heaven to help you and to lead him to the best in all things,—you should now draw near to His Throne of Grace and quietly lay your heart before Him for His loving comfort and support leave all to Him who careth for you; for only He Knoweth all that was thought and felt before the light of reason was dismissed and only He, the Lord, Knoweth how to judge all of a life. Try to learn your heart upon Him who gives us assurance that He pitieth us that fear Him as a father pitieth his children.

Instead of interpreting his suicide as a sign of Graves's moral weakness, those comforting Julia Graves chose to see his death as part of a divine plan that they could not fully comprehend. The ordered society that had existed in North Carolina before the Civil War had been replaced by a world in which only faith could make sense of the tremendous social upheaval. The death of her husband, wrote one correspondent to Julia Graves, proves that "truly God moves in a mysterious way!"[7]

The reaction to Graves's death stands in stark contrast to how antebellum white North Carolinians responded to similar acts and underscores a significant shift in the attitudes of white North Carolinians toward suicide after the Civil War. Although white North Carolinians never went so far as to embrace suicide as a noble choice, the discourse over suicide became much more sympathetic to the plight of those driven to end their own lives. Newspapers no longer classified suicides as "horrific" or "terrible"; instead, they were much more likely to label them as "sad" or "regrettable." In January 1871, for instance, the *Winston-Salem People's Press* headlined its article about the death of John Hester "Melancholy Suicide."[8] Although the same paper had in previous years routinely labeled suicides as "horrible," it now saw fit to affix a much less derogatory adjective to the act.

Newspaper editors were also more likely to emphasize the positive aspects of the deceased's life rather than dwell on the way in which that life ended. Downplaying Margarette Seybold's suicide in her death notice, the *Raleigh Daily Sentinel* noted in 1873 that her will left substantial "sums to orphan asylums, and to the church."[9] Reporting in 1885 on the death of William Crow, an Aetna insurance executive in Raleigh, the *News and Observer* noted that "the suicide of Mr. Crow was the topic of conversation yesterday. It caused general sadness among all classes of people, who felt the loss of a good citizen, whose position here for years had been prominent and who had been earnest in doing good." Unlike the suicide described by Woodbury Wheeler in 1859 when the victim received universal condemnation, William Crow's death brought only laudatory remarks. The newspaper concluded its assessment of Crow by observing that he "was thoroughly earnest in all his business work, and in his church affairs was equally devoted. He filled the measure of good citizenship."[10]

Part of this change in attitudes toward suicides resulted from a collective realization that while individuals chose to commit suicide, the community as a whole shared in some measure for the conditions that drove them to end their lives. Reporting on the suicide of a poor and disadvantaged woman, the *People's Press* asked its readers in its "Lesson for the Day" if her death "instinctively recalls to every generous mind the oldest of questions, 'Where is Abel, thy brother?'"[11] By the turn of the century, many white North Carolinians had concluded that suicide, though an individual act, had social causes.

Theological attitudes toward suicide victims underwent a similar shift. While newspaper articles about suicide before the Civil War routinely included religious language to damn suicide victims, such invectives rarely appeared afterward. In his *Homiletic Encyclopedia*, a popular reference work among southern clergy, R. A. Bertram argued that suicide was a comprehensible and understandable desire: "Overwhelmed by misery, not a few who are without hope in the world anticipate its [life's] period, and prematurely and violently terminate their earthly career. But no one can be so mistaken or so unhappy as the suicide. In their moments of despair, even good men have desired to be in the grave."[12] Although Bertram ultimately did not condone suicide, he accepted that good Christian men could wish their own deaths.

Not all clergy shared in this sentiment, especially when confronted with suicide as an abstract concept rather than in the form of an individual suicide. An unsigned article from the *Methodist Review* in 1894 claimed that suicide had become "one of the saddest and most painful features of modern civilization." Suicide was akin to atheism, as it "is the dire offspring of unbelief. It repudiates obligation to God and humanity." Although the author recognized that no specific biblical passage prohibited suicide, he claimed that "if no positive biblical precept prohibit[s] suicide [then] the whole spirit and tenor of the Bible forbid it." Even under the most traumatic of situations, the author notes, suicide can and should be avoided because of the eternal consequences on the soul. "Suicide," he concludes, "implies rebellion against God, is a sin that does not admit of repentance, and is, therefore, an unpardonable crime."[13]

This view, however, was in the minority. In 1885 an article in the *Quarterly Review of the Methodist Episcopal Church, South* noted that many virtuous Christians suffered from depression, which occasionally gave "rise to the thought, and even the act of suicide," observing that Goethe, Beethoven, Chateaubriand, and George Sand all suffered from suicidal depression.[14] A year earlier, an article in the same publication claimed that the suicidal impulse was almost universal among white southerners: "Who, we may seriously ask, is safe from his own hands? We may be safer from violence without than violence within. We may stand in less danger of assassination than self-destruction. . . . It may be seriously doubted if there is a man who has had a large share of the duties and vexations of life who has not at some time had the tempter to whisper in his ear wily words and delusive promises." Although he stopped well short of endorsing suicide, by normalizing the suicidal impulse the author, a Methodist preacher from Texas, recognized and sympathized with it. He also transferred the moral blame for the increase in suicide from the individual to society as a whole. To combat suicide, he claimed, "society must be reformed, made vulnerable, and given a conscience. It must become the guardian of our holy traditions, raise the standard of honor, and make holy the bridal and marital vows."[15]

This limited acceptance of suicide extended into private discourse. The dozens of condolence letters that Mattie McNair received after the suicide of her twenty-five-year-old brother Will in 1898 reassured her about the fate of his soul. At a young age, Will established himself as an "enterprising citizen and leading merchant" in Laurinburg. Because of his success in business, McNair made himself "a favorite among young people of this and other communities." On a cold January morning, Will, "whom all respected and many, very many truly loved, in the moment when his troubles pressed heaviest upon him, his mind gave way, that with the hand so unlike his own, used the razor and pistol by his side, with such fatal effect." News of his death spread rapidly through the community. "The best evidence of his worth," wrote one newspaper obituary, was that "the hold he had upon the people, for miles around, was attested by the vast congregation, one of the largest, if not the largest, ever assembled in the Presbyterian church of this place to hear the funeral sermon." Most important to his sister Mattie was that his soul would be preserved in heaven. Friends and family urged her to "remember that God in his goodness works in a mysterious way and he chasteneth those he loves and that your loss is his eternal gain, and that the time will be short when we will meet him to part no more."[16] Mattie must have been reassured to know that suicide victims could go to heaven.

Other white suicides in North Carolina at the turn of the century displayed similar characteristics. Writing in his diary in 1899, Abraham Oettinger of Kinston described the suicide of one of his closest friends and fellow businessmen, Sig Einstein. Upon hearing that his friend had shot himself, Oettinger rushed to Einstein's store, where he "found Sig on the bed in their private room, and with a bullet hole in his head. I remained in the room & he expired in about 15 minutes." As he prepared the body for the arrival of the undertaker, Oettinger witnessed numerous members of the Kinston elite coming to see the body, not out of horror or disgust but out of respect. Einstein's funeral the next day, Oettinger recorded, was one of the best attended Kinston had ever seen, a fact confirmed by a newspaper clipping Oettinger included with his diary. It claimed, "We think it was the largest crowd ever in attendance at a burial here. . . . The immense crowd and the sympathy and sorrow shown attests to the popularity of Sig with all our people." In another newspaper clipping included with the diary, Einstein was lauded as "one of the cleverest and most popular young men of Kinston and was a favorite with all."[17] Like Will McNair, Sig Einstein was praised in death despite the way in which he chose to end his life. Although suicide never became a noble act, many white North Carolinians came to understand that when their privileged young men took their own lives, it did not necessarily negate their accomplishments.

This reinterpretation occurred during what many white North Carolinians believed to be a significant increase in suicides since the Civil War, a phenomenon known variously as the "suicide mania," the "suicide epidemic," or the "self-slaying epidemic." The unreliability of suicide statistics during this period makes it difficult to determine whether this perception reflected a real phenomenon or merely an increased awareness of suicide. A survey of suicide articles in North Carolina newspapers from 1840 to 1893 reveals that suicide became dramatically more visible in the white public discourse after the Civil War (see Fig. 1).[18] In the two decades prior to the Civil War, North Carolina newspapers in this survey ran 70 suicide articles, representing 55 discrete individuals, amounting to fewer than 3 per year. The period during and immediately after the Civil War likewise displays very few suicides: only 3 per year between 1861 and 1870. However, as newspaper coverage during this period was considerably more fragmentary, especially during the final years of the Civil War and the early years of Reconstruction, suicides may have appeared in newspapers now lost.

FIGURE 1. Suicides reported in North Carolina newspapers, 1840–1893.

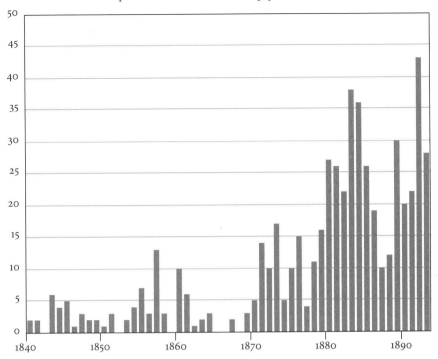

The situation changed radically after the Civil War. In 1871, for instance, North Carolina newspapers reported 14 suicides, more than twice as many as had been recorded in any single year during the previous three decades. After 1871, notices of suicides became more and more common in North Carolina newspapers, reaching an apex of 31 suicides in 1883. All told, between 1871 and 1893 the newspapers ran 459 articles about suicide, representing 386 individual deaths, an average of nearly 17 per year.

It is hard to say whether this dramatic increase in the coverage of suicides in North Carolina's white newspapers represents an actual change in the suicide rate. It can be argued that the increase in suicides documented in newspaper death notices represents only a change in newspaper coverage rather than in actual suicides. Indeed, a study of suicide articles in the *New York Times* between 1910 and 1920 indicated that an increase of suicide coverage in the newspaper had no bearing on the actual rate of suicide. Although the *New York Times* dramatically increased its coverage of suicides, particularly in sensational front-page articles, the actual suicide rate in New York remained relatively constant.[19] Several factors indicate, however, that contrary to the *New York Times* study, the increase in suicide articles in North

Carolina newspapers during the nineteenth century may have represented a real change in the suicide rate in the state. First, unlike the articles in the *New York Times* study, suicide articles in North Carolina newspapers were rarely on the front page. Instead, they were minor notices, buried in the interior of the paper, usually in sections entitled "Local News" or "State News." While the editors of the *New York Times* realized that placing suicide articles prominently on the front page could help sell newspapers, suicide articles in North Carolina newspapers rarely amounted to more than a paragraph and therefore would have had a negligible impact on sales. Second, before the Civil War, more than a quarter of the suicide articles in North Carolina newspapers described deaths that occurred outside the state. Presumably, had there been more suicides in North Carolina during this period, newspaper editors would have included them. After the Civil War, when suicides became more common in the state, editors reported out-of-state suicides less frequently.

The question of whether the increased coverage of suicides in the press represented a real change in the suicide rate occurred to contemporaries as well. In a series of articles on suicide in 1897, a *Leslie's Illustrated* editor pondered whether "perhaps there are not really any more suicides than there always have been, only nowadays we read about them all in detail in the newspapers." After pondering this problem, however, he concluded that "this theory is the veriest delusion — no serious investigator of the facts has ever entertained it for a moment."[20] Other contemporaries also believed that newspapers could provide the best indication of the level of violence in the South. When journalist Horace V. Redfield attempted to assess the frequency of homicide in the region in 1880, he turned to newspapers, believing that they more accurately measured the murder rate than official records.[21]

One of the few surviving public records supports the numbers provided by newspaper accounts. Between 1887 and 1893, the City of Raleigh collected information about each death within the city limits in a large bound folio now housed in the State Archives. All the suicides recorded in this volume received coverage in the city's newspapers, indicating that newspapers provided at least as accurate a measure of the frequency of suicides as any public records.[22] Furthermore, newspapers uncovered at least a dozen suicides in Raleigh that were not recorded in the city records. Therefore, although suicide articles may not perfectly gauge the suicide rate in North Carolina during the late nineteenth century, they present the best available source to assess changing rates of suicides in the state.

North Carolina newspapers did not, of course, report every suicide in the state. Undoubtedly, a number of North Carolinians took their own lives in relative anonymity, their deaths shielded from the newspapers by friends and family. In other cases, deaths that to the modern eye appear to have been suicides were not classified as such. For example, newspapers usually reported the deaths of those hit by trains while lying on tracks as accidents rather than suicides. Reporting on the death of James Wooten in 1871, the *People's Press* observed that "a railroad track is one of the strangest of all sleeping places, yet we are every now and then, compelled to record such accidents as above."[23] Wooten's death may not have been a suicide, of course; he may have been murdered and his body placed on the railroad tracks, or maybe he did indeed fall asleep as the newspaper indicated. Regardless, his case demonstrates some of the difficulties in identifying suicides in the historical record.[24]

Even if these newspaper accounts fail to provide a full record of suicide in postbellum North Carolina, they do provide meaningful insight into the social profile of suicide. Clear patterns emerge from newspaper accounts about who committed suicide, why they chose to end their lives, and the methods they employed. North Carolinians who chose to end their lives after the Civil War were disproportionately young white men with some degree of social standing. They killed themselves for a variety of reasons, including insanity, poor health, family problems, and financial problems. Similarly, they chose diverse methods for committing suicide, including firearms, hanging, drowning, and drug overdosing. Teasing apart this profile reveals how dramatically the Civil War undermined the social foundations of white society in North Carolina, leading some to end their own lives.

Men accounted for more than three-quarters of the white suicide victims after the Civil War, although the frequency of female suicide appears to have increased over time. Women accounted for less than 15 percent of the suicides in the three decades before 1870; by the 1880s, almost a third of suicides were women.[25] In this respect, North Carolina's suicide epidemic mirrored trends found elsewhere in the United States and in Europe, where, as suicide rates increased, the gender distribution became more balanced. Gender did not seem to factor heavily into how suicides were described in newspaper accounts, as journalists employed similar language to describe men and women who took their own lives.

Newspaper accounts indicate that the "suicide mania" afflicted North Carolinians of all ages. Suicides ranged in age from thirteen-year-old Ashby Carroll, who shot himself because of "mortified pride" in 1876, to the ninety-two-year-old Annie Hand, who ended her life with rat poison in 1891; the median age given for suicide victims was in the mid-thirties.[26] Many articles described the victims' ages qualitatively rather than quantitatively. Approximately a quarter of the suicide notices identify the victim as "a young man." Therefore, it may be said that although suicide preyed upon North Carolinians of all ages, a disproportionate number of its victims were in young adulthood.

Newspaper accounts indicate that the geographic distribution of suicides was relatively uniform throughout the state. While urban areas received their fair share, just as many suicides occurred in the state's rural areas. In Wake County, for instance, more suicides took place outside the Raleigh city limits than within, even though the majority of the population of Wake County lived in Raleigh. The central Piedmont region of the state appeared to have a slightly higher number of suicides, although these counties also had the largest populations and the most thorough newspaper coverage. All told, the "suicide mania" of the late nineteenth century stretched from one end of the state to the other.

Approximately half of the suicide articles offered some indication of the social status of the victim. Of these suicides, a disproportionate number appear to have come from the middle or upper class. At least thirty of the suicide victims were identified as "well-to-do farmers" or planters, approximately 20 percent of those whose status can be ascertained. For example, Fendal Southerland, who hanged himself in 1878, was at the time of his death Orange County's second largest planter, having owned dozens of slaves before the Civil War.[27] Likewise, the *Raleigh State Chronicle* reported that George Washington Wynn, a planter in Robersonville, was worth nearly $25,000 when he ended his life with a shotgun in 1890.[28] Less than two years later, the same newspaper described the suicide of David Avera, one of the state's wealthiest planters and the son-in-law of the governor.[29] In 1891, the *News and Observer* reported on the drowning suicide of Major W. W. Hampton, "a prominent and well-to-do citizen" of Surry County, who left an estate valued at $23,000, including "the famous 'Swan Pond' farm on the Yadkin River."[30] Members of the new professional elite that developed in the South after the Civil War also succumbed to the suicide mania, including two dozen merchants and businessmen, nine doctors, five lawyers, three ministers, and three newspaper editors. Suicide preyed upon many of North Carolina's wealthiest and most prominent citizens.

The suicides of women and young men were frequently linked to prominent men in their family. Reporting on the suicide of eighteen-year-old

David Cowles in 1890, the *State Chronicle* focused as much attention on the reaction of his father, Congressman William H. H. Cowles, as it did on the death itself, noting that the father "was informed of the accident by Senators Ransom and Vance, who received a telegram announcing the fact. He was completely prostrated, and had to be carried to the office of the Clerk of the House, where he remained for more than an hour before his friends deemed it wise to take him to his hotel."[31] Likewise, in 1880 the *Raleigh Farmer and Mechanic* reported on the suicide of a young man "who was a son of Rev. Henry M. Mood, the well-known clergyman," without even providing the deceased's name.[32] Probably the most extreme example of this tendency can be seen in the suicide of a woman identified as Mrs. Sullivan of Germantown in 1893. Neglecting to provide her first name, the *State Chronicle* did mention that she was the "wife of Dr. H. L. Sullivan," the daughter of Dr. Jones of Bethania, and "the sister of Miss Kate Jones, Senator E. B. Jones, of Winston, Dr. Robert Jones, of Salem, [and] Dr. Abe Jones of Walnut Cove."[33]

Many more articles indicated social standing without reference to occupation. For example, the *People's Press* described suicide victim John Hester as "a well-known citizen and one of the leading merchants at Kernersville."[34] Likewise, it described William Wolff, a drowning suicide, as "a prominent and highly respected old citizen of Surry county" and Thomas Eaton, who hanged himself in one of his tobacco barns, as "one of Davie county's prominent and worthy citizens."[35] More telling may be the relative absence of the poor and powerless among those who committed suicide. Fewer than a dozen suicide victims out of the nearly five hundred identified in this survey were described as poor or coming from poor families.

Almost all suicide articles called attention to the method that suicide victims used to end their lives (see Fig. 2). Approximately one-third chose firearms for the deed; hanging and throat cutting were also common methods. Drowning appeared to have been particularly common among women, as more than half of drowning suicides were women, including the aptly named Ophelia Ridenhour.[36] Almost 10 percent chose to take some form of poison. Opiates, such as laudanum and morphine, tended to be the poison of choice, as they ensured a painless death and were readily available in drug stores to cure a variety of ailments.[37]

Although newspaper editors never failed to indicate when someone committed suicide in a particularly spectacular or bloody way, as suicides among white North Carolinians became more common after the Civil War, suicide articles tended to devote less attention to the method employed and more

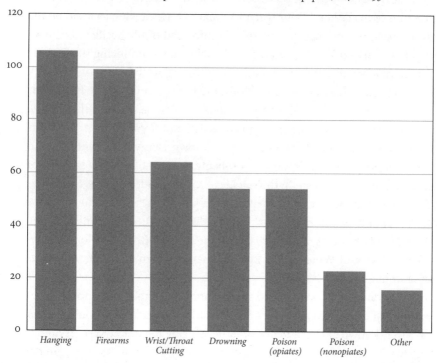

FIGURE 2. Suicide methods reported in North Carolina newspapers, 1840–1893.

attention to describing the life of the individual who committed the act. The graphic descriptions that characterized antebellum suicide articles gave way to more balanced accounts that focused on the overall narrative arc of the deceased's life rather than exclusively on its final downward spiral.

Articles describing attempted suicides did surface in North Carolina newspapers periodically. One of the earliest attempted suicides was described cryptically by the *Hillsborough Recorder* in 1869: "We are informed that a man named Crabtree living down in the neighborhood of Capt. Lyons has recently made two attempts to take his life. One time he was lectured on the impropriety of the deed by an old negro man, and he desisted in the attempt. But the next morning his wife was just in time to save him from hanging himself in the barn."[38]

As suicides became more common, however, descriptions of attempted suicide became more specific. In 1874, the *People's Press* reported that "Mr. R. E. Riddick, of Enfield, attempted suicide by swallowing laudanum. He was laboring under mental aberration at the time, consequent upon business pressure. When discovered he was walking the railroad track some distance from the town, and nearly exhausted. He is recovering slowly."[39]

Likewise, in 1889, the *News and Observer* described the attempted suicide of Lizzie Alexander, a fifty-year-old spinster from a prominent family living near Charlotte. According to the newspaper, Miss Alexander had attempted to take her own life on several previous occasions, only to be thwarted by family members. On this occasion she managed to cut her throat with her brother's recently sharpened razor, leaving a deep gash. Finding her soon after she had committed the act, her family summoned a doctor from Charlotte, who told them that the wound was serious but that he expected her to recover.[40] Similarly, in 1891, the *State Chronicle* reported that Robert Paylor "attempted suicide last night by drinking laudanum. The drug did not take its desired effect, and he is yet alive, though in a precarious condition."[41] The presence of these attempted suicides in the newspapers indicates the extent to which suicide was becoming more common in North Carolina.

In a pre-Freudian world, newspaper editors rarely looked beyond proximate causes to understand why individuals took their own lives. For instance, in 1884, the *Farmer and Mechanic* attributed "a perfect shower of suicides last week" to "the intense heat, joined with financial trouble."[42] When most postbellum North Carolinians constructed explanations for suicide, they looked to immediate stimuli, very rarely attempting to trace the causes to events in the deceased's past. In a little more than half of the suicide articles, newspaper editors offered some explanation of the causes that led the deceased to kill themselves. Insanity figured prominently in the vast majority of these. Indeed, suicide and insanity were so closely linked that many suicide victims were labeled as insane solely because they killed themselves. For example, the *News and Observer* noted that before Helen Woodward drowned herself, "the mind of the deceased had not previously been affected." Even so, the paper concluded that her suicide was evidence that she must have been insane.[43] Likewise, in describing the suicide of Col. Abner Parker, the *Hillsborough Recorder* concluded, "It is supposed that his mind was upset."[44] This conception that all suicide victims suffered from insanity conformed to mid-nineteenth-century medical opinion. In an 1847 article attributed to "A Southern Physician" published in the *American Whig Review*, the author indicated that most doctors believed "the Suicide is always insane."[45]

In those articles that identified a specific cause for the suicide beyond insanity, poor health ranked as the prime reason, factoring in almost a third of the cases. In describing the "Sad Suicide of Mrs. A. W. Frapps," the *News and Observer* attributed her death to "her mind [which] had been impaired by continued ill health."[46] Family problems placed a close second as a motivation for suicide. Although many of these suicides were ascribed to the vague grounds of "domestic troubles," newspaper editors found particular interest in suicides caused by unrequited or prohibited love. For example, the *People's Press* attributed Jeannie Anderson's 1886 suicide to the fact that "she was engaged to be married to a young man who disappointed her, and married another girl."[47] Likewise, it reported that a young woman named Westmoreland hanged herself in 1889 because "she was in love with a young man but on account of her youthfulness was informed [by her parents] that she must reach the age of twenty before she married and further that the young man would not be allowed to call again. She said that she could not stand this."[48] Similarly, the *State Chronicle* reported that Maggie May, a young woman from the city of Winston, killed herself in 1885 when she was "forced, by parental authority, to wed where her heart was not."[49]

Among the most bizarre of these suicides was that of William Harman, who thought that he was his own grandfather. The *News and Observer* reprinted his 1892 suicide note:

> I married a widow with a grown up daughter. My father visited our house very often, fell in love with my step daughter and married her. So my father became my son-in-law, and my step-daughter my mother, because she was my father's wife. Some time afterward wife had a son—he was my father's brother-in-law and my uncle, for he was the brother of my stepmother. My father's wife, i.e., my step-daughter, had also a son. He was, of course, my brother, and in the meantime my grandchild, for he was the son of my daughter. My wife was my grandmother, because she was my mother's mother, I was my wife's husband and grandchild at the same time. And, as the husband of a person's grandmother is his grandfather, I was my own grandfather.

The newspaper observed that "he can scarcely be blamed for killing himself under the circumstances."[50]

An equally bizarre suicide was reported by the *State Chronicle* in 1890, when it attributed the death of J. T. Bolling to his "peculiar and absorbing fascination" with a twelve-year-old boy. When Bolling first met Ed Lynn, he was struck by the similarities between the boy and his own deceased child. Convinced that Lynn was a reincarnation of his son, Bolling became obsessed with the child, going so far as to get a job teaching at his school. When the boy's father grew concerned about Bolling's obsession, he demanded that his son have no further contact with him. Believing that he had lost his son for a second time, Bolling went to the boy's house, handed a suicide note to an African American sharecropper working in a nearby cotton field, walked into the woods, and shot himself twice in the head with a .42-caliber pistol. In his letter, addressed to the object of his obsession, Bolling wrote, "If you had loved me as much as I loved you, you would have written to me, even if your father had whipped you every day. . . . I would give ten dollars in gold to see and talk with you for five minutes."[51]

Financial reasons ranked slightly lower than domestic problems as a cause for suicides. In a few cases, suicides were attributed to absolute poverty. When a woman attempted to drown herself and her three children, the *People's Press* claimed that the attempt was because "she had no home, no food, no work, no hope, and that death seemed the only relief possible."[52] Likewise, in 1861 it reprinted the suicide note of John Domler, a German immigrant: "You will find enclosed a letter, which will show you that a man who had charge of all the money I possess has absconded with the same, and left me totally ruined, without money and resources, among strangers in a strange country. Having no means to go any further, and without any chance to earn a livelihood, I am compelled to put an end to my miserable existence."[53] In many more cases, however, suicide resulted when prosperous white North Carolinians suffered shameful financial setbacks or embarrassments. Although the *People's Press* attributed A. V. Sullivan's 1875 suicide to financial embarrassment, it also noted that the High Point lawyer had several thousand dollars in cash and securities at the time of his death. When John Hester, a wealthy merchant from Kernersville, cut his throat in 1871, his death was attributed to "business cares and embarrassments," such that "his endeavors to overcome his embarrassments caused too severe a strain upon his mental organization, and he succumbed in the struggle."[54] In other cases, the obituary writers made a conscious effort to exclude financial motivations in their descriptions of suicides. When William Crow, an insurance executive in Raleigh, shot himself in 1885, the local newspaper made note of the fact that "his affairs are not thought to be in anywise embarrassed. He was a man of means."[55]

Because they looked primarily to proximate causes to explain individual suicides, white newspaper editors were never able to construct meaningful explanations for the "suicide mania." The increased visibility of suicide confused, shocked, and, at times, amused them. Despite the thousands of words used to describe how and why individual North Carolinians killed themselves, newspaper editors had difficulty finding any to explain the phenomenon as a whole. The *Farmer and Mechanic* may have come closest to crafting an overarching explanation when it stated simply, "It is the legacy of the war, we suppose."[56]

The suicide of Isaac Erwin Avery in 1904 demonstrates how much attitudes toward suicide had changed by the turn of the century. Born into one of the most prosperous families in the state, Avery could count among his ancestors North Carolina's first attorney general, a state supreme court justice, two governors, four Confederate generals (including Stonewall Jackson), and several wealthy planters. After graduating from Trinity College in 1893 and spending several years in China as the U.S. vice-consul general in Shanghai, Avery settled in Charlotte, where he gained prominence as an editor and columnist for the *Charlotte Observer*. When he took an overdose of laudanum on 2 April 1904, he stood at the height of his fame.[57] News of his death spread quickly. His own newspaper reported that "the intelligence of the death of Mr. Avery swept over the city like a flash, and excited the keenest grief. It is not an exaggeration of the fact to say that he was dearer to the heart of the community than any man in it."[58] Likewise, the *Greensboro Record* noted that "from friend to friend in whispered accent, from neighbor to neighbor in tender tone, from corridor to corridor, from room to room, from home to home over the busy phone in stifled voice the sad message sped."[59]

When North Carolinians received news of Avery's suicide, they reacted not by condemning him as they would have done a generation earlier but largely by ignoring the fact that his death had not come naturally. His obituaries, which in several newspapers ran for two or three pages, mentioned the circumstances of his death only in passing. Instead, they focused on Avery's ability and manly virtues. The *Raleigh Christian Advocate*, for instance, observed his "frank and tender nature" and noted that "everyone with whom he came in contact was his close friend." About his suicide, it simply stated that "the taking off of Mr. Avery was sudden. God knows best."[60] The most thorough coverage, naturally, came from the *Charlotte Observer*, which saw Avery as the culmination of southern manhood: "He closed as he began his career on earth and ever sustained it—a gentleman. He was descended from a knightly race, and illustrated in his life its loftiest virtues. He came of a people who regarded honor first, and who afterwards, were distinguished for intelligence, courage, for public service, for public and private virtues. There was never a man who discriminated more nicely between the right and wrong of things, or who lived more neatly to that ideal of a man as brave as a lion and as gentle as a woman."[61] Letters to Avery's father also reinforced this idea that his son lost no social standing or honor as a result of his suicide. Governor Charles Aycock wrote, "I beg to share your sorrow in the death of your noble son. Everybody loved and admired him." Another correspondent wrote that Avery was "a noble son by inheritance and conduct, and more, a nobleman in culture, aims, labors, ideals, hopes and accomplishment." He reassured the grieving father that "whilst you shall wait at the gate for his unreturning footsteps long and late, if our religion is not vain, his greeting will hail you at the gate of the Eternal City."[62]

A year after Isaac Avery's suicide, his friends and admirers published a collection of his essays entitled *Idle Comments*. Neither the lengthy introduction nor the biographical essay at the beginning of the collection mentioned Avery's suicide explicitly, although they did note his "untimely and tragic death." Instead, the volume's editors focused on Avery's virtuous life. They observed that he was "the most engaging of men. Handsome as Apollo, with a countenance clear-cut and proclaiming in every line his gentle birth; tall, massive of frame, he combined with these physical attributes a manner as genial as the sunshine." An aristocrat with a populist streak, Avery "thoroughly identified with the best phases of the city's life, and was a recognized leader in almost every movement that promised benefit to the people. While he was a leader in the best social life of the city, he was popular with all classes."[63]

Ignoring Avery's suicide in the introductory material, the editors did make a nod to it in the body of the text by reprinting an article Avery had written a couple of years earlier about suicide. In a description of a suicide that sounds eerily like his own, Avery focused on the victim's suicide note, which simply stated: "Just Tired." The victim, a "well-known" and "singularly handsome fellow," represented a conundrum to Avery. Had this man been insane, Avery could have understood how and why he committed suicide. But there was no indication of insanity. How could a sane man take his own life, especially when blessed with all the material comforts life had to offer? "The mind grasps such things feebly, and, in knowing suffering, shudders at the limitless possibilities of human agony."[64] While Avery did not understand how someone could choose to end his or her own life, his treatment of the event indicated a respect for the act and the actor.

ALTHOUGH WHITE NORTH CAROLINIANS filled the pages of their newspapers and private correspondence with references to suicide, fragmentary evidence suggests that black North Carolinians did not share in the "suicide mania." Looking through both white and black newspapers for references to African American suicides, one finds only a small fraction of the number of white suicides. Compared with the hundreds of references to white suicide, only fifteen black suicides appeared in either black or white newspapers in the three decades after emancipation.[65] Although this numerical imbalance probably overstates the extent to which suicide had become a predominantly white phenomenon, it indicates that white suicide had become very visible, while black suicide had become almost invisible.

Several possible explanations exist to account for the comparative absence of black suicide from the written record. First, it may reflect biases in late nineteenth-century journalistic practices. White newspaper editors may have considered the black suicides less newsworthy than their white counterparts. Black newspaper editors, who rarely referred to either black or white suicides, may have had different standards about the propriety of publicizing suicides, especially among those publications with a religious orientation, such as the *Star of Zion*. The comparative paucity and limited archival retention of black newspapers from North Carolina during this period would only compound this problem. Second, black families may have done a better job than whites in concealing the suicides of family members from the broader public. If true, this would suggest that black families on the whole felt a greater shame and dishonor associated with suicide than whites, leading them to take greater lengths to disguise or obscure suicides. Third, the comparative absence of black suicide in the written record could represent a real disparity in the number of African Americans who chose to end their own lives. Unfortunately, the available evidence does not readily reveal the extent to which these or other factors contributed to the relative invisibility of black suicide in the primary sources.

Regardless, the few references to suicide in African American sources indicate that many African Americans believed that suicide primarily affected whites and was rare in their community. One former slave interviewed by the Works Progress Administration in the 1930s introduced a description of her enslaved aunt's suicide by noting, "They say Negroes won't commit suicide."[66] She consciously contrasted the present reality, in which suicides were uncommon among African Americans, with the antebellum context in which her story took place.

This association between suicide and the slave past also manifested itself in a short story by one of North Carolina's most famous black authors. Originally published in 1889 in the *Atlantic Monthly*, Charles W. Chesnutt's

"Dave's Neckliss" describes the suicide of a virtuous slave driven mad by his owner's cruelties. In a tale within a tale, Uncle Julius, an aged former slave, recounted the story of Dave's suicide to two newcomers to the community. Chesnutt contrasted the revulsion of Julius's postbellum audience with the comparative composure of the slaves who witnessed Dave's suicide, indicating perhaps that although suicide had once been common in the black community under slavery, it had become rarer in freedom.[67]

According to Newell Ensley, a prominent African American educator who taught in Raleigh during Reconstruction, "There were three of the white men's vices which his people did not imitate—they were not skeptics, they were not infidels, and they did not commit suicide." His explanation for why African Americans did not commit suicide, however, strains credibility: "White reflects light, and therefore the face of the white man *reflects* the light, and he goes through life a melancholy creature; while the face of the black man *absorbs* light, which penetrates to his soul and makes him a glad, careless, jolly creature." As evidence, Ensley cited the case of Johnson C. Whitaker, a West Point cadet of mixed racial origins who had attempted suicide. Noting that Whitaker was "three parts white and two parts black," Ensley argued that "if he had been a black man, he would never have injured himself . . . ; if he had been a white man, he would have hung himself; but as he was neither white nor black, . . . he hurt himself just a little."[68]

As Ensley's account indicates, suicide had become coded as a white phenomenon after the Civil War. Like many African American intellectuals during the late nineteenth century, Ensley believed that the moral status of the black community had improved dramatically since emancipation. He saw the apparent absence of black suicide as evidence that African Americans increasingly led moral and godly lives.[69] Contrasted with the apparent increase in white suicides, African Americans' ostensible abstinence was considered to be a sign of their essential virtue. As we shall see in the next chapter, Ensley was not alone in racializing the discourse over suicide in postbellum North Carolina.

The abrupt shift in attitudes toward suicide indicates how radically different black and white communities in North Carolina experienced the Civil War and its aftermath. Black North Carolinians, who had demonstrated a limited acceptance of suicide before the Civil War, came to reject it outright after emancipation. White North Carolinians, who had demonized suicide during the antebellum period, moderated their stance as hundreds succumbed to the "suicide mania." These contrasting trajectories indicate that the Civil War had begun to unravel white North Carolinians' organic society while allowing black North Carolinians to construct new bonds of community that restrained individuals from taking their own lives.

ALTHOUGH NEWSPAPER ACCOUNTS about the spreading "suicide mania" indicate that many North Carolinians believed that white suicide had become increasing frequent since the Civil War, few attempted to create an overarching explanation to account for the phenomenon. Indeed, newspaper editors, who were quick to include accounts of individual suicides in their pages, never expounded a theory for the "suicide epidemic." North Carolinians looking to the national media to find such an explanation would have been baffled by what they read. Articles in publications such as *Leslie's Illustrated Weekly*, *Popular Science Monthly*, *Yale Review*, and *Galaxy* repeatedly attributed suicide to the increase in immigration, poverty, and urbanization—none of which appeared to hold in the case of North Carolina.[70]

Indeed, only within North Carolina's medical community could one find concerted efforts to craft an explanation for suicide in its local dimensions. In articles in the *North Carolina Medical Journal*, in their private writings, and in reports to the state legislature, doctors in North Carolina, particularly those associated with the state's insane asylums, devoted themselves to understanding and controlling the spreading threat of suicide. Authorized in 1848 by the North Carolina legislature and admitting its first patients in February 1856, the North Carolina Insane Asylum in Raleigh became the primary conduit through which North Carolina confronted the "suicide mania." Joined in 1880 by the Eastern (Colored) North Carolina Insane Asylum at Goldsboro and in 1883 by the Western North Carolina Asylum at Morganton, the North Carolina Insane Asylum functioned as the epicenter of contentious debate over the origins, meaning, and treatment of suicide.[71]

A couple of factors distinguish the history of North Carolina's public insane asylums from comparable institutions in other states. First, North Carolina lagged behind the national asylum movement, which had its highwater mark in the 1830s. North Carolina was the last of the original thirteen states to open an insane asylum; the state's failure to provide for the needs of its mentally ill residents was particularly egregious considering that the neighboring states of Virginia and South Carolina were the first two states in the country to open state-funded insane asylums, in 1773 and 1828 respectively.[72] Although some lawmakers advocated for opening an asylum before 1848, the most notable among them Governor John M. Morehead, not until Massachusetts asylum advocate Dorothea Dix petitioned the state legislature did significant momentum develop for opening an insane asylum. Personally witnessing the suffering of the state's mentally ill population, many of whom languished in county jails, Dix teamed with state Democratic leaders John W. Ellis and James C. Dobbin to present the case for an asylum. In a moving speech before the state legislature in December 1848, Representative Dobbin described his own wife's struggle with mental illness, which resulted in her death. In sympathy with Dobbin's loss, his colleagues voted to authorize the creation of an asylum. Even so, funding issues delayed its opening until 1856.[73]

Unlike its sister institutions in Virginia, South Carolina, Kentucky, Louisiana, and Maryland, the North Carolina Insane Asylum in Raleigh categorically refused to treat African American patients before the Civil War. To be sure, most state-sponsored southern insane asylums admitted only a handful of black patients. Asylum superintendents believed that mentally ill slaves could be effectively treated by their owners, while the number of free blacks suffering from mental illness was small enough not to burden the asylum facilities unduly. At Virginia's Eastern Lunatic Asylum in Williamsburg, which had the most liberal policy of admitting African Americans of all the southern insane asylums, the black population never exceeded 10 percent of the residents.[74]

Under the leadership of Superintendent Dr. Edward Fisher, the early years at the asylum in Raleigh were blessed with generous funding from the state legislature and comparatively few patients. Dr. Fisher, who had worked for several years at a Virginia asylum, devoted the majority of his time to the construction of the facility, set atop a large hill on the outskirts of Raleigh, surrounding the main buildings with gardens and orchards. Medical thought at the time dictated that such a bucolic setting was essential to the treatment of the insane. Although the facility was designed to house more than two hundred patients, Dr. Fisher rarely had to contend with half that number. Suicidal patients were relatively rare in the first five years of the asylum's operation. In his report to the state legislature in 1857, Fisher noted that suicide had claimed its first victim at the asylum. He wrote:

> The first case was that of an unfortunate individual, who, previous to and up to the day of his admission, labored under a suicidal form of mania for more than twelve months, during which time he had made more than one attempt at self-destruction, first by throwing himself into a well, and subsequently by means of a sharp instrument; the effects of which last attempt were plainly visible upon his

person when brought to us. Having failed in both, he finally resorted to the expedient of effecting his purpose, by abstaining from food and nourishment of all kind; and notwithstanding the continued and persevering efforts made to induce him to take nourishment, and the repeated efforts to administer it to him, by artificial means consistent with his enfeebled condition and emaciate frame, he finally sank a victim to this long cherished delusion.[75]

This incident indicates suicide's rarity in antebellum North Carolina and how unaccustomed even seasoned asylum administrators like Dr. Fisher were to dealing with suicidal patients. In later years, when suicide had become more common and its treatment at the asylum in Raleigh almost routine, suicidal patients would almost invariably be treated earlier and more effectively. Dr. Fisher cared for only a handful of other suicidal patients in the early years of the asylum; his report for 1858 referred to the fact that none of the other suicidal patients had been able to end their lives while at the asylum as a "cause of congratulation."[76] Fewer than a half dozen of the patients treated at the asylum prior to the Civil War were suicidal.

While the North Carolina Insane Asylum thrived before the Civil War, the years during and after the conflict were its most challenging. Funding for the asylum dropped dramatically during the war, and its facilities sustained considerable damage from occupying Union soldiers quartered there during the war's final months. The end of hostilities did not improve matters. Informed by Freedmen's Bureau officials that he would have to admit African American patients, Dr. Fisher saw the number of patients of both races applying for admission to the asylum increase dramatically.[77] His report for 1866 indicated that the asylum now housed five suicidal patients — as many as been treated in the five years prior to the war. The five, all white, had started to display suicidal behavior only since the end of the war. Unbeknownst to Dr. Fisher, these five patients served as a harbinger of what was to come in the subsequent decades.[78]

In 1868, Edward Fisher was replaced as superintendent by Dr. Eugene Grissom. This transition resulted more from the political effects of Reconstruction than any malfeasance or impropriety on Fisher's part, as the Republicans now in charge of state government replaced dozens of political appointments with those loyal to Governor William W. Holden. Despite the means by which he attained the position, Eugene Grissom was almost uniquely qualified to head the asylum. The son of a Granville County farmer, Grissom had trained as both a lawyer and a doctor before the Civil War. He

patients to beds to prevent them from hurting themselves. On 6 February 1889, Joseph Wilson, a farmer from Vance County, was admitted to the asylum after a suicide attempt. Grissom observed that Wilson "seems more or less hopeless and despondent and says he would be better off dead than alive." On his third day at the asylum, Wilson was able to evade the asylum attendants long enough to "slip off to his own room and ram his head against the wall with great force." To prevent Wilson from doing himself further damage, Grissom ordered that he be strapped to his bed and "kept there several hours, which seemed to distress him very much, and he made earnest protests and promises that he would never do such a thing again." According to the patient records, such a treatment was remarkably successful: Wilson never again attempted suicide, and he was released cured later that year.[87] Grissom's and Murphy's approaches to treating suicidal patients yielded radically different results. During Grissom's twenty-one-year tenure at the asylum in Raleigh, only one patient successfully committed suicide, while during Murphy's approximately equal tenure at Morganton, eleven patients took their own lives.

The account of Michael Cosgrove reveals the difference between Grissom's and Murphy's approaches to patient treatment. An Irish immigrant born in 1850, Cosgrove spent most of his adult life in and out of insane asylums on both sides of the Atlantic, including lengthy stays at the Morganton and Raleigh asylums. Publishing his account in 1906 in the hope of securing his release from a second stint at Raleigh, Cosgrove never definitively described the nature of his illness, claiming throughout that "there was nothing the matter with me." However, a few passages in his text indicate that he may have been diagnosed as suicidal. He described Grissom as cold, distant, and reserved. Grissom, Cosgrove claimed, did not comprehend his situation, but he was "not the only doctor who did not understand me; my whole life has been a mystery to many of them." Conversely, he had a very positive assessment of Murphy. During the fifteen months he spent in Morganton, Cosgrove believed his condition improved significantly as a result of Murphy's care, as he was "the only one that near understanding my trouble."[88]

Despite the severity with which Grissom treated suicidal patients, he also manifested a heartfelt sympathy for their pain. Although a devout Methodist, Grissom divorced whatever personal or religious ideas he held about suicide from his professional treatment of suicidal patients. "Should the physician attend the call of those whose maladies are the result of vice, and it may be loathsome and degraded wickedness?" Grissom asked the graduating class of Leonard Medical School in Raleigh in 1886. "Again the reply admits no question—disease is still disease, whether it be the sequel of the wine-cup or groveling licentiousness or even of abortion or suicide. The wages of sin is death, but the paymaster is a Power higher than man."[89] Grissom had seen too much to conclude otherwise.

Although Eugene Grissom and Patrick Murphy developed techniques for treating suicidal patients, neither doctor articulated a theory to explain why suicide had apparently become so common among white North Carolinians after the Civil War. Several of their medical colleagues, however, did, expressing their views in the pages of the North Carolina Medical Journal. Not all of these opinions were particularly insightful. In 1899, the Journal ran a brief piece describing the theory of a Dr. Haig, who "considers meat-eating, tobacco-smoking and tea, coffee and beer-drinking all contributory causes of suicide," a claim that the editors wisely rejected as "doubtful."[90]

One of the earliest theories proposed in the journal was presented by W. C. McDuffie, a Fayetteville physician. He argued that:

one whose tortured mind has dwelt for months upon suicide, finally destroys himself under some sudden impulse, not, however, without leaving behind evidence of 'method in his madness.' The reasons assigned, of course, the world pronounces unsound, but nevertheless the motive is patent. Perchance it may be the fear of poverty or the continued bitings of remorse, the balance wheel running crooked, until at last society itself becomes a burden and he seeks relief in death. A hundred causes almost might be named as calculated to produce this unhingement—this overwhelming emotional impulsive desire to get rid of one's self. Disappointment is probably one of, if not the most powerful.[91]

McDuffie's explanation attempted to rationalize the choice of suicide. Although outsiders might reject suicide as unsound, to someone so predisposed, suicide appeared as a reasonable response to hard circumstances. More important, McDuffie shifted the fundamental disjuncture that led to suicide from one that corrupted the victim's psyche to one that corrupted his or her relationship to and position in society. The less comfortable an individual felt in society, the more likely he or she was to commit suicide. When the social forces that tended to inform and create social positions and expectations weakened, disappointment, and ultimately suicide, were the result.[92]

These explanations, however, all appeared in the larger context of the treatment of insanity. The North Carolina Medical Journal did not run an article devoted exclusively to suicide until 1903. In this editorial, the Jour-

nal argued first that, under proper medical supervision, suicide could be treated like any other medical condition, though it recognized that "its entire prevention is impossible." It recommended asylum treatment for suicidal patients, though the editors admitted that there was "a certain stigma connected with being, or having been, an inmate of an insane asylum."[93]

Exactly why suicide had become so common, however, the editors were hesitant to say. "An exhaustive study of the causes of this increase in suicides would be timely," they argued, but "this study we do not propose to make." Instead, the editors presented what they termed "an idea in connection with the subject." They argued that "suicides are largely (but not wholly) epidemic." As suicides became more common and more widely reported, other people became inspired to emulate the act. The editors particularly blamed newspapers for publicizing suicides: "We believe that if less publicity were given to these cases the result would be beneficial." With newspapers functioning as the mode of transmission for this epidemic of suicide, the editors of the *North Carolina Medical Journal* hoped to stop its spread by attacking its host.

Although doctors in North Carolina never developed a comprehensive theory or explanation for the increase in suicides among white North Carolinians after the Civil War, their collective and individual responses to the "suicide epidemic" indicate the extent to which they believed it had become much more common and how, as doctors, much of the burden for controlling and treating suicide rested upon their shoulders. In their struggles to construct an explanation for suicide, North Carolina's doctors, like the suicide victims themselves, demonstrate the degree to which the state's social and culture landscape was changing.

While Grissom, Murphy, McDuffie, and other doctors sought to explain why suicide had become so common among white North Carolinians, the doctors at the African American asylum in Goldsboro puzzled over how few of their patients were suicidal. In an 1883 article entitled "Insanity in the Colored Race," Goldsboro superintendent Dr. J. D. Roberts reported, "I have been forcibly struck with the small percent of suicidal cases among the colored insane. Since my connection with the Eastern North Carolina Insane Asylum, I have had under my care near 200 cases of insanity without a single attempt to commit suicide. The histories received with the patients give a few as having threatened suicide, and also a small number as having made the attempt before being received."[94] When one of his patients killed himself later that year, Roberts maintained his original supposition that African Americans did not commit suicide in the Goldsboro asylum's annual report: "This is the first attempt, even, at suicide that has occurred during my administration, and as he was almost white, I still hold to my original opinion that the colored man is not as prone to suicide as his white brother. This man [the patient who committed suicide] would have easily have passed for a white man in any section where he was unknown."[95] Indeed, Roberts's sparse entry in the hospital's logbook indicates how central racial stereotypes were in his understanding of the deed. "Suicide by hanging, just before daybreak," he wrote; "Was almost white."[96]

In the following year, Roberts's report reiterated his opinion that black asylum patients did not commit suicide. He wrote, "I still see no reason to change that opinion, viz: that suicides are not as common with the negro as with the white." To support his claim, Roberts noted that of the 191 patients treated at Goldsboro that year, none were suicidal.[97] In 1896, Roberts's successor, Dr. J. F. Miller, confirmed that suicidal behavior was rare among his patients. While "insanity among the Negroes of the South has wonderfully increased since the close of the late war," he reported, "suicides are rare. I have seen but one well defined case of suicidal melancholia in the Eastern North Carolina Hospital for nine years."[98]

Roberts's and Miller's repeated declarations that African American asylum patients did not commit suicide indicate the extent to which suicide had become racialized in postbellum North Carolina. Roberts and Miller were not alone among southern asylum administrators in observing that black patients were rarely suicidal. Dr. J. W. Babcock, superintendent of the South Carolina Lunatic Asylum in Columbia, claimed that "we should expect to find, and do find, almost an absence of suicidal tendencies among the colored insane."[99]

These attitudes toward black suicide can be seen as part of a widespread belief among southern white doctors that black and white southerners suffered from different forms of mental illness. These doctors thought that white patients were predisposed to suffer from melancholias, while black patients were more likely to have manias.[100] This distinction grew out of and helped to reinforce ideas of black racial inferiority, as melancholias were thought to be the product of excessive civilization, whereas manias were a symptom of savagery and inferior mental capacity. According to Georgia Lunatic Asylum superintendent Dr. T. O. Powell, having "less mental equipoise" than whites, black asylum patients suffered "mental alienation from influences and agencies which would not affect a race mentally stronger."[101] Dr. Babcock of the South Carolina Lunatic Asylum concurred, claiming that "the comparative rarity of melancholia and the prevalence of mania" among African Americans resulted from "low developed brain function."[102] Mecklenburg County doctor John Brevard Alexander claimed that since the Civil War blacks lagged "far behind the whites in suicides, and will probably not equal them until their civilization is more advanced."[103] This distinction between the forms of mental illnesses that inflicted black and white asylum patients also helped to justify their segregation in separate institutions, as treatments could be specialized to the residents' needs. Because suicidal tendencies were thought to be the product of melancholias and rare among manias, white doctors at black asylums expected to see few suicidal patients.

Explanations for the absence of suicidal patients at the black asylum in Goldsboro proved as elusive as they were for the frequency of suicidal patients at the white asylums in Morganton and Raleigh. Roberts came closest to an explanation when he argued:

> Whether this small percent of suicides is from the Negro's inherent love of life I am unable to say, but so believe. The causes generally given for suicide are so many and exist to an equal extent in the Negro as in the white race, that some reason must be sought for the absence of a suicidal propensity in the Negro. Having no statistics I may be mistaken in this absence, I see no reason why the same causes operating on the white race and leading to suicide of the individual should not produce the same result if brought to bear on the Negro unless he has a greater inherent love of life. There are a few causes for suicide in the Caucasian that do not exist to the same extent in the two races, one of which is reverses in financial affairs. As the colored man pursues a mercantile life but little, the chances for his having reverses are few.[104]

Although Roberts never fully explained what he meant when he asserted that the African American "love of life" inhibited suicide, the implication was that a certain social cohesion in the African American community fostered self-preservation. Such a claim also implies that such a "love of life" had disappeared in the white community, resulting in the high frequency of suicide among white asylum patients.[105] Involvement in market forces, as many white North Carolinians increasingly experienced after the Civil War, only served to remove the individual from local community institutions, making them more susceptible to suicide.

CHAPTER THREE

The Legacy of the War We Suppose

Suicide in Medical & Social Thought

A S THE EVIDENCE in the preceding chapter has made clear, the Civil War fundamentally reoriented how white and black North Carolinians understood suicide. This evidence also suggests that the Civil War, at least at some level, effected some change in the frequency of suicide. The purpose of this chapter, therefore, is to present a series of hypotheses to account for the "suicide mania," employing the tools of modern psychology. To be sure, we cannot place nineteenth-century suicide victims "on the couch," and any analysis of a historical figure's individual psychology is constrained significantly by the available sources. Nevertheless, modern suicide research should allow us to discern patterns in the data that would not necessarily be apparent to contemporaries. Given the complex nature of the war and its effects on the North Carolina political, economic, social, and cultural order, seeking a monocausal explanation is both unsatisfying and unproductive. Rather, these dramatic changes in attitudes and practices concerning suicide almost certainly were the product of a complex interaction of factors brought about by the Civil War.

One possible explanation for the increased prominence of suicide among white North Carolinians is that many Confederate veterans of the Civil War suffered from post-traumatic stress disorder. Post-traumatic stress disorder, or PTSD, refers to a set of psychological consequences resulting from exposure to traumatic events, such as military combat, natural disasters, rape, or abuse. Originally defined in 1980 to describe symptoms displayed by Vietnam War veterans, PTSD has now been identified as the root cause behind what was known as "shell shock" in World War I and "combat fatigue" in World War II.[1]

PTSD can manifest itself in a variety of symptoms, including depression, irritability or fits of anger, nightmares, excessive anxiety, insomnia, emotional detachment, and flashbacks of the trauma. The severity and duration of these symptoms exhibit considerable variation among PTSD patients. While some PTSD victims manifest these symptoms almost immediately after experiencing or witnessing trauma, many others display a "delayed onset" of PTSD, going years or even decades before indications of the disorder manifest themselves. To be sure, not all victims of trauma develop PTSD; among Vietnam War veterans between 2 and 26 percent developed PTSD.[2]

The question of whether PTSD can result in higher suicide rates has vexed psychologists for decades, particularly in the case of Vietnam War veterans. The earliest studies indicated that the suicide rate among Vietnam War veterans was more than six times higher than in the civilian population. Indeed, some of these early estimates concluded that more soldiers killed themselves in the years after leaving Vietnam than died in combat.[3] However, these results were rejected by a study conducted by the Centers for Disease Control (CDC) in 1990, which concluded that fewer than nine thousand Vietnam veterans had committed suicide through the early 1980s, a figure no higher than in a civilian control cohort.[4] A more recent reevaluation of the CDC data, however, has indicated that veterans with PTSD displayed a statistically significant increase in the rate of suicide over veterans without PTSD. Moreover, many of these veterans did not display symptoms of PTSD or suicidal behavior until decades after leaving the combat theater.[5] Regardless of the data, many Vietnam veterans maintain that PTSD has resulted in a significant increase in suicide among veterans.[6]

Some historians have argued that Confederate soldiers did not experience PTSD like their Vietnam era counterparts. They claim that although a Civil War soldier's initial exposure to combat might be traumatic, after a period of "seasoning" he became largely immune to the psychological effects of witnessing and participating in the horrors of war. This line of argument concludes that Vietnam era soldiers experienced PTSD at such high rates because they never developed the "seasoning" that protected soldiers from an earlier generation.[7] Other historians have argued that the development of the Lost Cause ideology during Reconstruction effectively protected Confederate veterans from the mental trauma so common among Vietnam era veterans. According to historian Gaines M. Foster, "Returning Confederates received such ritualistic welcome; the returning Vietnam vets at first did not—a difference that helps explain why so many more

Vietnam than Confederate veterans had a difficult time putting the war behind them." The result, according to Foster, is that "little evidence of post-traumatic stress disorder appears . . . [among] Confederate veterans."[8]

More recent studies, however, indicate the Civil War soldiers, both Union and Confederate, experienced a significant degree of psychological trauma, verifying Captain Oliver Wendell Holmes Jr.'s assertion that "many a man has gone crazy since this campaign begun from the terrible pressure on the mind & body."[9] Eric T. Dean's study of 291 Civil War veterans at the Indiana Hospital for the Insane found that almost all of them displayed some symptoms of PTSD.[10] Similarly, a recent study sponsored by the National Institutes of Health and the National Science Foundation matched more than fifteen thousand Union soldiers with subsequent pension and health records. These records revealed that 44 percent of Union veterans suffered from some form of mental illness. Researchers concluded that a strong correlation existed linking traumatic experience during the Civil War to subsequent mental illness, a finding they believed indicated that PTSD was endemic among Civil War soldiers.[11] Unfortunately, a relative dearth of comparable postwar medical records makes an analogous study for Confederate veterans impossible. However, assuming that the Confederate military experience was at least as traumatic as that experienced by Union soldiers, one should expect that Confederate veterans would have had comparable levels of PTSD.

In a handful of cases, contemporary North Carolinians explicitly attributed suicidal behavior among Confederate veterans to their wartime experience. As the 1862 suicide of John Roland in the Second North Carolina Hospital indicates, the trauma of war had an immediate and devastating effect on some soldiers. In others, however, the psychological toll of war did not surface until years after the conflict ended. Of those with delayed-onset PTSD, the cases of Benjamin A. Withers and George J. Duke may be the most striking.

Benjamin A. Withers enlisted on 1 February 1862 in Mecklenburg County at the age of twenty-six, joining the notorious Bethel Regiment. He fought in several battles in defense of Wilmington, in eastern Virginia, and at Gettysburg, where he saw fifty members of his regiment killed in an hour. Later he fought at Bristoe Station, the Wilderness, Spotsylvania, Cold Harbor, and Petersburg. During the trench warfare that attended the lengthy defense of Petersburg, Withers spent weeks ankle-deep in mud and rats. When his unit was ordered to attack the Union position, according to one of his fellow soldiers, they had been "in that place of torment for 14 days," many of which had been sleepless because of the almost constant artillery barrage. During the ensuing Battle of Globe Tavern in August 1864, a bullet from a Union sharpshooter splintered the radius and ulna of Withers's right forearm.[12]

At a field hospital, a Confederate surgeon amputated Withers's right arm at the elbow, leaving a raw stump that never completely healed and caused him pain for the remainder of his life.[13] Although he was able to maintain himself as a painter in Davidson County for sixteen years after the Confederate surrender at Appomattox, he never regained his prewar vitality. Indeed, few were surprised when he killed himself in June 1881. Newspaper accounts of Withers's death report that he shot himself in the left side of head with a pistol he held in his remaining hand. According to both the *Charlotte Observer* and the *Raleigh Farmer and Mechanic*, Withers's unhealed wound provided the best explanation for his suicide.[14]

George J. Duke experienced many similar forms of trauma during his stint in the Confederate army. Born in 1836 in Warren County, Duke married as a young man, became a father, and sought to establish himself on the family farm. Joining the 30th North Carolina Regiment in August 1861, he would go on to see action in many of the Civil War's major campaigns. During the four years that he spent with the 30th, Duke participated in and witnessed some of the bloodiest fighting of the war, during which his unit suffered heavy casualties. Private Duke himself received minor wounds at Malvern Hill on 1 July 1862. After recovering from his injuries, he rejoined his regiment by the end of the year. Five months after returning to the front lines, however, Duke was wounded a second time, shot in the arm and side at Chancellorsville on 3 May 1863. Although serious, his wounds proved not to be fatal, and he spent the remainder of the war hospitalized in Lynchburg, Virginia.[15]

Duke's healed wound remained a constant reminder of his experience in the war and the friends he had lost. Powerless to cope with his wartime experience, Duke first became suicidal sometime in the early 1870s. Unable to care for him, his family committed him to the North Carolina Insane Asylum in Raleigh. Over the next two decades, he was in and out of the Raleigh asylum as bouts of suicidal impulses overwhelmed him. According to asylum records, Duke's threats of suicide always coincided with an unnatural obsession with his wounds. Unfortunately, these records do not indicate whether he eventually recovered, although they do reveal that through the summer of 1889, he continued to be treated for suicidal mania.[16]

Although the suicides of John Roland, Benjamin Withers, and George Duke provide glaring examples of PTSD among North Carolina Civil War veterans, only a handful of other postwar suicides can be attributed so explicitly. To be sure, many of the men who committed suicide during and after Reconstruction had fought in the Civil War. Comparing known male suicides in North Carolina with military records reveals that at least two-thirds of those men who killed themselves after 1865 had fought in the Confederate army.[17] Given the high rates of conscription into North Carolina's Confederate ranks, however, this finding should not be surprising. Under the Confederate Conscription Act of 1862, nearly all white men between the ages of eighteen and thirty-five (later raised to fifty) were drafted into military service. The net result was that an entire generation of white men from North Carolina was pressed into military service. One historian estimates that nearly 97 percent of white men between the ages of twenty and sixty living in North Carolina in 1860 would participate in some form of military activity during the Civil War.[18]

Although one is tempted to argue that all military experience is traumatic, not all of those North Carolinians who participated in military activity during the Civil War experienced or witnessed the type of trauma that would trigger PTSD. While a variety of different wartime experiences can trigger PTSD, studies of more recent military conflicts indicate that three wartime factors contribute in the majority of PTSD cases: being wounded in combat, experience as a prisoner of war, and the length of military service.[19] Almost all known Confederate veterans who either committed suicide or were treated for suicidal behavior at one of North Carolina's insane asylums had been wounded in battle or had spent time in a Union POW camp. In many cases, the unfortunate soldier had experienced both. For example, Joseph Hancock of Randolph County, who hanged himself in 1870, suffered bullet wounds in his foot at Gettysburg and in his right thigh at Bristoe Station before being captured by Union forces near Petersburg.[20] Twenty-one-year-old John T. Wescott, who cut his throat in 1870, was shot and captured in the Union assault on Fort Fisher in January 1865.[21] Enlisting in 1861 at the age of eighteen, Guilford Laws, a university student in Chapel Hill from Granville County, was wounded at South Mountain in September 1862 and at Fredericksburg three months later, before being captured at Rappahannock Station in November 1863. Laws spent almost a year as a prisoner at Point Lookout, Maryland, before he decided to change sides and joined the Union army in 1864. After the war, Laws became a farmer. In June 1877, Laws's body was found "suspended from the limbs of a small pine tree." Having gone out to plow his cornfield, Laws appeared to have "stopped his mule, taken off the lines, passed them round his neck, attached them to the limb, and swung off." Although no cause was assigned for his suicide, many noted that he had been "depressed for some time past."[22]

Guilford Laws spent almost the entire conflict in uniform, much of it at the front lines. Many of his fellow Confederates who later committed suicide also had extensive combat experience. Recent studies of soldiers in the Iraq War have indicated that a soldier's risk of developing PTSD is directly proportional to the length of time spent in the combat theater.[23] A similar experience seems to hold true with Confederate soldiers from North Carolina, as almost all of those who later committed suicide had enlisted in 1861 or 1862 and served for the duration of the war. Their repeated exposure to the trauma of combat, combined with their prolonged separation from home and family, probably contributed to deep psychological scars and eventual suicidal impulses.

In addition to its role in the postwar white suicide epidemic, PTSD might also explain one African American suicide after the Civil War. Wounded during his service in the 36th U.S Colored Troops, Washington Newby received his discharge in June 1865 and returned to eastern North Carolina, where he had hoped to create a new life for his emancipated family. His wartime experience, however, had left him with deep emotional scars. According to his widow, "We had to watch him constantly and one night we fell asleep and he got out and we could not find him." They found his body the next morning; Newby had drowned himself. His widow concluded that "he went crazy from the roaring of the guns in the war."[24]

As Washington Newby's suicide vividly illustrates, PTSD could affect black veterans just as significantly as white veterans. However, there is some evidence to suggest that black soldiers demonstrated greater psychological resiliency to the traumatic experience of combat. In his work on black Union soldiers and their white officers, historian Joseph T. Glatthaar found that after 1865 white officers often demonstrated symptoms of PTSD, including a significantly heightened rate of suicide, divorce, and substance abuse. Conversely, Glatthaar found that black soldiers, despite exposure to the same combat experiences as their white officers, did not manifest these symptoms to any significant degree. Glatthaar concludes that black soldiers' apparent resistance to PTSD came from "the excitement of freedom, the vision of genuine equality, and the enthusiastic response of the black population for their work."[25]

Although PTSD can be seen as one of the primary causes of suicide among white men in North Carolina after the Civil War, it does not help to explain why the suicides of white women or white men who did not fight in the Civil War also became more visible or why black suicide appears to have disappeared entirely. To be sure, the Civil War could also exact a psychological toll on those on the home front. In October 1861, Temperance Sirls of Raleigh hanged herself, "having lost her reason on account of her two sons volunteering and joining the army."[26] When James Little drowned himself in a well on his farm near Tarboro in 1864, the local newspaper concluded that "the distressed condition of the country was the cause of his mental derangement. All of his sons are in the army, one of whom has been very badly wounded."[27] In Forsythe County, Alexander Ridings hanged himself the same year because of "the present unhappy state of the country" and a "fear of being made to enter the service."[28] However, outside of these isolated episodes, little evidence exists to gauge how extensively the Civil War traumatized the noncombatant population.

If PTSD may have helped to institute the "suicide mania" among white North Carolinians, a phenomenon known as contagious suicide may help to explain why suicide was also common among the nonveteran population. For nearly a century, medical epidemiologists have recognized that suicides in a community can inspire others to take their own lives. They have identified two forms of contagious suicide. In the first form, personal experience with suicide — for instance, knowing someone who took his or her own life — significantly increases the likelihood that an individual might kill him- or herself. In the second form, often referred to as the "Werther effect" after a character in a Goethe novel, media reports of suicide inspire others to replicate the act.[29] Indeed, as we have seen, the editors of the *North Carolina Medical Journal* in 1903 presented a similar hypothesis when they argued that newspaper accounts of suicide tended to inspire others to take their own lives. White North Carolinians outside the medical community shared the belief that the decision to commit suicide could be inspired by the suicides of others. A folklorist recording oral traditions in North Carolina during the 1890s recorded, "Suicides never come singly. One is always followed by another."[30]

Some evidence suggests that suicide clusters like those described by epidemiologists developed in postbellum North Carolinians. One such cluster could be found in northern Orange County, where more than two dozen suicides took place. Many of these suicides were committed by members of the three Presbyterian churches that serviced this rural population. Hillsborough Presbyterian, the largest congregation, lost a prominent doctor, the wife of a well-known farmer, and a decorated Confederate veteran. Eno Presbyterian Church saw a devoted wife and mother hang herself after she had "ground the coffee and called the family to breakfast"; four years later her husband joined her, taking his own life with a rifle. Hardest hit was the remote congregation at Little River, which lost three of its most prominent members to suicide: George C. Ray, a prosperous farmer and descendant of one of the church's founders; John C. Wilkerson, "a worthy and most estimable citizen"; and Lambert W. Hall, a respected and honored judge, the last two of whom had served as deacons for the congregation. Presiding at all three congregations after his ordination in 1867, Rev. William Wilhelm oversaw funeral services for nearly a dozen suicide victims.[31]

Another such suicide cluster could be found at Abbott's Creek, a small community in Davidson County. According to the *Winston-Salem People's Press*, Abbott's Creek had been the site of "five suicides . . . within our recollection," including two a week apart during 1883. In the first of these two, Elizabeth Bodenhamer hanged herself from an attic rafter, leaving a distraught husband and eight children. Exactly one week later and less than a mile away, Jane Teague hanged herself, also from an attic rafter. The similarity of their deaths leaves little doubt that the former, at least in part, inspired the latter suicide. Indeed, according to the *Winston Sentinel*, Teague had "a week previous [to her suicide] attended the funeral of Mrs. Bodenhamer, and had inquired particularly of the method employed by that lady in effecting her demise . . . like the first unfortunate [she] chose an attic and a hank of flax thread as the place and instrument of death."[32]

Other suicide clusters focused on specific localities. When Peter Peeler, a Confederate veteran from Cleveland County, hanged himself from the rafters of his barn in 1875, it was noted that the farm's previous owner had hanged himself on that exact site.[33] Similarly, when Mary Kreeger drowned herself in 1886, the site of her death was well known in the community as the location where John Kiser had shot himself only months earlier.[34]

Family networks could also serve as a conduit for suicide clusters. For example, Amy Jones of Chatham County hanged herself in 1881, a dozen years after her husband had killed himself.[35] Similarly, Jana Faucett of Hillsborough hanged herself in 1881, eight years after her father, Alfred Brown, had shot himself.[36] The most striking case of a familial suicide cluster, however, is that of the Hester family of Forsyth County. Friends and family had noticed that John Hester, a Kernersville merchant, had not been himself ever since he was wounded at Gettysburg, often brooding and unable to concentrate on his work. On a cold January morning in 1871, he left his home, telling his family that he was going to supervise some hands assigned to chop wood in the forest adjacent to their house. When he did not return, his family went searching for him. Several hours later they found his body in the bushes, his throat cut several times and his son's pocketknife covered in blood at his side.[37]

In 1890, nineteen years after he had helped in the search for his father and had seen his own pocketknife dripping with his father's blood, Walter Hester boarded a train bound for Salem. Although he was a successful business-man, like his father, he had harbored a melancholy disposition since child-hood. As the train passed the site where his father had cut his throat, Walter Hester pulled a pistol from his coat pocket and shot himself in the head.[38] Although Walter Hester undoubtedly had his own motivations for ending his life and possibly had an inherited predisposition for depression, the cir-cumstances of his death suggest that the tragic experience with his father's suicide contributed to his own suicide. While such striking cases are rare, they speak to the extent to which individual suicides could inspire others to replicate the act.

If one concludes that heightened visibility of white suicide after the Civil War represented an actual increase in its frequency, the combination of PTSD and suicide clusters may provide a reasonable account for the phe-nomenon. The following scenario describes how these two factors might have generated the observed data. A small but significant number of Con-federate veterans returned to North Carolina psychologically devastated by their wartime experience. Emotionally crippled, they could not adjust to postwar civilian life, and incapable of coping with the strain, they com-mitted suicide. Widely publicized in local and statewide newspapers and a subject of public discussion, their suicides inspired others to replicate the act. These suicides in turn were reported and discussed, generating even more suicides. While such a scenario probably oversimplifies the mechan-ics of the "suicide epidemic," it explains why the number of white suicides appeared to increase after 1865.

Conversely, black North Carolinians found themselves immune to many of the factors that led white North Carolinians to end their own lives. As-sessing the apparent absence, or at least significantly less visible presence, of suicide among black North Carolinians proves even more challenging than understanding why white suicides appeared to increase after the Civil War. Nevertheless, the evidence suggests a couple of factors. First, unlike their white neighbors, black North Carolinians saw the Civil War as the be-ginning of a new era of potential personal advancement. Although scholars now recognize the myriad ways in which black efforts to secure full citizen-ship and economic equality were thwarted by resentful whites during Reconstruction, at the time most freed African Americans believed that emancipation was but the first step in creating a robust black community. Within this context, black North Carolinians created an individual and collective ethos that emphasized gradual economic and moral uplift. Because psychologists have long recognized that membership in a tight-knit community provides a strong counterindication for suicide, this ethos would have effectively created a brake on suicide in the black community. Second, Joseph Glatthaar's evidence suggests that black North Carolinians who fought in the Civil War demonstrated a greater psychological resiliency to the trauma of war than their white counterparts. Glatthaar's study also highlights the prominent role of the black community in insulating black veterans from the effects of PTSD. The same community institutions and networks that helped African Americans survive the upheavals of Reconstruction and Jim Crow helped to immunize black North Carolinians from the "self-slaying epidemic."

PROFESSOR RALPH GRAVES'S 1889 suicide probably could have been prevented. Returning from treatment at a private sanatorium in Baltimore, Graves decided to stay with friends in Raleigh rather than in his Chapel Hill home. In June 1889, Ralph and Julia Graves moved into the home of Spier Whitaker, a prominent Raleigh lawyer and Julia's brother-in-law. Surrounded by friends and family, Ralph Graves hoped to control his depression. Unfortunately, Spier Whitaker was involved in the most important trial of his career and therefore was unable to help monitor Graves. Fanny Whitaker, Julia Graves's sister, also found herself away from her house during most of the month, leaving Julia alone to care for her husband.[39]

Within weeks after returning to North Carolina, Ralph Graves's depression returned. Although he received periodic visits from doctors, Ralph's care was almost completely in his wife's hands. On the afternoon of 30 June, Ralph told her that he thought she looked fatigued and drained from his care and told her to take a walk outside. When Julia returned an hour later, she found her husband in the process of stabbing himself in the neck with a penknife. Rushing at her husband and knocking the knife from his hand, Julia screamed for help. Walking home from court accompanied by Raleigh mayor Alfred Thompson, Spier Whitaker heard the commotion and ran to her aid. While Whitaker and Thompson restrained her husband, Julia summoned a doctor to stitch up his wound, despite Ralph's repeated protestations that he wanted to die. The doctor told Mrs. Graves that her husband's prognosis was good: the knife had missed his jugular artery, and if he could be prevented from doing further harm to himself, he had "every reason to believe that he would recover." On the advice of his doctors, Julia Graves committed her husband to the North Carolina Insane Asylum.[40]

Under normal circumstances, Julia Graves could have been assured that her husband's life could be saved at the asylum. In the twenty years that Dr. Eugene Grissom had headed the asylum, no patient had ever successfully committed suicide there. If Grissom and the asylum staff could treat her husband as they had treated hundreds of suicidal patients in the past, Ralph Graves would be able to return with her to their home in Chapel Hill and maybe even resume his teaching career.

Unfortunately, these were not normal circumstances at the North Carolina Insane Asylum. Dr. Eugene Grissom, superintendent of the asylum for more than two decades, had been accused of serious misdeeds by two asylum employees. When these accusations were presented before the asylum's board of directors on 26 June 1889, the eight board members decided to assume a judicial role and try Dr. Grissom for impeachment from his post as superintendent. "The publication of these charges shocked and surprised the bulk of the people," wrote Josephus Daniels, "who believed that Dr. Grissom was both a great alienist and a man of high character."[41] Dominating North Carolina newspapers throughout the summer of 1889, Eugene Grissom's trial became a forum to discuss the role of the asylum and how far the state would go to prevent and control the suicide epidemic.

Spier Whitaker, Professor Graves's host in Raleigh, headed the small prosecutorial team. According to Josephus Daniels, Whitaker prepared himself for this unusual trial by buying "all the books on the treatment of the insane and read them and mastered them. When he came to discuss the right kind of treatment of the insane, he could quote the highest authorities in the world and could discuss their treatment as lucidly and clearly as if he had been an alienist all his life."[42] Whitaker argued that Dr. Grissom had committed two serious and impeachable offenses as superintendent of the North Carolina Insane Asylum. First, he claimed that Grissom had engaged in "gross immorality with the female attendants and others of this institution." Over the course of the trial, Whitaker named more than a dozen female attendants and asylum patients with whom he claimed Grissom had taken indecent liberties. The second, more damning accusation presented by Whitaker was the claim that Dr. Grissom routinely practiced "gross mistreatment of and cruelty to the patients under his charge."[43] Grissom's treatment of patients, Whitaker argued, frequently amounted to physical abuse. To support his claim, Whitaker produced more than a dozen witnesses who had seen Dr. Grissom order patients forcibly restrained, acts that Grissom, these witnesses claimed, often took part in leading by gripping the patient by the neck while the attendants strapped him or her to a bed or a chair. One witness testified Grissom had put his foot on an unruly patient's neck after he had been wrestled to the floor by a pair of attendants. For physical evidence, Whitaker had the asylum's restraining chair brought into the asylum chapel, for the time being functioning as a makeshift courtroom. It would stay there for the duration of the trial.

Eugene Grissom believed that the charges resulted from a conspiracy to remove him from office. On the opening day of his trial, Grissom marshaled newspaper editor Josephus Daniels into his office in order to "acquaint you with the conspiracy which I do not think you understand." Grissom told Daniels that rival doctors wished to replace him as the superintendent of the State Insane Asylum and had arranged these charges to usurp him. The whole affair, Grissom told Daniels, was "an attempt to break down my character and to destroy my reputation and put a stigma upon my family."[44]

Dr. Grissom did not let these charges go unanswered. To represent him during his three-week trial, he hired a team of the most visible lawyers in the state, including former governor Thomas Jarvis, former congressman Col. Thomas Fuller, and state legislator Charles Cooke. His lawyers argued that the use of physical restraints was fundamental to the successful treatment of patients. During the five days he spent on the witness stand, Grissom defended how he had treated his patients. On 8 July he testified that "the use of restraints were always intended for their own safety, the safety of others or to make a mental impression. It is for their good. In a majority of cases it has been beneficial."[45]

Unfortunately for Julia Graves, Dr. Grissom was unable to use such restraints on her husband. On 10 July, while Eugene Grissom was being cross-examined by her brother-in-law and the restraining chair sat as evidence, her husband was unattended less than one hundred yards away in his room at the asylum. There he completed the task he first attempted less than two weeks earlier, cutting his throat with a knife that he had somehow smuggled into his room. Out of respect to Graves, Grissom's trial was halted for the day, as lawyers from both sides and members of the board of directors "spoke in terms of deep regret at the death of Prof. Graves and eulogized his inestimable services to the State in the past."[46]

When the trial resumed, Grissom's lawyers continued their claims that the doctor had used physical restraints only when absolutely necessary. The treatment of suicidal patients received special attention from Grissom's lawyers as situations in which restraints were necessary and often beneficial. J. D. L. Smith, one of the patients whom Grissom was accused of abusing, was "a very dangerous criminal . . . a man who tried, time and again, to commit suicide by biting his arm and cutting himself with pieces of tin." Likewise, restraint had been necessary in the case of Mrs. M. S. Brown, as "her whole aim and purpose seemed to be to kill herself in any way possible— by choking herself, dashing herself against the floor or wall, or any way she could. It was impossible to prevent her injuring herself some, without restraining her." The use of force had also been necessary in the treatment of Mary Morse, who made "violent and determined attempts at suicide. . . . Her first night [at the asylum] on entering the dining-room at supper time, she seized a knife and attempted to kill herself. Her suicidal tendency became so violent that she could not be left alone a moment, and, even with an attendant at her side, she would dash herself against the wall or floor, choke herself, etc." After a lengthy period of confinement, much of it in the restraining chair that now graced the courtroom, Mary Morse had been cured of her suicidal tendencies.[47] In each of these cases, the use of restraints was a fundamental part of their treatment, and without their use many more patients would have died. On 15 July, as part of his closing arguments, Colonel Fuller declared that "during the twenty-one years of his superintendency there have been more than 1400 patients entrusted to his [Grissom's] charge and there has not been a single case of suicide."[48] As Julia Graves painfully knew, however, Fuller's statistics were one week out of date.

The debate over the use of restraints at Dr. Grissom's trial indicates the extent to which North Carolinians were divided over the issue of suicide. On the one hand, many felt a communal obligation to protect the lives of every citizen, even those who themselves no longer wished to live. Restraining suicidal patients, if it saved their lives, was not only a moral good but a societal requirement. "The whole theory of an insane asylum is one of restraint," argued Jarvis on Grissom's behalf.[49] On the other hand, many had increasingly come to reject the idea of community authority to force individuals to act against their will. Although they might have supported the treatment of suicidal and other insane patients at the North Carolina Insane Asylum, for many North Carolinians, the use of forcible restraints extended beyond the boundary of reasonable conduct.

After listening to three weeks of testimony, the board of directors resoundingly acquitted Dr. Grissom of all the charges leveled against him. Public opinion, however, had reached a different conclusion. Newspaper editorials and public meetings across the state called for Grissom's resignation. On 22 July, the day after Grissom's acquittal, more than two hundred people gathered in Raleigh's Metropolitan Hall declaring the verdict a fraud and demanding that both Grissom and the board of directors tender their resignations.[50] The *Raleigh News and Observer* remarked on how radically the trial had changed Grissom's public image: "A week before the trial began, Dr. Grissom was almost omnipotent in North Carolina in popularity and influence. No man was more so except Speaker Vance. Now, no man in the State is so unpopular with the masses."[51] While Grissom continued to maintain his innocence and the rightness of his actions, such repeated public condemnations must have struck deeply at his own sense of honor. On 22 August, bowing to public pressure, Eugene Grissom resigned from his position as superintendent of the North Carolina Insane Asylum.[52]

Eugene Grissom found himself unable to live in the community that had for nearly thirty years honored him and had recently come to revile him. Shortly after his resignation and the unexpected death of his wife a few months later, Grissom moved to Colorado to start his life over again. Although he briefly succeeded in restarting his medical practice in a small mining community, he had within months of moving to Colorado become a morphine addict, a habit that probably arose to mask the pain he felt from being cast out of the only community he had ever known. The scattered information that exists about Grissom's life in Colorado indicates that he had become mentally unhinged. Describing an interview Grissom gave to a Colorado newspaper about his trial, Josephus Daniels decried his "intemperate language" and claimed that he "was so vituperative that many who had stood with him and believed in his innocence were convinced that his whole conduct just before the trial and afterwards was due to a nervous breakdown."[53] In letters to his friend Albion Tourgée five years after his trial, Grissom revealed that he dwelled upon the past, believing himself

> the most severely punished victim of a personal & political con-
> spiracy planned & inflicted by a combination of ingrates and sanc-
> tioned by a people whom for almost a lifetime I had served with
> the fidelity of a dog and the labor and self-sacrifice of a galley slave.
> Falsely accused of charges . . . five years ago . . . by Thompson,
> Rogers, Fowle, Joe Daniels, Spier Whitaker, Alfred Waddell and a
> goodly number of the Editorial dogs. . . . But lost opportunities can
> never be regained in this life. Perhaps after all I merited some pun-
> ishment for sins either of commission or omission. Now, after it is
> too late, I have learned that moral cowardice never pays. . . . But no

man with any of the composition of fidelity in his character knows what he may submit to, after he has given "hostages to fortune."[54]

In an apparent suicide attempt, Grissom overdosed on chloroform sometime in 1895, after which he was committed to an insane asylum in Pueblo, Colorado.[55] For a man once considered among the foremost asylum administrators in the county, such a situation was a source of great shame, a shame doubled by the fact that several North Carolina newspapers published an account of his admission. "Are bloodhounds never satiated?" Grissom wrote to Tourgée. "Can they find no fields bearing other the crops of falsehood in which to beg their victims at the distance of 2500 miles?"[56] Grissom stayed at the asylum for most of the next six years, battling both drug addiction and deep depression, unable to reconcile the man he thought he was with the man he had become. In 1901, Grissom convinced the doctors at the asylum that he was well enough to be released and moved to Washington, D.C., to live with his son, then employed at the Pension Bureau.

In the early morning of 27 July 1902, Dr. Eugene Grissom committed suicide by firing the bullet of a revolver into his brain while standing on the front porch of his son's house. Eyewitnesses described seeing Grissom, now seventy-one years old with long white hair, remove the revolver from his pocket and fire the fatal shot; he then "staggered a moment and then sank into a large rustic chair standing near the door." Interviewed by the newspapers, Dr. Grissom's daughter expressed confusion about the weapon—her father had never owned a gun, she claimed. She had probably forgotten that nearly forty years earlier her father had dueled with a similar weapon inside the state capitol in Raleigh and had carried one at the Battle of the Seven Days.[57]

The public reaction in North Carolina to Grissom's suicide was quite muted, given the public stature he had once held in the state. The *Raleigh Morning Post* remarked on how much he had changed since his trial. Although once a "man of national fame," Grissom at the time of his death was no longer the "man of strength and force that the people of Raleigh knew."[58] Many publications, including the *North Carolina Medical Journal*, ignored his death completely. The *Charlotte Observer*, Isaac Avery's newspaper, noted that "news of the suicide of Dr. Eugene Grissom was not heard with any surprise by persons here."[59] Instead of directing his anger and frustration outward, as he had done as a young man, Grissom had, since his trial in 1889, internalized those emotions, leading to his deep depression and eventual suicide.

Eugene Grissom's life and death can be seen as representative of how cultural norms and social conditions changed in North Carolina during the nineteenth century. Confronting social disruption in the form of growing insanity after the Civil War, Grissom responded by trying to impose order through his work at the North Carolina Insane Asylum. His efforts to impose this order on an unruly society required him to resort to the use of force. Shamed and humiliated at his trial, he became a pariah in his own community. As a result, he succumbed to the very form of social disorder he had spent his life combating.

WHEN DR. EUGENE GRISSOM killed himself in July 1902, it had been forty years to the month since he had been wounded outside Richmond and had witnessed Private John Roland take his own life in a Confederate hospital in Petersburg. Whether he was aware of the anniversary or whether it influenced his decision to commit suicide is impossible to say, although newspaper coverage of an impending encampment of the Grand Army of the Republic not far from Grissom's house would suggest that he likely had some awareness of the significance of the date. During those forty years, Grissom had lived through a sea change in attitudes toward suicide, changes that he was probably more aware of than any other North Carolinian, and yet the full scale and complexity of the transformation probably eluded him.

The dramatic changes in attitudes and behaviors toward suicide suggest two tenets about the North Carolinians' moral frameworks during the nineteenth century. First, white and black North Carolinians never shared a common understanding or interpretation of suicide. Although, as we have seen, attitudes toward suicide changed radically over the course of the nineteenth century, black and white North Carolinians retained distinct interpretive frameworks for understanding suicide, frameworks that rarely overlapped or impacted each other. These distinct interpretative moral frameworks were reinforced by a racialized conception of suicide that coded suicide as black before the Civil War and white afterward. As upcoming chapters will illustrate, the interpretative frameworks that black and white North Carolinians used to understand suicide were part of a larger moral schema that helped them to make sense of other moral-social questions, such as divorce and debt.

Second, attitudes toward suicide appeared to change quickly and decisively. When comparing antebellum and postbellum white accounts of suicide, striking differences emerge in tone, rhetoric, and emphasis, differences that are fully apparent in the late 1860s and continue for decades thereafter.

Although the postemancipation black sources are comparatively silent on suicide, the immediate and almost total disappearance of suicide as a narrative trope after 1865 indicates that African American attitudes toward suicide also changed rapidly and decisively. Given the stability of antebellum attitudes toward suicide, these rapid changes indicate that the Civil War and emancipation fundamentally uprooted established moral frameworks and created the opportunity for transforming social and moral paradigms.

PART II

To Loosen the Bands of Society

Divorce

ADDIE MAY SPENT her whole life desperately longing for a successful marriage. Born in Pitt County near Farmville in 1863, at the height of the Civil War, she married Francis Dupree in 1882 when she was less than nineteen years old. Her husband began drinking heavily soon after their wedding, often returning home drunk and abusive. On their second wedding anniversary, an intoxicated Francis stumbled home and began verbally abusing his wife and infant son, breaking furniture, and throwing the fragments at his terrified spouse, who shielded their baby in her arms. Luckily for Addie, Francis's drunkenness impaired his aim, and she fled the house, running to her mother's with Francis pursuing them "with an unsheathed bowie knife in his hand."[1]

After receiving a legal separation in 1885 and a divorce in 1889, Addie moved to Texas to work as a governess for the two young children of Lorenzo DeVisconti. Italian-born and twenty-seven years her senior, DeVisconti was the only child of a count from the House of Milan and a French noblewoman. A series of political upheavals forced him to flee Milan, first to Austria, then Venice, then Mexico, and finally to Louisiana in 1863. Arriving in occupied New Orleans in the year of Addie's birth, DeVisconti was impressed into the Union army, though he never saw combat, absconding to New York City masquerading as a ship's cook. DeVisconti's itinerant lifestyle continued after the war. Teaching in several northern states, he married and was widowed twice. After the death of his second wife, by whom he had two young children, DeVisconti decided to move to Texas, where he had procured a teaching position. Placing newspaper advertisements for a governess, he hired the recently divorced Addie Dupree, who brought her own son to live in DeVisconti's house.

Less than a year later, Addie Dupree's relationship with Lorenzo DeVisconti transformed from one based on employment and the care of children to one of mutual romantic interest. After wedding in Texas, Addie and Lorenzo moved to her hometown of Farmville, North Carolina. Less than two years into their marriage, however, Lorenzo came to the conclusion that their union was "a humbug." A lapsed Roman Catholic at the time of their wedding, Lorenzo apparently rediscovered the religion of his childhood, concluding that since divorce was prohibited under Catholic doctrine, his marriage to Addie, although legally binding, had no spiritual or moral validity. Abandoning Addie, who was then pregnant with their second child, Lorenzo returned to Texas in November 1892.

Despite the circumstances under which they separated, Addie and Lorenzo carried on a lengthy and fairly friendly correspondence over the next eight years. In the letters between them, they reflected on their life together, their children, and the meaning of marriage in its social, legal, and religious contexts. Mainly, however, they discussed divorce. Their correspondence reveals deep fissures about the meaning of marriage and the significance of divorce.

Lorenzo maintained that their marriage was invalid because "according to nature's laws, or what is the same, God's laws, *no divorce is valid.*"[2] He later wrote her that "you will see that we have made a great mistake, that we both have sinned, and that this transgression of the Divine law must necessarily have a punishment to follow." His Catholic faith taught him that "a divorced person cannot [re]marry, while the divorced husband is living, and so we have *failed*, greatly sinned."[3] At the same time, he was willing to divorce Addie, since in his own mind their marriage had been critically flawed from the start. "My remaining days of my life shall be given to atone," he wrote her. "Before the civil law you are my wife, at least you were, but examine the scripture and [you] will find our error."[4]

Addie's position on divorce revealed little of the convoluted logic and internal contradictions found in Lorenzo's letters. "I think it best that we are divorced," she wrote bluntly. Addie believed that although she had tried to be his "beloved wife," the resulting "life of suffering" necessitated a divorce. For her, the act of terminating their relationship carried little of the moral baggage that Lorenzo described in such detail. Instead, she focused on the practical reality of their divorce. "Now answer me a few plain questions," she wrote; "don't give evasive answers but give plain truthful ones." Addie wanted to know how Lorenzo would respond to a divorce suit and how they would divide their property. "I have had enough of married life," she concluded one letter, "and never intend to live the married life again, with any man on earth."[5]

Despite her claims to the contrary, Addie did remarry shortly after her divorce from Lorenzo was finalized in March 1901. Although the circumstances of their reintroduction and courtship remain murky, Addie remarried Francis Dupree, her first husband, on 27 August 1901. Whether this marriage would have turned out differently than their first marriage is impossible to say, as Addie died less than a month later from an overdose of morphine.

Although there are many remarkable elements to Addie's story, one of the most notable is how the broader community responded to her various marriages and divorces. Instead of condemning her for her actions, local and regional newspapers considered her story almost poetic. The *Raleigh Morning Post* applauded Addie's remarriage to Francis Dupree as a "happy occasion" and believed their marriage "eclipsed . . . the pages of fiction, on which are founded the wild and fanciful imaginings of wonderful minds." The *Morning Post* justified Addie's first divorce on the grounds that her husband was "somewhat dissipated" and her second divorce because he "was also dissipated and in addition to his bad habits he was also lazy."[6] Several newspapers favorably compared her story to one penned by popular romance author Laura Jean Libbey entitled "Fell in Love with His Wife."[7] Addie's second divorce was considered so routine that her lawyer asked the judge to "withhold calling the docket until a divorce case could be disposed of, which would take only a few minutes. . . . The jury was only three minutes in answering the three issues 'yes' and granting the divorce."[8]

Had Addie lived a generation earlier, the broader community almost certainly would have responded very differently. Although Addie received blanket acceptance of her marital choices from everyone except her second husband, white men and women contemplating divorce in North Carolina during the decades before the Civil War faced prospects far removed from those Addie Dupree experienced. For them, filing for divorce meant public embarrassment, condemnation by religious leaders, politicians, and journalists, and ultimately social ostracism. Just as the Civil War forced a reinterpretation of suicide, the events of the early 1860s pushed white and black North Carolinians to reconsider how they understood divorce. As with suicide, this reinterpretation headed in very different directions for white and black North Carolinians, as whites became more accepting of divorce and blacks began to attach a greater stigma to it.

To be sure, both before and after the Civil War, many North Carolinians stuck in unhappy marriages found ways to exit those relationships without seeking divorce. They could (and often did) abandon their ill-matched partners, hoping to begin again in a new town or with a new paramour. Although abandonment was an important social phenomenon and may have at times been more numerically prevalent than divorce, divorce required the aggrieved spouse to appear in public before the community to justify his or her desire to be released from the marital bonds that the community had sanctioned.[9] It forced them to confront their friends and family members, their neighbors, and their clergymen, telling them in essence that they wanted their approval to dissolve a significant social relationship. Thus divorce presented an opportunity for conflict not only between spouses over the particulars of their relationship but also between the individual seeking the divorce and the broader community. By examining who filed for divorce and how they presented their claims and by exploring how their community responded to these arguments and actions, one can observe significant changes over the course of the nineteenth century concerning who felt able to seek divorce and how their actions were viewed by the broader community.

CHAPTER FOUR

The Country Is Also a Party

Antebellum Divorce in Black & White

ANTEBELLUM WHITE North Carolinians saw marriage not only as a commitment between a man and a woman but as a fundamental institution holding society together.[1] The *Southern Quarterly Review* concluded in 1854 that marriage was "the primal act by which human society was organized, the first social institution. . . . From the society formed by marriage, the whole social and political order in which man is placed has grown. The duties which arise in that society are permanent; there is no period at which they are ended."[2]

Within this context, divorce would serve to tear apart the fabric of society. According to a letter from "A Friend to Good Order & Religion" published in the *Raleigh Register* in 1809, many believed that divorce would "loosen the bands of Society and turn mankind upon each other like brutes."[3] Divorce, therefore, hinted at anarchy. Because marriage functioned as the fundamental social institution, ending marriage through divorce threatened every other form of social bond and hierarchy. Thus divorces, at least in theory, endangered not only the institution of marriage but all social institutions, including slavery.

North Carolina chief justice Thomas Ruffin delivered some of the most vehement criticisms of divorce in antebellum North Carolina. Serving as chief justice from 1833 to 1852, Ruffin saw divorce as a threat to the general welfare. In a series of opinions, he argued that the state ought to restrict access to divorce in order to preserve social order. He contended in an 1836 opinion that divorce was "not simply a cause between the two parties to the record; the country is also a party, and its best interests are at stake."[4] A decade later in another divorce case, he concluded that "the welfare of the community is to be consulted more than the wishes of the parties."[5] Ruffin argued that divorce posed such a threat to social order that "the public is concerned that divorces should not be improperly decreed, and this rule in particular is intended to protect the public morals and promote the public policy."[6]

As a foundational social institution, marriage retained in the minds of antebellum white North Carolinians many of the inequalities that characterized society as a whole. Inherited from the English common law, the legal status of women in marriage in North Carolina fell under the doctrine of coverture. Under this doctrine, women's entire legal identity after marriage was subsumed by that of her husband.[7] Indeed, the legal authority of the husband was such that Chief Justice Thomas Ruffin declared in 1862 that "the law gives the husband power to use such a degree of force necessary to make the wife behave and know her place."[8] However, the gender inequality in marriage described in legal texts did not always reflect the lived experience of real marriages. Some white women in North Carolina were able to maintain control over their own property, through either legal instruments or a personal agreement between spouses, and the complex power dynamics of individual marriages often deviated from the simple legal dictum of patriarchal authority.[9] Nevertheless, the conception of marriage held by most antebellum white North Carolinians reflected the belief that hierarchy and dominance were necessary components to maintain social harmony.

When a white woman from North Carolina filed for divorce before the Civil War, she was making not only a claim that she wanted to escape from a failed marriage but also a claim against white male authority. Since women initiated approximately two out of every three divorce suits in North Carolina and across the nation before the Civil War, divorce came to be seen as subverting gender hierarchies. Stephanie McCurry has argued that South Carolina never permitted divorce during the antebellum period (and only briefly during Reconstruction) because lawmakers and judges believed it would undermine male authority in the household. Any action, warned one justice, that would result in even "the partial dissolution of the husband's authority over the wife" should be avoided.[10]

Many scholars have attributed the low rate of divorce in North Carolina and across the antebellum South to a restrictive legal climate.[11] These scholars note that southern states fell behind the rest of the country in the transition from legislative to judicial divorce and that comparatively few legal grounds existed for divorce in the South. They also frequently cite legal opinions like those of Chief Justice Ruffin as representative of a broader legal prejudice against divorce. Yet although legal barriers to divorce certainly existed, the burden of social opinion may have weighed more heavily on the minds of those men and women considering divorce in antebellum North Carolina.[12]

Some scholars have pointed to the fact that southern states fell behind national trends in abandoning legislative divorce and adopting judicial divorce as evidence that legal barriers functioned as the primary obstacle to divorce. Noting that legislative divorces were much harder to obtain than judicial divorces, they argue that the delayed introduction of judicial divorce in the South should be read as indicative of a restrictive legal culture concerning divorce. Indeed, looking at the divorce petitions to the state legislature, one finds that the vast majority were denied. For example, in 1810, the North Carolina legislature approved only one of twenty divorce petitions; in 1813, only four out of twenty-two.[13]

However, these scholars do not examine why the state legislature denied most divorce petitions or why North Carolina eventually instituted judicial divorce. A look at the reasons for the failure of most petitions in the legislative system and for the eventual abandonment of that system suggests that the transition from legislative to judicial divorce was not as significant as some scholars have claimed.

Agitation for judicial divorce began in North Carolina as early as 1790. Instead of arguing that the state should adopt judicial divorce because it would make divorce easier, its proponents claimed that the legislature did not have the time or resources to deal properly with divorce cases. Moreover, they maintained that the legislature did not have the same tools as local courts to collect information about the particulars of divorce petitioners. William Gaston, a prominent lawyer, legislator, and jurist from New Bern, worried that, based on such an information deficit, the legislature might grant a divorce where it was unwarranted. "How would you feel," Gaston wrote, "if, on going through the proceedings of the legislature, you discovered you were no longer married to your wife?"[14]

In 1814, the North Carolina legislature authorized judicial divorce for the first time, granting jurisdiction to the superior courts, though still retaining the power to issue private bills of divorce. By 1827, the General Assembly had relinquished all authority over divorces, leaving the superior courts as the sole venue for legal divorce. If adopting judicial divorce did in fact make divorce easier, it did not appear to generate many divorce cases. In most counties, the superior court tackled few, if any, divorce cases in the decade after it was granted authority to issue divorces. The fact that few North Carolinians in failed marriages took advantage of the opportunity for judicial divorce upon its institution indicates that legal barriers did not function as the primary impediment to divorce.

Scholars have also noted how antebellum southern legal codes provided comparatively few grounds for filing divorce. North Carolina allowed absolute divorce only in cases of adultery or impotency and legal separations in the case of physical abuse or abandonment. In contrast, Indiana, infamous in the early nineteenth century for its liberal divorce laws, permitted absolute divorces for impotency, bigamy, adultery, abandonment, conviction of a felony, cruelty, and "in any other case, where the court in their discretion, shall consider it reasonable and proper that a divorce should be granted."[15] At first glance, these differences appear significant. However, in practice, the vast majority of divorces in both North Carolina and Indiana were filed on the grounds of adultery. Even if we only consider those Indiana divorces that fulfilled North Carolina legal requirements, Indiana's divorce rate was still significantly higher than North Carolina's.[16] Further, superior court records indicate that North Carolina judges and juries occasionally granted divorces that did not strictly meet the legal standard. For example, in at least two cases, antebellum women were granted divorces on the grounds that their husbands were alcoholics, and one man received a divorce because his wife refused "to enjoy the society of her husband."[17] This evidence indicates that differing grounds for divorce probably are not as significant as some have argued.

Scholars have also placed undue emphasis on the vitriolic rhetoric about divorce found in North Carolina Supreme Court opinions. However, only a small handful of divorce cases were appealed to the supreme court, and those cases probably were not representative of divorces cases in general. Examining the records from the superior court, the court of original jurisdiction in divorce cases, reveals that the experience of most North Carolinians seeking divorce differed significantly from what would be expected from reading supreme court opinions.

In order to assess the lived experience of divorce, I examined the superior court records from five counties—Perquimans, Hyde, Wayne, Orange, and Macon—from 1814 to 1900. Two factors shaped the selection of counties. First, their divorce records were among the most complete in the state. Divorce records from many counties are woefully incomplete, particularly before 1860, as the ravages of fire, war, and flooded basements have decimated fragile records in county courthouses.

Geographic and economic diversity functioned as a secondary criterion. Although not necessarily representative in a statistically demonstrable way, these five counties do provide a meaningful cross section of the North Carolina population. A brief tour of these counties will suffice. With more than one hundred miles of coastline and its soil nourished by the Perquimans, Little, and Yeopim rivers, Perquimans County was home to several of the state's largest plantations, resulting in a black majority. Its sandy soil and access to the Albemarle Sound sustained a substantial peanut crop and commercial fishing in addition to corn, wheat, and cotton. Fifty miles to the south of Perquimans and bounded by the Pamlico River to the west, Pamlico Sound to the south and east, and Tyrrell County to the north, Hyde County prospered on a mixed economy of subsistence farming, hunting, and fishing. Like Perquimans County, Hyde County had a handful of large plantations in the midst of small holdings. The gently rolling terrain of Wayne County, located in the Coastal Plain region, made it one of the most agriculturally productive counties in the state, cultivating hundreds of acres of cotton and tobacco. Goldsboro, Wayne's county seat and largest town, became an important railway hub in the 1840s, shipping the county's agricultural goods to regional and national markets. Bisected by the Eno, Haw, and Little rivers and home to the University of North Carolina, Orange County produced mainly corn and cotton during the antebellum period, though tobacco became a major crop after the Civil War. Although there were several sizable plantations within its borders, Orange County's population consisted primarily of small farmers, who raised cattle, pigs, and horses in addition to cash crops. Macon County is the western terminus of the tour. Bordering Georgia to the south and Tennessee to the north and set among the heavily forested Blue Ridge Mountains, Macon County was unsuitable for commercial agriculture because of its comparative isolation and cooler temperatures. As a consequence, slavery never flourished there, and its black population throughout the nineteenth century remained one of the smallest in the state.[18]

The first surprise that emerges from the divorce records from these counties is that the vast majority of filings were successful. Given the heated rhetoric of Justice Ruffin and others, one might expect courts to routinely deny divorce suits. In practice, however, more than 90 percent of those seeking divorce in each of the counties under consideration were successful. Indeed, the most common causes for denying divorce were the petitioner's failure to appear in court or the reconciliation of the couple. The success rate in divorce cases does not appear to have changed significantly over the course of the nineteenth century.

The second surprise is how few divorces were contested by the other marriage partner. In fewer than one in ten divorce cases did both spouses file petitions. Often, the reason was that one spouse had abandoned his or her partner and left the region. Although efforts were made through newspaper advertisements to locate wayward spouses, there is little evidence that these advertisements were effective. Often the petitioning spouse had been abandoned many years before and had no idea of his or her partner's whereabouts. For instance, Hyde County's Lucetta McPherson's husband abandoned her nine years before she filed for divorce.[19]

In other cases, couples who mutually agreed to separate arranged for only one of them to file for divorce. This arrangement existed to circumvent North Carolina law, which throughout the nineteenth century required that one partner in divorce cases be declared guilty and the other innocent. If both partners filed for divorce, it was theoretically possible for the court to deny the divorce on the grounds that both partners shared in the guilt for the marriage's failure.[20] Indeed, this adversarial conception continued well into the twentieth century. One Pitt County lawyer advised a client in 1907: "I know your unfortunate situation, but I regret to have to advise you that the law does not contemplate divorce by agreement between the husband and wife; and if the fact appear to any court, under existing laws, that husband and wife are both willing to divorce, this fact would prevent the court from granting the divorce."[21] In arranging her divorce from Lorenzo DeVisconti, Addie May informed him that she had "no money to waste on a divorce suit" and that he should remain "perfectly silent and take no steps" in the matter: "Do not answer the summons, and take no notice of it."[22] As Addie noted, such a contrivance also made divorce cheaper because of reduced legal fees associated with uncontested divorces.

The frequency of uncontested divorce cases helps to explain why so many divorce suits were successful. Assuming that the petitioner met the legal requirements for divorce and outlined them appropriately in the divorce petition, neither judges nor juries had much legal ground to deny the divorce. Examining the judge's instructions to juries in divorce cases reveals that only three legal questions needed resolution: was the couple legally married, did the defendant commit an offense (usually adultery) justifying divorce, and was the plaintiff a legal resident of the county where the suit was filed. With only one side of the case presented, judges and juries had no basis to dispute the facts of the case.

The fact that so few divorce suits were contested should lead us to question how representative those cases that reached the North Carolina Supreme Court were of divorce cases in general. Of the fifteen divorce cases that the supreme court addressed between 1828 (when judicial divorce began) and 1860, thirteen originated in cases of contested divorce. In almost all these cases, a substantial amount of property was in dispute. For instance, in the case of *Matilda Everton v. Major Everton*, the litigants were more concerned with the disposition of couple's plantation and slaves than in the termination of their marriage, which everyone agreed was moribund.[23] Therefore, the cases reviewed by the North Carolina Supreme Court were atypical of divorce cases in the state.

This evidence suggests that the legal barriers to divorce in antebellum North Carolina were not as burdensome as some scholars have suggested. Rather, the social stigma attached to divorce provided more of a barrier than the legal system for antebellum North Carolinians contemplating divorce. The act of divorce required standing before one's neighbors and friends and making a public declaration that one had failed to maintain an institution that most white North Carolinians considered sacred and fundamental to social order. As public events, divorce trials allowed the community to examine and judge the private lives of its members. The twice yearly meetings of the superior court in each county were as much public spectacle and social event as they were instruments of legal justice.[24] Although people petitioning for divorce could expect to leave the courthouse with the desired legal result, they could also expect public and private condemnation from their community. This social stigma provides the best explanation for the infrequency of divorce in antebellum North Carolina.

Divorce petitioners carefully crafted their legal filings not only to meet the legal requirements for divorce but also to minimize the impact that divorce would have on their social standing.[25] Particularly for female divorce petitioners, these documents provided the means to publicly demonstrate their virtue in the face of their partner's marital shortcomings. Indeed, the narratives provided in these divorce petitions emphasized how the innocent party maintained faith in marriage despite his or her spouse's repeated debasements.[26] For example, when the aptly named Prudence Briggs filed for divorce from her husband in 1849, instead of outlining the specific legal grounds for divorce, she crafted a narrative outlining her career as a virtuous wife contrasted with her husband's depravity. When Prudence's husband became cold and distant soon after their wedding, "persuading herself that it might be unintentional on his part; and willing to make every allowance for the increased care and anxieties necessarily accompanying the married life, she determined to bear this treatment with silent submission, and endeavored by redoubled efforts on her part to remove (if any these should be) the slightest cause of complaint from her husband." Despite her efforts, the relationship continued to deteriorate. According to Prudence's petition, her husband neglected his work, spent mindlessly, "consorted with dissolute company," and drank heavily. Throughout, Prudence maintained her position as a virtuous wife, as she "loved her husband, and anxiously strove to call him back to reason and duty." Indeed, she retained this posture at the end of their marriage when he accused her "with the fake charge of adulterous intercourse," made "outrageous threats of violence to her person," and finally drove her from her home.[27]

Prudence Briggs's account finds many echoes in Martha Trice's 1843 divorce petition. Remarried with eleven children and a sizable inheritance from her deceased first husband, Martha Trice discovered shortly after their wedding that her new husband possessed a sadistic streak. She argued that he "profanely cursed & abused her and continued to maltreat her in divers ways until he inflicted upon her a severe whipping with a cowhide." Despite his cruelty, like Prudence Briggs, Martha was "willing to forgive her numerous injuries & forget the past." When she discovered that he had been charged in the county court with the maintenance of a bastard child, she, despite being sick in bed, "complained [to] him of such treachery to her and to his religious professions," in response to which he "threatened to drag her from her bed and to beat her severely." Despite these repeated abuses over a long period of time, Martha Trice's account maintains that she "bore all these indignities with what patience she could command."[28]

The narratives contained in these divorce petitions repeatedly emphasized the wife's capacity to endure inhuman treatment at her husband's hands. Like Job, the level of abuse constantly escalated until it reached a point, in the words of one petitioner, of "cruelties and indignities perhaps unprecedented in civil society."[29] The contrast between the husband's brutality and the wife's steadfast saintliness could only serve to persuade the judge, jury, and audience of the wife's innocence, and she hoped it would lead them to the conclusion that her decision to seek a divorce was necessary rather than voluntary.

While women emphasized their humble submission and willingness to forgive in their divorce petitions, men constructed narratives that emphasized their partner's absolute degradation, particularly in sexual matters. These narratives also emphasize the husband's repeated efforts to redeem his wife from a life of debasement. Lemuel Ivey's 1837 petition provides a vivid, but not atypical, account:

Your Petitioner's wife actuated by the Devil and her own wicked propensities & forgetting that virtue of her sex which has elevated woman from the state of a mere mistress to that of a wife; and disregarding the advice and entreaties of your petitioner, and the moral restraints of civilized society, has wickedly abandoned his house and home, avowing to your Petitioner that she would live the life of an abandoned woman and wanton in her lusts; and indulging in adulterous conversation with men.[30]

Several aspects of Ivey's petition appear over and over again among male divorce petitions. First, many men contrasted their wives' behavior with an ideal of feminine temperament and behavior. For instance, because of his great faith in female virtue, Orange County's Green Partin went to great ends to overlook his wife's infidelity. His 1841 petition argues that while he had heard rumors for several years, "he endeavored to allay them as unjust to her character." Only after confronting his wife and her lover in their marital bed did he fully accept the reality of the situation. After unsuccessfully attempting to kill his wife's paramour, he took the children and filed for divorce.[31]

Second, male petitioners emphasized their wives' sexual depravity, often charging them with prostitution. Barnabas O'Fairhill charged that his wife Nancy's behavior had made him a "witness in his house of her habitual prostitution."[32] Similarly, William Jackson claimed that his wife "Lucinda left this county in a state of prostitution."[33] Willie Stagg's 1851 petition argues that his wife had descended into "a life of licentiousness and has become a common and notorious prostitute."[34] To be sure, in none of these cases did the husband present any evidence that his wife had exchanged sex for money. Instead, by labeling their wives' adulterous behavior as prostitution, these husbands hoped to demonize it sufficiently that it would justify their filing for divorce.

The narrative strategies pursued by Prudence Briggs, Lemuel Ivey, and other antebellum divorce petitioners reveal that they sought to minimize divorce's social stigma by crafting a narrative that absolved them of all guilt in the marriage's demise. Instead of choosing to file for divorce, the petitioners argued that they were driven to it by their partners' repeated abuses. That so many divorce petitioners chose to employ this particular narrative mode rather than a more legalistic description justifying the divorce indicates that it must have been a successful strategy both in persuading the judge and jury to grant the divorce and in mitigating the disgrace of divorce. However, the overall rarity of divorce in antebellum North Carolina indicates that it was not sufficient to remove this social barrier entirely.

The most overwhelming aspect about divorce in antebellum North Carolina may have been its rarity. As Figure 3 indicates, very few North Caro-

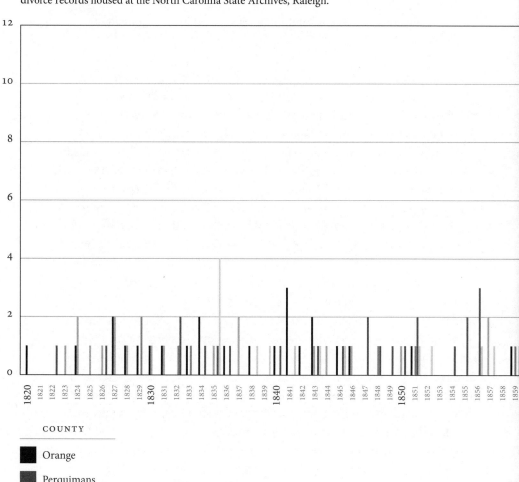

FIGURE 3. Number of divorce cases per year in Orange, Perquimans, Hyde, Wayne, and Macon counties, 1820–1900. The data were derived from extant divorce records housed at the North Carolina State Archives, Raleigh.

COUNTY

Orange

Perquimans

Hyde

Wayne

Macon

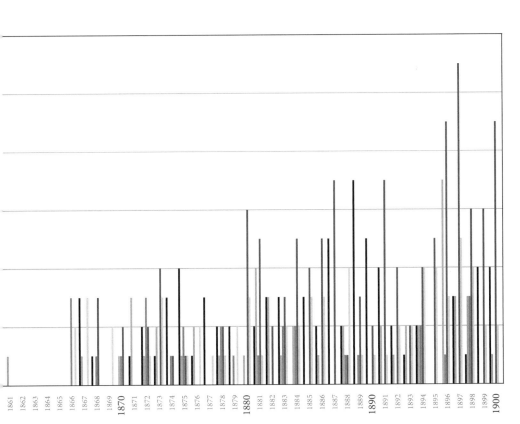

1861 1862 1863 1864 1865 1866 1867 1868 1869 1870 1871 1872 1873 1874 1875 1876 1877 1878 1879 1880 1881 1882 1883 1884 1885 1886 1887 1888 1889 1890 1891 1892 1893 1894 1895 1896 1897 1898 1899 1900

linians sought to legally terminate their marriage between 1820 and 1860. Many counties went years without any divorce cases. This low rate of divorce should not be read as an indication that marriages during this period were particularly blissful or without conflict. Rather, it indicates that social pressures kept many North Carolinians in dysfunctional marriages.

The few white divorced individuals in North Carolina bore a heavy social cost for their actions. Many became ostracized from the broader community, pariahs because of their divorce. Although assessing the degree of social ostracism faced by divorced people in antebellum North Carolina proves challenging, two factors indicate that local communities often made them feel unwelcome. First, many of them found themselves expelled from Christian fellowship, especially when they attempted to remarry after divorce. For instance, the Hay Street Methodist Church in Fayetteville expelled George Warden in 1815 for remarrying while his first wife was still alive.[35] Similarly, the Cove Creek Baptist Church in Sherwood, North Carolina, expelled George and Sary Davis in 1808 "for dubble marrdg" and decreed "that we never will receive any other under the same character." Later the same congregation expelled James Isaac and his wife in 1816 for "parting asunder" and three other couples over the next two decades on similar charges.[36] Indeed, many Baptist congregations categorically excluded divorced people from fellowship. Unlike the courts, churches rarely distinguished between the innocent and guilty parties in divorce cases.[37]

Second, some evidence indicates that divorced people often felt compelled to leave their communities. Comparing divorce records with the next decennial census returns indicates that more than 95 percent of divorced people between 1830 and 1860 no longer lived in the same county where they divorced.[38] Although a whole host of reasons can explain the absence of individual divorced people, their overwhelming disappearance indicates that few elected to remain in their community after their divorce. Those antebellum North Carolinians who remained in their communities after divorcing found that their actions had made them outcastes.

WHILE ANTEBELLUM WHITE North Carolinians held fairly rigid conceptions about marriage and divorce, black North Carolinians, both free and enslaved, developed more nuanced and situational schemes of judgment about marriage and divorce. Indeed, African Americans in antebellum North Carolina understood that marriage and divorce were not absolute categories but rather existed within particular social and cultural contexts, and the meaning of an individual marriage and divorce was predicated upon the particular circumstances that the couple faced. Black North Carolinians combined both African and European conceptions of marriage and divorce into a hybrid fundamentally shaped by the institution of slavery.[39] Although slave marriages were not legally recognized in North Carolina or anywhere in the South and the legal privileges of free black marriages were subject to various degrees of manipulation, marriage ties held no less significance for African Americans than for whites. However, African Americans judged a marriage's demise according to a very different set of standards.

Enslaved North Carolinians understood that many factors could result in the end of a marriage. First, one of the marriage partners could be sold and separated from his or her partner. Recounted in many fugitive slave and Works Progress Administration (WPA) narratives, this traumatic experience broke apart numerous black families, often separating parents from children as well as husbands from wives. Second, a slave owner could forcibly demand that particular slaves abandon their current partners to form a union of his choosing. Although rare, the occasional appearance of such demands in accounts of slave life in North Carolina reveal the extent to which slave unions fell under the dictates of slave owners. Finally, slaves could voluntarily choose to end a marriage of their own volition. In each of these three cases, the end of the marriage fell somewhere in a liminal zone between "till death do you part" and formal divorce.

Only in the final case, however, did the termination of a slave marriage approximate the moral quandary posed by divorce. Almost all slave marriages received some form of sanction, either from a slave owner, the church, the slave community, or some combination of the three.[40] How elaborate or formal this sanction was varied tremendously; nevertheless, the vast majority of slave marriages bore some form of endorsement by the broader community. For slaves who left failed marriages, therefore, their choice echoed many of the same social realities that befell whites who chose to divorce. Although their actions did not have the same legal significance as divorce in the white community, the fact that both whites and blacks commonly referred to this form of marriage termination as divorce indicates the extent to which the two were considered conceptual equivalents. Indeed, each of the three sanctioning entities for slave marriages sought to exert its influence over slave divorce and passed judgment over its validity and morality.

Slave owners held considerable interest in and authority over the married lives of their slaves, though the extent to which they exercised this influence varied considerably. A small handful of slave owners exerted dictatorial authority in arranging slave marriages. Many more slave owners allowed their slaves to choose their own partners, believing (probably correctly) that slaves who formed meaningful partnerships and stable families would enjoy higher morale and offer less resistance. Most slave owners, however, fell somewhere between these two extremes, choosing to encourage and sanction some relationships while discouraging others. Indeed, slave owners in North Carolina and across the South often took the place of a minister at slave weddings, offering their own sanction to a marriage in place of a legal or clerical one.

Slave owners demonstrated the same authority in ending slave marriages. Much has been written about the extent to which slave owners broke up marriages by selling one of the partners.[41] Less, however, has been said about how slave owners understood and reacted to slaves who chose to end their marriage. A handful of slave owners across the South actively attempted to prevent slave divorce through force. South Carolina's James Henry Hammond allowed slaves to divorce for "sufficient cause," but only after submitting to one hundred lashes. Similarly, a Louisiana sugar planter permitted slaves to divorce if given a month's notice and permitted remarriage after the individual received twenty-five lashes.[42]

Many more slave owners sought to dissuade slaves from ending their marriage through moral suasion, though most found this approach both tiresome and unprofitable. "As to their habits of amalgamation and intercourse," wrote one planter in 1851, "I know no means whereby to regulate them. I attempted to for many years by preaching virtue and decency, encouraging marriages, and by punishing, with some severity, departures from marital obligations, but it was all in vain." Another planter claimed that although he considered "the settlement of family troubles" among slaves an essential aspect of plantation management, "some owners become disgusted and wearied out, and finally leave the people to their own way."[43]

Most slave owners, however, appeared to take a hands-off approach to slave divorce, recognizing that forcing slaves to stay married against their will only served to undermine morale and decrease productivity. Others apparently adopted a passive response to slave divorce out of apathy rather than intention. One Florida planter claimed that he "never interfered in their connubial or domestic affairs, but let them regulate those after their own manner."[44] This attitude could reflect a begrudging respect for slave autonomy or, more likely, a belief that the marriage of slaves functioned only as a shadow of its white counterpart. "The relation between the slaves is essentially different from that of man and wife joined in lawful wedlock," wrote one North Carolina justice in 1858; "with slaves it may be dissolved at the pleasure of either party."[45] According to one former slave from Orange County, "Gettin married an' having a family was a joke [to slave owners] in the days of slavery, as the main thing in allowing any form of matrimony among the slaves was to raise more slaves."[46]

Southern religious institutions also weighed in on the subject. Slave divorce, like most aspects of slave marriage, presented a vexing problem to antebellum biracial churches because it forced them to reconcile the fiction that all members needed to be held to the same moral standard and the extralegal reality of slave marriage. Throughout the antebellum period, churches across the South struggled with the questions raised by the termination of slave marriages. Did the extralegal status of slave marriage affect the moral obligations of the couple to each other or to the community? What was the marital status of a slave whose spouse had been sold? Could this slave remarry? Were slaves who voluntarily separated subject to the same degree of ecclesiastical condemnation as whites who divorced? The Flat River Primitive Baptist Church in Person County was among the first to address these questions. In 1790, it took up the case of "Negro Sam," a slave whose wife had been sold and taken to South Carolina. Sympathetically, the congregation concluded that "where a man and wife is parted by their owners, who being in bondage cannot help themselves, as such we have come to the conclusion that it shall not brake [sic] fellowship with us if Sam should git another wife."[47]

In the next seven decades, most churches in North Carolina concluded that slaves forcibly separated from their husbands or wives could remarry. After the Civil War, one white man recalled that sale of a spouse to a location more than thirty miles away "was considered by the clergy equivalent to a divorce because the husband could not walk to his wife and back again between Saturday at sundown and Monday at sunrise."[48] Not all churches and religious organizations conformed to this view. The Broad River Baptist Association of North Carolina concluded in 1820 that slaves whose partners had been sold and relocated could not remarry and remain part of the religious fellowship.[49] This position, however, was rare. According to Moses Grandy, a fugitive slave born in Camden County, in most churches, "ministers, some years ago, . . . decided that such a separation might be considered as the death of the parties to each other, and that they therefore agreed to consider subsequent marriages not immoral. The practice is common."[50]

Although churches generally absolved slaves of moral fault when they remarried after being forcibly separated from a spouse, they demonstrated no hesitancy in condemning slave members who voluntarily separated from a spouse. Indeed, slaves who voluntarily abandoned a church-sanctioned marriage were frequently reprimanded or even excommunicated, especially in those cases in which the slave then went on to live with another partner.[51]

Some slaves internalized the marriage ethic espoused by their church and refused to marry after being forcibly separated from a spouse. For instance, a sixty-two-year-old enslaved carpenter from Weldon, North Carolina, told abolitionist-journalist James Redpath in 1854 that he remarried after his first wife, with whom he had twelve children, was sold and relocated. However, after his second wife was also sold, he decided that he would not seek another wife. "I hasn't had anyding to do wid women since," he told Redpath. "I's a Baptist; and it's agin my religion to have anything to do wid anybody 'cept my wife. I's never bothered anybody since my last wife was sold away from me."[52]

The slave community provided the third sanctioning entity for slave marriage and divorce. Fellow slaves, including those from surrounding farms and plantations, often provided a fundamental social context for any slave marriage. Indeed, according to Herbert Gutman, approximately half of slave marriages received no official sanction from either owners or white clergy.[53] For some slave couples, their marriage was sanctioned in a slave community ritual, officiated by a slave preacher or another community leader. Other slave couples simply decided that their relationship was significant enough to consider themselves married. Even in this second case, sometimes referred to as "blanket marriages," the slave couple relied upon tacit community approval to sustain the relationship.[54] Had a slave community determined that a particular union did not meet local standards, it is likely that it would have intervened.

Some historians have argued that the extralegal nature of slave marriage resulted in a comparatively tolerant attitude in the slave community concerning divorce and a high rate of voluntary separations among slave couples. Notably, Eugene Genovese argued that slave morality permitted "a wider standard of behavior that sanctioned divorce" and that this "easy attitude toward divorce was strongly reinforced by the knowledge that the blow to the children would be greatly softened in a community in which all looked after all and the master had to feed all." Additionally, Genovese claims that the prevalence of early marriage among slaves "set the stage for a high rate of divorce."[55]

Although Genovese is correct in concluding that many slaves did not share white southerners' aversion to divorce, he fails to recognize that discourse over divorce in the slave community resulted from a variety of alternate conceptions of marriage. Even if he does not say so explicitly, Genovese's argument implies that slaves did not consider marriage important or did not believe that upholding the obligations of marriage was significant. However, the evidence indicates that many slaves in North Carolina valued marriage just as much as whites did. While slaves in some communities tolerated voluntary separations much more than whites, each slave community could establish well-defined boundaries delineating how and why slaves could end marriages. Although the position of these social-moral boundaries varied temporally and geographically, there is good evidence to suggest that slaves knew their local community's expectations concerning marriage and divorce.

Wayne Durrill's study of Somerset Place Plantation indicates that slaves there subscribed to the idea that in marriage couples formed a permanent union. Located near the Albemarle Sound on the northwestern rim of Lake Phelps, Somerset was among the state's largest plantations, home to more than two hundred enslaved men, women, and children. According to the owner of a neighboring plantation, slave women metaphorically compared entering a marriage to tying "a knot with her tongue which she can't untie with her teeth." Durrill notes that plantation records indicate many of the slave unions at Somerset lasted for decades, while providing no evidence that slaves voluntarily parted from spouses. He concludes that "voluntary divorce occurred rarely at Somerset Place."[56]

Divorce also seems to have been rare among slaves at Stagville Plantation, located in what is today northern Durham County. An analysis of detailed genealogical charts reconstructed from plantation records and oral histories of Stagville Plantation indicates that slave marriages were remarkably stable and slave-initiated divorce was rare or even nonexistent.[57] However, although the evidence from Somerset Place and Stagville is compelling about the strength of slave marriages on those particular plantations, it would be a mistake to extrapolate from these examples to the broader slave population. Somerset and Stagville slaves lived in atypical social conditions. Among the largest plantations in the state, they each had slave populations that numbered in the hundreds. Owned by wealthy and secure families who seldom saw the need to sell their human property, slaves at Somerset and Stagville had less reason to fear being sold than those who belonged to financially insecure owners. Young slaves had a comparatively large pool of potential marriage partners, and a large slave community existed to support and counsel young couples. Under such circumstances, noted Mecklenburg

County doctor James B. Alexander, "it was almost an unheard of thing for a negro to ask for a divorce."[58]

These favorable conditions for stable marriages did not exist for most slaves, especially in North Carolina, a state with comparatively few large plantations. Living on small plantations and farms, most slaves had significantly constrained choices about potential spouses, usually limited to slaves living on their own or neighboring plantations or occasionally nearby free blacks. They had more reason to fear being forcibly separated from loved ones, as small slave owners were more likely than large slave owners to sell their human property to pay their debts. Finally, slaves on small plantations had greater difficulty maintaining the robust social support networks that slaves on large plantations relied upon to support marriages in troubled times. Although many North Carolina slaves maintained healthy and robust "abroad" marriages, the inherent difficulty in sustaining these relationships potentially made divorce or long-term estrangement more likely than would have been the case for slave relationships confined to one plantation.[59]

Unfortunately, small slaveholders on the whole left less robust records of slave kinship than their compatriots with larger holdings, and therefore it is difficult to quantify the extent to which divorce was more common for slaves living on small farms than those living on large plantations. However, anecdotal evidence, particularly from WPA slave narratives, indicates that a form of community-recognized divorce was relatively common among non-plantation slaves and that the slave community attached little stigma to the practice. This practice, sometimes referred to as "quitting," allowed slaves in unhappy marriages to separate, either through mutual agreement or by individual initiative on the part of one of the partners.[60] According to Hilliard Yellerday, who had been a slave on a small farm in Warren County, "Some slave women would have dozen of men during their life. Negro women who had had a half dozen mock husbands in slavery time were plentiful. The holy bonds of matrimony did not mean much to a slave."[61] A North Carolina slave questioned by James Redpath in 1854 echoed this sentiment when asked about his marital status: "Ah was married, but ah didn't like my old woman, and ah lives wid another now."[62] His readiness and openness in discussing the end of this marriage indicate that he did not feel ashamed of his actions.

This evidence suggests that, unlike their white owners and neighbors, North Carolina slaves did not adhere to a universal conception of divorce or marriage termination.[63] Instead, what emerges is a patchwork of beliefs and attitudes dependent on local conditions, experiences, and values. In large measure, slaves in North Carolina never developed a single common understanding of divorce because they never shared a common understanding of marriage. What slaves thought about marriage, both generally and in reference to individual unions, reflected the particularities of their local conditions. Consequentially, the way that they interpreted divorce depended on local marriage practices and sentiments.

It is difficult to assess the meaning and role of divorce among North Carolina's free black population. Unlike slaves, free blacks could obtain legally recognized marriages and therefore could, if they so desired, also obtain a divorce. Comparing free black North Carolinians' understanding of divorce with that of either whites or slaves is complicated by the fact that many free blacks maintained long-term relationships with partners who were enslaved, and these unions were not cloaked in legal protections and thus not subject to divorce.[64] Although an ordinance passed by the General Assembly in 1830 prohibited intermarriage or cohabitation between free blacks and slaves, many free blacks in North Carolina nevertheless sustained relationships with enslaved partners.[65] Therefore, a free black person's access to marriage and divorce was predicated upon the legal status of his or her partner.

Historians are divided on the extent to which free blacks exercised their right to marriage. In her study of Petersburg, Virginia, Suzanne Lebsock argued that free black women often chose not to exercise their legal right to marry because they believed that marriage would deprive them of the autonomy they enjoyed as free women.[66] However, as Michael Johnson and James Roark have observed, because Petersburg (like most southern cities) had significantly more free black women than free black men, marriage practices there may have differed significantly from practices in those places with a more even gender balance. They argue that Petersburg's free black women's failure to marry legally reflected their inability to find an available free black man as a partner rather than a statement of personal independence. They conclude that whenever and wherever possible, free black families sought to protect themselves through legal institutions, including marriage.[67] The prevalence of legal marriage among free blacks remains, therefore, an open question.[68] This scholarly disagreement may indicate that free black marriage practices, like slave marriage practices, varied according to local conditions.

No cases of free black divorce appear in any of the five counties under examination. Several possible explanations present themselves for free blacks' absence from divorce records, but the mostly likely cause may have been that free blacks found the financial costs of divorce prohibitive. The fees associated with divorce could amount to several dollars, and in those few cases in which the divorce was contested, they could run much higher. This financial disincentive to divorce would also help to explain why comparatively few poor whites sought divorce during the antebellum period. For both free blacks and poor whites, a de facto divorce often served as a substitute for legal divorce, although without the possibility of legal remarriage and often with messy complications in inheritance and personal finances.

White and black North Carolinians saw divorce very differently during the antebellum period. This difference was shaped primarily by their conceptions of and experience with marriage. From the perspective of marriage as a fundamental social institution, white North Carolinians almost categorically abhorred divorce as a threat to public order, stigmatizing divorced people as social pariahs. Black North Carolinians, in contrast, viewed marriage from a variety of perspectives, depending on their legal status, the attitudes of their owners, and local social and demographic conditions. As we shall see, the Civil War challenged and changed how white and black North Carolinians saw marriage and divorce in two significant ways. First, the wartime experience placed an unprecedented stress on marital relationships. Second, it forced white and black North Carolinians to conform to a single marital standard. The results were devastating.

CHAPTER FIVE

Connubial Bliss until He
Entered the Army by Conscription

Civil War & Divorce

W HEN TWENTY-THREE-YEAR-OLD James Wells enlisted in his
local regiment on 6 June 1861, he knew that his service for the
Confederate cause would take him farther from his Caswell
County home than he had ever traveled. He also knew that it would take
him away from his young wife, Nancy, whom he had married only months
earlier. At her request, Wells escorted his wife to her father's home in Orange
County, "to remain until he could return and take charge of her." After three
months in uniform, Wells secured a two-week furlough to visit his wife, returning to his unit "happy in the belief that he had obtained a virtuous and
loving wife and one every way suited to him."[1]

James Wells spent the next eighteen months away from North Carolina,
engaged in one battle after another along the Virginia-Maryland border.
Battle scarred and longing to return home, he heard rumors that his wife
"had proved false to her marriage vows" and "become a common prostitute."
Obtaining a brief furlough in February 1863, Wells traveled to his father-in-
law's home, hoping against hope that the rumors would prove false. After
being questioned by her husband, however, Nancy Wells admitted that she
had indeed been unfaithful. He stormed out of the house, determined never
to see her again.

Enraged by his wife's behavior, Wells returned to his unit. After receiving
a minor bullet wound at Gettysburg in July 1863, he was captured by Union
forces near Rappahannock Station, Virginia, in November 1863. Spending
the next year as a prisoner at the Union prison at Point Lookout, Maryland,
Wells was eventually exchanged in February 1865. Furloughed at Richmond
in early March 1865, Wells returned to North Carolina, where he learned that

his estranged wife had borne a "bastard child" a year earlier. He promptly filed for divorce in the Orange County Superior Court.

The Civil War had a radically different effect on the married life of James McCullom, a slave laboring on a plantation near Lumberton. As a young man, McCullom had married and fathered two young children. At some point during the early 1850s, his owner sold his wife and children. Not knowing where his family had been taken and resigning himself to the fact that he would never see them again, he began to adjust to life in their absence. Although heartbroken, McCullom remarried four years later. After emancipation, however, his first wife and children reappeared, having sought him out immediately after obtaining their freedom. His first family's reappearance forced McCullom to choose between two marriages, neither of which had legal sanction but both of which he had entered with the expectation that he would uphold his marital obligations. In the end, he concluded, after some deliberation, that his first marriage had precedence and remarried his first wife in 1867.[2]

The experiences of the Wellses and the McCulloms were not uncommon. For many white and black North Carolinians, the Civil War placed a strain on both actual marriages and conceptions of marriage. For many whites, the wartime experience separated husbands from wives, as men joined the Confederate army, while women tended their homes and farms as best they could. Although most white North Carolinians found separation temporary and reunion joyful, for a significant number of others, the war had long-term consequences for their relationships. For black North Carolinians, the Civil War also strained marital bonds, bonds that were already fragile because of the peculiar burdens of slavery. Especially in coastal regions of North Carolina, where a significant Federal presence existed from the early months of the conflict, slave owners uprooted slaves and often split families in order to prevent this most valuable property from falling into enemy hands.[3] At the same time, however, many enslaved African Americans found opportunities either to flee to Union lines or to reconnect with loved ones long separated. With emancipation, freedmen and freedwomen confronted the prospect of legalized marriage and the possibility of legal divorce.[4] Thus, for both whites and blacks, the Civil War transformed their understanding of the role of marriage in society and the meaning of divorce.

The desire to legalize long-standing relationships among newly liberated black North Carolinians indicates how radically the Civil War transformed the meaning of marriage and family. Across the South, freed slaves sought out lost family members and hoped to cloak their family relationships with the legal protections marriage provided. However, as Ira Berlin has noted, the black family that emerged from slavery was more than the slave family given legal sanction.[5] Freedom transformed how African Americans understood familial institutions, including the obligations of marriage and the meaning of divorce.

As soon as Union forces had a foothold in North Carolina's coastal counties, refugee slaves sought to celebrate their freedom by seeking out Federal officers and army chaplains to perform marriage ceremonies.[6] Huddled in refugee camps that became communities, many fugitive slave couples believed that these ceremonies would secure their uncertain legal status. During the summer and fall of 1862, Union army chaplain T. W. Conway married dozens of black couples. "Some of them," he noted, "on inquiring about the institution of marriage, ascertained that they were not properly married; that they were simply joined together at the will and pleasure of their masters. . . . While they agree very well, and live very happy, they somehow or other think themselves to have begun wrong, and accordingly make up their minds to begin over again."[7]

However, not all refugee slave couples believed that they needed outside approval to validate their marriage, and the presence of so many "unmarried" couples deeply troubled some Union officials in charge of managing the refugee population. They worried that, without legal sanctions for their unions, refugee slaves would defile the institution of marriage. The presence of slave women with children and without visible husbands particularly troubled them. The wife of one Union official remarked that these women "supposed they had no partner & were at liberty to marry again."[8]

The behavior of refugee slaves indicates that even though obtaining legal marriage was a priority for some slaves on North Carolina's eastern coast, this desire was not universal. They did not always see the same distinctions between legal and extralegal marriages that Freedmen's Bureau officials did.[9] A significant number of refugee slaves believed either that a marriage ceremony officiated by a Union official was unnecessary or that such a ceremony would not add any significant legal or social sanction to their union. This range of opinions reflects in part the diversity of marriage practices among North Carolina slaves. Slaves brought with them a multiplicity of conceptions about the meaning of marriage as they sought to rebuild their families behind Union lines, leading some to demand immediate official recognition of their marriage while others saw no such need. As we shall see, fugitive slaves demonstrated a range of behaviors and attitudes toward marriage during the war that would manifest themselves on much larger scale after the war ended, when tens of thousands of freedmen and freedwomen decided what their freedom meant to their marriage.

In the summer of 1865, many freed people celebrated their liberation by wedding their loved ones. Wake County's Mattie Curtis remembered that "right atter de war northern preachers come round wid a little book a-marrying slaves an' I seed one of dem marry my pappy an' mammy."[10] Over a two-day period in late August 1865 at Warrenton, an Episcopal minister married approximately 150 freed couples who were eager to obtain legal and social sanction for their marriage.[11]

The fervor with which some freed persons sought to reaffirm slave relationships indicates that many of them saw a meaningful difference between the socially sanctioned slave marriage and the legal marriage now available to them. Wake County freedman Parker Pool remembered that although slaves formed meaningful bonds, "dere wuz no marriage — till after the surrender." Similarly, freedwoman Rena Raines recalled that although her parents had married as slaves by "jumpin' de broom," after emancipation, they "come ter Raleigh atter de surrender an wus married right."[12] Although almost all slave marriages had received some form of social sanction, many freedmen and freedwomen believed that officially recording their marriage would add an additional layer of respectability. One former slave noted that, although she and her husband had lived together for thirty-five years and raised twelve children, she wanted to "buy a 'ticket'" because "all 'spectable folk is to be married, and we's 'spectable."[13]

While most former slaves married of their own volition, the freed community at times exerted pressure on those who did not abide by the evolving community standards regarding marriage. A Freedmen's Bureau official in Bladenboro, North Carolina, wrote in July 1867,

> The Colored people of this place are trying to make their colored bretheren [sic] pay some respect to themselves and the laws of the country by making them pay some respect to the marriage bond and stop the slave style of living to gather [sic] without being married. . . . A colored man has been promising to marry a girl for the last year [and] has been begging with her most of the time. They have had four times set for marriage but at each time he has put her of[f] with some excuse. The colored men of this place appointed a committee to wait on him and see if they could not influence him to do better but no satisfaction could be obtained.[14]

To be sure, freedmen and freedwomen were not alone in seeing the necessity to legitimize slave marriages. Whites from a variety of backgrounds saw the legalization of black marriage as a pressing need in the immediate aftermath of emancipation, although their motivations were often quite different from those of the newly liberated slaves. Union military officials, both in Washington and locally, acted to provide some legal protection for slave marriages.[15] Northern teachers and missionaries who traveled to Union-occupied territory insisted that freed persons formalize their relationships out of the belief that legal sanctions inculcated moral and sexual restraint.[16] For instance, Col. Eliphalet Whittlesey, the Freedmen's Bureau assistant commissioner in North Carolina, reported that in the six months after the end of the war, "as a result of moral instruction, 512 marriages have been reported."[17] To be sure, the motivations of the Freedmen's Bureau were not always altruistic. Some bureau officials believed that marriage would transfer the responsibility for impoverished freedwomen and their children from the bureau to their husbands and fathers.[18]

Many native whites, however, did not believe that freed persons could maintain the moral standards of marriage. According to Rev. James Sinclair, a Freedmen's Bureau agent in Lumberton, black marriage "is a matter of ridicule among the whites. They do not believe the negroes will ever respect those relations more than the brutes." Although his own experience in presiding over two hundred black marriages convinced him of their earnest intentions and commitment, "the whites laugh at the very idea of the thing."[19] Similarly, according to journalist John Richard Dennett, a delegate to the 1865 Constitutional Convention in Raleigh claimed that he had heard "from a gentleman of undoubted veracity" that of seventy former slave couples who had obtained legal marriage in one town since emancipation, sixty-five had "within a week left other wives or husbands to take new ones."[20] While the veracity of this third- or fourth-hand tale is to be questioned, it indicates the extent to which many white North Carolinians doubted that their newly liberated black population could uphold marital obligations.

In March 1866, the state legislature decided to intervene on the issue of freed-person marriages by passing "An Act Concerning Negroes and Persons of Color or of Mixed Blood." Most former Confederate states legalized slave marriages by fiat; they were considered legally valid without further action on behalf of the partners and without the need to document the union.[21] Other states considered all freed people to be unmarried until they sought formal marriage under the law.[22] North Carolina's legislation was somewhat unique in that it neither immediately granted legitimacy to slave marriages nor required freed people to undergo the entire ritual of marriage again.[23] Instead, the state adopted an intermediary position whereby freed couples were required to register their union with the local clerk of the county court or justice of the peace, paying a fee of twenty-five cents for the privilege.

Many freedmen and freedwomen responded swiftly to register their marriage. In the months that followed the act's passage, at least 22,400 former slave couples registered their marriage.[24] Indeed, many who had sought legal sanction for their marriage immediately after emancipation also registered their marriage, believing that the redundant documentation would provide greater legal protection for their unions.

However, not all freedmen and freedwomen decided to exercise the provisions of the new marriage registration law. Herbert Gutman estimated that approximately half of former slave couples in North Carolina legalized their union in the immediate postwar period, arriving at this figure by comparing marriage registers with 1860 census data.[25] From this, Gutman concluded that most former slaves embraced legal marriage. However, his own calculations indicate that approximately half of slave couples chose not to register their union, despite legal penalties for failing to do so.[26]

Assessing why approximately half of North Carolina's slave couples did not register their union is more challenging than explaining why half did exercise that option. First, many freed couples who had already obtained what they considered a legal marriage, either by a military or Freedmen's Bureau official or by a minister, perhaps believed that further registration was unnecessary. Second, other couples evidently believed that the social sanction that their slave marriage had enjoyed was sufficient and that no further action was necessary to legitimize it, despite the legal penalties for failing to register.[27] Third, the cost of marriage registration, while lower than the cost of a full marriage, proved prohibitively expensive for some freed slaves.

In all likelihood, these explanations account for the vast majority of nonregistrants. However, a fourth explanation also existed. Although emancipation meant that former slaves had the right to marry those whom they loved, it also permitted slaves stuck in undesirable marriages to obtain a de facto divorce by not solemnizing their slave marriage.[28] The particularities of North Carolina's marriage registration statute meant that someone seeking such a de facto divorce could do so easily. The case of Tony Alston, a black Union veteran originally from Georgia, demonstrates how failing to register a marriage functioned as a divorce. Settling after the war with his wife in Goldsboro, North Carolina, Alston apparently failed to register in 1867, deciding instead to abandon his wife and move to Savannah, Georgia, where he married another woman.[29]

While some former slaves faced the dilemma of whether or not to register their marriage, others confronted more challenging issues. As Leon Litwack has observed, "The question facing numerous freedmen and freedwomen was not whether to formalize their slave marriage but which one should take precedence."[30] At times, black couples called upon outside authorities to arbitrate between vying claimants. For example, Freedmen's Bureau agent Rev. James Sinclair remarked, "Whenever a negro appears before me with two or three wives who have equal claim upon him, I marry him to the woman who has the greatest number of helpless children who otherwise would be a charge on the Bureau."[31]

But in most cases freedmen and freedwomen made these difficult decisions on their own, weighing carefully their own needs and desires against those of their loved ones. A former slave of Rev. Billy Boone in Northampton County, Andrew Boone recalled that his father had to choose between several wives, all of whom had borne him children. "He had several women besides mother. . . . Dese women wuz given to him [by Rev. Boone] an' no udder man wus allowed to have anything to do wid 'em." When given the chance to arrange his own household after emancipation, Boone's father rejected all his slave marriages, choosing instead to begin a new family.[32]

This evidence of divorces and de facto divorces among freedmen and freedwomen indicates that emancipation had a devastating effect on some black marriages. Emancipation and the access to legal marriage forced the great variety of local slave marriage practices to conform to a single standard, a standard that not all marriages or marriage partners could match. While most black couples jumped at the opportunity to cloak their marriage in legal protections, for a significant number the transition from slavery to freedom proved an unbearable strain on their intimate relationships.

THE CIVIL WAR also transformed how white North Carolinians understood marriage and divorce. For men and women deeply invested in local community and kinship networks, the military experience placed deep strains on marital ties. Even though Confederates often sentimentalized the wartime experience, the physical separation of husbands and wives exposed marital fissures.[33] The Civil War also created new wounds, as the temptations created by the physical distance and the uncertain reunion with one's spouse proved irresistible. The consequences led many white North Carolinians to reinterpret the nature of marriage and a significant number to seek divorce.

The onset of war spawned many hasty marriages. For unmarried white women watching young soldiers march off to battle, the sight of a landscape increasingly devoid of white men brought up fears of spinsterhood. As the war's lethality became increasingly apparent, many young women realized that a significant number of the young men marching off to war would never return and therefore their marriage prospects would not improve significantly after hostilities ended. "The reflection has been brought to my mind with a great force," wrote one young woman in early 1864, "that after this war is closed, how vast a difference there will be in the numbers of males and females."[34] According to a letter to Governor Zebulon Vance from concerned women living near New Bern, by the summer of 1863, only 20 of the 250 white people remaining in town were men.[35] "There is but few men at home," wrote Mittie Williams of Montgomery County, "and what there is I reckon has declined the idea of ever marrying."[36] For young men entering the Confederate army, marriage before enlistment helped to legitimize their manhood and strengthen their connection with home. The resulting enthusiasm for marriage among young North Carolinians shocked many of their parents' generation. As the demands of war pressed, the antebellum customs of deliberation and careful selection of marriage partners fell away in favor of brief courtships and engagements.[37] The newlyweds in these hastily arranged marriages scarcely had time to set up housekeeping before being separated.[38]

Very few white North Carolinians sought divorces during the war itself. In the five counties under examination, the slow trickle of antebellum divorces ran dry between 1861 and 1865. No divorces were filed in Wayne, Hyde, Macon, or Orange counties during the war itself. The Perquimans County Superior Court granted only one divorce during the war, and that in its spring term of 1861, before major combat had commenced. The almost total absence of divorce in North Carolina courts during the Civil War may have resulted in part from the fact that the superior courts met irregularly, especially in those counties on the coast where the threat from Union forces was the highest.

More significant, however, individuals in failed marriages could reap many of the benefits of divorce without incurring the social or financial costs. With their husbands away, many would-be divorcées had the de facto autonomy and control over property that divorce would provide. Further, North Carolina, like many Confederate states, provided some benefits to soldiers' wives. Albeit meager, these benefits would have disappeared were they to divorce.[39] Moreover, for women in abusive relationships, the war would have been a welcome reprieve from their husband's cruelty. They might have also concluded that the courts would have been less sympathetic to their arguments while their husbands were away at war and unable to defend themselves.

Court records after 1865, however, reveal that white North Carolinians' experiences during the war led to a significant number of divorces immediately afterward. With many husbands and wives separated by time and distance, the stage was set for marital breakdown on a vast scale. The Civil War, like most military conflicts, placed extreme strains on marital relationships. Although most white southern marriages healed from the wounds inflicted by war and some even grew stronger, for a significant minority, the conflict had undermined their union and exposed latent flaws in their relationship.

The number of divorce cases in the immediate aftermath of the war increased dramatically. In Hyde County, the superior court authorized three divorces in its fall session of 1866. Although apparently a small quantity, it exceeded the total number of divorces granted in the entire previous decade. Between 1866 and 1870, twenty couples divorced in the five counties under consideration, a significant amount compared with the one divorce issued between 1861 and 1865.

One thread running through these postwar divorces was the central role of the war itself. Like James and Nancy Wells's, other Orange County marriages were destroyed by wartime separations. According to his divorce petition, John Bowling had lived happily with his wife, Elizabeth, "from the time of his marriage to 1861." Enlisting in September 1861, John returned home a year later on furlough to find that "his house had been converted to a brothel, [and] that his said wife Elizabeth disregarding the sacred ties by which they were bound together, had prostituted herself to the embraces of other men."[40] Similarly, Willie Couch claimed that after his 1860 marriage to his wife, Emma, "he took his wife to a home he had provided for them where they lived contented and happy . . . until the breaking out of the late civil war when as one of the young men of the South he was called upon to take up arms for his State." When he returned home in May 1865 after more than three years in the army, he was "shocked & overwhelmed to find that his wife had left their home he had provided for her & had proved false to his marriage vows and had given birth to a bastard child. . . . Emma had become a hard woman and common prostitute."[41]

The remarkable similarities between the Wells, Bowling, and Couch divorces find echoes outside Orange County. Married in 1863, Macon County's Eli Patton "lived in the enjoyment of connubial bliss until he entered the army by conscription. . . . Shortly after his departure for the army his said wife abandoned his home," moving to Tennessee with a paramour.[42] Similarly, Joseph and Charlotte Shepard "lived together as man and wife enjoying all the comforts and happiness incident and pertaining to the marriage relation without any disturbance whatever, each discharging their duties without complaint and without suspicion on either side until about the 14th May of 1861, when your petitioner volunteered and entered the Confederate Army." Returning home on furlough in December 1862, he found his wife carrying an infant born more than eleven months after he departed. Thus "satisfied of his wife's whoredom," Joseph Shepard returned to his unit. The shock of his wife's infidelity, however, had sapped him of all desire to fight, and "smarting under the betrayal of the wife of his bosom and the infidelity of those most dear to him," he abandoned his unit and crossed into Union territory, where he spent the remainder of the war as a noncombatant.[43]

One of the striking elements of this postwar divorce surge is that husbands initiated the majority of divorces cases. During the five years after the Confederate surrender at Bennett Place, husbands began the proceedings in three-quarters of the cases. This is in sharp contrast to antebellum practice, when wives petitioned for divorce in approximately two-thirds of the cases. To be sure, there were female equivalents of the "soldier returning to find unfaithful wife" narratives described above, although they were significantly rarer. For instance, Orange County's Mary Herndon claimed that "till about the month of June 1861 she and the defendant [Chesley Herndon] lived happily as man & wife & that she conducted herself in all respects as a dutiful wife should." After his enlistment, they maintained an "affectionate correspondence" until he was captured by Union forces at Gettysburg in 1863. At the end of the war, to Mary Herndon's great surprise, he refused to see her. According to her petition, she "wrote to him & inquired the reason for his conduct. He refused (by silence) to give any & would have nothing to do with or say to" her. Although she had little evidence to substantiate the claim, Mary Herndon concluded that adultery was the only possible explanation for her husband's behavior.[44]

Even though wartime female adultery appears as the dominant theme in these postwar divorce cases, men were probably not any more loyal to their marital vows. While it is impossible to gauge the frequency of infidelity during the Civil War, the history of warfare has shown few examples of army camps that did not generate the occasional extramarital tryst. Accounts of Confederate camps attest to the presence of prostitutes and other "lewd women" throughout the war.[45] The predominance of the female adultery in postbellum divorce records can be attributed to several factors. First, men had a greater capacity to conceal their extramarital activities than their wives. Far from home and often among strangers, soldiers had the freedom of anonymity that would have been impossible for their wives at home. Second, a double standard allowed husbands to engage in the occasional discreet liaison while denying that same liberality to wives. Finally, soldiers did not have to contend with pregnancy testifying to their infidelity as women like Charlotte Shepard did.

The superior courts were not the only avenue by which postbellum North Carolinians sought to dissolve failed marriages. Dozens of North Carolinians petitioned delegates to the 1868 Constitutional Convention in Raleigh for divorces. Called in response to the Reconstruction Act of 1867's requirement that former Confederate states draft constitutions guaranteeing African American men the right to vote and that the states ratify the Fourteenth Amendment, the 1868 Constitutional Convention became a forum not only for political reforms but also on marriage and divorce in postwar North Carolina. Elections in the fall of 1867 had resulted in an overwhelming Republican slate of delegates. Indeed, 107 of the 120 delegates were Republicans, 15 of whom were African Americans. Meeting from 14 January to 17 March, the convention produced a document that revolutionized North Carolinians' political structure by expanding the franchise and increasing the level of local democracy. While the most contentious issues arising out of the new constitution revolved around its guarantee of a "general and uniform system of Public Schools" and its promise of universal manhood suffrage, the convention also extensively debated the role of divorce in postbellum North Carolina. Although political cleavages between Republicans and Conservatives characterized the discourse on most issues, the topic of divorce elicited novel coalitions and unlikely alliances.[46]

D. J. Rich, a representative from Pitt County, presented the first divorce petition on 23 January on the behalf of DeWitt and Nancy Wilson. Although some delegates expressed doubt whether they had the authority to grant divorces, the petition was forwarded to the Judicial Committee, one of thirteen standing committees at the convention. Two days later, the convention's second divorce petition was introduced on the behalf of Martha Hopkins of Granville County, which was also referred to the Judicial Committee. Although the two divorce petitions were introduced only two days apart, the debate on them revealed deeply mixed attitudes toward divorce.

A week after its referral, William Blount Rodman, the Judicial Committee's chairman, reported on the Wilson divorce petition. Of the delegates to the 1868 Constitutional Convention, Rodman was probably the most famous and influential. Born in 1817, he graduated first in his class at the University of North Carolina at the age of nineteen. Admitted to the bar in 1838, he established a lucrative law practice in Hyde, Pitt, Beaufort, and Martin counties. His professional success led to his selection in 1854 as part of a commission to revise the North Carolina State Code. A Breckinridge elector in 1860, he advocated secession upon Lincoln's election.

In 1861, Rodman organized an artillery company known as "Rodman's Battery." Over the next four years, Rodman served the Confederate government in a variety of roles, including stints as a quartermaster and as a military judge. During the war, Rodman's plantation near Washington, North Carolina, was pillaged by Union soldiers, destroying most of his personal property. Despite his personal loss and his involvement in the Confederate cause, Rodman joined the Republicans after the war, believing that as a moderate he could temper some of the party's more radical impulses.[47]

Rodman's experience in law, politics, and war gave his words a gravitas that transcended partisan divisions. Although the divorce issue was complex, he concluded that "if the Convention determines to legislate on private matters, they recommend a favorable consideration" of Wilson's divorce petition.[48] Rodman's statement raised immediate objections. An outraged E. W. Jones of Washington County protested the convention's taking up divorce cases. "The policy of the State has been against divorce," he argued.

> The more tenacious laws are upon the subject, the better the population. The regulations of other States are regarded as loose — tending, it appeared, to bastardize the issue of marriages. There was no proof of impotency, or adultery or other just cause in this case. But because of incompatibility of temper, these parties call upon this Convention to ignore all precedent. Because a man and woman do not choose to live together, a divorce is to be granted here, and it is set down in the journal of this Convention in order to permit each to

choose another partner. Why did not they apply to the Courts? The presumption is that, being known too well, they knew that no advantage could be gained there. Why come here? Because the parties believe there is less regard for law here.[49]

Given such rhetoric, one might expect Jones to oppose vehemently every divorce petition presented to the convention.

Two days later, however, when Rodman's committee reported favorably on the Hopkins divorce petition, Jones of Washington reversed his position on the issue, arguing that "this was a case of cruelty and required action." Other delegates joined Jones in his assessment that the Hopkins case warranted a response. Albion Tourgée, a Union veteran from Ohio representing Guilford County, "opposed on principle to granting divorces by legislation. But this was a case of hardship and he would make no resistance." Although usually at loggerheads, both Rev. James Walker Hood, a black clergyman representing Cumberland County, and Orange County Conservative John W. Graham, the son of a former governor, a Confederate war hero, and a militant white supremacist, argued that the delegates should be briefed on the "merits of the case."[50]

The conflicting reactions to the Wilson and Hopkins cases indicate that many delegates saw clear distinctions between the two divorce petitions. Although more than a dozen divorce petitions remain in the archival record of the convention's proceedings, the Wilson petition is missing, and the sparse accounts provided in the official transcript and newspaper accounts of the convention offer no indication of its contents. More can be said about reasons why Martha Hopkins sought a divorce. According to her petition and letters sent by her father to convention delegates, Martha meet her husband-to-be in 1862. William T. Hopkins claimed that he was the son of a Kentucky judge and that he had been recently discharged from the Confederate army owing to poor health. William and Martha married after a brief courtship, and their union quickly soured. When Martha's father began to question the veracity of his son-in-law's back story, William abandoned Martha, after one year of marriage and shortly before the birth of their child. After several years of trying to locate her wayward husband, Martha reconciled herself to life without him.[51]

After some debate, the delegates decided to postpone action on both divorce cases while they tackled more pressing constitutional questions. Tabling their petitions did not, however, prevent more from being introduced. Over the next four weeks, delegates from across North Carolina presented petitions for more than two dozen divorces. In a convention deeply divided along party lines, divorce petitions were introduced by Republicans and Conservatives alike.

Some delegates were deeply worried that if they began granting divorces, they would be overwhelmed in divorce petitions. New Hanover delegate Samuel S. Ashley argued, "If divorces were granted here, the desks of the delegates would be covered." Richard W. King of Lenoir conjectured that "if one divorce was granted, twenty thousand would pour in."[52] One Conservative delegate introduced a resolution that no more divorce petitions be considered, while a Republican thought that it would be less work if they passed an ordinance whereby "all men in North Carolina were thereby divorced and at liberty to marry again."[53]

Many delegates thought that these cases belonged in the courts. Because divorce cases had been the superior courts' exclusive purview before the Civil War, they wondered why that venue would not the proper place to address these petitions now. On several occasions, Republican Albion Tourgée objected to their considering divorce petitions, arguing, "I am opposed to granting divorces here. The parties can go the Courts." Similarly, Conservative Phillip Hodnett of Caswell County declared that he "was opposed to taking up the subject of divorce—he held that the Convention was called to form a constitution," not to issue divorces.[54] In response to the crippling number of divorce petitions, two leading Republicans, Convention president Calvin J. Cowles and John Q. A. Bryan, entered an official protest: "Being of the opinion that all cases of divorce properly belong to the Courts, we dissent from granting the same otherwise."[55] Their objection stemmed primarily from their belief that that the convention had other priorities, not from a moral opposition to divorce per se. "The Convention has unfortunately wasted some of its valuable time," Cowles wrote home, "but it now seems to have seen the error of its way & determined to attend to the legitimate work for which it was convened."[56]

Although it is impossible to ascertain why each of the divorce petitioners sought redress at the convention rather than in the courts, surviving petitions and other evidence indicate that financial incentives and impatience may have factored in the decision-making process. Harmon Merritt of Bladen County addressed this issue directly in his petition:

> Your Petitioner, in answer to the question which may arise: Why he has not applied, or does not now apply to the Courts for redress? Respectfully answer: That he is poor, very poor, old and infirm, and

that although, through the indulgence of the law, he might obtain permission to sue in forma pauperis, yet so large is the docket of the Superior Court of his County as that at least two hundred and fifty cases would have precedence over his as to trial and that, associated as he is with this abandoned woman, he cannot afford (when a speedier delivery is offered him) to wait the law's delays.[57]

James and Nancy Brady's petition made the same point more succinctly: "They are unable to petition the courts, as the matter of costs would be difficult to meet, hence the application to this body."[58] A letter to Albion Tourgée accompanying a divorce petition noted that the impoverished petitioner "is not able to pay the costs of a court and it is a quicker manner of getting it from the convention. She is a woman of good character and without property and she wishes to be relieved from the bonds of matrimony as her husband is married to another woman."[59] Despite earlier statements that such cases belonged to the courts, Tourgée ended up introducing at least two divorce petitions to the convention, testifying to the rhetorical effectiveness of these petitions.

Of all the delegates, William Blount Rodman presented the most spirited case for the convention granting divorces. He doubted whether the overwhelmed postwar court system could adequately address the delicate questions posed by divorce. As chairman of the Judiciary Committee, he had greater familiarity with the petitions than any other delegate and could see the desperate situation many in broken marriages faced. Instead of having the whole convention address the petitions, Rodman proposed that a special committee of five examine their merits, "otherwise indelicate disclosures would be made, destructive to the peace of the families."[60] After deliberating, the special divorce committee would report to the whole convention, which Rodman hoped would approve its recommendations without debate. Although Rodman's proposal failed because of opposition from fellow Republicans, it represented a new conception of divorce. Rodman thought that, instead of exposing the divorcing couple to public examination, divorce should be a largely private matter, shielded from public scrutiny. Unlike Thomas Ruffin, Rodman believed that the desires of the public did not outweigh those of the individual in divorce cases.

Even though the debate over divorce largely ignored party lines, when the time came to vote on actually granting divorces in the convention's final week, the verdict was strictly partisan. On the three divorce cases for which the vote was recorded, all the Conservative delegates, with one exception, voted against them. Approximately two-thirds of white Republicans voted for divorce. Many white Republicans voted for some divorce petitions and against others, indicating that the merits of individual petitions influenced their voting. Black Republicans, in contrast, unanimously voted to approve divorce petitions, although in approximately half of the cases, black delegates abstained, failed to register a vote, or were absent from the convention when the balloting took place.

The black delegates' commitment to legal access to divorce was clearest in the one black divorce petition presented at the convention.[61] According to the petition introduced by James Harris of Wake County, free blacks Gilliam and Ann Underdue had married in 1858. At the end of the war, he had left her, taking with him eight hundred dollars, and remarried in Ohio. Born a free mulatto in Granville County, Harris could have first met Ann Underdue when he worked as a carpenter in Raleigh during the late 1850s or more likely when he returned to the city after the war as a teacher for the New England's Freedmen's Aid Society. In either case, he knew her well enough to vouch that she was a "woman of unblemished character." According to Harris, her primary motivation in seeking divorce was to prevent her "unworthy husband" from inheriting her property in the event that she predeceased him.[62] In large measure because of Harris's advocacy on the convention floor and Rodman's support in committee, the convention granted Ann Underdue her divorce.[63]

Another divorce petition introduced by James Harris indicates that African Americans sought redress at the convention for many of the same reasons as their white counterparts. Littleton Perry, "a freed man and citizen of Wake County," had legally married Esther Mangum, "a freedwoman of said county," in 1866, though his petition noted that they had "lived together as man and wife for some years before that time." After discovering his wife's infidelity, Perry hoped that the convention would grant him a divorce, as "he is a poor man, barely able to support three young children he has had by his said wife, that he has not the means to apply to the courts, and if he could by pledging his labor of himself for two or three years raise sufficient funds to file a petition for divorce, the dockets are so crowded that there would be no prospect of the same being decided for a number of years."[64] Like many white petitioners, African Americans who sought divorces at the 1868 Constitutional Convention believed that the courts were inaccessible and unaffordable, leaving the convention as their only possible remedy.

Black delegates' willingness to grant divorces at the 1868 Constitutional Convention does not necessarily mean that they held more liberal attitudes toward divorce than their white counterparts. For instance, Rev. James W. Hood supported the convention's assumption of divorce cases and voted in the affirmative on the one divorce petition at which he was present. However, as we shall see, in the upcoming decades, after Hood became the presiding AME Zion bishop for North Carolina, he regularly and clearly denounced divorce as immoral. In Hood's mind, the problem of divorce was not primarily a legal problem but a moral one. He believed that the best way to reduce divorce was not to restrict its legal availability but to instill a respect for moral values generally and the institution of marriage specifically, thereby reducing the demand for divorce.

By the convention's conclusion, the delegates had considered at least thirty-three divorce petitions, granting fourteen of them. In those cases in which they refused to grant divorces, the evidence suggests that their opposition stemmed primarily from incomplete information about the particulars of the situation rather than a moral or political opposition to divorce. By antebellum standards, the rate at which the convention granted divorces was significantly higher than that of most legislative bodies.[65] The number of divorce petitions and the willingness of convention delegates to grant them indicate how the Civil War and the immediate postbellum period effected a sea change in attitudes toward divorce in North Carolina.

William Blount Rodman and many other convention delegates endorsed a new contractual conception of marriage and divorce in which the state and community had little legal or moral standing. A decade after the Constitutional Convention, Rodman, now a North Carolina Supreme Court justice, argued that "it is universally admitted that although marriage is a political and social institution, and creates a certain status of the parties, yet it is begun by a contract, which like all other contracts may be voided."[66] Although he recognized that marriage differed in important respects from other contracts, Rodman believed that the needs and desires of individual divorced people outweighed those of the broader community. Compared with antebellum pronouncements on divorce, the position taken by Rodman and other convention delegates amounted to something of a moral revolution.

CHAPTER SIX

The Divorce Mill Runs Over Time

Marital Breakdown & Reform in the New South

T HE CIVIL WAR placed unprecedented and acute pressures on both black and white marriages, often separating partners and submitting them to severe mental and emotional burdens. Although divorces in the immediate postwar period can be attributed to the particular strains of wartime and emancipation, they heralded a period of skyrocketing divorce rates in North Carolina that would last for four decades, during which the number of divorces in the state approximately doubled every decade (see Fig. 4). For most of this period, white North Carolinians disregarded divorce's increase, ignoring it in their church pulpits and newspaper pages. By the turn of the century, however, this "divorce crisis" had reached such a point that the highest levels of the white political and ecclesiastical leadership worried that it would tear the society apart. Black North Carolinians, however, quickly addressed the issues presented by the divorce contagion in the immediate postwar period. An activist black clergy committed to moral uplift repeatedly railed against divorce as destructive to social order. Further, these clergymen maintained that upholding marital bonds provided evidence for attaining social and political rights.

Several aspects of this postwar increase are worth noting. First, men initiated the majority of divorce cases. This is significant in that it deviated from national trends, in which two out of every three divorces were initiated by women, and from North Carolina's antebellum practice, when women also filed two out of three divorce petitions. As Figure 5 indicates, southern states had many more divorces initiated by men than anywhere else in the country. Indeed, North Carolina had the nation's highest rate of male-initiated divorce between 1867 and 1886.[1]

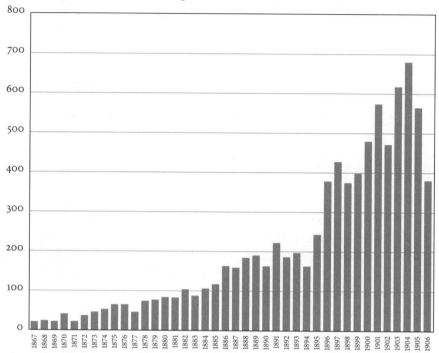

FIGURE 4. Divorces in North Carolina, 1867–1906. Wright, *Report on Marriage and Divorce*, 139; *Marriage and Divorce, 1916*, 50.

Historian Victoria Bynum attributes this male-petitioner majority to a revision in North Carolina's divorce law enacted by the state legislature during its 1871–72 session. This revision permitted men to file for absolute divorce if their wives committed adultery, while women could file only if their husbands committed adultery and abandoned them. According to Bynum, this change in North Carolina's divorce law "strengthen[ed] the authority of husbands" and "encouraged dissatisfied husbands to seek divorces."[2]

Although this change in the statutory law of divorce may have contributed to the predominance of husband-initiated divorce, several factors indicate that it was not the primary cause. First, as we have seen, men filed the majority of divorce petitions between 1866 and 1871, before this particular change in the law took effect, and the percentage of divorce petitions filed by husbands did not change significantly with its enactment. Second, despite statutory law to the contrary, superior courts occasionally granted divorces to women whose husbands had committed adultery but who had not abandoned them.[3] Third, North Carolina was not alone in having the majority of its divorce petitions filed by husbands, as similar conditions prevailed in

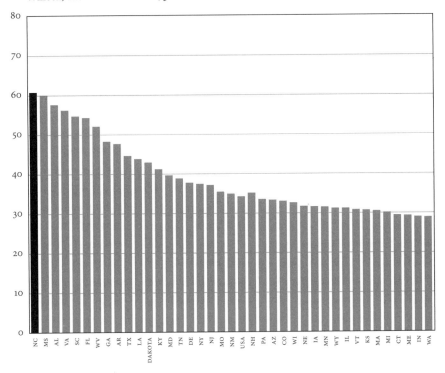

FIGURE 5. Percentage of divorces granted to men, 1867–1886.
Willcox, *The Divorce Problem*, 36.

Virginia, Alabama, and Mississippi. In each of these states, women filed the
majority of divorce petitions in the decades before the Civil War, only to
have men initiate the majority of the divorce cases in the decades afterward.
None of these other states, however, had divorce laws that significantly discriminated on the basis of gender.[4]

This final point indicates that the significant transition to male-initiated
divorce resulted from regional factors rather than changes in North Carolina's divorce statutes. All four states where men filed the majority of divorce petitions belonged to the former Confederacy. Further, in many other
southern states, the number of divorce cases initiated by men and women
were close to parity; such was the case in Louisiana, Florida, Georgia, and
Arkansas.[5] In almost every state outside the South, however, the number of
divorces initiated by wives significantly outnumbered those begun by husbands, often by a ratio of two to one.[6]

Several features of the postwar southern social landscape may help to explain why so many men in North Carolina filed for divorce after 1865 when
so few did before the Civil War. First, according to the 1870 census, women

outnumbered men in almost every county in North Carolina, often by a substantial margin, a result due in part to the death of more than forty thousand North Carolina men during the war. This imbalance would have allowed men who wished to remarry after divorce to be reasonably certain that a potential new partner would be available. Conversely, women in unhappy marriages might have been dissuaded from seeking divorce on the grounds that finding a new partner would have been challenging. Second, although the vast majority of both men and women filed for divorce on the grounds of their spouse's adultery, the ways in which adultery was understood was gendered. In 1875, North Carolina Supreme Court justice Richmond M. Pearson observed that "there is a difference between adultery committed by a husband and adultery committed by a wife—the difference being in favor of the husband." He argued that while a wife's adultery rendered the husband "cuckolded," in the reverse situation, the wife would be "pitied."[7] Although Richmond was pronouncing a legal opinion, he was also reflecting a broad cultural conception that not all adultery was created equal.

A second notable feature of the postbellum divorce epidemic is that the emotional rhetoric characteristic of antebellum divorce petitions largely disappeared. Although one finds elements of pathos employed in divorce petitions in the immediate postwar period, after 1870 divorce petitions almost universally took on a purely legalistic mode of argument. Clearly delineating the legal foundation for divorce, these petitions lack any clear attempt to justify the divorce on moral grounds, eschewing the narrative form often found in antebellum petitions in favor of a formulaic outline.[8] One consequence of this shift is that divorce petitions became radically shorter. Events that would generate several pages of complex narrative during the antebellum period were now summed up in a few brief paragraphs.

The disappearance of emotional language and narrative structure from divorce petitions indicates that the petitioners did not feel the same overwhelming need to justify their actions to the community that their antebellum predecessors did. As Addie May's three-minute divorce from Lorenzo DeVisconti indicated, North Carolina's superior courts routinely dispatched divorce cases in fairly short order, and extended legal proceedings in divorce cases were rare. Indeed, one newspaper reporter indicated that one Wake County judge dispatched five divorces in five minutes and that "the usual procedure, so we are told, is for divorce cases to be tried while waiting on witnesses for some 'important case!'"[9] Although court days still figured prominently in the social calendar in many communities, divorce cases had ceased to provide the kind of moral theater that they did before the Civil

War. Because communities no longer demanded that divorce petitioners publicly justify their actions, the petitioners no longer felt the need to play that role.

By the 1890s, divorce trials had ceased to function as a social forum for the litigants to justify their actions. Some North Carolinians, therefore, sought to substantiate their decision to seek a divorce in other venues. Two white women, Pattie Arrington and Ida May Beard, published books to explain publicly how their marriages fell apart. First published in 1893 and 1898 respectively, both Arrington's and Beard's accounts broadly adopted a narrative tone similar to that of antebellum divorce petitions, albeit considerably longer in length. For example, Arrington described her husband subjecting her to "the most brutal treatment . . . whipped, cursed, kicked, slandered, and made to endure all the cruelty a miserable wretch could endure."[10] Similarly, Beard described her husband's repeated physical abuse and adultery, noting several occasions when she thought he attempted to kill her, including an attempt with poisoned candy.

However, unlike antebellum divorce petitions, Arrington's and Beard's books actively drew attention to their status as divorced women. If antebellum women saw divorce petitions as a necessary evil to justify their divorce to the court and their community, Pattie Arrington and Ida May Beard chose to publicize, and even profit from, their divorce. Indeed, Beard published at least seven editions of her book between 1898 and 1911 and appears to have derived her primary livelihood from it. Beard justified her account by claiming that two ghosts of her "dead-and-gone ancestors" had instructed her to so, telling her that the "heroine would be crowned 'Queen of All,' while the villain who wrecked my young life died the death of a murderer upon the gallows."[11] More practical and less supernatural, Arrington asked "the men of North Carolina if they are willing to permit a woman and her helpless children to be imposed upon year after year."[12]

The demise of the narrative mode in divorce petitions indicates that the meaning of divorce in white society had changed. With each passing year, as more white North Carolinians sought to dissolve their marital bonds, the social stigma attached to divorce decreased. Although it retained a certain taint of disrespectability, divorce had ceased to be deviant in the eyes of many North Carolinians. Many had come to the conclusion that their decision to divorce was personal rather than social. For instance, Thomasville resident J. Howard Jones rebuked an acquaintance who spoke disparagingly of his divorce: "Your comments concerning my divorce from Mrs. Jones . . . I consider very unnecessary trouble on the part of yourself & think it would be best to reconcile your own domestic strife before you undertake the discussion of that which you are not invested in at all."[13] As Jones's statement indicates, what once had been public had become private.

Unfortunately, available evidence does not allow us to compare black and white divorce rates during the postbellum period. In many states during the nineteenth century, including North Carolina, divorce records very rarely documented the litigants' race. Further, in a significant number of cases, the litigants were identified only by last name and first initials, making racial identification through census records or other public records difficult. Two large federally funded studies of postbellum divorce reached the conclusion that they could not assess the racial component in divorce for most states. The first national study, under the aegis of the Bureau of Labor Statistics, claimed that 390 of 1,338 divorces in North Carolina between 1867 and 1887 were black.[14] If these statistics were accurate, it would mean that approximately 29 percent of divorced people were black, a figure somewhat less than their 38 percent of the total population. However, while presenting these figures, Carroll Wright, the commissioner of labor and the report's author, was careful to indicate that he had little faith in their accuracy. The second, even larger report conducted by the Census Bureau did not even consider its tentative calculations worthy of publication. It concluded that "the statistics can not be regarded, therefore as having established any definite fact in regard to the comparative prevalence of divorce among the two races."[15]

Unable to calculate the racial composition of divorces directly, several scholars attempted to employ indirect methods. Working from the data collected in the Bureau of Labor Statistics study, Cornell University sociologist Walter F. Willcox calculated that counties with high black populations had comparatively low divorce rates. "On the whole," Willcox concluded from this evidence, "it seems probable that the average negro divorce-rate is rather below that of the southern whites."[16] However, when census officials attempted to reproduce Willcox's results using their data in 1906, their results were inconclusive.[17]

While the absence of clear data concerning the racial composition of postbellum divorce closes certain avenues of inquiry, the differing rhetorical atmospheres indicate that the tremendous increase in divorce after the Civil War was understood very differently in the black and white communities. In both communities, clergymen served as the rhetorical font for radically distinct discourses about what the rising prevalence of divorce meant and how to respond to it.

The postbellum black church in North Carolina took an active role in discouraging divorce, linking marriage to morality.[18] Black church leaders were not imitating white middle-class values; rather, they saw a strict stance on divorce as part of a multifaceted social and political agenda. They believed that strengthening the institution of marriage served as a vehicle for moral uplift. A critical element in postbellum southern black theology, the doctrine of uplift posited that slavery had deprived African Americans of a strong moral culture and that creating such a culture would strengthened the black community and provide evidence that blacks deserved political and social equality.[19]

One might object, with some justification, to an analysis of the "black church's" response to divorce because it obscures meaningful distinctions between African American religious denominations and equally important divisions within these denominations. To be sure, the largest black denominations in North Carolina (Baptists, African Methodist Episcopal, and AME Zion) did not see eye to eye on many issues, both theological and social. However, with regard to divorce, they spoke essentially with one voice, and similar arguments about the nature of the marriage vow appear across denominational lines within the black community. Therefore, for the purposes of understanding how African American religious thought in North Carolina assessed divorce, the term "black church" will encompass organized African American religion as a totality, obscuring distinctions that are important in other contexts.

Black clergymen believed that slavery had prevented African Americans from developing a proper conception of marriage. "During his slavery days," Rev. George W. Clinton told congregants at an AME Zion church in Shelby, North Carolina, in 1885, "the Negro had no polar star, no compass by which to guide his moral bark. The sacred marriage institution which God established among men was disregarded and sneered at by his master when the Negro desired to marry."[20] In the rhetoric of uplift, black marriage had reached its nadir under slavery, and the black clergy had an obligation to teach freedmen and freedwomen how to progress from this point to the ideal of Christian marriage.

Among the postbellum black clergy in North Carolina, AME Zion minister Rev. Joseph C. Price presented the most lucid arguments linking the strength of black marriage at emancipation to slavery. Until his premature death in 1893, Price believed that the church could improve the stability of the black family through a program of uplift that included a firm opposition to divorce. Price's oratorical talents led one white Methodist to describe him as "the ebony Demosthenes of North Carolina."[21] Price used these skills to deliver a powerful critique of how white slave owners had corrupted African Americans' inherent sense of moral marriage. "The Negro's moral condition," Price remarked on one occasion, "is the result of his training in the peculiar institution. It taught him no moral obligation of the home, for it recognized no home in the civilized sense of the term; it rather encouraged him to violate the sacred bonds of husband and wife, because, in so doing, he was taught the advancement of the interest of his master in adding to the number and value of his human stock for the plantation or the market."[22] On another occasion he remarked that "for 240 years the Negro was taught by precept and example to call vice, virtue, and immorality, morality, and thereby add to the Master's human stock in trade."[23] Indeed, Price took every opportunity to attribute black North Carolinians' moral shortcomings to the heritage of slavery, noting that "this heartless system made no claims or even pretensions to morality. It was the greatest legalized system of moral prostitution and vicious defilement the world has ever seen, and its single purpose in all this work of corruption was the increase of human stock in trade."[24]

Price's opposition to divorce and his commitment to strengthening the black family derived in part from his own childhood experience. Born in 1854 in Elizabeth City, North Carolina, Price saw how slavery could destroy black families. His father was a shipbuilder's slave, and his mother was a free woman. Because of his mother's status, Price was born free, but his relationship with his father was predicated upon the whims of his father's owner. When Price was still very young, his father's owner moved to Baltimore, taking his slaves with him. Price knew, therefore, the terrible emotional toil that such separations had on every member of the family. Still grieving over the loss of her husband, Price's mother remarried, and during the Civil War, the family fled to Union-occupied New Bern. There Price met Rev. James Walker Hood, an AME Zion clergyman who had been sent to the refugee slave colony in 1863 as a missionary.[25]

Although Joseph Price was only a child when he met Rev. James Hood, he eventually became his protégé. During the 1880s and 1890s, after Hood's elevation to bishop in 1872 and Price's ordination in 1879, they became the most visible black religious leaders in North Carolina. In 1882 they founded Livingstone College in Salisbury, an institution devoted to instilling the values of moral uplift in young black men. They worked together on temperance campaigns across the state. They also worked consistently to improve the state of black marriage in North Carolina, a crusade that included a firm opposition to divorce.

Hood and Price recognized that significant advances in moral uplift, especially with regard to marriage, could not be expected overnight. Just before his death in 1893, Rev. Joseph Price remarked that "as a race we are in what may be termed the formative period in intellectual and moral culture." Slavery, he noted, had "perverted the moral sensibility" but it "could not be destroyed." Undoing the damage done by centuries of enslavement and moral degradation, Price believed, would not be immediate, as old customs and practices die slowly. However, emancipation had provided an opportunity for blacks to reclaim their proper moral stance, though the work might take decades.[26]

This recognition that moral uplift required decades to attain helps to explain why James Walker Hood generally supported divorce petitions as a delegate at the 1868 Constitutional Convention while taking a strict line on divorce in later years. Hood may have recognized that three years removed from slavery, freedmen and freedwomen in North Carolina had had little opportunity to improve their moral condition. In later years, Hood held his congregants to a stricter standard. "The [AME Zion] Church has taken a high stand on moral questions," Hood wrote in 1895, particularly "the subjects of marriage and divorce." Under Hood's direction, the AME Zion church did not permit divorce, except for the biblically sanctioned cause of adultery. He directed ministers to investigate all divorce cases to ensure that they fulfilled this strict standard and punished those who failed to do so. However, he permitted an exception for those "unavoidably separated by slavery." The church retained this exception despite its obsolescence, Hood noted, "as a relic of the accused institution, and [it] reminds children of what their parents endured."[27]

Across denominations, black churches exerted a strict discipline on parishioners accused of sexual transgressions, including those who divorced for nonbiblical causes. Indeed, one study of discipline in Southern Baptist churches indicated that postbellum black churches disciplined their members at a significantly higher rate than their postbellum white counterparts, and even at a slightly higher rate than biracial antebellum churches. Further, black churches found sexual offenses particularly heinous and prosecuted them harshly.[28] As we shall see, the vigilance of the postbellum black churches to discipline their members contrasted sharply with events in white churches, where church discipline declined precipitously after the Civil War.

Black churches also demonstrated a particular wariness in the remarriage of divorced persons. According to Rev. J. A. Whitted, the most prominent black Baptist in North Carolina, the issue of remarriage for divorced people created a fissure in the Lane's Creek Association in Union County and "constantly brought confusion in the ranks." Apparently, one minister performed marriages for divorced persons on several occasions, evoking the ire of his colleagues. Whitted believed that this dispute eventually contributed to the Lane's Creek Association's demise.[29]

Black church leaders did not believe that restricting divorce through legal measures was an effective tool to improve morality. Although "there is no Church more pronounced in its opposition to loose marriage laws," wrote Bishop Hood, "the law is sufficient and its administration rigid."[30] Similarly, Bishop George W. Clinton observed that although "the evils which stalk abroad in society are giant-like in stature and countless in number . . . we cannot depend on legislation" to combat them.[31] They believed that the proper venue to combat divorce was the church, not the courts or the legislative halls. Baptist clergyman P. F. Maloy observed in 1901 that "500 divorces in one year bring us face to face with a fearful and awful crisis." Maloy argued that to combat this crisis "the pastors and churches must be a unit."[32] As we shall see, this attitude stood in stark contrast to that of white ministers, who increasingly sought to fight divorce through legislative reform of the state's divorce laws.

Much of black church leaders' effort to combat divorce took the form of creating and maintaining healthy black marriages. They believed that if women and men entered marriage with a proper conception of its role in divine and social order, they would form robust unions. "When on this sea of matrimony so many are wrecked," observed the *Star of Zion*, "remember that a mistake here is a mistake forever."[33] A self-improvement guide used by students at Livingstone College informed them that "marriage is for life . . . how despicable to separate husbands and wives!"[34]

By the start of the twentieth century, black church leaders saw what they believed to be significant improvement in marital conditions in North Carolina. According to Rev. George W. Clinton in 1885, "The marriage institution, once but a mockery among the Negro race, is now the respected institution. . . . What more can we boast of?"[35] Even some white North Carolinians conceded that marital conditions among the state's black population had improved. Describing his black students, the white president of Scotia Seminary in Concord noted, "Their marital fidelity is beyond question."[36]

In 1900, the *A.M.E. Zion Quarterly Review*, quoting black Episcopalian Alexander Crummell, presented the clearest summation of the role of marriage in racial uplift:

> For two hundred and fifty years we were as a race deprived of the family and robbed of the home. . . . A generation of freedom has not yet sufficed for our recovery of these grand organic elements of being. . . . If we don't get back the family and the family idea; if we don't restore the home; if we don't cultivate wide-spread family feeling among our people; if we don't inspire, everywhere family allegiance, family devotedness, family reverence, and obedience, we shall be a lost people in this land. . . . Proclaim constantly the dignity of marriage, the sanctity of motherhood, the glory of continuity of blood and lineage, and the abomination of lust and illegitimacy. Next to godliness, let this be the beginning of race-reform and race-progress.[37]

Succinctly phrased, this statement outlined the philosophy that James Walker Hood, Joseph C. Price, George W. Clinton, and countless other black clergymen in North Carolina adopted in their campaign to strengthen black marriage. Within this context, divorce served as a marker that the institution of marriage needed to be strengthened. In their eyes, however, they consistently saw signs of progress. On the eve of the twentieth century, they believed that they had made significant headway in creating a firm foundation for black marriage.

NOT ALL AFRICAN AMERICANS shared in the black clergy's conception of marriage or abhorrence of divorce. Scattered evidence from divorce records indicates that many African Americans saw marriage as a more flexible institution than their ordained brethren envisioned. Instead of conforming to a legal and religious conception of marriage espoused by black and white elites, some black North Carolinians saw marriage primarily as a social institution. They believed that marriage entailed a set of social obligations and responsibilities between husband and wife. When either partner failed to uphold his or her end of the relationship, divorce and separation were the natural consequence. Although the legality of the marriage held some significance, it was secondary to its social role. Ultimately, many African Americans saw the final arbiter of a marriage's status not as the court or the church but the community.[38]

A couple of examples illustrate how this socially sanctioned but extralegal conception of divorce functioned within the black community. In 1899, Haywood Hargrove of Orange County sought a divorce from his wife, Harriet. According to his divorce petition, the couple had been "slaves prior to and during the Civil War" and had begun to "live together and cohabit in the relation of husband and wife" during "the second year of said war." After emancipation, Harriet and Haywood had their union recorded by the Orange County clerk of court "in compliance with the law . . . and the said Clerk gave [the couple] a certificate." In 1896, after more than thirty years together, Harriet abandoned her husband. Haywood Hargrove's petition indicates that he drew an important distinction between his marriage, which began when he and Harriet started to "cohabit in the relation of husband and wife" and ended when she abandoned him, and his legal union, which began when the clerk of court certified their legal relationship and which he sought to end with a legal divorce.[39] An 1876 Granville County divorce case manifests a similar dichotomy between socially and legally sanctioned divorce. E. B. Bullock's petition indicated that he and his wife, Jane, had been separated for many years and she had subsequently taken on other partners, presumably with the tacit approval of their community. He accounted for the lengthy interval between the effective dissolution of his marriage and the beginning of legal divorce proceedings on the grounds that he was unaware that a legal divorce was necessary.[40]

Some black North Carolinians did not believe that a court's intervention was necessary to dissolve their marriage. For instance, Irvin Thompson, a veteran of the 37th Colored Regiment, married shortly after the war's conclusion. After living with his wife for approximately one year, "she associated with other men and left me," Thompson revealed to a pension examiner. "I did not get any divorce. She just went off a whoring and I lost track of her." Evidentially, Thompson considered his wife's behavior to amount to a de facto divorce, as he shortly thereafter married another woman in a socially and legally sanctioned marriage ceremony.[41]

Black North Carolinians such as Irvin Thompson had multiple reasons for forgoing the state court system. First, the court costs associated with divorce cases, although usually lower than other forms of litigation, often proved insurmountable. Although these costs did not make divorce prohibitively expensive for poor black North Carolinians, they certainly provided a disincentive. Second, divorce proceedings required black couples to enter into a local court system dominated by whites. Given the negative association that most African Americans had between the southern courts and white supremacy, many black North Carolinians would have been naturally hesitant before turning to the courts to resolve their marital disharmony.[42]

UNLIKE THEIR BLACK NEIGHBORS, white North Carolinians showed little public interest or awareness of divorce in the two decades after 1865. Newspapers rarely commented on divorce cases, and if they were aware that divorce was becoming more common, they did not mention it. Similarly, white preachers in North Carolina did not consider the subject worthy of attention in their sermons, focusing instead on other social ills, like drinking or (in some denominations) dancing.[43] The divorce epidemic also occurred in a context in which white churches exercised less oversight and control over the behavior of their members. The robust antebellum culture of church discipline declined markedly in the decades after the Civil War as the responsibility for maintaining social order was transferred from churches to local and state governments.[44]

Lawyers and judges were the only white North Carolinians who paid particular attention to divorce, outside of divorced people themselves. As the number of divorces rose, a significant number of lawyers and law firms came to specialize in divorce cases, the most notable among them the Raleigh firm of Busbee and Busbee. Like their antebellum predecessors, justices on the North Carolina Supreme Court handled a significant number of divorce cases. On the whole, their divorce decisions handed down between 1865 and 1905 were not more sympathetic to the plight of those seeking divorce than their antebellum precursors, such that Justice Edwin G. Reade argued in an 1877 opinion, "There are with us no such things as 'divorces made easy,' 'divorces without publicity,' and the like, as are said to prevail elsewhere."[45] Despite this fundamental hostility to divorce, the rhetoric employed to describe the nature of marriage and divorce shifted significantly. Increasingly North Carolina Supreme Court justices referred to marriage in terms of a contract and divorce as the termination of a contract.[46] This emphasis on the contractual nature of marriage conflicted with the rhetoric employed in antebellum opinions, which denied that marriage was a contract and stressed the role that the broader community played in marriage and the interest that community had in preventing divorce. In describing marriage as a contract, however, postbellum justices were quick to point out that marriage represented a particular type of contract, distinct in many ways. For instance, in 1890, Justice Alphonso Avery opined in one divorce case, "The marriage contract is the most important to society in the catalogue of contracts."[47] In another case, Justice William Blount Rodman claimed that marriage "is begun by a contract," albeit one of an "important and peculiar character."[48]

The publication in 1889 of the Bureau of Labor Statistics study on divorce since the end of the Civil War began to rouse whites from their apathy toward divorce. When the report's initial findings were announced, but before the report itself was published, the *Raleigh News and Observer* asserted that although "the figures for North Carolina and other Southern States we have not yet seen, they must certainly be lower very much than those of the other States of the Union."[49] When the figures finally did become available, they indicated that the newspaper was half right. Although North Carolina and many other southern states had fewer divorces per capita than most other states, the divorce rate since the Civil War had increased alarmingly.

This finding deeply disturbed those white North Carolinians who had assumed that divorce was primarily a northern and western phenomenon. The *Biblical Recorder* of Raleigh quipped in May 1889 that evidently "all the divorces are not up North."[50] An 1889 editorial in the *Baptist Quarterly Review* lamented how the South had joined the rest of the country in the divorce epidemic: "It is not in the West, but in the South that the percentage of divorces to population is greatest, and where the increase of percentage is most rapid." While the divorce rate was actually decreasing in many northern states, North Carolina's had increased 676 percent over the previous two decades, with other southern states demonstrating similarly dramatic increases. The editorial blamed these results on a gradual "drift of opinion" since 1865, a counterweight to which must come in the form of "enlightenment and education of conscience through the Christian pulpit and the Christian press." If moral suasion failed to produce the desired result, a constitutional amendment might be the only means to combat "this great evil."[51]

Episcopal bishop Joseph Blount Cheshire Jr. also read Wright's report with shock and disbelief. He saw the rapid increase in divorce in North Carolina as a fundamental threat to social order and divine law. Although Wright's report made clear that North Carolina's divorce statutes were among the strictest in the country, Cheshire concluded that only by restricting the legal access to divorce could North Carolina reduce the threat posed by divorce.

Born in 1850, Cheshire was raised in the Episcopal Church. Cheshire's father had served as the rector of Trinity Church in Scotland Neck and Calvary Church in Tarboro since 1842. After graduating from Trinity College in Connecticut in 1869, Cheshire studied law under William K. Ruffin, son of Chief Justice Thomas Ruffin. In 1876, Cheshire abandoned the law to enter holy orders, studying theology under his father. Following his ordination two years later, he was assigned to Chapel of the Cross in Chapel Hill. In 1881, he accepted a call to become rector at St. Peter's Church in Charlotte, one of the largest parishes in the state. In 1893, at the age of forty-three, he became the bishop of the Diocese of North Carolina. Serving as bishop for nearly forty years, Cheshire sought to revitalize the Episcopal Church in North Carolina, which had since 1840 entered a period of decline.[52] Although his interests and activities as bishop were varied, Cheshire regularly and repeatedly returned to divorce reform as one of his consuming passions.

Cheshire preached his first sermon on divorce at St. Peter's in Charlotte in January 1890, about six months after Wright's published report on divorce became available. Entitled "Marriage," the sermon would become one of Cheshire's favorites, a text that he returned to over and over again. With slight revisions, he would deliver it more than two dozen times over the next fifteen years. In this sermon, Cheshire presented the thesis that divorce presented a threat to marriage as a divine institution and to social order and that North Carolina needed to reform its divorce laws to conform with biblical commandments and prevent social breakdown.

Cheshire began his sermon by evoking the spiritual meaning of marriage. Like his antebellum forebearers, Cheshire thought that marriage stood at the root of human society. Marriage, he said, is "the only foundation for human, life, for society, and for the State." While he recognized that civil regulations had some authority over marriage, "human laws cannot alter its essential character, nor can they annul its divine obligation." Any legislation that weakened the institution of marriage by making divorce easier only mocked God and harmed society.

Cheshire rejected the idea adopted by some legislators and jurists that the marriage functioned like a contract. Although he admitted that certain elements of marriage resembled a contract, such a conception ignored marriage's "real character." When state legislators adopted a contractual conception of marriage, they ignored "its character as an institution essential to human life and social and civil stability. They have legislated for the individual at the expense of the interests of society and the State." He argued that public officials should instead regulate marriage as "a State of life involving the interest of the community."

Cheshire concluded his sermon by directly rebuking the North Carolina legislature for the present state of marriage and advocating immediate divorce reform. "Many dangers threaten our land," he said. "Not the least of these is the growing indifference with which the public mind regards the loosening of the marriage tie." He implored his congregants to lobby for divorce reform, telling that "the public conscience in North Carolina has been sadly dull to the perception of the importance of this question." Cheshire believed that North Carolina could be saved, as "the evil is not so great in our immediate section as in some others," but only immediate action could prevent social degeneration.[53]

In the decade after he first delivered his jeremiad on divorce in 1890, Cheshire recognized that his efforts to motivate divorce reform from the Episcopal pulpit had failed. He understood that although he had substantial influence within the Episcopal community in North Carolina, he needed to transcend denominational boundaries if he wished to effect meaningful change. He needed to develop a coalition of religious leaders, especially from the numerically superior Baptist and Methodist faiths, to exert meaningful pressure on state officials. Writing to and meeting with influential leaders such as Baptists Livingston Johnson and *Biblical Recorder* editor J. W. Bailey, Methodist Rev. Dr. E. A. Moore, and Presbyterian Rev. John M. Rose, Cheshire hoped that their combined efforts could succeed where his own had failed. Unfortunately for Cheshire, however, his arguments found little traction with those he attempted to recruit. Although they generally agreed with Cheshire's basic premise, that weak laws promoted divorce, few of them were willing to actively lobby for divorce reform.

Their reluctance to join Cheshire's crusade stemmed from a general antipathy by North Carolina Protestant clergymen toward active involvement in politics. Many believed that religion and politics should not mix and that political solutions could not resolve moral questions.[54] They were particularly wary of challenging political leaders, preferring to take a supporting role, if they took any role at all. Prominent Methodist Rev. E. A. Yates argued that the church "is necessarily a conservative power . . . , an antagonist to all disorder. . . . It can but align itself with the powers that be, for 'they are ordained by God.'"[55]

One of the few who did immediately join Cheshire was Rev. Charles W. Blanchard. A prominent Baptist minister from Kinston, Blanchard was somewhat reluctant to participate in political questions, arguing once that it was "doubtless best for the minister of the Gospel to be as non-partisan in his politics as possible."[56] However, he believed that for this cause, at least, he needed to violate that dictum. "It is perhaps no bad omen that the subject of divorcement is much agitated in this State," he wrote in a 1901 editorial in the Baptist organ the *Biblical Recorder*. Blanchard found many North Carolina legislators ignorant of basic Christian beliefs and argued that "it were well for our State if our legislature knew more of the teachings of the Scriptures, in word and in spirit, on many points of moral interest to the people." When one legislator declared that "it was a custom of Baptist ministers to unite divorced persons in marriage," Blanchard declared that it "was either a willful slander of our ministry or the result of bad instruction." While he admitted that North Carolina Baptists had never officially prohibited their clergymen from marrying divorced persons, Blanchard declared that most did not and that he "had decided it was not lawful for divorced persons to marry" and therefore had "never married such and am careful not to marry strangers without investigating this point."[57]

Cheshire's ecumenicalism did not extend to African Americans, even those within his own denomination.[58] Although he contacted white religious leaders from comparatively insignificant denominations, he never sought out prominent black clergymen such Bishop James W. Hood, Rev. J. A. Whitted, or Rev. George W. Clinton. Nor did Cheshire visit the large black denominational meetings as he did with their white counterparts. His failure to incorporate African Americans into his crusade probably reflected a belief that a politically disenfranchised group could not effectively lobby for a change in the divorce laws. After the Wilmington Riot of 1898, the political power of the black community had been significantly curtailed, and white supremacists like Governor Charles B. Aycock were unlikely to be receptive to a religious coalition that included African Americans. Further, although both whites and blacks were subject to the same divorce laws, many whites evidently believed that divorce in the white and black communities existed independently. An editorial published in the Raleigh *News and Observer* in 1904 began with this premise: "We will omit any reference to the negroes. What the negro does, thinks or says is not chargeable to our white people. While we have no statistics at hand, still we are much within the mark when we say that that two-thirds of the divorces in this State are by negroes."[59]

Cheshire also did not attempt to involve women or women's groups in his crusade. This is surprising considering the prominent role that women had played in the state's prohibition movement, a cause that stressed many of the same moral themes as divorce reform. Male prohibition advocates in North Carolina had sought female support since the 1880s. The North Carolina chapter of the Woman's Christian Temperance Union, nearly three thousand members strong in 1903, had advocated sexual morality (though not explicitly divorce reform) for two decades and had been instrumental in the passage of two significant temperance bills in the North Carolina legislature in 1903.[60] Groups such as the Woman's Christian Temperance Union and the newly founded North Carolina Federation of Women's Clubs might have joined Cheshire's effort had he asked them. Cheshire evidently believed that white men needed to lead the effort to reform the state's divorce laws.

Between 1890 and 1903, Cheshire noted critically how the North Carolina legislature repeatedly expanded the legal grounds for obtaining divorce. Instead of strengthening the institution of marriage by restricting access to divorce, as Cheshire had hoped and advocated, the legislature had done the opposite. "At almost every session of the Legislature," Cheshire complained, "'a little bill' that sounds very harmless is introduced to grind out more divorces."[61] To be sure, none of these expansions significantly altered the basic legal framework for divorce in the state, and there is no evidence from either the superior or supreme court records to indicate that any more than a handful of North Carolinians filed for divorce under these provisions who would not have been able to do so earlier. Further, the legislature made these additions to the state's divorce law with little, if any, debate, and newspapers did not comment on their significance.[62] Cheshire had two primary objections to these new laws. First, they symbolically deteriorated what he considered already too weak divorce laws. Every further departure from the divine conception of marriage, Cheshire thought, indicated how the "moral atmosphere" had declined.[63] Second, Cheshire, among many others, believed that the legislature had enacted these "little bills" primarily for the benefit of wealthy or influential individuals. "The several amendments and changes in the law of divorce," he argued, "have not been based upon any general principles of moral and of social science—but have notoriously been for the purpose of relieving particular persons."[64]

Although he made this claim repeatedly, Cheshire never explicitly said which "particular persons" had pressured the state legislature to craft special divorce provisions. It is likely, however, that Brodie Leonidas Duke was among those Cheshire had in mind. Born in 1848, Brodie Duke was the eldest son of tobacco magnate Washington Duke and half brother of industrialists James B. Duke and Benjamin Duke. In 1868, he opened the family's first tobacco warehouse in Durham and helped to found the company that would become American Tobacco. His business acumen had made him one of the state's wealthiest men by 1890. His alcoholism and erratic behavior, however, made him the black sheep of the Duke family.

After the death of his first wife, Brodie married Minnie Woodard, a younger woman from a wealthy Chattanooga family. Within months after their wedding, it became clear that the union was troubled. They rarely saw each other, as Brodie lived primarily in Durham and Minnie in California. In March 1904, after thirteen years of marriage, Brodie sought to divorce his wife, publicly declaring that his primary purpose was to have clear title to his property. He claimed the divorce under a statute passed a year earlier that allowed for absolute divorce in the case of abandonment for two years.

Many expected that the Duke divorce case would drag on for more than a week, an eternity by turn-of-the-century divorce trial standards, as each party had hired a corps of attorneys and brought a host of character witnesses to Durham. Although it "promised to be long drawn out and sensational litigation," the trial itself took less than fifteen minutes. At the start of the trial, while most of the newspaper reporters eager to cover the case finished their American Tobacco cigarettes outside the courthouse, Brodie Duke's lawyers called him to testify. He briefly stated that his wife had abandoned him and that he wished to be granted a divorce under the recently passed statute. His wife's attorneys did not cross-examine him, and no further witnesses were called. Faced only with Brodie's testimony as evidence, the jury granted him his divorce. Brodie Duke and his lawyers left the courthouse before many of those lingering outside had even realized the proceedings had commenced.[65] This unexpected resolution led many to conclude that Brodie Duke and Minnie Woodard had arrived at some form of compromise. Rumors spread through the community that Brodie had paid his wife between $30 and $100,000 to avoid a public trial.[66]

Brodie Duke's divorce brought unprecedented public attention to the issue. A day after running an article describing the trial's conclusion, the *News and Observer* ran two pieces condemning the spread of divorce in the state. In a lengthy letter to the editor headlined "Divorce, Whose Spread Threatens Purity of Home and Nation, May Be Crushed If the Church Will Act," Rev. W. H. S. McLaurin presented an argument not dissimilar from that which Bishop Cheshire had been making for almost a decade. "Why should there be," he asked, "such lax laws and such wholesome slaughtering of this sacred institution, in our fair State?" A Methodist, McLaurin argued that churches ought to pressure legislators to reform divorce laws to conform to biblical standards. Failure to act now, McLaurin claimed, meant disaster, "for nothing could so effectively destroy our civilization, and uproot the foundations of our faith; striking as [divorce] does at the vitals of all true civilizations." A second, shorter piece in the same issue observed that "the divorce mill runs over time and legalizes 'progressive polygamy.'"[67]

In the months after the public spectacle of Brodie Duke's divorce in 1904,

Bishop Cheshire redoubled his efforts to lobby for meaningful divorce reform. To this end, Bishop Cheshire embarked on a frantic public speaking tour in the fall of 1904 to convince religious leaders to join him in a united effort, a crusade that would take him from one end of the state to the other. With the attention to the issue brought by Brodie Duke's divorce, Cheshire found his audiences receptive. During a three-week period in late 1904, Cheshire visited the Presbyterian Synod in Durham, the Baptist State Convention in Elizabeth City, and Methodist conventions in Henderson and Charlotte. At each event, he secured the denomination's support for a petition to the state legislature demanding immediate divorce reform.[68] He told the Methodists that "the statute law of a State is, in a measure, the expression of the civic conscience of the people of the State. Yielding to the influence of particular cases of individual hardship, this civic conscience, during the last twenty years, has in North Carolina been brought down from the higher standard which we had inherited from our fathers."[69] Cheshire evoked a similar tone of social decline when he told the Presbyterians, "If North Carolina did not change her laws and do something to check this growing evil, she would ere long be taking a hand in the new and very popular game, now in vogue at Newport and other places, known as progressive matrimony."[70] The *News and Observer* applauded Cheshire's efforts to bridge denominational barriers to combat divorce. "It is a good sign," declared a November 1904 editorial, "for any cause to see the churches touching elbow to elbow for the protection of the home." Although the paper warned that "the war against lax divorce laws will not be easily won," it expressed confidence that the growing religious coalition headed by Bishop Cheshire would be successful. Its main obstacle, the paper cautioned, was "the growing lax conception of the idea of marriage and the sanctity of the home."[71]

By the end of 1904, Cheshire had secured the support not only of religious leaders but of political ones as well, the most significant of whom was Governor Charles B. Aycock. In a letter to Cheshire in December 1904, Aycock wrote, "I have been following with much interest the discussion of the divorce laws in recent months and have come to the conclusion to recommend to the Legislature that we repeal all divorce laws."[72] Like Cheshire, Aycock had become disgusted by the way in which men such as Brodie Duke had used North Carolina's divorce laws and concluded that only meaningful divorce reform could prevent social collapse.[73] Later that month, in his final message to the General Assembly as governor, Aycock argued that "the conscience of the State has recently been greatly awakened on the subject of divorce." He applauded the efforts made by Bishop Cheshire and other religious leaders in drawing attention to "the great evil of frequent divorces" and supported their campaign to reform the state's divorce laws. Like them, Aycock saw divorce as a menace to social order: "Divorces have become more and more frequent until their number has challenged the consideration of thoughtful people and threatened in no small degree to undermine family life, out of which grow society and the State." He argued that the legislature should repeal all divorce statutes passed in the past twenty years. "It is better," Aycock concluded, "that a few individuals should suffer from being unhappily married than the public view with reference to the solemnity and permanence of the marriage relation should be in the slightest degree weakened. Wedlock ought not to be entered into lightly, but when it is once entered into it ought, save for scriptural causes, to be inviolable."[74]

When the North Carolina legislature convened in January 1905, growing public pressure indicated that divorce reform would be high on its agenda. The *News and Observer* declared that "there is no duty with reference to any change in the statute law of the State so important as the repeal of those laws that have let down the bars and made divorce easy. . . . The best sentiment of the State would be disappointed if this Legislature should fail to wipe out the new laws responsible for the invitation to men and women to violate their sacred vows."[75] Legislators eager to respond to the public outcry introduced several competing, though fairly similar, bills that would repeal all divorce statutes passed in the previous twenty years. Charles Aycock's successor, Governor Robert B. Glenn, lent his support to the measures, claiming that "divorces are now too easily obtained and are often granted . . . when the people find they cannot be easily separated, but indeed take each other for 'better or for worse,' they will 'bear and forbear' with each other's frailties, thus preserving the sanctity of the marriage vow and adding to the safety, purity, and peace of home life."[76]

On the afternoon of 17 January 1905, Bishop Cheshire marched to the state capitol to present his petition demanding immediate reform of the state's divorce laws. He headed a delegation that included some the most important religious leaders in North Carolina, including Rev. E. A. Yates, Rev. John M. Rose, and Rev. Livingston Johnston. He was also joined by political leaders such as former governor Thomas Jarvis, former chief justice James E. Sheperd, and University of North Carolina president Francis P. Venable. "The arguments of the distinguished gentlemen made a profound impression upon those present," concluded the *News and Observer*, "and it is now almost certain that the divorce evil will be lessened in this State."[77]

During the six weeks that the legislature debated divorce reform, Raleigh ministers used Sunday sermons to urge lawmakers to enact divorce reform. Preaching at Edenton Street Methodist, Rev. W. H. Moore said that "men may be made moral, if not Christian, by legislation, and no man is worthy to sit in a legislative seat who does not recognize this fact." At First Presbyterian, Rev. Dr. A. H. Moment told parishioners that weak divorce laws threatened to destroy the very foundation of society. "Had the American nation been preceded by ten generations of Anglo-Saxons having such divorce laws as now exist in Connecticut, Indiana, South Dakota, and other states I'll leave you to add," he told them, "there would have been no American nation."[78] Rev. R. H. Whitaker concluded that "if the members vote here as they talked at home and as they were understood to be at home, they will pass such a divorce law as will be in line with the express teaching of Christ."[79]

On 6 March 1905, the General Assembly passed legislation repealing all divorce laws passed since the codification of 1883. On the eve of its passage, the *Presbyterian Standard* of Charlotte hoped that it would end the period in which "the divorce evil has about wrought its own curse in the good old State of North Carolina."[80] The reform resulted, according to the *News and Observer*, from "the crusade set in motion by a vast number of citizens of the State including 400,000 church members for the repeal of lax divorce laws."[81] It concluded that "no single piece of legislation in a decade has been so generally approved as the Eller-McNinch-Biggs law that passed the General Assembly. . . . Under that law we shall see the number of divorces steadily decrease in North Carolina."[82]

For Bishop Cheshire, the passage of divorce reform legislation was but a temporary victory. Although the number of divorces declined in 1905 and 1906, by 1907 the number of divorces in North Carolina reached an all-time high. In a 1907 letter to Charles Aycock, his former ally in his divorce crusade, Cheshire lamented how he had become "mortified and disappointed" that the General Assembly recently had liberalized divorce laws. Particularly troubling, wrote Cheshire, were rumors that Aycock himself had used his influence in the legislature to secure passage of the measure for the benefit of one of his legal clients. "If it be true as is alleged that you have exerted your personal influence to secure what is in effect the repeal for a particular and private interest, of an enactment specifically urged by yourself two years ago upon general principles of right and of utility," Cheshire wrote, "I must take the liberty of saying that I and many others most deeply deplore your action."[83]

He voiced a similar disgust in a letter published in the *News and Observer*. Claiming to represent "the Christian sentiment of North Carolina on this subject," he said that he "deeply deplore[d] the action of our law makers, and cannot but feel that they have made a grievous error." He lamented that he had recently been out of the state on church and personal business and therefore had been unaware of the proposed legislation. He concluded that this addition to the divorce statute could only be the result of influential lawyers advocating for prominent clients. He felt that lawmakers had been swayed by these lobbying efforts despite "very wide spread feeling [among North Carolinians] of mortification and distress at this retrograde movement."[84]

Ensuing years indicated that Cheshire's 1905 campaign had been a Pyrrhic victory. In 1913, Cheshire's friend and *News and Observer* editor Josephus Daniels wrote to him that the General Assembly had again passed legislation weakening the reforms made in 1905.[85] By 1916, census figures indicated that the divorce rate in North Carolina had increased 9 percent since 1900 and 16 percent since 1890.[86] Throughout his lengthy tenure as bishop, Cheshire continued to maintain that the state needed to reform its divorce laws to prevent social deterioration. Indeed, he regularly delivered his sermon on the evils of divorce until January 1928, four years before his death.

Black and white clergymen's diverging interpretations and approaches to divorce in postbellum North Carolina reflect radically different opinions of the moral state of the South since the Civil War. For many white North Carolinians, the Confederate loss of the Civil War heralded a period of moral decay and decline. To combat this decline they believed that the state needed to intervene to control the slide into depravity and, it was hoped, even return to what they considered a morally superior antebellum past. Conversely, many black North Carolinians saw the period since emancipation as one of gradual and incremental moral improvement. Black North Carolinians remained skeptical about the capacity of the state to enact positive change. Their experience, both in slavery and in freedom, taught them to distrust any form of legislation, especially laws that interfered with family and personal relationships.[87] Instead, they looked inward, to their family, neighborhoods, and churches, to enforce moral standards.

PART III

Enslaved by Debt

The Culture of Credit & Debt

I N ITS INAUGURAL REPORT, the North Carolina Bureau of Labor Statistics concluded in 1887 that North Carolinians across the state shouldered debts they could not pay. A teacher from Rutherford County observed that "the working people of this county, as a rule, are in debt." A Gaston County farmer concurred, noting that "people in this section are generally in debt." A Montgomery County clerk advised, "Be more cautious about going into debt and I think we will improve." The ubiquity of crushing debts led the report's authors to conclude that debt was "a worse curse to North Carolina that drouths [sic], floods, cyclones, storms, rust, caterpillar and every other evil."[1]

Although the report's conclusions reflected the particular conditions of its time, debt would not have been a new problem for most North Carolinians. Throughout the nineteenth century, the structure of the southern agricultural economy meant that many of the region's residents, black and white, rich and poor, frequently went into debt. Three factors account for southerners' apparently perpetual indebtedness. First, because farmers could expect to receive payment for their crops only at harvest time, unexpected expenses, particularly in the summer months preceding the harvest, meant going into debt. Second, the limited amount of hard currency in circulation in the South both before and after the Civil War meant that most financial transactions had to be conducted on credit. Third, the South never developed the robust banking system that existed in other regions of the country, limiting the number of bank notes that served as economic lubrication elsewhere.[2] One scholar has estimated that the cumulative effect of these factors meant that between two-thirds and three-quarters of all transactions in the antebellum South were conducted on the basis of credit; after the Civil War rates may have been even higher.[3]

North Carolinians employed a variety of strategies over the course of the nineteenth century to deal with the problem of debt in its social, cultural, and economic components. These strategies were not static; black and white North Carolinians changed how they understood and coped with debt depending on shifting economic conditions and social norms. Although market fluctuations constantly pushed North Carolinians to re-valuate their relationship to debt, the Civil War placed unprecedented stress on North Carolina's culture and system of credit. The experience of white North Carolinians during the Civil War fundamentally transformed their attitudes toward and strategies for coping with debt. Before the Civil War, white North Carolinians built complex informal networks of credit between and among local community members. These networks grew out of and re-inforced a deep commitment to and investment in interpersonal relation-ships. In a variety of ways, the Civil War decimated this system. In its wake arose a new understanding of the role of debt that emphasized the needs of the individual over those of the society. After 1865, white North Carolinians employed strategies for dealing with debt that were antithetical to antebel-lum mores. Among the most important and visible of these strategies were the dramatic increase in personal bankruptcies, the rise of female-owned boardinghouses, and the growth of new credit-granting institutions, includ-ing general stores and pawnshops. These new strategies resulted from deep structural changes in the southern economy and a revolution in white atti-tudes about the relationship between individual and community.

The Civil War also transformed how black North Carolinians understood the social meaning of debt. Slaves could not legally contract debts, and free blacks were routinely shut out from white credit networks. After emancipa-tion, black North Carolinians recognized the potential material advantages that credit provided and the potential peril that debt posed to their free-dom. Because emancipation left black North Carolinians with "nothing but freedom," control over capital, and hence over credit, remained primarily in white hands.[4] Out of necessity, freedmen and freedwomen in North Caro-lina relied on new credit institutions such as sharecropping, the crop-lien system, and general stores to meet their most basic needs. Although this newfound access to credit theoretically provided a means to material im-provement and upward mobility, it created the potential for debilitating levels of debt. Consequentially, black North Carolinians sought to avoid in-debting themselves to whites, fearing that such indebtedness would return them to a state of peonage. Credit, therefore, acted as a double-edged sword for African Americans in postwar North Carolina.

Debt can be seen as both a financial instrument and an intellectual and moral construct. This study emphasizes the latter, while never entirely abandoning the former. The intent here is not to reinvent how scholars should think about various manifestations of debt, many of which have been thoroughly examined by economic historians, but rather to explore how these phenomena reveal cultural ideas about debt and to observe how the changes in the ways in which black and white North Carolinians thought and talked about debt paralleled changes in the ways in which they discussed suicide and divorce.

CHAPTER SEVEN

Sacredness of Obligations

Debt in Antebellum North Carolina

A LTHOUGH DEBT of one form or another was ubiquitous throughout the South during the nineteenth century, indebtedness carried
a significant social stigma for white North Carolinians during the
antebellum period. Debt functioned as a fundamental threat to an individual's independence because it made the debtor assume a subordinate
position to his or her creditor. Antebellum white southerners recoiled at
the idea of dependence because they associated it with slavery. One of the
distinguishing features of slaves, thought white southerners, was their sub-
ordination to and dependence upon their master. Therefore, to enter into
debt was to assume the position of a slave. While the metaphor comparing
indebtedness to slavery was common throughout the United States during
the nineteenth century, the symbol of the debt slave was particularly palpable in the context of a slave society.[1] As a result, most antebellum white
North Carolinians sought to avoid indebtedness at all costs.

At the same time, a desire for upward mobility and social standing often
compelled them to enter into debt. More than almost anything else, owning land and slaves demarcated social status in antebellum North Carolina. Tangible and visible, these forms of property offered antebellum white
men access to the domain of mastery. To this end, they routinely violated
the social prohibitions against debt in order to acquire these culturally and
economically significant forms of property. Antebellum yeoman farmers
often justified purchasing slaves on credit as a vehicle for social mobility.
Indeed, buying slaves on credit was probably the greatest source of debt in
antebellum North Carolina and across the South.[2] White North Carolinians
justified buying slaves on credit for four reasons. First, they could consider
the purchase of slaves as a financial investment, as the price of slaves more

than tripled between 1805 and 1860.[3] Second, the productive labor of slaves in the fields meant that most slaves would pay for themselves in less than five years. Third, the reproductive labor of slaves meant that buying slaves functioned as a tool for upward mobility not only for a yeoman farmer but also for his sons and grandsons.[4] Fourth, slave owners recognized that in times of financial trouble their human property was a very liquid form of capital. Unlike crops or real estate, whose liquidity depended upon fluctuations of geographic and seasonal demand, the market for slaves was relatively inelastic. Because slaves could be sold to settle other debts, slave owning functioned as a form of insurance against indebtedness. Furthermore, slaves could function as collateral to secure credit in the future. Indeed, one historian has concluded that slaves functioned as collateral in the majority of antebellum southern credit agreements. Therefore the structure of the southern slave society encouraged indebtedness, while at the same time attaching a heavy social stigma to debt.[5]

Antebellum white North Carolinians mediated the contradictory aspects of debt through the development of what anthropologists call a gift economy. Blurring distinctions between market and interpersonal transactions, gift giving flourished in the antebellum white South because it functioned as needed credit without publicly making the recipient into a debtor. While these gifts existed in a myriad of forms, the type of gift that antebellum white southerners gave most often and desired most desperately was currency. By engaging in reciprocal gift giving, white North Carolinians created an informal credit system that simultaneously bound them horizontally and vertically in the community and served a necessary economic role. This network of loans between white North Carolinians helped to create a system of mutual indebtedness that did not threaten to "enslave" its participants.[6]

Antebellum white North Carolinians did not, however, participate in this system indiscriminately. Instead, they established a socially sanctioned, informal set of rules that dictated to whom they could loan money and in what amounts, rules that one historian has described as an "etiquette of debt."[7] Although these rules varied from community to community and their interpretation was often determined by individual idiosyncrasies, they broadly required that participants in debtor-creditor relationships recognize each other as social peers, though not necessarily equals. To be sure, individual reputation played a significant role when a creditor decided whether to provide a loan; however, because the possible social ramifications of refusing to loan money to a peer were so significant, most creditors were willing to overlook an imperfect reputation except in the most egregious cases. The practical consequences of this "etiquette of debt" was that white men with strong ties to a community participated most heavily in the gift economy, while women (with the possible exception of widows), African Americans (both slave and free), and outsiders or newcomers were excluded.[8]

Although these credit relationships helped to provide a meaningful form of connection between white men, this informal and personal credit system was inherently unstable. Because the only person who knew how much money a debtor owed to various creditors was the debtor himself, external manifestations of financial security and success could be illusory. While individuals within the gift economy were aware of the bonds of debt that connected them to their neighbors, the full articulation of these credit networks escaped them, allowing the unscrupulous to borrow money well in excess of their capacity to repay. Therefore, although the gift economy was in one sense a manifestation of the trust that creditors placed in their community, they constantly questioned whether their trust had been misplaced.[9]

THE LIFE OF Dr. James Webb provides insight into the nature of the gift economy in the antebellum South. Born in 1774, Webb was the oldest son of a Granville County planter. After attending the University of North Carolina at Chapel Hill and studying medicine under Benjamin Rush at the University of Pennsylvania, Webb established himself as a doctor and planter in Hillsborough.[10] He quickly acquired property, including an eighty-acre farm outside town and a half dozen lots on the town common. Even though he considered his agricultural pursuits secondary to his professional calling as a physician, Webb also became one of Orange County's largest slave owners, acquiring at least thirty slaves by the mid-1830s.

Webb forged close friendships with many of his fellow slave owners, including Justice Thomas Ruffin, Thomas Bennehan, and Duncan Cameron. He sought out positions of leadership within the community, serving as a trustee of the University of North Carolina, as vice president of the North Carolina Medical Society, and as an elder of the Hillsborough Presbyterian Church. In short, Webb participated fully in almost every facet of social interaction in his community, often taking leadership positions.

In this context, providing credit was another aspect of participating fully in the life of his community. Webb's surviving correspondence indicates that he routinely received requests for funds from friends and relatives, requests that he almost uniformly fulfilled. These donations of money functioned as a halfway position between gifts and loans. Although he expected repayment, Webb rarely requested that his debtors pay on any particular schedule. Instead, he relied upon the honor of his debtors to pay when they could. This lax attitude toward repayment can be seen in a letter from Archibald Murphey, an old college classmate, a member of the state legislature, and one of Webb's heaviest debtors. In 1817, he wrote to Webb, "I am not able to send you as much money as I wished, several people having promised to pay me considerable funds lately and almost all having failed."[11] This letter reveals much about the informal nature of the credit system created by the gift economy. Murphey apologized for not being able to repay because his own debtors had not been able to repay him. Each participant in the credit network realized that demanding immediate and timely payments could be interpreted as a challenge to his debtor's honor.[12] Webb responded to Murphey's letter by granting him as much time as he required to repay this debt, relying upon Murphey's reputation as sufficient collateral.

Many requests for money were phrased in the language of community rather than finance. Four months after requesting an extension on his own debt, Archibald Murphey wrote asking Webb to join him in a loan to their mutual friend M. L. Prather, who had fallen into significant debt. Murphey argued that only by this financial donation could Prather be "assisted to redeem his reputation" and "bring into useful life a Man."[13] Such an act would not, of course, reduce the size of Prather's debt, but it would allow Prather to reestablish some of the honor that his debts appeared to have cost him. By joining Murphey in lending money to Prather, James Webb demonstrated that his motivations in becoming a creditor sometimes depended more on social than financial considerations.

The language employed in these requests for money also indicates an ambiguity as to whether these transactions were loans or gifts. Indeed, few potential debtors referred to the money in question as a loan, preferring in most cases to ask Webb to "send" them money. Only a handful of the dozens of written requests for funds that Webb received over the years provide any indication of the terms of the loan, the date due, or the amount of interest. This reluctance to describe these loans in financial terms reveals the extent to which Webb's debtors and southerners in general had negative associations with the idea of debt, regardless of how many of them lived beyond their means.

Although some of the debts owed to Webb were contracted through written correspondence, most of Webb's credit relations were conducted in person. Instead of requiring collateral, a formal contract, or some other form of security, Webb appears to have been satisfied primarily with his debtors' pledging an oath that the money would be repaid. Oaths had an almost mystical power among antebellum southern whites. Historian Bertram Wyatt-Brown describes the oath as "something impressive, particularly to Southern whites . . . who prized oral, personal ways over rationalistic, formalistic ones."[14] A debt oath, like a marriage oath or an oath sworn in court, rested entirely on the honor of the pledger. James Webb evidently felt that such oaths were sufficient security to distribute his money.

Although these examples indicate that Webb was generous in how he participated in the gift economy, he was far from indiscriminate. In late 1842, for instance, Webb had outstanding loans to 109 individuals.[15] Comparing these names against manuscript census returns reveals that more than half of those indebted to Webb were slave owners.[16] Indeed, a handful of those who owed Webb money held as many slaves as he did. For example, Fendal Southerland, who owed Webb $16.50, owned more than fifty slaves. Andrew Borland, a planter with over 170 acres in cultivation, owed $10. Not only were most of Webb's debtors within his social class, but many lived in close proximity to his house in Hillsborough. Moreover, church records indicate that at least a third of those who owed Webb money saw him every week at Hillsborough Presbyterian Church.[17] Therefore, while Webb was willing to distribute loans to a large number of his neighbors, he was selective about which neighbors were worthy of such allotments. He opened his coffers only to those whom he saw as having a comparable investment in the community.

Most of these loans were for fairly modest amounts. Indeed, out of the 109 debts recorded in 1842, most were for sums less than twenty dollars; a handful were for less than five dollars. William Garrard, for instance owed Webb three dollars, while his brother James owed him six dollars. William and Thomas Freeland each owed Webb four dollars. Some of these small debts may have originated in unpaid medical services rendered by Dr. Webb, although little manuscript material concerning Webb's medical practice has survived. Despite, or perhaps because of, the modest sums involved, Webb often allowed these debts to remain outstanding for extended periods of time, as at least ten of the debts recorded in 1842 had been contracted more than five years earlier.

Despite James Webb's apparent ability to offer credit to his neighbors, he also regularly found himself in need of money. Instead of calling in debts owed to him, Webb himself would contract debts with other planters, particularly Thomas Ruffin, Duncan Cameron, and Thomas Bennehan. Although the number of men to whom Webb owed money was substantially smaller than the number indebted to him, the amounts in question were often significantly larger. At one point, for instance, Webb owed Thomas

Bennehan more than one thousand dollars. For much of Webb's life, it is unclear whether he owed more than he was owed. Indeed, his correspondence and behavior suggest that Webb neither knew nor cared about the balance between his debts and credits.

Webb's willingness to contract debts for himself rather than call in debts owed to him indicates how Webb viewed the role of credit. Webb granted credit to those whom he considered respected members of the community, individuals who were his social equals or close to it. Webb loaned money, therefore, not for financial advancement on his own part but as a means of building relationships with men he considered his peers.[18] To demand payment of these debts could be interpreted as an affront to the debtor's honor because it indicated that the debtor-creditor relationship was more hierarchical than egalitarian. In other words, if Webb were to demand repayment, it would indicate that the money in question was in fact a loan and not a gift. Webb decided, therefore, that it was better to contract his own debts rather than potentially challenge the honor of his debtors.

To be sure, many antebellum creditors did attempt to collect on delinquent debts. North Carolina county court records indicate that many creditors sought to bring their debt relationships into the public domain. The preponderance of debt cases in county courts does not mean, however, that white North Carolinians believed that credit relationships should be exposed in public forums or needed the force of law to sustain. Although the number of debt suits brought in county courts appears significant at first glance, they represent only a small fraction of potential debt suits that would have been brought had creditors like James Webb been interested in maintaining rigid credit relationships. Many creditors hesitated before hauling their debtors into court, perhaps believing that interpersonal credit relationships ought to resolve themselves in private. Furthermore, a significant number of debt suits filed in county courts did not result in judgments. Rather, creditors brought these suits to create a public record, thereby providing a legal basis for recovery were the need to arise. Therefore, debt recovery suits represent an aberration within the context of the social credit system. In most cases, they indicate those cases in which interpersonal debt relationships had broken down.

North Carolina planters rarely unmasked themselves as debtors. However, on those rare occasions when they did admit their own indebtedness, it was cause of considerable anxiety and shame and rarely of their own volition. Three years after pleading with James Webb for forbearance on his debt, Archibald Murphey wrote to another creditor expressing his shame in his chronic indebtedness. "Now the Cup of my Humiliation is full to the Brim," Murphey wrote to Thomas Ruffin. His debt had left him "degraded in the World and pointed at even by the Common Vulgar." According to Murphey, who had spent most of the past decade deeply in debt to a variety of creditor-neighbors, his shame began not with the debt itself but when some of his creditors had publicly exposed him as a debtor by registering his debts in court. According to Murphey, "To be harassed by my Creditors is worse than Death to me."[19]

Dr. James Webb was but one participant in a complex web of credit that extended across Orange County. Financial records of Orange County's white residents reveal how these credit transactions helped to reinforce social relationships. An intensely local system, this web created ties of credit and debt that bound white residents into a community; to stand outside this complex network was to be outside the community, and to be within it was to proclaim membership in the social order. Although this credit system projected a façade of white male egalitarianism, its inherent instability and capricious nature often resulted in disastrous consequences, especially for poor debtors.[20]

The existence of this complex local credit network also indicates a broad antipathy among southern whites toward patronizing formalized credit institutions located outside the community. In addition to his medical practice and his agricultural pursuits, Dr. James Webb served as the local agent for the Bank of the Cape Fear, one of North Carolina's oldest and largest banking institutions. Yet despite his access to funds considerably greater than his own personal fortune, Webb's neighbors in need of a loan were much more likely to approach Webb as a friend and private creditor than Webb as the local agent of a distant bank.

Although Webb and other planter-creditors maintained the façade of white male egalitarianism in their debtor-creditor relationships, poor white debtors recognized that their use of credit placed them in a subservient position and thereby threatened their liberty. For more than half of the antebellum white population in North Carolina who held little or no property, indebting themselves to their wealthier neighbors became the only way to sustain themselves. When the availability of credit contracted, particularly in times of economic depression, these poor debtors suffered. In many cases, the calamity of their situation came not as much from their outstanding debts as from their inability to tap into new sources of credit. Largely self-sustaining, at least compared with their postbellum descendants, poor white North Carolinians often needed to borrow money to pay their taxes.

When hard times prevented them from borrowing the needed funds, many poor farmers lost whatever property they owned to pay taxes in arrears. "A large majority of the people are farmers and are deeply in debt," farmers from Moore County wrote to the state legislature in 1843 during one of the deepest depressions the country had known. "The consequence will be serious. . . . In vain have the people toiled laboured and economized. . . . The property of the poore is rapidly passing into the hands of the rich—for a mere trifle."[21]

The failure of North Carolina's legislature to pass homestead legislation complicated the plight of poor debtors. In many southern states, homestead laws protected debtors from losing all their property when they found themselves helplessly in debt. Georgia's law, for instance, proclaimed that "it does not comport with the principles of justice, humanity, or sound policy to deprive the family of an unfortunate debtor of a home and a means of subsistence." Entitled an "Act for Relief of Honest Debtors," the Georgia statute protected fifty acres of land, one horse or mule, and thirty dollars in provisions, among other items, thereby allowing poor debtors to hold on to enough property to sustain themselves and a chance for escape from under their debt in the future.[22] Because North Carolina did not have homestead legislation during the antebellum period, poor debtors could and did lose all their property, including the shirts off their back.

In lieu of a homestead exemption, North Carolina's Insolvent Debtor Law provided a modicum of protection for poor debtors. Passed during the colonial era and periodically revised, the law allowed debtors who evoked its provisions to retain "one cow and calf, ten bushels of corn or wheat, fifty pounds of bacon, beef, or pork, or one barrel of fish, all necessary farming tools for one laborer, one bed, bedstead, and covering for every two members of the family."[23] Although the Insolvent Debtor Law undoubtedly saved many North Carolinians from absolute destitution, it provided only a fraction of the relief provided by homestead exemptions. First, the Insolvent Debtor Law did not protect real property, forcing small independent farmers to become tenants. Second, it did not absolve the debtor of paying the debt itself. If his financial conditions improved, he would still be held liable for the old debts at full value.

If poor whites suffered under the antebellum credit system, yeoman whites faired only slightly better.[24] Even yeomen who wished to avoid debt could hardly avoid participating in local credit networks. Basil Armstrong Thomasson, a yeoman farmer and schoolteacher in Yadkin and Iredell counties, struggled throughout his life to balance his distaste of debt and the practical needs of his family.[25] In January 1859, he noted in his diary,

> I've set in this year to get out of debt, and if we live and have health
> and strength enough to "push along, and keep moving," I think
> I'll come it. I do not intend to buy anything on time this year, un-
> less its [sic] a bit of land, if I can help it. I must stop going in [debt]
> if I would get out. "Better to go to bed supperless," said Franklin,
> I think, "than get up in debt." Its bad to get up in debt, but I guess
> it would be well enough, generaly [sic], to go to bed supperless, or
> nearly so. We should eat to live, and not live to eat. O that I could
> govern myself in this matter of eating.[26]

Benjamin Franklin's aphorisms about the virtues of frugality made regular appearances in Thomasson's diary, as did the biblical dictate that "the bor-rower is a slave to the lender."[27] Indeed, the perils of debt was a reoccur-ring motif in Thomasson's diary. In one of his earliest entries, he notes, "I must curtail my expense and live on economy awhile." He was also critical of those who lived beyond their means, noting that "there is great danger of 'living too fast,' and most persons that buy on credit live in advance of their means" and that "paying interest is bad business."[28]

Thomasson sought to avoid debt because he felt, in proper republican tradition, that debt threatened his independence. In October 1856, he noted that he had "been keeping house upwards of nine months, and living on borrowed salt. . . . I concluded to go to them that sold [salt] and buy for my-self, as I am, and of right out to be free and indipenant."[29] Many yeoman farmers in North Carolina continued to espouse the Jefferson ideal of the independent farmer, while increasingly becoming embedded in the market economy.[30] Like most yeoman farmers in the western Piedmont, Thomasson practiced a "safety first" model of agricultural production, growing most of his crops for his family's use rather than for the market.[31] However, Thomas-son's efforts do not necessarily indicate a rejection of the market economy, as Thomasson devoted a significant portion of his seventy-one-acre farm to tobacco, despite his personal repugnance to tobacco products. His forays into the market, however, rarely netted Thomasson the kinds of returns that he desired. For most of the diary, Thomasson's career as a teacher generated far more income than his work on the farm. Indeed, Thomasson often ne-glected his farm to teach, despite the low pay, because it provided a consis-tent source of income. He noted in his diary in 1859, "I fear I shall lose as much by teaching school as I shall gain. I ought to be doing up my fences, ditching and cleaning up the swa[m]p. But I *must* have money."[32]

Thomasson's need for money pushed him into the local debt economy. Despite his efforts to the contrary, he relied upon local credit sources to meet his daily needs. He borrowed money from his neighbors, including local planters, and from shopkeepers. Like James Webb, Thomasson became an integral part of a credit network based in kinship and social relationships, borrowing money from (and occasionally loaning to) his social peers.

Thomasson's efforts to secure credit sometimes failed. In February 1857, he traveled "to Doweltown to borrow some money of Dr. H. Willson, but did not get any, as he said he had not 'a particle.'" While such a refusal to lend money might have been interpreted as an affront by many white North Carolinians, the even-tempered Thomasson used the event as an opportunity to reflect upon his experiences in the local credit network. "I've tried a few times in my life to hire money, and I've found it hard to get," he wrote in his diary. "Hope I shall find it necessary but seldom to make the tryal."[33] Here Thomasson's account contradicts the rest of the diary. Although he claimed to have borrowed money only "a few times in my life," his diary indicates that he regularly sought out and used credit. This contradiction speaks to how yeoman farmers like Thomasson thought about debt. Although they practiced credit relationships out of necessity, they did not like to think of themselves as debtors. Yet, as his repeated pledges to extricate himself from debt indicate, Thomasson recognized on some level that he needed credit to sustain even his frugal lifestyle. In January 1855, after taking account of his debts, Thomasson remarked, "If my debts were paid I should not be worth more than 10 [dollars]," an observation that led him to recommit to living within his means, a pledge he broke almost as soon as he made it.

Although both James Webb and Basil Armstrong Thomasson participated in local credit networks, Thomasson's participation differed from Webb's in a couple of important aspects. First, unlike Webb, Thomasson often described his debts as debts. While Webb and other planters eschewed the language of debt because it indicated dependence, Thomasson made no pretense in his diary that his credit relationships masqueraded as gifts, even when the credit relationships were with close friends. Second, Thomasson, unlike Webb, kept a detailed account of his debts and credits, not only in his diary but also in an account book that he referred to as his "Cost of Living." This document, now unfortunately lost, indicates that Thomasson felt a need to assess his standing in the local credit network, a sentiment that was some-what foreign to Webb and many planters. The paucity of yeoman sources comparable to Thomasson's diary makes it difficult to assess whether the differences between Thomasson's and Webb's use of credit reflect a mean-ingful distinction between yeomen's and planters' thoughts about debt. The differences do indicate, however, that white North Carolinians possessed a range of opinions about debt, even if these opinions were often inchoate.

North Carolina's black population, both slave and free, fell outside the gift economy credit system. Although scholars are increasingly recognizing the informal (and often illegal) economic relationships that transcended the color line during the antebellum period, the vast majority of these trans-actions were conducted through cash or barter.[34] John Hope Franklin's seminal study of free blacks in antebellum North Carolina indicates that even under the best of conditions free African Americans had difficulty securing credit.[35] Planters such as James Webb were unwilling to grant credit to their black neighbors because doing so would effectively label them as an equal.[36] Conversely, according to Charles Ball, their inability to secure credit made slaves the preferred customers at antebellum general stores, as "the store-keepers are always ready to accommodate the slaves, who are fre-quently better customers than any white people; because the former always pay cash, whilst the latter almost always require credit."[37]

Ironically, because they stood outside white credit networks, African Americans sometimes could see the contradictory elements in southern debt culture that remained invisible to their white neighbors. Enslaved poet George Moses Horton ranked among the most observant. Born in 1797 in Northampton County, Horton learned to read by eavesdropping on lessons given to his owner's children. After he moved with his owner to Chatham County in 1815, Horton's duties included taking surplus produce to Chapel Hill to sell to college students. Although originally they "were fond of pranking with the country servants," these college students discovered that the poetic muses had blessed Horton and started paying him to compose poetry, particularly love sonnets.[38] Continuing to labor in the fields, Horton routinely sold more than a dozen poems a week to students. With the assis-tance of a faculty member's wife, Horton eventually published many of his poems in the *Raleigh Register* and the *Southern Literary Messenger*, later compiled into two volumes of verse. Although most of his poems address pastoral themes, two of them speak to the role of debt in southern society.

In a poem entitled "The Woodsman and the Money Hunter," Horton compares money to a fox. While the woods abound with other types of game such as the "opossum, coon, and coney," men often reject them in pursuit of the sly fox. Horton warns his readers of the perils of money:

> And she lies in the bankrupt shade;
> The cunning fox is funny;
> When thus the public debts are paid,
> Deceitful cash is not afraid,
> Where funds are hid for private trade,
> There's nothing paid but money.[39]

Here Horton recognizes that debtors often disguised their real assets, preferring some creditors to others. Knowing that only they had complete knowledge of their finances, these debtors realized that they could refuse to pay back creditors whom they considered socially less important, while at the same time maintaining those social credit relationships they thought significant. Indeed, as we shall see, one of the aspects of legal bankruptcy that repulsed antebellum white North Carolinians was its prohibition against preferring creditors.

Another of Horton's poems, entitled "The Creditor to His Proud Debtor," explores the role of debt in southern white society even more pointedly. The poem begins with a creditor rebuking one of his debtors for living beyond his means. He criticizes his "dandy" mode of dress and compares him to a peacock, strutting through town. Although the debtor gives the public appearance of success with his "pocket jingling loud with cash," the creditor/narrator sees through this: "But, alas! dear boy, you would be trash, / If your accounts were paid." Although the creditor/narrator condemns the debtor for his lifestyle in the first half of the poem, in the second half he recognizes that he too wants to appear wealthier than he is. He longs for the ability to "gird my neck with a light cravat, / And creaning wear my bell-crown hat." Here Horton captures one of the paradoxes of debt in the antebellum South. White men rejected debt because it made them dependent upon another, but at the same time they felt drawn to debt because it allowed them to appear gentlemanly.[40] Because Horton stood outside white credit networks, he had the capacity and distance to expose this paradox, which whites understood but could not articulate.

Although African Americans were largely excluded from local credit networks, enslaved North Carolinians suffered the heaviest costs when white debts went bad. Because debtors often used slave property as collateral or to settle debts, white debts often tore apart black families. Accounts of North

Carolina slave life reveal that debt settlement was probably the most common reason that slave families were forcibly divided. Fugitive slave Moses Grandy described how his brother was abruptly clamped into irons and taken away from his family because "his master had failed; and he was sold towards paying the debts." Grandy's terse assessment concluded that "this is the usual treatment under such circumstances." Shortly thereafter, Grandy lost his wife because her owner found himself in debt.[41] Near the end of his narrative, Grandy remarked that slave owners, "though they live in luxury, generally die in debt. . . . At the death of a proprietor, it commonly happens that his coloured people are sold towards paying his debts. So it must and will be with masters, while slavery continues."[42]

George Moses Horton also described the devastating experience of forced separation from family members. A recurring theme in Horton's poetry, the auction symbolized slaves' powerlessness and subjugation. In "A Slave's Reflections the Eve before His Sale," Horton observed,

O' comrades! To-morrow we try,
The fate of an exit unknowing—
Tears tricked from every eye—
'Tis going, 'tis going, 'tis going![43]

Horton voiced a similar sentiment in "Division of an Estate," lamenting, "O, the state, / The dark suspense in which poor vassals stand; / Each mind upon the spire of chance hangs, fluctuant, / The day of separation is at hand."[44] Horton's words grew out of personal experience: in 1819 he was separated from his parents and siblings in just such an auction.

Among white North Carolinians, the most insightful comments about the meaning of debt came from the evangelical pulpit. Clergymen saw that indebtedness had reached epidemic proportions in many of their congregations. While many of these debts had grown out of friendships developed in the context of Christian fellowship, the tensions inherent in credit relationships undermined their spiritual community. Indeed, several divines noted that debtors occasionally feigned illness on Sunday mornings in order to avoid a confrontation with a creditor. According to one anonymous sermon reprinted in the *Biblical Recorder* in 1848, "To be in debt is to be in a state of anxiety, if not of danger. Whether the debtor is asked for the money he owes or not, he is constantly expecting to be asked for it, which is almost as bad. The best thing, then, in money matters, is to keep out of debt; and the next best, if you owe anything, is to pay it as soon as you can."[45]

At the same time, clergymen recognized that no ready alternative existed to the local interpersonal credit networks. Indeed, most evangelical clergy-men themselves regularly participated in them as both creditors and debtors. Grossly underpaid, southern clergymen often had to rely upon loans and charity from their congregants to make ends meet.[46] Consequentially, their public pronouncements on debt revealed a muted criticism, warning their congregants about the potential problems inherent in debt but stopping short of condemning the practice outright.

Church discipline also reflected a muted criticism of the southern debt culture. Across denominations, church leaders sought to mediate between congregants engaged in disputes over debts, often actively trying to dis-suade them from taking the matter to civil courts. While churches could punish or expel members who defaulted on debts, most distinguished be-tween honest debts that, due to misfortune, could not be paid and fraudu-lent debts that the debtor never had any intention of repaying. For example, the Methodist Church in North Carolina authorized ministers to investigate the affairs of bankrupt members. If the investigation revealed that debts had been accrued imprudently or fraudulently, the minister could and did expel members. After 1812, the Methodists also formed three-member panels to discipline recalcitrant debtors. By 1840, most other denominations were em-ploying similar mechanisms. While disciplinary actions for debt were rare, their occasional appearance in church records indicated that white North Carolinians recognized some of the peril involved in chronic indebted-ness.[47]

IN NOVEMBER 1842, Dr. James Webb declared bankruptcy. Since he was burdened by debts he could not pay, this act absolved him of his heavy finan-cial obligations, but it also separated him from most of his property, as his slaves and most of his land holdings were auctioned off as part of the settle-ment. Declaring bankruptcy, however, also severed Webb from the local web of credit and debt in which he had participated so extensively. He had violated the oaths that he had made to his creditors, including his onetime friend Thomas Bennehan. Many of those who owed Webb money now saw the personal and informal credit relationship they had established with a neighbor and friend transformed into an asset in Webb's estate, to be auc-tioned off to the highest bidder. While Webb reacquired much of his per-sonal property over the next few years, he was never able to repair the dam-age that declaring bankruptcy inflicted upon his standing in the community. His surviving correspondence indicates that many of Webb's friends refused to speak to him ever again.

Only death and selective memory allowed Webb to reclaim the honor he lost the day he declared bankruptcy. An obituary published in the *Hillsborough Register* noted his deep involvement in the gift economy, noting that Webb was "ever ready to sympathize with, and to counsel and advise those whom misfortune had involved in difficulties, and to lend a helping hand when such assistance promised to be useful." The obituary omitted any mention of Webb's bankruptcy, claiming instead that "his business habits were characterized in a remarkable degree by punctuality, regularity, and care." Erasing this blemish from Webb's record, the obituary was able to conclude that "all who knew him honor and respect his virtues and his character."[48]

Dr. James Webb was one of a handful of prominent antebellum southerners to take advantage of the Bankruptcy Act of 1841. Passed in response to the Panics of 1837 and 1839, the Bankruptcy Act of 1841 granted debtors liberal terms in discharging their debts. While the financial troubles of the late 1830s and early 1840s were national in their implications, the South responded to the idea that debts could be dissolved in a distinctly different manner than other regions of the country. Outside the South, most observers saw debt and bankruptcy as unfortunate consequences of living in a growing market economy. To most white southerners in 1841, however, debts existed within a network of bonds that held society together.[49]

The congressional debate over the Bankruptcy Act of 1841 indicates a fundamental sectional divide concerning the social role of credit and debt. Northern congressmen, particularly Whigs such as Daniel Webster, advocated most heavily for the creation of a bankruptcy law. They argued that bankruptcy legislation was necessary to help rehabilitate entrepreneurs who had fallen hopelessly into debt. In Webster's words, bankruptcy legislation would aid "probably one or two hundred thousand debtors, honest, sober, and industrious, who drag out lives useless to themselves, useless to their families, and useless to their country, for no reason but that they cannot be legally discharged from their debts."[50] According to this argument, bankruptcy would grant such honest debtors a fresh start at life.

Southern congressmen interpreted Webster's proposed bankruptcy law in very different terms. Led by Missouri senator and former Orange County, North Carolina, resident Thomas Hart Benton, southern congressmen saw bankruptcy as a threat to the organic relationships between neighbors embedded in credit obligations. Benton argued that Congress had "no moral right to pass" bankruptcy legislation because under such a law "the natural order of things is reversed." Benton opposed bankruptcy because it failed to recognize how debts were contracted within the context of social relationships. He noted that credit was not granted purely on the basis of financial conditions: "Men are credited upon their character—upon their station in society—from the office which they fill—upon the prospect of future earnings or acquisitions; men are credited upon all these considerations; and creditors have a right to retain these chances in their hands, and look out for future payment, if they cannot receive it at present." Benton worried that the end result of bankruptcy legislation would be a culture in which debtors sought legal absolution rather than to fulfill their obligations to their creditors.[51]

Outside the South, debtors by the thousands took full advantage of provisions of the new bankruptcy law. Indebted farmers, merchants, clerks, artisans, laborers, and "gentlemen" alike saw bankruptcy as a way to restart lives shackled by debt. Indeed, bankruptcy became so common that one New York newspaper described debtors clogging the city's streets in front of the federal court more than "ten thousand in number" awaiting the opportunity to file.[52] Although the Bankruptcy Act of 1841 was repealed after only a year, nearly thirty thousand northerners took advantage of its provisions.[53]

In contrast, most southerners, even those heavily in debt, refused to take advantage of the provisions of the 1841 Bankruptcy Act. Bankruptcy rates across the South were only a fraction of those found in other regions. As Figure 6 indicates, they were on average three times lower in the South than elsewhere. In trying to explain why so few southerners filed for bankruptcy, one Florida district attorney noted that "the general sentiment of the community here is opposed to the moral propriety of taking advantage of the [bankruptcy] law, and that many have been deterred from seeking the relief it affords, either by their own conscientious scruples or by the force of public opinion."[54] In other words, even heavily indebted southerners bypassed the opportunity to wipe their financial slate clean because of the powerful stigma attached to bankruptcy.

The case of Dr. James Webb indicates how significantly this communal disapproval of bankruptcy could negatively affect an individual's position in society. Not only was Webb's decision to declare bankruptcy uncommon, but also his social position made him unusual among North Carolina's bankrupts. While outside the South bankruptcy appealed to debtors from a wide range of social conditions, within the South bankruptcy appears to have been primarily a phenomenon of social outsiders. An analysis of known North Carolina bankruptcy filers from 1842 indicates that Webb

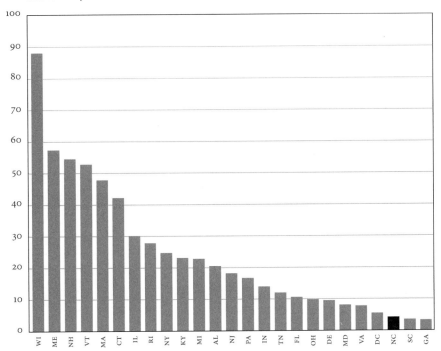

FIGURE 6. Bankruptcy filings per 10,000 free residents in 1842. Data for most states derived from Senate Document 19, 27th Congress, 3rd sess., *Report of the Secretary of State* [Daniel Webster]. Data for North Carolina extrapolated from Edwin Robeson Papers, SHC, and from extant but grossly incomplete bankruptcy records at the National Archives–Southeast Region in Atlanta. See Bennett, *Index of North Carolina Bankrupts*, 10–13. Data not available for Mississippi, Louisiana, Missouri, and Arkansas. State populations taken from the 1840 U.S. Census.

may have been the only large slaveholder in the state to file for bankruptcy. Many known bankrupts do not appear in the manuscript census returns for 1840, indicating that they were probably recent immigrants to the area. Despite their difficulty in procuring credit, free blacks appear in disproportionate numbers among bankruptcy filers in 1842, accounting for more than 10 percent of the total.[55] Thus, the Bankruptcy Act of 1841 appealed primarily to those outside the gift economy. As Dr. James Webb found out, bankruptcy had a heavy social cost for those within that culture.

Outraged at the perceived threat that the Bankruptcy Act of 1841 posed to the social order, southerners led the way in its repeal. The state legislatures of Mississippi and North Carolina sent petitions to Congress demanding its repeal. In arguing for its repeal on the floor of Congress, North Carolina representative Kenneth Raynor claimed that it fostered "a disregard for the sacredness of obligations." These obligations, Raynor asserted, formed the foundation not only of business and credit relations but of society itself. He hoped that bankrupts who had taken advantage of the law would eventually pay their debts, "debts from which they had been released — debts which honor called on them to provide for."[56]

CHAPTER EIGHT

Out of Debt before I Die

The Credit Crisis of the Civil War

T HE EXPERIENCE OF WHITE North Carolinians during the Civil War fundamentally transformed their conception of debt. Their faith in the sanctity of the debtor-creditor relationship rapidly eroded as wartime economic conditions made predictable credit relations almost impossible. Instead of returning to antebellum practices at the war's end, white North Carolinians struggled to construct a new conception of debt after 1865, reflecting postbellum economic and social conditions. Black North Carolinians experienced an equally radical reevaluation of the meaning of debt. Emancipation at the war's conclusion created the potential for many black North Carolinians to participate in white credit networks and to create credit networks and institutions of their own.

Although a variety of factors contributed to economic dislocation during the Civil War, unprecedented levels of inflation did more than anything else to undermine white credit networks in North Carolina. Especially after 1863, the proliferation of Confederate paper money, coupled with myriad state currencies and widespread counterfeiting, and shortages of both consumer and agricultural goods resulted in hyperinflation in excess of 9,000 percent.[1] By 1865, prices had risen so much that shoes in Wilmington sold for more than $600 and wool overcoats for $1,500. Even in comparatively self-sufficient western counties, prices for foodstuffs increased dramatically, such that over the course of the war, the price of eggs increased 1,666 percent, flour 2,777 percent, and corn more than 3,000 percent.[2]

Catherine Ann Devereux Edmondston described inflation's disastrous consequences in her plantation diary. Thirty-eight years old when the Civil War began, Edmondston lived on nearly two thousand acres in Halifax County with her husband, children, and eighty-eight slaves. Her financial position insulated her somewhat from the immediate effects of Confederate inflation. By the midpoint of the war, however, even women of Edmondston's status could not overlook inflated prices that were well above prewar levels. In April 1863, she remarked that "prices too are ruinous. I do not see how salaried men can live . . . so much has our currency depreciated." In March 1864, she complained that the price of sugar had reached "$12.50; flour, $300 to 325 per bll; . . . Corn & Meal, $10 per bu; Peas & Beans, $25 to 30 do." One month later she claimed that Confederate currency had become "now little but waste paper."[3]

Much of the inflationary pressure can be attributed to the Confederate government's excessive printing of treasury notes and other forms of paper currency to finance the war effort. By July 1861, more than one million dollars in Confederate treasury notes circulated. Five months later, the figure had reached thirty million dollars. By the fall of 1862, the Confederate treasury had printed nearly half a billion dollars and by February 1864 nearly one billion dollars.[4] Although the Confederate treasury generated the vast majority of inflated currency, state and local governments also contributed to the glut of paper money. North Carolina issued at least $8.5 million in state treasury notes.[5] At least a dozen counties and towns in North Carolina also issued notes that served as mediums of exchange.[6] To keep pace with the rapid devaluation of treasury notes, North Carolina banks also increased their circulation of bank notes from approximately $5.2 million in 1860 to more than $7.1 million in 1865.[7] At its height in 1864, the Confederate monetary expansion totaled more than a billion dollars, some twenty-two times its 1861 level.[8] Although the Confederate government attempted at various times to contract its runaway currency, particularly in 1864, these measures were largely ineffectual and may have actually increased the velocity of money (and therefore inflation) as note holders attempted to liquidate their holdings.[9] Taken together, these myriad currency issues flooded the market, diluting the currencies' value, and spreading financial uncertainty.

This proliferation of paper currency had an immediate inflationary effect on prices. In November 1862, the *Newbern Progress* reported that "party after party began to issue this trash, until our community has become flooded. . . . Unless some speedly [sic] and summary measures are taken, we soon shall have a brilliant array of worthless currency. . . . As for ourselves, we refuse this kind of stuff."[10] Several months later, the same newspaper noted that "the locusts which persecuted Pharaoh were scarcely more plentiful than paper currency in the South. Confederate notes, soft paper shinplasters, pasteboard chips, brass, iron and everything else that be converted into a circulating medium abounds everywhere. Everybody's pockets are lined with stuff which is scattered broadcast with a looseness. Nobody seems to place any value on paper money, and no other kind if to be had."[11]

Chronic shortages also contributed to inflationary pressures in Confederate North Carolina. Decreased agricultural production, heavy in-kind taxation, and the Union blockade all contributed to drive up prices on many goods.[12] On small farms, the loss of male agricultural labor to conscription left fields unplowed and crops unharvested, as their already overburdened wives and children struggled with an increasing workload. As early as October 1862, a Fayetteville farmer wrote that "nearly every man, woman, and child . . . [has] a long face, . . . since goods have advanced 100 percent each one grins a ghastly smile."[13] Those farming families that did manage to produce a crop had to contend with the regressive Confederate tax in kind. Passed in 1863, this tax assessed farmers with a debt of one-tenth of their agricultural production. Confederate officials hoped that this measure would provide the army with an inexpensive food source and simultaneously curb inflation by decreasing the need for the Confederate treasury to print new bills to purchase war supplies. Unfortunately for them, the measure did neither. Expensive and grossly inefficient to collect, the tithe tax often resulted in tons of food rotting on railway sidings in one part of the Confederacy while soldiers rationed hardtack hundreds of miles away. In addition to being ineffectual, the tithe tax proved to be wildly unpopular. Public meetings across North Carolina during the summer after its passage denounced it as "unjust," "tyrannical," "unconstitutional," "antirepublican," "oppressive," and "taking one-tenth of the people's living."[14] Its anti-inflationary measures also proved unsuccessful. Because the tithe tax reduced the amount of goods available for sale and created a disincentive for farmers to produce more, it exacerbated already critical shortages. Indeed, one economic historian concluded that the tax in kind may have contributed more to inflationary pressures than if the Confederacy had simply printed more notes to buy food for the army.[15]

In November 1862, Governor Zebulon Vance complained to the legislature that shortages had become so severe that "flour . . . can now be used only by the rich."[16] While the rich may have been able to afford flour, all North Carolinians found that some products had become so scarce that they could only be acquired for more than one hundred times their antebellum price.

For instance, the Union blockade of coastal ports led to dramatically inflated prices for such diverse items as bonnet ribbon, pepper, playing cards, corset stays, sewing needles, and children's dolls.[17] More significant to most North Carolinians, however, was the dramatic shortage of imported salt, a needed food preservative. In October 1861, the *Newbern Progress* reported that "the scarcity of spirits of turpentine and other descriptions of naval stores, has caused quite a demand for them, and prices have consequently run up to an unprecedented figure. . . . In a few months it is expected, should the blockade prove effectual, that the price will become so high as to almost forbid consumption."[18]

Under such conditions, even planters heavily invested in the gift economy realized the folly of lending money. Many creditors refused to accept Confederate currency, recognizing that its inflated value effectively negated the cost of the loan. North Carolina state treasurer and future governor Jonathan Worth found that he could not pay his personal debts with Confederate currency. Mentored as a young lawyer by Archibald Murphey, Worth had relied on a complex network of creditors throughout his life. In a letter dated 1 August 1863, Worth observed that he had more than enough money in Confederate currency to pay off his debts but that none of his creditors would accept it. He concluded, "I am getting old and want to feel *out of debt* before I die."[19] Worth's difficulty in maintaining the antebellum system of credit reveals the extent to which the Civil War fundamentally challenged the gift economy in North Carolina.

N. A. Waller, a Granville County farmer, and John Kinyoun, a Yadkin County doctor, had similar experiences with creditors refusing Confederate currency. In November 1862, both men wrote to Zebulon B. Vance, hoping that the North Carolina governor would support them in their disputes with creditors. "What ought to be done with a man who refuses to take Confederate notes in payment of Debt[?]" Waller asked. Like many poor farmers, Waller faced pressure to repay his debts, debts that his primary creditor insisted could be paid only in specie. "I consider such men an enemy to our country, for if we had enough such men our Country would be ruined for the credit of the southern Confederacy would be ruined." He urged Vance to pressure the state legislature to require creditors to accept Confederate currency.[20] After his discharge from the Confederate army, Dr. Kinyoun sought to pay off some long-standing debts with Confederate notes, as "of corse [*sic*] this is all the mony [*sic*] that I have to offer them." His creditors refused to accept payment in Confederate currency, presumably because of its inflated value. "I would like to know what we are to do with such men," Kinyoun wrote to Vance, "that strike Such blows at our Cause and County." Vance's answer, scrawled on the reverse of Kinyoun's letter, expressed the futility of the situation: "I don't know any remedy. ZBV."[21]

Hyperinflation and the uncertain result of the Confederate war effort also encouraged widespread speculation on currency and commodities prices. Because the amount of currency in circulation fluctuated in unexpected and unpredictable ways, merchants and bankers constantly had to reevaluate the worth of their holdings. As early as 1862, Jonathan Worth recognized how the existence of so much paper money instilled fear in many. "Confederate money must be nearly useless at the end of the war," he wrote. "Nobody doubts this, and all who hold any considerable amount of it are anxious."[22] Speculation increased the already excessive velocity of money, further exacerbating the inflationary pressures.[23] The *Wilmington Journal* reported that "the speculators have caused the present high prices, and they are determined to make money even if one-half of the people starve."[24] Positive and negative reports from the battlefield spurred rapid shifts in currency values. "There is likely to be a great mania for speculation," wrote the *Raleigh Standard* in 1862; "the condition of the currency has a great deal to do with it."[25] In the same year, a Methodist minister from Marion, North Carolina, wrote to Zebulon Vance that "if it is Constitutional, and if your position as Governor of N. Carolina gives you the power to do so, in the name of God, of suffering humanity, of the cries of widows and orphans, do put down the Speculation and extortion in this portion of the State."[26] In the war's final months, with Confederate defeat looming, speculation in Confederate and state currency and bonds reached a frantic pace, further undermining the antebellum credit system.[27]

Some North Carolina lawmakers recognized the threat that wartime conditions posed to antebellum credit networks. Even before Lincoln's inauguration and in the midst of rampant speculation, many southern states entertained the possibility of suspending debt suits until normal economic conditions resumed. Proponents argued that a stay law would protect both creditors and debtors from the uncertainty and rapid fluctuations in currency prices. The measure faced significant opposition from the beginning, in large part because it posed a threat to the traditional understanding of the nature of debt. Opponents believed that, by allowing debtors to delay repayment, the stay law unnecessarily and unnaturally interposed the state between community members. "So far from remedying the evil of hard times," opined the *Raleigh Register* in February 1861, the stay law "will greatly increase it by putting an end to credit and confidence between man and man."[28] Several days later, it added:

> We do not believe the people demand any such law, and are posi-
> tively sure that those who do ask for a Stay Law, in the hope that it
> will afford relief to the debtor class, will, in the event of its passage,
> however honest may have been their motives, find themselves egre-
> giously mistaken. Such a law would bear particularly hard on the
> debtor class, unless it is the first step to utter repudiation. . . . Any
> such law will be destructive to many and beneficial to none. . . . Such
> a law here would only place a stain upon the reputation of our good
> Old State without benefiting any class of the community, and we
> hope it will never pass. We belong to the "poor class" that needs re-
> lief and who are in debt, but we want no *stay law*.[29]

The *Newbern Progress* concurred, arguing, "We feel that it [the stay law] would benefit neither the creditors or debtors, and as to the 'relief for the people' that can only come by a restoration of harmony in our National Affairs and a return to confidence in the stability of government. . . . No stay laws can benefit us. The panic is national, not local, and nothing but a satisfactory and permanent settlement of our national affairs will restore confidence and give business its wonted activity."[30] Despite this opposition, the stay law passed in May 1861.[31]

The measure proved thoroughly unpopular with many of the state's elite. Jonathan Worth wrote to Asheville lawmaker A. G. Foster that the state legislature "ought to repeal the Stay Law" because "it disorganizes Civilized society."[32] B. F. Moore concurred with Worth's assessment, claiming that "the Stay law is a revolutionary measure, radical, unwise, demoralizing, disgraceful to the state, to the age and the Southern Confederacy. . . . A heavier blow was never struck at our liberties than the Stay law. . . . It is the beginning . . . of continued efforts to discharge all debts." He argued that the stay represented the victory of "the profligate, the spendthrifts, reckless, insolvents."[33] Those debtors who did take advantage of the stay law's provisions risked social ostracism. Like James Webb's bankruptcy twenty years earlier, availing oneself of the 1861 stay law meant violating social dictates and thereby suffering significant social consequences. Hillsborough lawyer George Lacus advised Greensboro merchant Robert Lindsay that he doubted one of his debtors would take advantage of the new stay law: "I do not think [Lindsay's debtor, W. W.] Guess is the man to take advantage of the —— stay law. Any man that has ought to blatted out of state and I would not trust the man that voted for it for ten cents."[34] Facing such overwhelming elite opposition, the stay law was repealed less than half a year after its passage. A second, somewhat weaker stay law passed in February 1863, only to be repealed shortly thereafter.[35] North Carolina's failure to pass meaningful legislation to protect debtors during the Civil War indicates the extent to which antebellum conceptions of debt held firm despite radical social and economic upheaval.

The Confederate loss, however, forced white North Carolinians to reassess the meaning of debt. Wartime conditions so decimated antebellum credit networks that they could not easily be resumed or reconstructed. Further, at the war's end, most white North Carolinians found themselves even more deeply in debt than they had been when the war began. For example, the McBee family of Lincoln County, North Carolina, emerged from the war more than twenty thousand dollars in debt, most of it from antebellum slave purchases. "I am perfectly satisfied in my own mind," wrote Alexander McBee to his brother Vardy, "that these *debts* will force me into *Bankruptcy* & that very soon."[36] Although their farm had survived the war unscathed, the loss of their slave property through emancipation meant that they now had to pay off debts on property they no longer owned. For the McBees and many other white families, the loss of their slave property meant the loss of almost half of their household wealth.[37]

White North Carolinians also confronted the fact that any wealth they held in Confederate currency was now worthless. Catherine Edmondston recorded in her diary a walk she took with her husband in November 1865. "We picked up some pieces of Confederate notes of the value of $10 & further on some NC Treasury notes," she wrote, "thrown there in all probability by some negro who had learned their worthlessness. It gave me a pang, thus to see 'Mine honour in the Dust.'"[38] Mariah Barnes, who had been only a child when the war ended, recalled that when her owner announced his slaves' emancipation, he advised them, "'Don't let nobody pay you for your work wid Confederate money; it ain't no good now.' I 'member dey gin we chil'en Confederate money to play wid."[39] In short, white North Carolinians shouldered greater debts than they ever had before and had no possible means of paying them off. In 1866, Governor Jonathan Worth wrote to a friend that accumulated debts had caused "the almost destitution of many among the masses . . . and even among those who possess large real estate."[40]

In response to the economic crisis immediately after the Civil War, many southern states, including North Carolina, passed stay laws to protect insolvent debtors, a category that included a significant segment of the population. These stay laws interposed the state between the debtor and his creditors in unprecedented ways. Under North Carolina's legislation passed in 1866, creditors could not use state courts to collect on debts contracted prior to 1865 until 1868. "We are in favor of holding every man to the performance of his contracts," opined the *Raleigh Daily Sentinel*, but "the conviction is forced upon us that if, at the present time, our people are forced to pay their individual debts, two-thirds of the real estate in the State must be forced onto the market." Somewhat begrudgingly, therefore, many North Carolinians came to accept that abiding by antebellum debt conventions was untenable in the aftermath of the war.[41] Indeed, the new stay laws proved to be among the most popular moves of the Reconstruction legislature.[42]

This new attitude toward debt was also reflected in how many white southerners took advantage of the new Bankruptcy Act of 1867, the first such legislation since the 1841 act's repeal. As Figure 7 indicates, southerners were on average seven times more likely than nonsoutherners to file for bankruptcy after the Civil War. The popularity of the Bankruptcy Act of 1867 among southerners is doubly puzzling considering that it was passed as part of the Reconstruction program of Radical Republicans and was intended by its congressional framers primarily to benefit northern creditors.[43] The popularity of the new bankruptcy act in the South reflected both the dire economic conditions in the immediate aftermath of the Civil War and a new conception of debt.

Many North Carolina newspapers encouraged their readers to take advantage of the new bankruptcy act. They recognized that although many white North Carolinians held entrenched attitudes about the sacred obligations of debt, the Civil War had changed economic conditions in the South so dramatically that many of their readers would benefit from wiping their financial slates clean. "Some people hesitate to avail themselves of the bankrupt law, supposing that it is dishonest, or at least dishonorable," wrote the *North Carolina Daily Standard*. "This is a great mistake. The bankrupt law is a wise and beneficent provision and is designed to relieve the sufferings of our debt burdened people." Insolvent debtors, the paper argued, did not find themselves unable to pay their debts out of their own misdeeds but rather because of the myriad ways in which the Civil War destroyed the basic economic and social assumptions that undergirded credit relationships. "It is not necessarily from any fault of his own that the unfortunate debtor will never be able to meet his obligations. This disaster has been the result of a revolution, which has upheaved the foundations of our former systems and

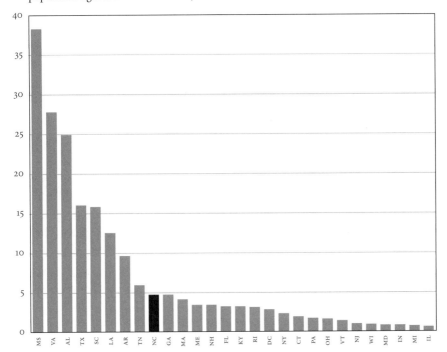

FIGURE 7. Bankruptcy filings per 10,000 free residents in 1868. Data derived from U.S. Senate, *Letter from the Attorney-General, Communicating, in Compliance with a Senate Resolution of February 24, 1873, Information in Relation to the Expenses of Proceedings in Bankruptcy in United States Courts.* 43rd Cong., 1st sess., 1874. S. Ex. Doc. 19. State population figures taken from the 1870 U.S. Census.

which was not contemplated by either party when the obligations were assumed. The inability of the debtor, then, to pay his debts is a calamity, and the debtor himself, instead of being the subject of reproach, deserves the sympathy of all fair-minded men." Not only should insolvent debtors receive sympathy, the paper concluded, but also society should no longer stigmatize those who felt the need to declare bankruptcy: "It is to be presumed that a man is honest who goes into bankruptcy, until the contrary is shown. We advise all those who can not pay their debts, and who are honestly disposed to surrender all their property and take the benefits of the act, and begin life anew, to go into bankruptcy."[44]

Other newspapers advocated a more moderate course of action. "We advise no one to go into bankruptcy who can possibly meet his obligations," opined the *Raleigh Standard*. "We regard the law as a beneficent one in many respects, but we should regret to see it perverted or abused. In many cases it is the only refuge left to the unfortunate from the pressure of debts they cannot pay." The *Standard* also drew a distinction between a debt's financial and social obligations. "The release thus given him from his debts is merely legal, not moral. He is as much bound in honor as before to pay his just debts, and if he be an honest man he will do it, if he should ever be able. We know men who in 1842 took the benefit of the law, and afterwards paid every cent they owed; and we have no doubt that such will be the case with many under the present law."[45]

A recent study of the Bankruptcy Act of 1867 in the South reveals that those most likely to file for bankruptcy during Reconstruction were also those mostly likely to have opposed bankruptcy during the antebellum period. More than 80 percent of bankruptcy filers under the Bankruptcy Act of 1867 were native southerners; indeed, more than half filed in the same county in which they were born. Planters, merchants, and professionals accounted for more than 90 percent of filers, and at least 70 percent of filers had owned slaves before the Civil War. Based on these data, one can conclude that those who had wielded the most political and economic power in the antebellum South formed the core of bankruptcy filers during Reconstruction. Noting that many of these bankruptcy filers quickly recovered much of their property, historian Elizabeth Lee Thompson has argued that the Bankruptcy Act of 1867 was one of the primary mechanisms through which antebellum southern elites reestablished themselves as a potent economic and political force after the Civil War.[46]

Not all southern debtors after the Civil War took advantage of the new bankruptcy and stay laws, however. African Americans are almost totally absent from the bankruptcy rolls. Indeed, in several former Confederate states, no African American filed for bankruptcy. While freed slaves, who accounted for more than 90 percent of the African American population in North Carolina and across the South, had little opportunity to accumulate debt when the Bankruptcy Act took effect in 1867, by the time of its repeal in 1878, most of the black population was heavily in debt.[47]

Although a variety of factors contributed to the dearth of black bankruptcy filers, two stand out as most significant. First, the provisions of the Bankruptcy Act of 1867 required that debtors owe at least three hundred dollars before they could declare bankruptcy. Because black debtors often owed less than this amount, they found themselves ineligible to declare bankruptcy, even if they had less of a capacity to repay their debts than many white southerners, who had greater absolute levels of debt but at the same time had a greater capacity to repay. Further, because black debtors tended to owe money to a limited number of creditors, those creditors could effectively prevent them from declaring bankruptcy by limiting their access to credit just below the threshold needed to declare bankruptcy.

A second factor limiting black participation in the postbellum bankruptcy epidemic was a developing belief within the African American community that fulfilling debt obligations was one means of legitimizing their new legal and economic status. Indeed, many African Americans during Reconstruction were resistant to legal measures that interfered with debtor-creditor relationships. One early manifestation of this reticence occurred at the Constitutional Convention of 1868. Just as the delegates manifested deeply divided attitudes toward divorce, they also held radically different ideas about debt.

Both white and black delegates to the 1868 Constitutional Convention recognized that debts had become a crushing burden on many North Carolinians. "WHAT CAN BE DONE!" opined the *North Carolina Daily Standard*. "We are daily in receipt of communications from parties from all parts of the State, East, West, North, and South, praying for relief from debt. . . . We are told that unless some measure of the kind be taken by which to relieve the great masses of the people, any Constitution which may be framed by the Convention will be voted down by the people."[48] Letters from across the state implored delegates to take immediate action. "The people & planters in this section are in a hard fix," wrote a Rocky Mount farmer to delegate William Blount Rodman. "None can pay up & it seems many had to have one creditor come down on thru & collect his money."[49] A letter Rodman received from a farmer from Wilson expressed similar sentiments: "There are but very few who are not completely paralyzed and rendered powerless by the impoverished condition of the country, and weight of old debts. We seem already on the eve of a famine on account of the short crops of last year, and if the collection of old debts are allowed to go on, our country's ruin is inevitable." The letter writer could see that the intricate networks of debt that had helped to stabilize his community during the antebellum period had become a liability. So many debtors had defaulted that the entire system of credit appeared on the verge of collapse. "My own debts do not trouble me as far as I myself am concerned," he wrote, "but what is most galling to me is to think that other men (my securities) should have to suffer on my account, and have my debts to pay. I know that I cannot pay my debts and I make my mind as easy as possible on that point, but I hate for this to have them pay."[50] Greene County delegate John M. Patrick expressed the situation most succinctly: "From the mountains to the seaboard, our citizens were burdened with debt."[51]

Amid the clamoring for debt relief, white North Carolinians expressed deep divisions over what specific reforms the convention should enact. The *North Carolina Daily Standard* analyzed some of the alternatives: "Some urge of the absolute necessity of the repudiation of all debts, principal and interest, up to the surrender of Gen. Lee to Gen. Grant. This of course would embrace all ante-war debts and all debts contracted during the war. Others urge the necessity of homesteads, free from all past, present and future liabilities. . . . Others, again, are in favor of scaling all debts and paying about twenty-five cents to the dollar."[52]

Each of these options, the newspaper recognized, had distinct costs and benefits. One route that the paper rejected was absolute debt relief. Such a measure would benefit, the newspaper argued, only "the landed *aristocracy* of the State. . . . The very men who forced war upon the country, and forced *poor men* into the war to fight their battles and to protect their lands and their negroes." If the planter class could avoid paying their debts, "the poor white men, as well as the colored, would be forced to become their tenants at will, which would be the greatest evil that could possibly befall the poorer classes of all races. . . . It would be a financial death and ruin of all poor men." Alternatively, if the planter class were required to pay their debts, it would most likely require them to sell property, making "millions of acres of land" available for purchase.[53]

Black convention delegates expressed dismay at the apparent willingness of white delegates to suspend debts, especially those of wealthy landholders. Rev. James Walker Hood, representing Cumberland County, argued that "he did not believe in stay laws at all. They were usually for the benefit of the rich and detriment of the poor."[54] Such legislation, he argued, would profit "those who now hold lands" and would "prevent the poor people from ever getting land."[55] Similarly, James H. Harris of Wake County argued that although "he desired to vote as to give substantial relief to the working men of the State, white and black," he could not favor measures that aided the planter class. Instead he advocated "relief [for] all the people, and the small farmers and laboring men, who were oppressed by debt."[56]

Black delegates were no doubt aware than in the three years since the end of the Civil War African Americans in North Carolina had often and repeatedly been cheated out of wages owed to them by white landowners for agricultural labor. Freedmen's Bureau records from North Carolina indicate that hundreds of black labors believed that they had been defrauded of money or shares owed to them, often working for months while receiving no compensation. These records also indicate that in their efforts to seek redress from the Freedmen's Bureau, other federal agencies, and state courts, freedmen often protested in vain.[57] Black delegates to the 1868 Constitutional Convention could see in debt relief efforts part of a continuing pattern by white North Carolinians to deny black laborers back wages and to continue a system of racial hierarchy and hegemony.

Black delegates also developed their own conception of what constituted "honest debts." Abraham Galloway, a thirty-one-year-old black Union army veteran and delegate from Wilmington, recognized that debt had become a significant burden for many freed persons, yet "he would never vote to repudiate honest debt." He hoped that the convention would require that "all debts for slaves since '63 and all debts contracted to aid the rebellion" go on "forever."[58] Because both slavery and the Confederacy were moral wrongs, Galloway contended, debts contracted in their support should remain intact, and those debtors should be required to suffer the consequences of their choices.[59]

Only a handful of white delegates joined black Republicans Hood, Harris, and Galloway in opposing universal debt relief. E. W. Jones of Washington County argued that any form of debt repudiation would undermine the social honor that formed the foundation of credit relationships. North Carolina, he claimed, "had lost every thing but her honor [in the Civil War], that was the only thing now left her. And shall she not preserve that almost sacred relic?"[60] Buncombe delegate Thomas J. Candler claimed that he could never "vote for a constitution repudiating honest debts."[61] Although a minority view, many North Carolinians believed that any measure interfering in credit relationships was dishonest and immoral. "The poor men of the country are honest men still," a farmer from the hamlet of Marshall in Madison County wrote to the *North Carolina Daily Standard*. "Away then with any endorsement of ideas inconsistent with the personal and individual equality of men before the law, and of the recognition of the doctrine that honest men pay honest debts."[62]

Despite the objections of black Republicans and others, the constitution drafted in 1868 contained strong and unprecedented protections for insolvent debtors. First, it prohibited imprisonment for debt, except in cases of fraud.[63] Although comparatively few North Carolinians were jailed for debt during the antebellum period, especially after 1844, the abolition of debt imprisonment marked a significant ideological departure from antebellum practice.[64] Second, the convention extended the duration of the 1866 stay law, allowing debtors to postpone payments of debts contracted prior to May 1865 until January 1869.[65] Sponsored by Republican carpetbagger

Albion Tourgée, this measure recognized that credit relations had not immediately returned to antebellum standards upon the war's end, as many had expected, but would require a significantly longer period. Third, the new constitution created a strong homestead exemption. This provision allowed insolvent debtors to hold on to $1,000 in real property and $500 in personal effects.[66] These measures represent a watershed in how North Carolinians understood debt. By creating new legal protections for debtors, they reinterpreted the nature of the debtor-creditor relationship.

ARGUING IN VAIN against the Bankruptcy Act's repeal in 1878, North Carolina senator Augustus Merrimon extolled the role that law played in his native state: "It was a great boon, a great blessing, to the southern people ... [it] relieved thousands of people [in North Carolina] who otherwise would have been practically *slaves to their debts* and debtors for life."[67] Here Merrimon recognized the debtor's dependent role, linking it explicitly with slavery. Merrimon's statement also indicates how the culture of debt had fundamentally changed since the Civil War. Although before the Civil War debt had served to bind white North Carolinians together in community, afterward most tried to distance themselves as much as possible from indebtedness. By embracing bankruptcy after the Civil War, they sought to emancipate themselves from their debts.

CHAPTER NINE

What the Landlord and
the Storeman Choose to Make It
General Stores, Pawnshops, & Boardinghouses in the New South

I F THE EXPERIENCE of Dr. James Webb serves as a useful example of
the antebellum gift economy, the life of his son, James Webb Jr., epito-
mizes the new system of credit that developed after the Civil War. While
his father liberally extended credit as a pillar of the local gift economy, only
to be disgraced by bankruptcy, his son made his living extending credit as
the proprietor of Hillsborough's largest general store. Whereas the father
saw lending money as the social obligation of a prosperous member of the
community, the son believed that the primary role of credit was to facili-
tate his own financial interests. The difference between their experiences,
choices, and concepts of debt underscores the revolutionary change brought
about in southern society as a consequence of the Civil War. Within the deep
gulf that separated father and son, North Carolinians were simultaneously
liberated and enslaved by their debts.

This new conception of debt that emerged among white North Carolinians in the decades after the Civil War differed in two important respects
from its antebellum precursor. First, it lacked the heavy moral overtones
that characterized antebellum debt. To be sure, debt maintained certain
negative connotations throughout the nineteenth century and beyond, but
white North Carolinians increasingly thought and wrote about debt in pragmatic terms. Whereas men like Dr. James Webb engaged in rhetorical feats
to disguise their indebtedness, using the language of the gift economy, postbellum white North Carolinians routinely unmasked themselves as debtors.
By thus exposing themselves as debtors, they created opportunities to recognize structural elements of the economy that maintained and exacerbated
their indebtedness. This recognition that they belonged to a community of

debtors prompted many North Carolinians to push for political and economic reform in the final decades of the nineteenth century.

The abolition of slavery contributed to the demise of the stigma that white North Carolinians pinned to debt. Without the pressing need to maintain the illusion of mastery, white North Carolinians became less attached to the idea that indebtedness implied dependence and, by association, slavery. As the metaphor of the debt slave lost its connection to actual chattel slavery, white North Carolinians found that they could contract debts without assuming the ideologically submissive position of a slave.

For black North Carolinians, however, the debt-slave metaphor continued to have deep reverberations. Having secured their freedom in 1865, African Americans avoided situations that resembled the exploitation they experienced in slavery. Some African Americans sought to avoid debt altogether because of the taint of dependence that it created. In September 1865, the *Journal of Freedom*, a black newspaper in Raleigh, urged its readers to "trade with and patronize your friends, but, above all, each other. — Encourage your brethren who embark in trade or any mechanical or other useful industry, though at some personal inconvenience; keep out of debt; work if possible, for men whom you esteem and trust; and each of you become land-holders so soon as you can without running into debt."[1] Although avoiding debt became a goal for many African Americans, the economic realities of the postwar South necessitated that they enter into credit relationships, most often with white landlords and shopkeepers. While debt never developed the social stigma among postbellum African Americans that it had among antebellum whites, they often imbued debt with moral connotations that no longer had much currency in the white community.

A second factor in the creation of a new postbellum conception of debt can be traced to the disappearance of antebellum social credit networks after the Civil War, replaced by more centralized models of credit in which many debtors owed money to an individual or entity. North Carolinians reconceived of debt in increasingly pecuniary terms, downplaying, although never entirely abandoning, its social aspects. This new conception of debt was shaped fundamentally by North Carolinians' experience during the Civil War and Reconstruction. The disastrous economic conditions during that period decimated the antebellum credit system and undermined whatever desire North Carolinians might have had in revitalizing it. At the same time, the rapid modernization of the southern economy after 1865 pushed North Carolinians into novel credit relationships.[2]

More than almost any other institution after the Civil War, general stores catered to a broad spectrum of southern society across lines of class, race, and gender. Selling a wide variety of products from groceries, whiskey, tobacco plugs, and dry goods to clothing, children's toys, farming implements, and patent medicines, general stores functioned as the primary locus of trade in most North Carolina communities. General stores also served a valuable social function; they were places where neighbors could congregate, exchange news, and socialize.[3] In a cash-strapped economy, general stores also served as a central conduit for credit. Indeed, very few southerners could avoid routinely and repeatedly being indebted to general stores.[4] An examination of general store account books from postbellum North Carolina indicates how the store centralized credit, tying community members from a range of backgrounds to a focal node. At the same time, these account books reveal how individual customers sought to mediate and control their indebtedness.

Although general stores were well-established fixtures on the southern landscape before the Civil War, their numbers increased significantly in the decades after 1865. According to the records of the R. G. Dun Mercantile Agency, the number of general stores in North Carolina increased from 2,428 in 1870 to 3,153 in 1875 to 4,521 in 1890.[5] These records also indicate that the average capitalization of general stores doubled during the same period. Several factors help to explain this significant increase in the number and size of general stores. After the Civil War, small farmers increasingly produced crops for the market, especially cotton. Whereas yeoman farmers grew most of their own food before the Civil War, the transition to market farming meant that food production in the South actually decreased nearly 50 percent between 1860 and 1890.[6] As a result, small farmers now had to turn to general stores to stock their pantries.[7] The rise of sharecropping also increased demand for general stores, as sharecropping contracts almost invariably required tenants to produce crops for the market rather than to fill their own larders.[8] Improved transportation networks across the region after the Civil War allowed consumer goods to infiltrate the southern interior, creating both the supply and the demand that fueled the growth of general stores.

General stores conducted the majority of their business on credit.[9] Instead of charging a distinct interest rate, most general stores employed the dual price system. Under this system, general stores charged one price for cash purchases and another, significantly higher price for credit purchases. Although the differences between these two prices varied depending on the product and the locality, a 50 percent markup was not uncommon. This system not only made accounting practices easier but also allowed general store owners to bypass state usury laws. Many southerners railed against what they viewed as excessive interest charges levied by general stores, yet they mirrored the comparatively high interest rates charged to southern general stores by northern wholesalers. Indeed, despite the stereotype held by many southerners that general stores were widely profitable, about a third of general stores went out of business within any given five-year period.[10]

In many rural North Carolina communities, the general store functioned as the only source of consumer goods and credit. As a consequence, many general stores had an effective monopoly on the local market.[11] Ubiquitous in the postbellum landscape, general stores attracted a primarily local clientele. These conditions allowed general store owners to know more about the finances of their debtors than had ever been possible under the antebellum informal credit networks. This knowledge allowed them to extend credit with greater confidence that the debtor had the capacity to repay.

While indebtedness to a local general store was pervasive, general store account books reveal a broad diversity of strategies for dealing with this debt. William Patterson's general store in Alamance County, North Carolina, catered almost exclusively to the Piedmont farming community in and around Cobles Township. Cataloging the period from 1866 to 1892, his account books provide one of longest continuous records for credit relationships in a North Carolina community. They record the credit histories of more than 80 percent of local farmers and indicate that the composition of his customer base broadly reflected the racial makeup of the community, which, according to census records, remained approximately one-third African American throughout the nineteenth century. The records of two of Patterson's customers serve as a useful vehicle to understand how postbellum North Carolinians coped with the problem of debt.[12]

Essex Geeringer relied upon William Patterson's general store to provide him with the goods he could not produce on his small farm. Visiting Patterson's store on average once a week, Geeringer amassed more than forty dollars in debt every year between 1877 and 1882. His account indicates that he rarely splurged; indeed, outside of food staples such as flour and salt or household necessities such as soap, Geeringer purchased very little. Although Geeringer undoubtedly hoped to pay off his debt to Patterson's store at harvest time, in most years his estimated return on his cotton crop exceeded what he actually produced. Without the money to settle the account at year's end, Geeringer relied upon other means to satisfy his debt. On several occasions, Geeringer sold excess foodstuffs to Patterson, including eggs, hogs, and oats. More regularly, however, Geeringer paid off his debt through labor on Patterson's farm. Patterson's account books indicate that Geeringer worked for extensive periods after the cotton harvest to pay down his debts, including stints of seventy-two days in 1879 and ninety-seven days in 1880. Because Patterson paid him only thirty cents a day for this labor, however, Geeringer usually ended the year still in debt, a debt that Patterson carried over into the next year. As cotton prices declined, farmers like Geeringer found it harder and harder to pay their debts.

Another of William Patterson's customers demonstrated debt strategies that subtly differed from those employed by Essex Geeringer. Born into slavery in 1860, Will Isley worked as a sharecropper on his former owner's land. Like Geeringer, Isley relied upon Patterson's store to supply himself and his family with basic staples, rarely purchasing anything other than necessities. Indeed, Isley accumulated only half the level of debt in any given year that Geeringer did. Isley's reduced debt level may have been in part due to his own caution or frugality, though the fact that Geeringer owned his farm while Isley sharecropped might have influenced Patterson to extend less credit to Isley.[13] Like Geeringer, Isley also routinely used his labor to pay off his debts to Patterson's store. Unlike Geeringer, however, Isley did not wait until he had accumulated a significant amount of debt before offering Patterson his labor. Instead, Isley worked a variety of tasks for a day or two at a time, shucking corn, striping tobacco, or plowing a field on Patterson's farm.

The differences between Geeringer's and Isley's accounts reveal the dialectical nature of credit within the southern general store. While William Patterson's effective monopoly on local credit and consumer goods meant that he could broadly dictate terms to his debtors, the behavior of debtors like Essex Geeringer and Will Isley indicates that they sought to control their own indebtedness. Although both men realized that some level of indebtedness was unavoidable, they endeavored to minimize its effects through debt-management strategies that maximized their access to credit while minimizing their social and financial exposure.[14]

William Patterson's general store displayed a typical pattern of debt relationships for general stores in the rural South, though it was by no means universal. The account books of Henry Patterson's general store in Chapel Hill reveal an alternative set of credit strategies. Catering primarily to university faculty members, Henry Patterson's (apparently unrelated to William Patterson) store differed in several significant ways from the stores that furnished farmers. First, Henry Patterson's customers demanded a greater diversity and quality of goods than were typically available in general stores. In addition to stocking staples, Henry Patterson regularly sold luxury items such as silk ribbons, canned salmon, and sheet music. Second, Henry Patterson's account books reveal that the total number of debt entries was significantly higher than that of a typical general store. Patterson's store was located on Franklin Street adjacent to the University of North Carolina campus, and many of his customers visited the store several times per week, accumulating small debts with each visit. Finally, owing to the comparative wealth of his consumers, Henry Patterson granted significantly more credit per account than most general stores. These differences fundamentally changed the nature of the debt relationships Henry Patterson developed with his customers and consequentially affected their strategies for managing debt.[15]

Dating from 1882 to 1915, Henry Patterson's account books reveal that most of his customers were associated with the University of North Carolina. Unlike farmers who relied upon credit to sustain them until the harvest, Henry Patterson's customers consisted of university faculty members and their families, students, and the handful of other Chapel Hill residents who derived their livelihood from the university. For most of these customers, credit was more of a luxury and convenience than an absolute necessity.

Professor Ralph Graves's account typified how university faculty members (almost all of whom shopped at Patterson's) employed credit. Passing by Patterson's store twice per day walking between his classroom and his home, Graves stopped at least three times a week to shop. Although Graves's income as a university professor meant that he could have paid cash for these purchases, he regularly allowed the clerk to record his purchases as debts in Patterson's account books.[16] Over the course of an average month, Graves accumulated approximately one hundred dollars of debt at Patterson's store, a figure that exceeded what most farmers spent in a year. Despite the size of this debt, Graves routinely paid off his balance at Patterson's store with cash at the beginning of every month. The accounts of Graves's faculty colleagues, including Kemp Battle, Francis Venable, and George Winston, reveal similar patterns of debt and repayment.

With Ralph Graves's suicide in July 1889, his wife demonstrated a different pattern of debt in her dealings with Patterson's store. Without the steady source of income that her husband's job provided, Julia Graves quickly accumulated a sizable debt in Patterson's ledgers. Although most of this debt came from her purchases at the store itself, Julia Graves also used Patterson's store as a source of cash loans. Indeed, among dozens of other cash loans in Patterson's account books, she borrowed $3.00 on 11 July and $1.25 on 27 July of that year to pay for "digging grave": the first presumably to bury her husband and the second to bury her infant child. Julia Graves's situation required her to rely upon cash loans more than most of Patterson's customers, yet their regular presence in his ledgers indicates the central role of general stores as credit providers. By the end of the nineteenth century, they had become the primary, and sometimes only, source of credit for many North Carolinians.

When Julia Graves opened a boardinghouse in the autumn after her husband's death, her struggles with debt only intensified. Her need for generous credit from Patterson's store increased significantly once she had undertaken the responsibility of feeding a half dozen boarders in addition to her own family. Indeed, from 1890 onward, Henry Patterson placed Julia Graves's name first in his annual account book, indicating perhaps that he saw her as his most important customer.

Examining Julia Graves's account at Patterson's store over the course of the next decade reveals a distinctly seasonal pattern to her debt. Not unlike farmers, whose debts ebbed and flowed with the harvest, Julia Graves's debt fluctuated according to the academic calendar. Her debt reached its highest level during the early fall, when she had a houseful of boarders to feed. Usually by the end of the school year, her boarders had settled their accounts with her, allowing her to pay down most of her debt at Patterson's in May. Throughout the summer, without the benefit of many boarders, Julia Graves's debt gradually increased, even though her total expenditures dropped significantly with only herself and her family to feed. Despite her best efforts, Julia Graves never escaped from this annual cycle of debt until her grown sons helped her to settle her account and close her boardinghouse in 1902. Although he may have been moved in part by her tragic story, Henry Patterson's decision to extend liberal amounts of credit to Julia Graves was shaped by the realization that their mutual self-interests depended upon credit.

The unspoken threat inherent in these negotiated credit relations between general storekeepers and their customers was the possibility that the storekeeper would prosecute on bad debts. For those who owned land, defaulting on debts owed to a merchant could mean losing the family farm, descending into the ranks of tenancy.[17] For tenant farmers, such a default could result in a condition of virtual peonage from which they had little chance of escape.

This relationship was not without risk for the creditor, however, particularly when he loaned money to landless farmers. A series of North Carolina Supreme Court decisions in the 1870s and 1880s concluded that even when merchants had a lien on a tenant farmer's crop, the landlord's superior claim could leave storekeepers without recourse in the case of a poor harvest.[18] Any time, therefore, that general storekeepers extended credit to tenant farmers, they were gambling with an essentially unsecured loan. "A good man has to pay for a bad man's account, which ought not to be," argued one southern general store owner. "But you cannot tell who is a good man; one may be good this year and bad another."[19] Two significant consequences resulted from the risky nature of general store credit. First, in poor harvest years, general stores had to contend with many of their patrons defaulting on their loans. The general store itself often had to close its doors as a consequence; one study indicated that about one out of every three southern general stores between 1877 and 1900 closed within any given five-year period.[20] Second, the high rate of default inflated general store prices and interest rates, as storekeepers had to transfer the costs from bad loans to other customers.

Because of general stores' perceived prosperity, however, many North Carolinians came to resent them as parasites preying on the vulnerabilities of poor farmers. For men and women who toiled in the fields for hours under the sun, the apparent leisure enjoyed by general store keepers bred resentment. Many North Carolinians suspected that general store owners manipulated their account books to ensure that their customers remained indebted. According to George H. White, a black congressmen from Edgecombe County, illiterate farmers suffered particularly from the tyranny of dishonest accounting, noting in 1900 that "there is a great deal of fraud perpetrated on the ignorant; they keep no books, and in the fall the account is what the landlord and the storeman choose to make it."[21]

The most exploitative general stores were run by textile mills and mining companies to supply their workers. Situated in remote locations, these company stores had an effective monopoly on their employees' business. Whereas most general stores offered credit as a necessary component of a cash-poor economy, company stores used their customers/employees' indebtedness as a means of controlling their labor. Workers' company stores debts effectively tied them to their employer; so long as they remained indebted to the company store, they became slaves to their debts.[22]

Some employers reinforced their workers' dependence upon the company store by paying them partially or wholly in scrip. Workers recognized that such payments allowed their employer to keep them in perpetual debt. A sawyer at the Parkwood Mill-Stone Company in Moore County observed in 1887, "We are paid weekly in trade tickets, which are good only at the company's store. All goods cost us more than they would if we could buy for cash. They charge high for their goods, but we must pay it."[23]

Hoping to avoid indebtedness to company stores, many miners and mill workers practiced thrift and self-sufficiency. Many workers raised chickens and hogs, tended small vegetable gardens, and made their own clothes to evade inflated company store prices. Others bartered with company store managers, exchanging surplus vegetables or even animal pelts for store credit. Twelve-hour workdays, however, kept most mill workers and miners from fully employing these strategies.[24] Burdened by their chronic indebtedness to company stores, many workers could not see any way they could ever be free of their debts.

SOME STOREKEEPERS SOUGHT to avoid the public animosity and other inherent problems in the general store system by functioning on a cash-only basis. The obvious drawback of this model was that it limited the amount of business that the store could entertain to the cash resources of its customers. The advantage of this model was that it could often offer lower prices than its credit-granting cousin because it did not have to factor credit costs into its prices. Cash stores also positioned themselves very differently in relation to their customers than credit-granting stores. Instead of assuming the superior position of creditor, cash stores functioned as equals to their customers. This alternative social positioning reveals itself in the name that future Farmers' Alliance and Populist leader Leonidas L. Polk gave to the store he opened in Anson County the 1870s: "Farmer's Cheap Cash Store."[25]

To be sure, the cash store model rarely competed with credit stores in most communities. Of the more than four thousand general stores open in North Carolina in 1890, fewer than one in ten operated on a cash-only basis. The majority of these were in urban areas, where general stores often specialized. Besides Polk's Farmer's Cheap Cash Store, the most important cash store in North Carolina was William Henry Belk's New York Racket Store in Monroe, the seat of Union County. Opening his store in 1888, Belk modeled his business on northern department stores. Unlike his credit-granting competitors, Belk offered a single cash price. "It [general store's not offering credit] was a new thing in our part of the county," Belk remembered. "I don't think anybody had ever tried it out down this way and mighty few anywhere." His friends warned him that such a scheme could not work, especially in a rural community like Monroe, where most of his farmer-customers had little cash and were accustomed to purchasing on credit. "Folks aren't accustomed to that way of trading," they told him. "They won't like it and they won't trade with you. They won't have the money to trade with, in fact. It'll put you out of business before you get started." Belk responded, "It would save me money and it would save the customers money. . . . Our idea was to sell goods just as cheap as we could and at the same time make a small profit, and to have a quick turnover. We figured that if we could undersell the other fellow and get cash for our goods, we'd be doing better than to accept credit business and run the risk of losing out in the fall, when the farmers sold their crops, in the hope of making a bigger profit." To his friends' great surprise, the endeavor succeeded. Belk credited a great deal of his success to the fact that his customers appreciated the feeling of shopping without the looming burden of debt. "When a fellow buys something and pays cash," Belk argued, "he just naturally feels good. He doesn't have that trade hanging over him." Belk's venture was so successful that he was able to open a second store in 1893, beginning the chain that would eventually evolve into the modern Belk's department store.[26]

The small number of general stores owned by African Americans often adopted the cash model. Located primary in eastern North Carolina communities with high black populations, at least fifty-three black general stores between 1865 and 1879 generated enough business to attract the attention of northern credit agencies. Unfortunately, no business ledgers from black general stores have survived from nineteenth-century North Carolina, and therefore it is difficult to assess how credit practices differed in black and white general stores. The little anecdotal evidence suggests that black general store keepers were more conservative than their white counterparts in extending credit. For instance, in the 1890s, York Garrett's general store in Tarboro offered credit to fewer than half of its customers, all of whom were black.[27]

The failure of black general stores to offer credit hints at an ambivalence within the African American community over the entire idea of credit. Livingstone College president Rev. J. C. Price stood at one end of a wide spectrum of beliefs. He argued that African Americans would be well served to borrow money from prominent whites. Not only would these loans help in the formation of black business, but they would also give white community leaders a financial and personal interest in their black debtors.[28] The unstated implication of Price's argument was that a white creditor might protect a black debtor from dishonest merchants or even from racial violence. At the same time, Price urged black North Carolinians to demonstrate due diligence in paying off these debts. As one of Price's protégés noted in 1898, "The first test of a man's honesty is his disposition to pay his debts. If he seeks every possible excuse to avoid these it must be taken for granted the he lacks the essentials of true honesty."[29]

Many more black North Carolinians, however, saw with their own eyes that debt rarely resulted in "uplift," as Price suggested. Rather, debt had become just another form of slavery as black debtors perpetually found themselves unable to pay their debts. Many black North Carolinians argued that debt should be avoided at all costs, or if necessary, only to other African Americans. Debt, some argued, was not only a poor financial situation but also immoral. "DEBT," argued the *Christian Recorder*, a national black newspaper popular in North Carolina, "is an inexhaustible fountain of dishonesty. . . . Whoever runs in debt . . . is A DISHONEST MAN."[30] Yet, regardless of what they felt about the idea of debt, black North Carolinians could not escape the practical reality that debt had become a necessary aspect of life for those at the bottom of the South's social and economic order. In *The Souls of Black Folk*, W. E. B. DuBois described black southerners' pervasive indebted condition as "a pall of debt [that] hangs over the beautiful land; the merchants are in debt to the wholesalers, the planters are in debt to the merchants, the tenants owe the planters, and laborers bow and bend beneath the burden of it all."[31] DuBois's rival, Booker T. Washington, expressed a similar sentiment in 1888 when he observed that the "colored people on these plantations are held in a kind of slavery that is in one sense as bad as the slavery of antebellum days." The poor black farmer's debt, Washington argued, "binds him, robs him of independence, allures him and winds him deeper and deeper in its meshes each year till he is lost and bewildered."[32]

The rise of general stores in postbellum North Carolina provides insight into the changing relationship between credit and community. Before the Civil War, credit and debt relationships functioned as *network*, linking myriad individuals together. Community members were expected to act as both creditors and debtors. General stores, however, centralized credit into a handful of institutions. Therefore, although most North Carolinians remained debtors as they always had, fewer and fewer of them had experience as creditors. They could no longer envision their debts as a component of community dynamics. Rather, debt had become a symptom of their economic dependence on storekeepers' credit.

IF GENERAL STORES functioned as the dominant credit-granting institution in the postbellum South, pawnshops served as their subaltern counterparts. Although pawnshops were ubiquitous in urban areas throughout the North and West by the middle of the nineteenth century, they were almost totally absent from the southern landscape. Even after the collapse of the gift economy after the Civil War, the number of pawnshops in the South increased only slightly. Indeed, pawnshops did not become a permanent part of North Carolina's debt economy until the eve of the twentieth century.

Studies of pawnshops in Britain and in the American North indicate that pawnshops flourished in communities ill served by more formal banking institutions.[33] Given the abysmal state of banking and the scarcity of currency in North Carolina and across the South after the Civil War, it is surprising that a greater number of pawnshops did not arise to fill the economic void. Pawnshops could have served a useful role as the provider of short-term loans to cash-strapped southerners. The fact that pawnbroking never established itself as a viable source of credit in the South during the nineteenth century indicates how entrenched antebellum conceptions about debt persisted into the postbellum period.

Searching nineteenth-century census records and business directories turns up only a small handful of pawnshops in North Carolina, all of which disappear from the historical record just as quickly as they appear.[34] Black businessman Thomas C. Miller's dockside pawnshop closed in Wilmington less than a year after it opened in 1897.[35] Raleigh saw two pawnshops open their doors in 1899 and 1901, respectively, only to see them close before the year was out.[36] Although pawnbroking was an inherently risky profession and the rate of business failures in the postbellum South was significant, the degree to which pawnbroking repeatedly failed to find a niche for itself within the southern credit system cannot be explained by these factors alone.

Ida Beard's description of visiting a pawnshop in Winston-Salem in 1895 provides insight into postbellum southern attitudes toward pawnbroking:

> Often 9 o'clock at night found me standing in A. Savery's pawnshop, disposing of my jewelry and other trinkets given me when a child. I was forced to do this in order to obtain food and shelter for myself and children. During my girlhood I had heard of women being

compelled to earn a livelihood in this way, but little did I think at the time that I, Ida May Crumpler, who was reared in luxury, would ever come to want, and be seen standing in a public pawnshop disposing of my wares in order to obtain food and lodging.[37]

Her description exposes a deep antipathy toward pawning as a form of credit, particularly among those, in Beard's words, "reared in luxury." However, this passage also reveals that despite her repulsion, Ida Beard frequently employed pawnbroking services. Indeed, other passages from her account demonstrate the central role that pawnbroking played in providing Beard with needed credit. These occasions indicate that she used pawnbroking to help pay other debts in addition to feeding her children. In the most touching of these episodes, she pawned her engagement ring to pay a debt owned to a boardinghouse. Although she received only $2.50 for pawning the ring, "this amount seemed almost a fortune to me that morning, as the ground was covered with snow, and two hungry children standing at my side crying for bread. After leaving the pawnshop, I purchased a load of wood, then food for the children's breakfast and the remaining portion of the money I paid to H. Montague for rent due him. As the coins fell upon his desk I said to myself, 'There's the end of another fatal wedding.'"[38]

Despite how crucial pawning was to Beard's financial survival, she clearly saw it as a source of great shame. With no other source of credit available to her, she had little alternative than to pawn her few remaining possessions. She saw her dependence on pawnshops as symbolic of her destitution and her moral decline. Her attitude indicates that the antebellum aversion to debt as a form of dependence continued to reverberate in southern society.

Harry Finkelstein opened North Carolina's first permanent pawnshop in 1903. Located on the cusp between white and black neighborhoods in Asheville not far from Julia Wolfe's boardinghouse, Finkelstein's pawnshop attracted a clientele from a broad spectrum of the community.[39] A Jewish immigrant from Lithuania, Finkelstein knew that his position as an outsider to the community required him to work diligently to earn its trust. To this end, he joined or founded more than a dozen civic or fraternal organizations with the hope that by doing so he would establish the legitimacy of his business.

Providing small loans to rich and poor Ashevillians alike (including a retired William Jennings Bryan), Finkelstein's pawnshop functioned as a central source of credit in much the same way that general stores did. However, unlike general store keepers, who generally had the respect of the community despite occasional tirades against their excessive profits, pawnbrokers like Harry Finkelstein had difficulty obtaining and maintaining their public reputation. Only after operating his pawnshop for more than a quarter century could he claim to be legitimately ensconced in Asheville.[40]

North Carolinians' reluctance to embrace pawnshops indicates the degree to which antebellum conceptions of debt continued to influence postbellum attitudes. Of the forms of credit described in this chapter, pawning presented the debt in its rawest form. Although North Carolinians found a variety of ways of masking their debts both before and after the Civil War, convincing themselves and others that they did not depend on credit, the nature of the pawning relationship unmasked the debtor. Not until the dawn of the twentieth century, therefore, could enough North Carolinians sufficiently relieve themselves of the fear of debt slavery to patronize a pawnshop.

WHILE WHITE MEN took full advantage of new bankruptcy and stay legislation after the Civil War, white women rarely did so. Limited occupational opportunities for white women made debt particularly problematic. With fewer opportunities to pay off even fairly small debts, white women retained a more traditional aversion to living beyond their means. Yet, in their quest to avoid debt, many white women challenged other cultural conventions and assumptions about the place of women in society. Among the most significant of these innovations was the development of female-run boardinghouses.

For many white women, of course, their debts were commingled with those of their husband. Yet, for unmarried women and particularly for widows, the problem of debt was often a significant one. The Civil War itself created at least 20,000 widows in North Carolina and more than 100,000 across the Confederacy.[41] While poor women returned to the fields and entered the burgeoning textile mills, upper-class white women found that the financial strategies employed by their antebellum predecessors were increasingly untenable. As a recent study of antebellum slaveholding widows indicates, upper-class white widows managed to sustain themselves financially either through remarriage or by relying upon the generosity of relatives.[42] With the massive increase in the number of widows after the Civil War, however, the chances for remarriage declined significantly. Similarly, many families that would have had the means to support a widowed relative before the Civil War now were either unable or unwilling to do so. As a result, an increasing number of privileged white women sought employment outside the home. At an unprecedented level, they worked as teachers, authors, and governesses, each of which brought in much-needed money while at the same time maintaining established class and gender roles.[43]

A significant number of white women burdened by debt also transformed their home into a place of work by opening a boardinghouse. Widows with children found this option particularly appealing, as it allowed them to stay at home while providing for their family. At the same time, however, opening a boardinghouse posed a potential threat to the proprietor's honor because it introduced strange men into the household. For antebellum upper-class women to be seen in public accompanied by unrelated men was scandalous; to be seen in private spaces, especially after dark, was almost criminal.[44]

Southerners had long associated boardinghouses with prostitution. Since the colonial period, some boardinghouses had doubled as brothels, especially in port cities such as Wilmington, Charleston, Richmond, and New Orleans. Serving a clientele primarily of sailors and itinerant merchants, antebellum urban boardinghouses often blended the legitimate business of providing room and board with the illicit sex trade. More often than not, police turned a blind eye to prostitution in boardinghouses, preferring it to remain behind closed doors rather than paraded on the streets.[45] To be sure, while most antebellum boardinghouses did not double as brothels, the public association between them was strong enough to make prospective boardinghouse operators wary.

Opening a boardinghouse, therefore, exposed privileged white women to accusations of sexual impropriety. The fact that they increasingly opened boardinghouses after the Civil War indicates that their financial needs took precedence over the cultural prohibitions against such domestic arrangements. However, while most women who opened boardinghouses in the years immediately following the war did so out of financial necessity, by the end of the century, many southern white women had come to realize that running a boardinghouse provided both personal independence and financial security. Therefore, what began as a suspect strategy undertaken to deal with looming debt became a vehicle for women's financial and personal empowerment.[46]

Boardinghouses began to lose some of their negative connotations during the Civil War, as a refugee crisis, a housing shortage, and economic necessity forced women to open the doors of their home to strangers. Perceived as one of the safest areas within the Confederacy, North Carolina became a destination for thousands of refugees from throughout the South. Communities in central and western North Carolina became crowded with refugees, overwhelming the available housing supply. One North Carolina woman who opened her home in 1863 as "a boarding establishment for Refugees" found herself immediately swamped with applicants. A widow whose sons were fighting in the Confederate army, Phila Calder felt that she had little option but to convert her home into a boardinghouse in order to remain financially solvent.[47] However, this wartime boardinghouse, and hundreds more like it, were seen as temporary responses to unusual circumstances, and very few of the boardinghouses opened during the Civil War remained open after 1865. Yet they foreshadowed a dramatic rise in female-owned boardinghouses in the postwar period.

The meteoric increase in female-owned boardinghouses after the Civil War can be explained in part by changing economic and demographic patterns within North Carolina. In the forty years after 1865, the state transformed itself from an almost purely agricultural economy to one with a significant manufacturing component, primarily in the textile and tobacco industries. Between 1865 and 1900, nearly two hundred thousand North Carolinians moved from their farms to towns or factory villages across the state seeking employment.[48] This change resulted in an increased demand for temporary residences, a demand that boardinghouses were well positioned to meet. However, comparing the number of female-owned boardinghouses and hotels with their male-owned counterparts in Wilmington and Raleigh, North Carolina's two largest cities during the nineteenth century, reveals that simple market demand is an inadequate explanation for the rise of female-owned boardinghouses. While female-owned establishments increased in numbers in both cities during the four decades after the Civil War (Figures 8 and 9), the number of their male-owned equivalents remained essentially static throughout this period.[49] Had the growth of female-owned boardinghouses been primarily the result of economic and demographic factors, one would have expected that their male-owned equivalents would have demonstrated a comparable increase. The fact that they did not indicates how the rise of female-owned boardinghouses resulted from a combination of economic and cultural changes.

To tell the story of female-owned boardinghouses in late nineteenth-century North Carolina, one must look beyond the statistics to the experiences of individual women who ran these boardinghouses. At first glance, their lives appear tedious and tiring, an endless repetition of laundry, cooking, housecleaning, and child rearing—all the tasks that went into running a large household. They spent their days meeting the needs of their family and the strangers who shared a roof with them, leaving little time or energy for

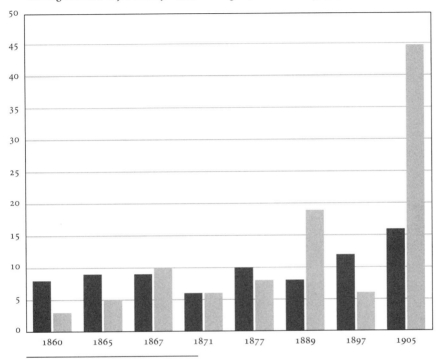

FIGURE 8. Boardinghouses and hotels in Wilmington, 1860–1905. Statistics derived from *Kelley's City Directory* (1860); *Wilmington Directory* (1865); *Smaw's Wilmington Directory* (1867); *Sherriff's Wilmington Directory* (1877); *Directory of the City of Wilmington* (1889); *Wilmington, N.C. City Directory 1897*); *Wilmington, N.C. Directory, 1905.*

■ Male-Owned Establishments
▨ Female-Owned Establishments

reflection or relaxation. At the same time, by running boardinghouses, they challenged received notions about the place of women and the role of the home. The experience of four of these women (Alice Houston, Julia Graves, Ida Beard, and Julia Wolfe) reveals how southern ideas about boardinghouses changed significantly over the course of the late nineteenth century. Between them, they represent four distinct generations of boardinghouse operators. Each of them led demanding lives for which their privileged backgrounds left them ill prepared. Each ran her boardinghouse essentially on her own. While Alice Houston and Julia Graves were both widows, Ida Beard opened her boardinghouse when her husband abandoned her, and Julia Wolfe started hers in order to escape from an abusive and alcoholic husband. All were mothers and struggled to balance their roles as a single parent and as a provider. Finally, each of them, to one degree or another,

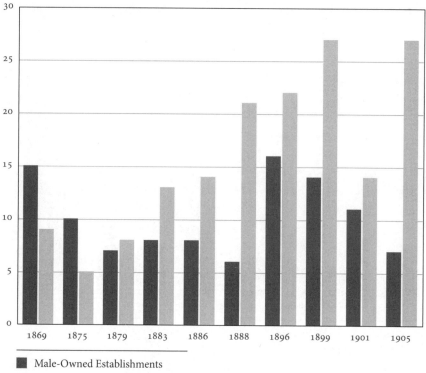

FIGURE 9. Boardinghouses and hotels in Raleigh, 1869–1905. Statistics derived from *Branson's North Carolina Business Directory* (1869); *Chataigne's Raleigh City Directory* (1875); *Chas. Emerson & Co.'s Raleigh Directory* (1879); *Raleigh City Directory* (1883); *Raleigh City Directory* (1886); *Directory of the City of Raleigh* (1888); *Directory of the City of Raleigh* (1896); *Maloney's Raleigh City Directory* (1899); *Maloney's Raleigh City Directory* (1901); *Raleigh, N.C. Directory* (1905).

■ Male-Owned Establishments
▨ Female-Owned Establishments

struggled with debt. Faced with few other options to maintain solvency, they saw their boardinghouses as their only means of supporting their families and maintaining their independence. Without their boardinghouses, they feared that they would become "enslaved by debt."

"TONIGHT I COMMENCE a new journal and with it almost a new life," Alice Houston wrote into a new leather-bound diary on a brisk February evening in 1870. Her husband, a prosperous lawyer in Wilmington, had died the week before, leaving her "alone—utterly alone—with only these mute and yet unstained pages to confide in."[50] To be sure, Houston was not literally alone—she had two young children and two aged parents to care for. But her husband's unexpected demise left her in despair and unprepared to deal with the financial and practical responsibilities of caring for a family on her own. Her diary entries in the weeks after her husband's death reveal a deep dread of the future. While she realized that her husband's estate was inadequate to support her and her children, she hesitated about which course of action to take.

She contemplated both remarriage and moving in with relatives as potential remedies for her delicate financial position. For antebellum widows of her social background, these were often the only options available. Yet after a thorough examination, Alice Houston rejected both. When urged by her family, she briefly moved in with her cousins, but reluctantly. "This home is mine at least," she wrote in her diary the night before she was to move in with them, "and here I can do as I please and would rather stay here, but don't like to seem obstinate."[51] Houston had long believed that her family did not understand her, and a day after moving in with her cousins she realized she had made a mistake. Resolving to move out as soon as possible, she wrote, "It seems so queer to me this feeling of dependence that I cannot get used to it and don't think I ever shall."[52] Although her attitude toward her relatives improved somewhat over the nine months spent living with them, she was never completely at ease. In one of her last diary entries before striking out on her own, she wrote, "If it were not for this suffocating sense of *dependence*, I would feel content and happy amid old friends and old scenes."[53]

Alice Houston rejected the idea of remarriage even more vehemently than she did the idea of living with relatives. Although she received no fewer than seven marriage proposals in the two years after her husband's death, she rejected them all out of hand. While she longed for a man of stature to replace her deceased husband, the thought of marriage purely for financial security repulsed her. After spurning one potential suitor, she wrote in her diary, "How any woman can thus legally prostitute herself I cannot understand for marriage without love is in my opinion nothing less."[54] Indeed, while her marriage had been a critical period during her life, she did not see her current status as in any way inferior. "Some women make marriage the pinnacle of their ambition," she wrote. "Well, I don't think it is so important."[55]

Although she considered teaching more seriously than remarriage or living with relatives, Houston also rejected that means of supporting herself. As Jane Turner Censer has pointed out, most teaching positions for educated women in North Carolina were at residential schools. These posts had a considerable appeal to single women and childless widows, as the percentage of teaching positions held by women increased from less than 10 percent in 1860 to more than 50 percent in 1900.[56] For women with children, however, these positions were largely unavailable, as the schools provided lodging only for an individual teacher and not for a family. Therefore, while Alice Houston received several respectable offers to teach in the months after her husband's death, she turned down each of them, as they would have required her to live apart from her children. In declining one position in Wilmington, she wrote in her diary, "I cannot separate from them: I should feel so unhappy."[57]

Nine months after her husband's death, Houston had not decided on a course for her life. Much of those months she spent in bed from a combination of depression and illness, including severe bouts with consumption and typhoid fever. The deaths of her father and youngest child in November 1870 led her into a deep despair, followed quickly by a newfound resolve. Unsuccessfully trying to hold back the tears that stained her diary, she recognized that "my grief is making me selfish, and I must strive to conquer this, as I have others of less magnitude." With the death of her father, she realized that she now had responsibility not only for her living child but also for her aged and infirm mother and her adolescent sister. "Father's death," she wrote, "leaves Mother and little Rose homeless, and though neither of them realize the fact yet, the time will come very soon when they must." With this knowledge, Houston took it upon herself to open a boardinghouse to support her family.[58]

When first presented with the idea, Houston recoiled at the thought of opening a boardinghouse. "I am advised to open a private boarding house," she wrote in her diary, but "I dislike that idea very much, but I see no other way." Although she never says so explicitly, the thought of living in close proximity to strange men may have factored into her apprehension. The records from a contemporary boardinghouse in Raleigh reveal the extent to which the boardinghouse clientele was overwhelming male. Of the 317 boarders who stayed at Howell House in Raleigh between January 1871 and January 1873, 303 were single men, 6 were married couples, and 2 were single women. Although a handful of the boarders stayed with the widowed Mrs. N. J. Howell for months at a time, most stayed for less than a week.[59] For a woman like Alice Houston who carefully protected her reputation by always being circumspect in her relationships with men, the thought of living in a boardinghouse must have been one step away from prostitution. Indeed, in rejecting one of her many marriage proposals, she pleaded in her diary,

"God help me and deliver me from prostituting myself thus for the stake of a home and luxuries."[60]

When Houston eventually opened her boardinghouse in January 1871 on the outskirts of Wilmington, she found that her fears were unwarranted. Unexpectedly, she found the experience liberating, writing in her diary, "I have today 'turned a new leaf' . . . I have taken possession of my new home; made new resolves and it is a new year in which to commence a new life." To her surprise, Houston quickly took to her initial crop of four boarders, remarking, "I like their manners better than I feared I would."[61] Two weeks later, she had taken on two additional boarders. Although she found herself busier than she had ever been, her diary now displayed a vitality absent from her earlier entries. Indeed, maintaining the boardinghouse kept her so busy that she often neglected her nightly ritual of diary writing. "What a regular busy-body I've become!" she wrote after a three-night hiatus. "Between waiting on Rose [her ill sister], attending to my household, and serving—I can't find time even to 'chat' with my good old confidant. Every one is so kind to me—I'm almost happy once more."[62] After four months of running her boardinghouse, Houston found herself happier than she had ever been: "Twelve months ago I was a homeless miserable waif: moneyless and sometimes I thought and felt friendless. Now, though plain and simple, I have a *home* and many friends."[63]

As happy as her new boardinghouse made her, Houston had difficulty paying her bills. Although she regularly had between four and six boarders throughout the summer and fall of 1871, she found that her location on Wilmington's outskirts made it impossible to charge more than five dollars a week. With every passing month, she fell deeper and deeper into debt, almost all of it to a neighboring general store where she purchased groceries for her family and her boarders. Realizing that her current position was untenable and facing bankruptcy, Houston decided to move closer to Wilmington's business district, where she would be able to attract more boarders and charge a higher weekly rate. "Today I moved into a new home—left the quiet of 6th street for the noise and bustle of the heart of Town and find the change decidedly pleasant," she wrote in her diary that night. "I wonder have I taken a wise step? I know not—the future alone can determine, but God will take care of me let the issue be as it may."[64]

Located on Front Street between Dock and Orange streets, Alice Houston's new boardinghouse was situated near Wilmington's busy port. By moving her boardinghouse, Houston not only improved her financial prospects but also placed herself in direct competition with the city's male-owned hotels. In this respect, Alice Houston was personifying a long-term trend in Wilmington's economic topography. A map of Wilmington's boarding-houses and hotels in 1865 indicates that male-owned establishments tended to dominate the waterfront and Market Street, Wilmington's main commercial artery, while female-owned establishments were scattered randomly throughout the city, often at a distance from business distinct. By 1905, a different pattern emerged. While male-owned hotels continued to occupy prime real estate, now they were surrounded by female-owned boarding-houses (Figure 10). This pattern of increasing concentration of boarding-houses in business districts and competition with male-owned hotels found in Wilmington parallels trends in other North Carolina cities, including Raleigh, Salem, and Charlotte.

Alice Houston's diary ends shortly after she relocated her boarding-house. Newspaper and public records show no trace of her or her business after early 1872, and her boardinghouse is conspicuously absent in a listing of boardinghouses in an 1877 business directory.[65] In all likelihood, she closed her boardinghouse either because she could not make it profitable or because brighter prospects presented themselves elsewhere. Here again, Alice Houston's experience was typical of boardinghouse proprietors. While a few boardinghouses stayed open for more than a decade, the vast majority closed after a few years. This trait appears particularly common among boardinghouses opened before 1880, when opening a boarding-house was primarily a temporary solution to an economic crisis. After 1880, the trend was for boardinghouses to stay open longer, indicating that running boardinghouses had become less a remedy for immediate needs and more of a business.

LIKE ALICE HOUSTON'S, Julia Graves's boardinghouse emerged from tragedy. Although she had known for some time that her husband was mentally ill and she had been present at his first attempt at self-destruction, his suicide in July 1889 shocked and bewildered her.[66] A woman of extraordinary personal strength, Julia Graves received the support of a wide array of friends and relations. On the morning after Ralph's death, his faculty colleague Francis Venable wrote her that he was "deeply pained to learn this morning of the death of your husband. In his death the whole state has sustained a great loss; this however is not comparable to your loss and affliction." In the coming days, dozens of similar missives arrived. Later that month, when Julia Graves's youngest child died, she again received the emo-

FIGURE 10. Map of Wilmington boardinghouses and hotels, 1865 (top) and 1905. Stars indicate male-owned establishments. Circles indicate female-owned establishments. Locations of boardinghouses and hotels taken from *Wilmington Directory* (1865); *Wilmington, N.C. Directory, 1905*. Adapted from a map by Kathleen T. Cox.

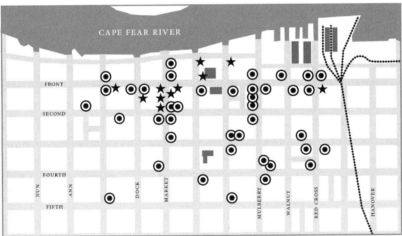

tional and spiritual support of the community. While she undoubtedly appreciated the prayers, thoughts, and kind words of so many, she realized that they would not help her provide for herself and her four living children in the years to come. Fearing destitution, that autumn she converted her stately Chapel Hill home into a boardinghouse.[67]

In its broad outlines, Julia Graves's situation upon her husband's death resembled Alice Houston's. Like Houston, she had grown up in a privileged slaveholding family, descended from a signer of the Declaration of Independence. Raised on the campus of the University of North Carolina, where her father taught Latin, Greek, and French, she married mathematics professor Ralph Graves in 1877 at the age of twenty-one. He provided well for her, purchasing a large antebellum house on seven acres adjacent to campus. By the time of his death, they had five children, ranging in age from an infant to eleven years old.

Unlike Alice Houston, however, Julia Graves demonstrated little trepidation at the prospect of converting her home into a boardinghouse. Instead, she was more concerned about what type of boardinghouse hers should be. Over tea at her house, the other faculty wives unanimously endorsed the idea of a boardinghouse, and together they decided that she should try to attract only prosperous boarders by charging a hefty thirteen dollars per month. (Only W. P. Mallett, another faculty widow, charged more.) Such a rate would help to ensure that her home would remain exclusive and thereby help to maintain her social position. Cornelia Phillips Spencer, the reigning arbiter of public morals in Chapel Hill, wrote to Julia, saying that the boardinghouse idea was "brilliant." University president Edwin A. Alderman made a more public validation of Graves's enterprise by boarding there himself.[68] Julia Graves's comparative willingness to open a boardinghouse may have reflected the subtle evolution in attitudes in the eighteen-year interval that separated her boardinghouse from Alice Houston's.

While Julia Graves saw running a boardinghouse as a means of staying out of debt, she often found that the costs of running a boardinghouse exceeded what she took in from her boarders. One of her sons later recalled that she saw herself more as a hostess and maternal figure to her boarders than as a proprietor of a business. Graves's ingrained sense of hospitality led her to furnish the dining room table with more than she could afford. Indeed, her son remembers that she fed her boarders on a daily basis like honored guests: "There was often veal steak with gravy for breakfast, in addition to eggs, and unlimited butter, and hot biscuits, and battercakes. I remember the vast quantities of chicken consumed in our house; and, at the evening meal (then called supper), the black molasses—with the hot buttered biscuits, again—that most of the students were so fond of."[69]

Julia Graves paid the cost of her extravagance at the boarding table. Over the course of the thirteen years she ran a boardinghouse in Chapel Hill, she found herself perpetually in debt, mainly to the local general store where she purchased her supplies. According to its account books, she often carried a balance of more than two hundred dollars, most of it to pay for groceries.[70] Her son described the panic that set in on his mother's face upon seeing "those bills at the end of the month! They were always much larger than [she] expected them to be. Her thoughts had been centered on giving the students at her table all they wanted to eat, and she had not had time to pay attention to what she was going to have to pay out. One of my earliest memories is of my mother's worried, strained face when she looked at the columns of figures that came once a month from the store where she did most of her trading."[71] Indeed, she accumulated so much debt while running her boardinghouse that her son marveled that she was not forced to declare bankruptcy during its first year of operation.

Graves closed her boardinghouse in 1902 when her youngest child reached adulthood. Her experience indicates that running a boardinghouse could function as a long-term debt management strategy under the proper circumstances. At the same time, however, Graves continually struggled with debt throughout her dozen-year tenure as a boardinghouse operator. As we have seen, the account books of her local general store indicates that Julia Graves accumulated significant amounts of debt, increasing each year from 1889 to 1902. Henry Patterson's willingness to extend so much credit to Graves over more than a decade probably stemmed in part from a personal sympathy with the tragedy of her story. However, it is also likely that he recognized that her boardinghouse represented one of the only possible avenues that Graves had available to her to manage her debt.

THE EVENTS THAT LED Ida Beard to open a boardinghouse in 1896 differed significantly from those of Alice Houston and Julia Graves. Born during the Civil War in Forsythe County, North Carolina, Ida Beard was raised, by her own account, in "the lap of luxury."[72] Although her family might be more accurately described as prosperous rather than wealthy, Beard's account of her early life indicates that she never went without. On her eighteenth birthday, she married John Beard against the wishes of her parents. Deeply in love with John from an early age, Ida Beard soon found that her new husband did not live up to her idealized conception of him. Throughout their sixteen-year marriage, during which she bore him three children (one of which died in infancy), Ida Beard was rarely happy. Indeed, in her written account of their marriage, she titled one of her chapters "Misery! Misery! More Misery!" At times, she considered suicide.[73]

Ida's account of her marriage to John Beard can be read as a compendium of troubles that could befall a Victorian era marriage. She describes her husband's alcoholism and opium abuse, gambling, adultery, physical abuse, and eventually abandonment. However, according to Ida Beard, among the most serious of her husband's flaws was how he dealt with money and debt. Spending lavishly on himself while denying his wife and children basic necessities, John Beard rarely held a job for more than a few weeks. To Ida's horror, John often defaulted on his debts, moving from town to town to escape his creditors. On one occasion, when she caught him trying to defraud his creditors, she rebuked him: "I will not dishonor the mother who bore me by being your accomplice in this affair; but I will leave the State's uniform for you."[74]

Although she may have been somewhat relieved when her husband abandoned her in 1896, Ida Beard's immediate concern was that he had left her practically penniless to fend for herself and their two children. Indeed, her position was even more desperate because he left her responsible for the sizable debts he had accrued. Although her account does not indicate the extent of her legal liability for his debts, she evidently believed that she had some responsibility for his lavish spending, even if she disapproved of it. She was able to rent an unheated room in Winston-Salem's slums, where she and her children "huddled together in that cold, bare room . . . nothing with which to build a fire; neither had we a light, save that of the moon."[75] Unable to find work, she reluctantly accepted the charity of friends and family to feed her family.

Facing destitution, Ida Beard decided to open a boardinghouse. However, her financial position was very different from that of Alice Houston or Julia Graves. While they at least owned their homes, providing the venue for their boardinghouses, Ida Beard was almost homeless, living in a rented room in Winston-Salem's notoriously squalid Starbuck Block. She described her situation succinctly: "After I had made a thorough canvas of the city in order to obtain employment, I at last decided to upon opening up a boardinghouse; but how was I to begin, with nothing?"[76] Determining that the alternative was starvation, however, Beard managed with the help of friends to rent a dilapidated house. Laboring day and night to make it habitable, she recorded, "I almost felt though I could tear my eyeballs from their sockets."[77]

Surprisingly, her initial experience running a boardinghouse did not differ significantly from that of Alice Houston and Julia Graves, despite how significantly her financial and personal situations varied from theirs. Drawing upon the example provided by her mother and her privileged upbringing, Ida Beard felt obligated to function as a hostess. "I will always remember the first table I spread for the boarders," she wrote in her account. "I was so afraid that something would be wrong, and that it wouldn't seem like a boarding house. I prepared for my boarders as though they were guests coming to tea, and on leaving the dining room, they each declared themselves highly pleased with their first meal."[78] Indeed, if her detailed description of the initial meal is accurate, she probably spent all her remaining cash.

Despite the terrible impact that her marriage had upon her psyche, Ida Beard's experiences prepared her to run a boardinghouse in ways unavailable to Alice Houston and Julia Graves. Unlike them, she had grown up in a world where boardinghouses were common and had spent much her adult life living in them, as her husband flitted from town to town and from job to job. She had stayed in boardinghouses of varying quality, ranging from lavish and comfortable, when her husband was feeling generous, to seedy and putrid, when he wasn't. Indeed, one of them disgusted her so much that she compared it to "purgatory" because upon entering it she caught a "glimpse of about seventy-five men and women . . . playing pool."[79] She was also aware that not all boardinghouse patrons paid their debts, as her husband routinely had left them without paying, to Ida's considerable horror. Because of this firsthand experience, Ida Beard knew more about what to expect from a boardinghouse than most women of her background and much more than those born a generation earlier.

Regardless of her experience, Ida Beard's boardinghouse did not stay open for very long. Only weeks after it opened, her eldest son contracted typhoid fever, requiring her constant attention. Forced to choose between maintaining her boardinghouse and tending to her ailing child, Beard decided on the latter. Unfortunately, her choice had immediate financial repercussions: unable to pay the rent, she was quickly evicted. Moving from house to house over the next couple of years, Ida Beard finally found a way to support her family through writing.[80]

Although her boardinghouse was open only a few short weeks, Ida Beard's experience indicates one of the significant problems that faced many of her peers: how to balance the demands of running a boardinghouse with those of caring for a family. Julia Graves in particular went to great lengths to preserve her family's integrity within the context of running a boardinghouse. She spatially arranged her boardinghouse so that she and her children lived on the ground floor while her boarders lived upstairs. This arrangement helped to preserve a private domestic space within her public home. Graves also maintained a separate family dining table with a distinct set of tableware for her and her children.[81] Thus, she was able to maintain the semblance of a Victorian middle-class family dinner in the context of a bustling boardinghouse.

Ida Beard's experience also indicates the precarious nature of opening a boardinghouse. Because she rented rather than owned her boardinghouse, Ida Beard was unable to weather unexpected reverses in the way that Alice Houston or Julia Graves could. Without the benefit of their material and social resources, Beard could not maintain such a demanding enterprising on her own. Therefore, Beard's experience indicates how running a boardinghouse was not a practical option for most indebted single women.

The absence of these material prerequisites may explain the paucity of African American boardinghouses in North Carolina during the nineteenth century. Only three black boardinghouses appear in extant city directories from Raleigh; none appear in directories for Wilmington. This last fact is even more surprising considering Wilmington's majority black population and its reputation as a center for African American businesses. Indeed, according to economic historians Roger Ransom and Richard Sutch, boardinghouse operator was among the most racially exclusive female occupations in the late nineteenth-century South. Based on occupational data from the 1890 census, they conclude that only teaching, merchandising, and clerking discriminated more heavily against black women.[82]

IMMORTALIZED AS "Dixieland" in her son Thomas's autobiographical novel *Look Homeward, Angel*, Julia Wolfe's boardinghouse in Asheville (which she called "Old Kentucky Home") easily ranks as North Carolina's best known. Julia Westall Wolfe was born in 1860 in Swannanoa, a remote mountain town in western North Carolina. Her experience as a boardinghouse operator represents the culmination of a forty-year period of development that started shortly after the Civil War. What began with Alice Houston as a somewhat suspect strategy for providing for a family and coping with debt had become a venerated southern institution that could, under the right circumstances, be a significant source of profit.

Opened in 1906, Old Kentucky Home was Julia Wolfe's third attempt at running a boardinghouse. Her first effort started in 1885 shortly after she married W. O. Wolfe and became pregnant with her first child. Unlike the other boardinghouse keepers described in this chapter, Julia Wolfe had extensive work experience before marriage as a schoolteacher and door-to-door book agent.[83] Now that she was pregnant, however, Wolfe felt that continuing to work in public would be both socially inappropriate and bad for her health.[84] She recognized that Asheville had begun to develop a national reputation as a health resort, particularly for those with respiratory illnesses.[85] Ever the entrepreneur, she took in a handful of boarders for the summer, hoping that the revenue would supplement her new husband's income as a stonecutter.

One of the distinguishing features of Julia Wolfe's initial foray into the boardinghouse business was that she was not in or threatened by debt, in contrast to Alice Houston, Julia Graves, and Ida Beard. While the Wolfes were not wealthy, according to one biographer, W. O. Wolfe's income as a stonecutter alone made the Wolfes better off than nine out of ten families in Asheville.[86] Julia Wolfe saw her boardinghouse as a means of maintaining some financial and personal independence from her new husband, who, she realized early in their marriage, was an incurable alcoholic and occasionally abusive. Indeed, Julia's quest for financial independence from her husband led her to buy their house from him during the first year of their marriage.

Julia Wolfe closed her first boardinghouse a year later, in July 1886, when her infant daughter died. Although Wolfe herself attributed the baby's death to bad milk from a neighbor's cow, her symptoms indicate she may have died from cholera contracted from one of her mother's boarders.[87] Unlike Ida Beard, who closed her boardinghouse at the first sign of illness, Julia Wolfe attempted to care for her ailing child while running a boardinghouse. Although she kept summer boarders occasionally over the next decade, Wolfe did not seriously consider opening another boardinghouse until 1904. In that year she traveled with five of her seven living children to St. Louis to run a boardinghouse for visitors to the World's Fair. Catering primarily to North Carolinians, Wolfe's St. Louis boardinghouse proved to be a tremendous financial success. These benefits came at a tremendous cost, however, as Wolfe lost a second child to disease when one of her twelve-year old twin boys succumbed to typhoid fever.

Even though her experience in St. Louis proved both rewarding and traumatic, it inspired her to open a permanent boardinghouse in Asheville. Unlike with her 1885 venture, however, Julia Wolfe decided not to convert her own house on Woodfin Street into a boardinghouse but to purchase a separate building for the purpose on Spruce Street. Built in 1883, the house on Spruce Street had several previous incarnations as a boardinghouse. Indeed, the name "Old Kentucky Home" had been inherited from an earlier proprietor. Tom Wolfe described the structure as a "big cheaply constructed frame house of eighteen or twenty drafty high-ceilinged rooms: it had a rambling, unplanned, gabular appearance, and was painted a dirty yellow."[88] Although the thirty-year history of the Old Kentucky Home rests outside the chronological parameters of this study, several aspects of its founding and its initial years of operation demonstrate how the role of boardinghouses in southern society had changed by the dawn of the twentieth century.

If the growth of female-owned boardinghouses after the Civil War can be tied to women's desire to preserve their families, Julia Wolfe's decision to open a boardinghouse at a location other than her home eventually split her family into two. Although she originally attempted to run her boarding-house while still living with her family, she quickly discovered that its effective operation required that she live on the premises. Therefore, she moved into the Spruce Street boardinghouse, leaving all but her youngest son, Tom, to live with their father. In *Look Homeward, Angel*, Thomas Wolfe described his distaste for living in his mother's boardinghouse:

> He hated the indecency of his life, the loss of dignity and seclu-
> sion, the surrender of the tumultuous rabble of the four walls
> which shielded us from them. He felt, rather than understood, the
> waste, the confusion, the blind cruelty of their lives—his spirit was
> stretched out on the rack of despair and bafflement as there came to
> him more and more the conviction that their lives could not be more
> hopelessly distorted, wrenched, mutilated, and perverted away from
> all simple comfort, repose, happiness. He saw plainly by this time
> that their poverty, the threat of the poorhouse, the lurid references
> to the pauper's grave, belonged to the insensate mythology of hoard-
> ing; anger smoldered like a brand in him at their sorry greed. There
> was no place sacred unto themselves, no place fixed for their own in-
> habitation, no place proof against the invasion of the boarders.[89]

Tom's invective demonstrates how his mother's boardinghouse destroyed any sense of home that women like Julia Graves attempted so hard to preserve. He remembered being shuttled from room to room throughout his childhood to accommodate the boarders' needs. Indeed, it was Tom's deep unhappiness with his upbringing that led him as an adult to produce his most successful literary works.

This passage also reveals how the Wolfes were never as poor as his mother maintained. While the boardinghouse offered the outward appearance of creeping poverty, Julia Wolfe rarely found herself in debt. Indeed, until the Great Depression, Old Kentucky Home generated steady and significant profits, money that Wolfe funneled into a variety of real estate ventures or into expanding the physical structure of her boardinghouse.[90] When Wolfe purchased the property in 1906, Old Kentucky Home already had the capacity to house nineteen boarders, significantly larger than any other boardinghouse examined in this study. Over the next twenty years, she built additions onto the house so that it could host as many as twenty-six boarders. These measures indicate how, at least in the hands of Julia Wolfe, running a boardinghouse had ceased to function as a debt-management strategy and had become a business.

This examination of nineteenth-century North Carolina boardinghouses reveals several broad patterns. The number of female-owned boarding-houses increased significantly after the Civil War. Most of the women who opened boardinghouses did so in the aftermath of a significant trauma, most frequently the death of a husband. They saw their boardinghouses primarily as a means of supporting their family and mediating the threats of debt. At the same time, they frequently struggled financially. The experience of these women, who came primarily from privileged backgrounds, indicates how middle-class white North Carolinians struggled significantly to free themselves from the bonds of debt in the decades after the Civil War.

CHAPTER TEN

Nothing Less than a Question of Slavery or Freedom

Populism & the Crisis of Debt in the New South

H ARD TIMES IS the cry," argued a tenant farmer from Johnston County in 1887. "Tenants are far behind, caused by short crops for three years. If we could get cash for our work and produce and pay cash for what we buy we would soon be out of debt and doing well. As it is nearly everyone is in debt and getting worse every year."[1] A rural physician from Rowan County concurred that many farmworkers had descended into a morass of debt from which they could not escape. "All are more or less involved in debt," he argued in 1889, "and many beyond their ability to pay."[2] Although many North Carolinians suffered from debts that they could not pay, the state's farmers shouldered the heaviest burden.

This chapter explores how North Carolina farmers understood the problem of debt in the final decades of the nineteenth century. Declining crop prices drove farmers to work harder every year in an attempt to pull themselves out of debt, only to find that the harvest yielded more bushels and less money than the year before. Exacerbated by the demonetization of silver in 1873, a deflationary federal monetary policy punished debtors, who found it progressively harder to pay off their debts.[3] The resulting agrarian revolt challenged the existing political, social, and economic order in unprecedented ways. Debt stood at the heart of the agrarian critique of American capitalist society. By the 1880s, farmers recognized that they could not combat their chronic indebtedness through individual effort; rather, only collective political action could sufficiently reform the exploitive economic system.[4] Although both black and white farmers at the end of the nineteenth century both found themselves mired in debt, this chapter argues that black and white agrarians in North Carolina interpreted debt very differently. Although briefly politically allied, black and white agrarians brought with them two distinct interpretative schemata about the social, cultural, moral, and financial meaning of debt. White agrarians saw debt as a fundamental threat to their liberty and advocated for the creation of a new credit culture. They hoped to construct a new credit system that allowed farmers to have credit without social stigma, increased the role of the state in credit relationships, and reflected the economic realities of Gilded Age society. Black agrarians, however, were skeptical about debt reform measures such as the subtreasury plan or bimetallism advocated by white agrarians. While easing the crushing burden of debt experienced by black farmers in North Carolina was a political priority for black agrarians in the state, other issues, notably voting rights and election reform, remained higher priorities.[5]

In the late 1870s, the Grange (officially the Patrons of Husbandry) became the first statewide organization with the specific purpose of improving the condition of farmers. Established in 1873, the Grange grew quickly in North Carolina; at its peak a decade later, it had approximately five hundred lodges and more than fifteen thousand members. A secret, fraternal organization, the Grange provided indebted farmers with a necessary social network, allowing them to see, perhaps for the first time, that their problems with debt were not individual and situational but rather universal and chronic.[6]

Although the apolitical Grange could help farmers identify the origins of their indebtedness, it could not provide them the needed political tools to effect change. Leonidas Polk recognized that farmers in North Carolina needed some vehicle outside the Grange to make their voices heard. His experience with the Farmer's Cheap Cash Store, as North Carolina's first agriculture commissioner, and other ventures convinced him that their unremitting indebtedness financially crippled poor farmers to the extent that they could not resolve their debts on their own. In 1886, Polk established the *Progressive Farmer*, a newspaper intended not only to educate and inform farmers but also to advocate and foment political action. Within a year, the *Progressive Farmer* had the largest circulation of any newspaper in the state. In 1887, Polk founded the North Carolina Farmers' Association, shortly thereafter to become the North Carolina Farmers' Alliance. Like his newspaper, Polk's insurgent agrarian organization experienced explosive growth. By August 1888, North Carolina hosted 1,018 subordinate Alliances in 53 counties, membership of 42,000; a year later, there were 1,816 subordinate Alliances in 89 counties and more than 72,000 members.[7] Excluded from the white Alliance (along with lawyers, merchants, and atheists), black farmers formed a Colored Alliance in 1888, attracting more than

55,000 members by 1890.[8] Although the two organizations pursued similar economic goals and maintained tenuous organizational ties, they never developed a fully biracial movement.

From the beginning, the North Carolina Farmers' Alliance proposed an ambitious political program, including the creation of a state railroad commission, the expansion of educational opportunities for rural children, and reform of the convict leasing system. At the heart of its agenda, however, was a series of proposals to reduce the crushing burden of debt of North Carolina's farmers. Its three most significant proposals (the subtreasury plan, the abolition the state's homestead law, and a reduction in the maximum interest rate) each sought to create a new system of credit that would enable the state's farmers to liberate themselves from their debts. Indeed, many agrarians believed, in the words of agitator James Murdock, that "revolution demands the abolition of the credit system. . . . There can be no compromise with the present financial system. It must be destroyed root and branch."[9]

The cornerstone of the white Farmers' Alliance agenda, both nationally and in North Carolina, was an ambitious program known as the "subtreasury plan." The plan called for the federal government to build agricultural warehouses, known as "subtreasuries," in every county with more than half a million dollars in agricultural commodities per year. Farmers would be able to store nonperishable crops in these subtreasuries, waiting until crop prices rebounded from their harvest-time nadir. When farmers deposited their crops in the subtreasury, they would be able to borrow up to 80 percent of their value in treasury notes, paying only a nominal interest rate until they removed the crops for sale.[10]

White agrarians argued that the subtreasury plan would relieve at least some of the burden of indebted farmers in two ways. First, it promised that farmers would receive higher prices for their crops. By allowing farmers to choose when to sell, instead of forcing them to sell during the harvest, when the market was glutted, the subtreasury plan would permit farmers to benefit from the higher off-season crop prices that middlemen and speculators usually reaped. Indeed, many agrarians hoped that the subtreasury plan would effectively remove this entire parasitic class. Second, the subtreasury plan would create a flexible and expanded currency, inducing the inflationary pressures that would effectively reduce the relative size of farmers' debts. Agrarians argued that, unlike the hyperinflated Confederate currency, the treasury notes issued by the subtreasuries would be a legitimate currency expansion because their volume would be proportional to agricultural production, in their eyes the only legitimate source of wealth. "We take the position," argued Leonidas Polk in the *Progressive Farmer*, "that no country can prosper when the farming industry does not prosper. That is the foundation of all prosperity. That is the producer of wealth; the others are simply manipulators who turn one thing already in existence into another, enhancing its value by converting it."[11]

Although the subtreasury plan originated in Texas, white agrarians in North Carolina became some of its most vocal proponents.[12] Elias Carr, who became president of the North Carolina Alliance when Polk became president of the national Alliance, said of the subtreasury plan, "The one thing needful in the present financial condition of the people is a debt-paying system of finance in comparison with which all other questions sink into utter insignificance."[13] In 1891, Leonidas Polk argued that currency expansion by means of the subtreasury plan was "the great and paramount issue now before the American people."[14] Although North Carolina agrarians favored inflationary monetary policy, they for the most part rejected the Greenback panacea that high inflation rates would effectively erase their debts. Instead, they advocated that a moderately inflated currency would create parity now absent in creditor-debtor relationships. The object, according to the *Caucasian*, was an "honest dollar" that respected the needs of creditors and debtors alike.[15]

White agrarians also blamed the state's homestead law for exacerbating poor farmers' credit problems. Originally passed in 1859 and significantly expanded several times after the Civil War, North Carolina's homestead law, like similar measures across the South, was intended to protect insolvent debtors from losing all their property by excluding certain forms of property from debt suits. One unforeseen consequence, however, of this exclusion was that creditors demanded that farmers pay higher interest rates to compensate for their reduced collateral. "I believe," argued J. J. Goldston, an elderly Chatham County farmer, that "the homestead law has been one of the main causes of the indebtedness of the average farmer."[16] A landlord from Cleveland Country agreed. "One of our needs is the removal of the homestead law or greatly reducing it," he argued in 1887. "Take away the homestead and make people honest and responsible for their debts."[17] So too did a farmer from Harnett County, employing very similar language: "Repeal the homestead law and make all honest debts collectible. Enact such laws as will tend to the restoration of confidence between all classes of trade."[18]

White agrarians also argued that the state should restrict maximum interest rates. "Interest hangs on like grim death to a dead pig," concluded an editorial in the *Carolina Watchman*, using language familiar to its agrarian readers. "The increase of wealth in this country is not more than three percent; so if Shylock gets more than that in the shape of interest, it is only a question of time when he will have all the wealth of the country. Usury must go!"[19] White agrarians proposed that the state reduce the maximum rate of interest from 8 percent to 6 percent and crack down on business practices, such as general stores' dual price system, that bypassed usury laws.

Indeed, many white agrarians concluded that any form of interest amounted to usury and was, therefore, immoral. Usury, claimed one North Carolina Populist in 1896, was "the most gigantic power for the subjection of industrial humanity that has ever appeared on earth."[20] Many agrarians believed that creditors artificially employed distinctions between usury and interest to justify their exploitation of indebted farmers. "By changing the name from usury to interest," argued Farmers' Alliance president Marion Butler, somewhat tongue in cheek, "good people escape the penalty of disobedience to the Biblical injunction while they gather the fruit of their brother's toil."[21] Agrarians' opposition to interest grew naturally out of their belief in the labor theory of value. Farmers, agrarians believed, earned their money through physical and mental toil. Creditors who profited through interest, in contrast, did not labor, and therefore their profits must be dishonest.[22] "What do they [creditors] produce?" asked the *Caucasian*, Marion Butler's agrarian newspaper. "What do they distribute? What moral right have they to cumber the earth?"[23]

Many North Carolina agrarians concluded that any form of credit should be avoided and that a pure-cash system ought to replace it.[24] For some, this rejection of credit was a moral matter as much as it was one of personal and political economy. James Murdock, an essayist for the *Progressive Farmer*, claimed that credit encouraged "recklessness in buying" and "rascality and laziness." The solution, according to Murdock, was a system of "pay as you go."[25] To be sure, most agrarians realized that, as a practical matter, a credit-free economy was impossible. Debt and farming had become so intermeshed in the minds of many North Carolinians that few could envision an alternative system. "The credit system of farming," claimed the *Tarboro Farmers Advocate* in 1891, "has become so habitual to many of our farmers as to be second nature, and they do not believe they could live under any other system."[26]

The relationship between debt and race proved to be a thorn in the side of the agrarian movement throughout its history in North Carolina. Most white agrarians recognized that black farmers also suffered from debts they could not pay, prompting agrarian leader Marion Butler to conclude that "what is good for a white laborer in the South . . . is equally good for a colored laborer."[27] Indeed, most white agrarians recognized that black farmers had even more difficulty in paying their debts than their white neighbors. According to a white mechanic from Hyde County in 1887, compared with whites, "black laborers [are] very poor: they are always in debt."[28] White agrarians also understood that the support of a black electoral majority in some eastern counties would be necessary for any statewide agrarian reform movement.[29] However, they rejected the idea of a completely biracial organization, always keeping black agrarians at arm's length. Whatever parallels they drew between their plight and those of their black neighbors, most white agrarians supported white supremacy and rejected racial egalitarianism. This racial ambivalence manifested itself in an 1892 *Progressive Farmer* editorial: "Whatever hurts the white farmer or mechanic injures the colored farmer or mechanic. Naturally they should not be arrayed against each other . . . but the fact remains that the Anglo Saxons must rule this country and we believe all honest, intelligent negroes know the importance of this."[30]

Black agrarians recognized that their problems with debt were not identical to those of white agrarians. Because the vast majority of black agrarians did not own their own land but toiled as tenants, sharecroppers, or wage laborers, their relationship to debt differed in significant ways from their white counterparts, many of whom owned their farms. Therefore, although black agrarians desired many of the same goals as white agrarians, they did not necessarily advocate the same political measures to attain those goals. They recognized, for instance, that abolishing the homestead exemption would expand credit only for those who owned their land. Similarly, they understood that the subtreasury plan would not profit farmers who worked for wages and were skeptical of its benefits for tenant farmers and sharecroppers. Conversely, black agrarians were consistently frustrated by white agrarians' refusal to advocate reform of the Landlord-Tenant Act of 1875, which granted landlords first lien on crops and criminalized the removal of crops without the landlord's authorization.[31]

The Farmers' Alliance demonstrated considerable success in electing favorable candidates to the North Carolina General Assembly. By 1891, 110 of 170 members of the General Assembly were Alliancemen, most of whom were Democrats.[32] Yet, despite their numerical superiority, the Alliance had difficulty in transforming this legislative majority into the envisioned economic reforms. A measure to reduce the maximum interest rate introduced by Allianceman Willis R. Williams of Pitt County, for instance, died in the

Judiciary Committee despite widespread public support.[33] The Alliance's failure to enact more meaningful change can be attributed to two main causes. First, many of the most devoted Alliancemen in the state legislature were political neophytes. They had been elected in large measure because they were farmers and not lawyers or professional politicians, and their inexperience with the legislative process handicapped their effort to enact the Alliance agenda. Second, although the Farmers' Alliance had at least the nominal support of a majority of the legislators, it did not have the support of the majority Democratic Party. Non-Alliance ("Straight-Out") Democrats such as Edward Chambers Smith and Spier Whitaker wielded enough political influence to keep the Alliance program in check.

Even though the Alliance failed to enact meaningful change in debt's legal parameters, many local chapters of the Farmers' Alliance found that they could take steps to reduce their debts and lessen their dependence on credit. They saw cooperative purchasing as an alternative to the credit monopoly enjoyed by rural general stores. Such collective endeavors, they hoped, would remove farmers from the crushing seasonal burden of debt. Some initial forays into collective purchasing were moderately successful. For instance, the Bethany Alliance in northern Davidson County arranged a collective purchase of fertilizer in September 1889. Although such efforts enabled farmers to bypass the local general store temporarily, it did not absolve them of the fundamental credit crisis. When farmers attempted to escalate their collective purchasing power into exchange stores as a collective alternative to general stores, they usually failed. For instance, the Mt. Sylvan Alliance in northern Durham County voted to create such a store in 1889 and started to collect money in 1890. The store, however, never opened. The Jamestown Alliance in Davie County did only slightly better, opening a small store in Mocksville. It, however, closed eighteen months later.[34] The failure of exchange stores to become a meaningful alternative to general stores helped to convince many agrarians that debt reform within the existing political-economic paradigms would be almost impossible.

Despite the robust efforts of thousands of North Carolina Alliancemen, financial conditions did not improve significantly. If anything, between 1887 and 1892, North Carolina farmers faced deeper and deeper levels of debt. "Farmers in my county have hard times," complained one Montgomery County farmer in 1891. "Farm products are so low and goods so high that the farmers can't make both ends meet. I would be glad if some remedy could be found for it. I am a farmer myself, and own a good farm, and work hard, but I am in debt at this time, and I do not see how I can help myself."[35] A petition from the Farmers' Alliance of Chatham County to the General Assembly claimed that "there is very little money in the hands of the farmers. Almost every farmer is depressed; many are disheartened; labor is unremunerative. . . . They are gradually but steadily becoming poorer and poorer every year."[36]

By 1892, many North Carolina agrarians had came to the conclusion that existing political leaders and institutions could not or would not act decisively to address the growing debt burden under which many farmers labored. Agrarians seemed particularly incensed with Democratic politicians who had pledged solidarity with Alliance goals but failed to act decisively to enact their agenda. Elderly senator Zeb Vance was a particular source of frustration and ire. "Nine-tenths of the people in this State are carrying a burden of debt," wrote A. D. Taylor to Senator Zeb Vance in July 1890. "I can not believe you will turn a deaf ear to their cry at this the time of their extremity."[37] That same month, Vance received a disheartening letter from Eugene Beddingfield, the secretary of the North Carolina Farmers' Alliance: "The people are very restless. We are on the verge of a revolution. God grant it may be bloodless. . . . You cannot stand before the tide if it turns in your direction. No living power can withstand it."[38] In what many agrarians saw as a particular act of betrayal, Vance sponsored a subtreasury bill in 1890, largely to placate Polk, but conspicuously failed to do anything to secure its passage.[39]

The Vance affair fundamentally divided the agrarian movement in North Carolina. Some, like Leonidas Polk, decided that only a new political party, the People's Party, could adequately address the farmers' need for radical reform. Others concluded that reform could happen only within the context of the Democratic Party and that any third party would result in a Republican victory at the polls, an election that potentially threatened white supremacy. A few agrarians, the most notable of whom was Marion Butler, initially endorsed this latter course of action, only to later embrace Populism. This division spelled the end of the Farmers' Alliance as an effective political entity within North Carolina, as agrarians divided over how best to pursue their agenda.

Unfortunately for North Carolina Populists, the creation of their party began inauspiciously when Leonidas Polk died unexpectedly in June 1892. Polk had been widely considered as a potential presidential candidate, but his death sent the new party into disarray. Although they carried only three counties in 1892, North Carolina Populists recognized that the Democratic Party no longer had an electoral majority. Joining forces with Republicans in 1894, Populists formed a coalition ticket (though maintaining separate organizational hierarchies) for the 1894 election that handily defeated the Democrats, gaining control over both houses of the General Assembly.[40]

Although usually referred to as the Fusion movement, the alliance between Populists and Republicans was founded more on their mutual hatred of Democrats and their desire for political power than on a common agenda or political philosophy. Ideological differences between Populists and Republicans on economic questions consistently threatened this marriage of convenience. Unlike their new Populist bedfellows, Republicans, particularly white Republicans, strongly rejected bimetallism (which by 1894 had replaced the subtreasury plan as the Populists' preferred inflationary measure) and opposed measures to reduce the maximum legal interest rate and abolish the homestead law.[41] Black Republicans, who composed approximately two-thirds of the party in North Carolina, were not as hostile as white Republicans to bimetallism, though they rarely endorsed it with enthusiasm.[42] Although the Fusion legislature enacted a number of meaningful reforms, particularly in democratizing the state's election law, decentralizing county government, and improving education funding, it failed to enact most of the Populists' core debt-relief program.

Despite its centrality in the Populist Party's formation and ideology, debt relief legislation was rarely considered by the North Carolina General Assembly during its two sessions under Fusionist control. Recognizing that their Republican allies did not share in the economic vision, Populists introduced only two significant pieces of debt-relief legislation. In the first session, the Fusion legislature in 1895 successfully passed a measure to restrict interest rates to 6 percent. Historian Allen Trelease's roll call analysis of fourteen votes taken on this bill indicates that Populists and black Republicans supported it resoundingly, 96.8 and 93.6 percent, respectively, while only 14 percent of Democrats supported it. The Republicans, Trelease argues, voted for this bill largely to secure Populist support for their election reform proposal rather than because of the interest bill's merits. According to the *Raleigh News and Observer*, the Republicans, if left to their own devices, would have voted against any measure lowering the maximum interest rate.[43]

In the second legislative session, the Populists proposed a bill in 1897 to prevent discrimination against silver as a legal tender. Here the Populists found that the Republicans abandoned them completely, with only 2.4 percent of Republicans voting for silver in four roll call votes. Further, Republicans successfully added a crippling amendment to the measure, requiring that debts contracted in one form of money be repaid in the same kind of money. Thus gutted, the bill died, opposed by nearly all Democrats, most Populists, and approximately half of Republicans.[44] These two measures indicate the extent to which Fusion politics effectively undercut North Carolina Populists in their efforts to bring about meaningful debt reform.

In the end, the Populists' failure was more political than ideological. Although Fusion temporarily placed Populists in a position of political power, their coalition with Republicans was inherently unstable. The Democrats' white supremacy campaign of 1898 effectively exploited this political weakness, frightening white voters with tales of black domination and dissuading black voters through threatened and actual violence. Yet, despite this political failure, North Carolina's agrarian movement represented the culmination of three decades of cultural and intellectual transformation about the meaning, economics, and morality of debt. In the thirty years that separated the end of the Civil War and the Fusionist legislature of 1895, black and white North Carolinians considered and reconsidered the role that debt would play in their lives.

Historians have categorized the Populists variously as petty backward-looking reactionaries, pragmatic reformers, agrarian capitalists, innovative protoprogressives, radical democratic egalitarians, and socialists. Their stance on debt, at least as manifested in North Carolina, indicates that most agrarians wanted to be liberated from their debts, to have a clean slate, and to have an opportunity to lead productive lives unburdened by debt. They did not manifest a desire to return to informal antebellum credit networks but envisioned a new credit system that incorporated significant government intervention and supervision. Agrarians saw debt, like many North Carolinians before them, as a form of slavery. One of North Carolina's most prominent agrarians, Marion Butler repeatedly compared the plight of the state's farmers to that of slaves. "For my own part," Butler argued, farmers' debts were "nothing less than a question of slavery or freedom."[45] Similarly, an elderly agrarian from Catawba County argued that "North Carolina is oppressed with debt and mortgages. . . . The people of this country have tasted liberty and they never will submit to be enslaved by a few. A revolution must come."[46]

DEBT PLAYED A significant role in the lives of North Carolinians throughout the nineteenth century. Torn between their need for credit and their abhorrence of debt, they employed a variety of strategies to mediate between them. Social and economic upheaval during the Civil War resulted in a fundamental shift in these strategies. Before the Civil War, white North Carolinians overwhelmingly chose strategies that emphasized the relationship between an individual debtor and his or her community. Local networks of credit helped to place the debt in an acceptable social context that reinforced interpersonal bonds. The Civil War decimated this credit system, and in its wake arose a new conception of debt that placed significantly more emphasis on the needs of the individual over those of the community. By declaring bankruptcy or visiting a general store or pawnshop, individuals sought solutions for the problem of credit in ways that were anathema to the antebellum culture of debt. The agrarian revolt at the century's end posed a fundamental but unsuccessful challenge to this new credit system.

Conclusion

I N 1908, at the age of seventy-four, John Brevard Alexander sat at his desk in Charlotte to write his memoirs. In *Reminiscences of the Past Sixty Years*, the Confederate veteran and Mecklenburg County doctor fondly recalled his youth, a period he referred to as "the best days of our Republic" and "a civilization that has never been excelled." He lamented that so much of this antebellum culture had vanished, such that "the civilization of the first half of the 19th century is but a misty remembrance of an almost forgotten period." In Alexander's narrative, the Civil War functioned as "a revolution of gigantic proportions" that cost the South "everything but honor."[1]

Dr. Alexander saw suicide, divorce, and debt as symptomatic of the "Dangers of Civilization" that plagued North Carolina since the Civil War. "In the olden times," Alexander noted, "we seldom heard of divorces—and then it was a long ways from home; but of late years we have a dozen cases in one court." White North Carolinians' understanding of debt, Alexander claimed, had been transformed for the worse since his antebellum childhood. "Fifty years ago dishonesty was under par; money was borrowed and loaned among neighbors without taking a take, or giving any evidence of debt, and to ask what interest was charged would be an insult." He complained that the antebellum culture of debt had become a memory, such that "a man can now live in [an] elegant style—if he wants to, and never pay a just debt." Similarly, suicide symbolized a form of social decay that had infected North Carolina to the extent that "it is patent to all observers that this fearful crime is increasing at a rapid pace."[2]

Suicide, divorce, and debt functioned in Dr. Alexander's narrative as barometers of social conduct and responsibility. He saw the Civil War as a point of deep social and cultural disjuncture, separating an idealized past from a corrupt present. Many black North Carolinians also came to the conclusion that the Civil War had resulted in profound moral upheaval. The nature of this change, however, was radically different from that envisioned by Dr. Alexander and other white North Carolinians. Many black North Carolinians believed that the moral condition of their community had improved dramatically since emancipation and that this improvement was manifested in particular behaviors. Bishop James W. Hood observed in 1884 that "there is no better evidence of a change of heart than a change in our conduct — our manner of life."[3] Despite repeated efforts by whites to keep African Americans from attaining political and economic power, black North Carolinians found solace in the belief that they had achieved significant advances on certain moral questions. "In spite of the present difficulty," noted the *A.M.E. Zion Quarterly Review* in 1902 in the aftermath of a militant white supremacy campaign that disenfranchised most black voters, "the fact remains that the Negro is doing better today than in any time in his history."[4]

Suicide, divorce, and debt can be among the most profound and defining events in an individual's life. This study has argued that they provide a meaningful window into both personal tragedies and broader patterns of social experience. The dramatic changes in both behaviors and attitudes toward suicide, divorce, and debt indicate that the Civil War had lasting repercussions in lives of and opportunities for white and black North Carolinians. From this perspective, the story of nineteenth-century North Carolina is one of deep discontinuity and revolutionary cultural change. Although persuasive continuity narratives can be constructed to describe economic or political conditions over the course of the nineteenth century, at a deeply personal level the Civil War forced white and black North Carolinians to see the world and their place in it with new eyes. This new perspective shaped the ways in which they judged their own conduct and that of others.

Suicide, divorce, and debt also shed light on the complex story of community change over the course of the nineteenth century. Historians have often described the nineteenth century in terms of community decline and collapse. Robert Wiebe famously described this transition as one from isolated "island communities" to a national bureaucratic and impersonal state.[5] His argument mirrored that of nineteenth-century intellectuals and social critics, who worried that modernity heralded the decline of traditional community values. Wiebe and his intellectual descendants envisioned this transformation in fairly linear, unidirectional terms, as localism gradually evolved into cosmopolitanism.

Yet we should hesitate before applying such a broad brush. The term "community," as Thomas Bender has noted, has often proved difficult to define with precision. Communities, even "island communities," can contain very different populations whose experiences, beliefs, and social organizations vary dramatically.[6] Nineteenth-century North Carolina provides a cogent example of such a divided community. Black and white North Carolinians rarely saw themselves as members of a single community. Despite living and working in close physical proximity, white and black North Carolinians lived in separate social and moral worlds. As this study of suicide, divorce, and debt indicates, black and white North Carolinians began the nineteenth century with very different conceptions of the role and meaning of community. Both communities were transformed by the Civil War, as white North Carolinians suffered the tragedy of Confederate defeat and African Americans experienced the elation of emancipation. Both black and white North Carolinians adopted new moral perspectives after the Civil War, taking the communities in divergent directions. The gulf between their two perspectives reflected their radically difference experiences.

This study also opens up broad questions about how white and black North Carolinians' wartime experience shaped their understanding of fundamental social and cultural constructs. Historians have long recognized that wars open up the potential for significant social and cultural change, yet they have not fully explored how the most significant and bloody war in American history could result in momentous and long-term changes in the country's moral, social, and cultural landscape. Drew Faust has recently argued that the unprecedented scale of death and carnage in the American Civil War "planted seeds of a more profound doubt about human ability to know and to understand." She argues that the Civil War experience forced its survivors to assume new identities and worldviews.[7] By examining the Civil War's long chronological shadow, historians will uncover what one North Carolina soldier realized only months into the conflict: that the South had become a "strange world" in which "one does not know what to believe, or what to think. Things have all got into a sort of whirlwind, and are whirling and kicking & jumping around at such a rate, that half the time, a man hardly knows whether he is standing on his head or feet."[8] If this study of suicide, divorce, and debt in North Carolina is any indication, the Civil War will continue to provide fertile ground for social and cultural historians for generations to come.

Appendix

Methodological Problems in Studying the History of Suicide

UNLIKE MANY HISTORICAL STUDIES of suicide, this study does not attempt to enumerate how many North Carolinians took their own lives during the nineteenth century or to calculate a suicide rate for this period. Methods that have proved fruitful in other contexts fail to provide much insight when applied to nineteenth-century North Carolina. For example, coroner's inquests have been used successfully to explore the frequency of suicide in medieval and Victorian England, where suicide resulted in the forfeiture of property to the Crown, resulting in complete and comprehensive records.[1] An examination of nineteenth-century coroner's records from North Carolina, however, reveals that these records pale in comparison in both detail and accuracy with their English counterparts. Whereas suicide in England resulted in specific legal consequences for the deceased's property, North Carolina never enacted legal consequences for taking one's own life.[2] Therefore, while coroner's inquests were required in all possible suicide cases in England, most suicides in North Carolina did not result in a coroner's examination. In several cases, a coroner was called to the scene of a suicide, only to conclude that "the facts in the case deemed an inquest unnecessary and none was held."[3] Furthermore, because coroners operated at the local level without centralized state supervision and oversight, inquest records were infrequently retained, and comparatively few remain in state archives. Coroner's records from many counties are missing entirely. North Carolina's medical community concluded that most coroners were guilty of gross incompetence. An editorial in the *North Carolina Medical Journal* asked, "How is it in North Carolina? Bad enough. In Wilmington, the largest town in the State, the coroner is elected by the people. The choice has fallen for years upon a mulatto man, a barber or barber's apprentice, whose fitness for office is the respect he pays to the advice of educated white persons, and another merit being that he at times uses the prerogative of his office and decides that the county should not be put to the expense of an examination."[4] However, although coroner's records are inadequate for providing a picture of the overall level of suicides in North Carolina, on occasion they provide information unavailable elsewhere, particularly on those rare occasions when witness testimony has been saved along with the coroner's report. North Carolina also fell behind most of the nation in collecting vital statistics, as the state did not record the births and deaths of its citizens until 1913. Therefore, mining public records fails to provide a meaningful assessment of the suicide rate in nineteenth-century North Carolina.

Federal records are equally disappointing. Although the federal census attempted to enumerate suicides after 1850, these records present at best an incomplete picture. As census officials repeatedly admitted, mortality data were among the most difficult to collect, as regular enumeration techniques habitually underestimated the mortality rate. To compensate for this mortality undercount, census officials double-checked their figures with state records. North Carolina, lacking such records, could not employ this method of adjustment and was left with unadjusted figures. Although census records do indicate some increase in suicides during the nineteenth century, on the whole they undercount how many North Carolinians killed themselves during that time. For example, while 1880 census records indicated that only six North Carolinians committed suicide in that year, a combination of other records identifies the names of at least twenty-six suicide victims.[5]

Even if good statistical information were available, suicide data often prove remarkably unreliable. Recent studies indicate that in a significant number of cases modern medical examiners often cannot conclusively determine whether individual deaths were caused by suicide and that the examiners' own prejudices about suicide often determine how they interpret particular cases.[6] Furthermore, in a society in which suicide carried a heavy social stigma, families had a strong incentive to hide suicides from public scrutiny and attribute a family member's death to a less dishonorable cause. Instead of attempting to uncover these hidden suicides, I have employed a simple test to determine whether to include particular cases in this study. I included all those cases in which the death was explicitly referred to as a suicide in the primary sources and excluded all others. This method undoubtedly excluded those suicides that were misattributed or hidden by friends and family from public view. It also excluded those North Carolinians who engaged in chronic behavior that could lead to premature death, such as drug abuse and alcoholism, which some modern psychologists classify as a form of suicide. Despite these limitations, this method provides insight into how nineteenth-century North Carolinians understood suicide. By looking at the ways in which individual North Carolinians described and responded to cases of suicide, one can assess how attitudes toward suicide evolved over time.

Notes

ABBREVIATIONS

DU   Rare Book, Manuscript, and Special Collections Library,
         Perkins Library, Duke University, Durham, North Carolina.
ECU   Special Collections, Joyner Library, East Carolina University,
         Greenville, North Carolina.
NCDAH   North Carolina Department of Archives and History,
         Raleigh, North Carolina.
SHC   Southern Historical Collection, Wilson Library,
         University of North Carolina, Chapel Hill, North Carolina.

INTRODUCTION

1 Reid, "Duty and Destiny of the Church," 175–76.
2 *Raleigh Farmer and Mechanic*, 24 February 1881.
3 Reidy, "Economic Consequences of the Civil War and Reconstruction," 303–17.
4 Camus, *The Myth of Sisyphus and Other Essays*, 3.
5 Erikson, *Wayward Puritans*. Also see Durkheim, *Rules of Sociological Method*, and Durkheim, *Suicide*.
6 Kushner, *Self-Destruction in the Promised Land*; Bell, "Do Not Despair"; Minois, *History of Suicide*; Coontz, *Marriage, a History*; Cott, *Public Vows*; May, *Great Expectations*; Balleisen, *Navigating Failure*; Mann, *Republic of Debtors*; Coleman, *Debtors and Creditors in America*; Sandage, *Born Losers*.
7 Roark, *Masters without Slaves*, 157, 203.
8 On the nineteenth century as a conceptual whole, see Barney, *Passage of the Republic*.
9 Warren, *Legacy of the Civil War*. Also see Ayers, "Worrying about the Civil War," 150–51.

PART I

1 Faust, *This Republic of Suffering*, 57.

2 McPherson, *Battle Cry of Freedom*, 461; Wright, *City under Siege*, 119–20; Thomas, *Confederate State of Richmond*, 55–56, 97; Warren, *Doctor's Experiences in Three Continents*, 293–309; Wiley, *Life of Johnny Reb*, 261–69; Manarin, *North Carolina Troops*, 8:352; Stowe, *Doctoring the South*; Greene, *Civil War Petersburg*, 94–95; Betts, *Experiences of a Civil War Chaplain*, 8; Norris, "'For the Benefit of Our Gallant Volunteers,'" 320–23.

3 *Wilmington Daily Journal*, 27 August 1862; *Richmond Daily Dispatch*, 30 June 1862, 26 August 1862; Alexander, *Reminiscences of the Past Sixty Years*, 71–73; Scrapbooks, Eugene Grissom Papers, DU.

4 *Report of the Board of Directors and Superintendent of the North Carolina Insane Asylum*, 1872, 1877.

5 *Winston-Salem People's Press*, 25 August 1892.

6 Ibid., 19 July 1883.

7 *Raleigh Farmer and Mechanic*, 22 January 1880, 25 November 1880.

8 *Farmer and Mechanic*, 29 January 1880.

9 Ibid., 6 October 1881, 13 October 1881.

10 Ibid., 29 July 1882 and 30 August 1882.

11 Ibid., 11 April 1883.

12 Wyatt-Brown, *Southern Honor*; Greenberg, *Honor and Slavery*; Franklin, *Militant South*; Brundage, *Lynching in the New South*; Edwards, "Law, Domestic Violence, and the Limits of Patriarchal Authority," 733–70; Hackney, "Southern Violence," 906–25; Ayers, *Vengeance and Justice*; Bruce, *Violence and Culture in the Antebellum South*; Vandal, *Rethinking Southern Violence*; Stevenson, "Distress and Discord in Virginia Slave Families"; Forret, "Conflict and the 'Slave Community'"; Gorn, "'Gouge and Bite, Pull Hair and Scratch'"; Baptist, "'My Mind Is to Drown You and Leave You Behind'"; Genovese, *From Rebellion to Revolution*; Aptheker, *American Negro Slave Revolts*; Wood, *Black Majority*.

13 The suicides of a few individual southerners have attracted scholarly attention. See Klotter, *Kentucky Justice, Southern Honor, and American Manhood*; Ruffin, *Diary of Edmund Ruffin*; Allmendinger and Scarborough, "Days Ruffin Died"; and Guice, *By His Own Hand?*

CHAPTER ONE

1 Battle, *History of the University of North Carolina*, 1:80; Minutes of the Philanthropic Society, SHC.

2 *Winston-Salem People's Press*, 3 May 1861.

3 *Highland Messenger*, 2 June 1843.

4 *People's Press*, 25 September 1857.

5 *Raleigh Register*, 2 May 1851.

6 *Highland Messenger*, 24 November 1843.

7 Enoch Faw Diary, 25 October 1858, 5 May 1859, Enoch Faw Papers, DU.

8 H. T. Brown Diary, 11 December 1857, 11 January 1858, Hamilton Brown Papers, SHC. On the biblical injunction against suicide, Brown voiced a common misconception, as neither the Old nor New Testament contains a specific prohibition against suicide and in the case of Samson appears to endorse the act under certain circumstances. Most scholars date the Christian prohibition against suicide from the writings of Saint Augustine. The belief, however, that Christianity prohibited suicide and those who committed suicide were doomed was widespread throughout the South and helped to shape southern attitudes toward self-murder. See "Christianity" in Evans and Farberow, *Encyclopedia of Suicide*, 44–46.

9 *Highland Messenger*, 25 December 1840, 5 September 1845.

10 John Wesley Halliburton to Juliet Halliburton, 14 February 1861, John Wesley Halliburton Papers. SHC.

11 J. Edward Horton to Octavia Wyche Otey, 29 May 1852. Wyche and Otey Family Papers, SHC.

12 Woodbury Wheeler to Kate Wheeler, 19 November 1859. Kate Wheeler Cooper Papers. ECU.

13 Brame, "Folly and Danger of Making a Covenant with Death," 147–48.

14 Sloane, *Last Great Necessity*, 27.

15 Jeter, *Evils of Gaming*, 4.

16 On some the methodological problems associated with fugitive slave and WPA narratives, see Bailey, "Divided Prism"; Blassingame, *Slave Testimony*; and Escott, *Slavery Remembered*.

17 Roper, *Narrative*, 62.

18 Ibid., 68.

19 Grandy, *Narrative of the Life*, 168.

20 There is a lively historiographical debate about the extent to which slave suicide amounted to a form of resistance. See Genovese, *Roll, Jordan, Roll*, 639–40.

21 Grandy, *Narrative of the Life*, 173.

22 Several months later Grandy was able to purchase his son's freedom through an intermediary.

23 Rawick, *American Slave*, 19:182.

24 Ibid., 15(2):333–34.

25 Keckley, *Behind the Scenes*, 30.

26 Ball, *Slavery in the United States*, 69.

27 Ball, *Fifty Years in Chains*, 35.

28 *National Era*, 17 October 1850; Schantz, *Awaiting the Heavenly Country*, 143.

29 *North Star*, 5 September 1850; Schantz, *Awaiting the Heavenly Country*, 143.

30 Schantz, *Awaiting the Heavenly Country*, 151.

31 Ibid., 144.

32 Ball, *Slavery in the United States*, 69–70.

33 Pierson, "White Cannibals, Black Martyrs"; Brown, "Spiritual Terror and Sacred Authority," 180–81.

34 Ball, *Slavery in the United States*, 69.

35 *Rutherford Gazette*, reprinted in *Colored American*, 17 February 1838.

36 Pierson, "White Cannibals, Black Martyrs," 149–52; Gomez, *Exchanging Our Country Marks*, 119–20.

37 Bassett, *Slavery in the State of North Carolina*, 92–93. Although Bassett does not explicitly state on which plantation this event took place, Somerset Place would be a likely candidate.

38 Painter, *Southern History across the Color Line*, 15–39.

39 On slavery as a total institution, see Elkins, *Slavery*. For a discussion of the controversy over Elkins's thesis, see Franklin, "Slavery, Personality, and Black Culture," and Lane, *Debate over Slavery*.

40 Ball, *Slavery in the United States*, 70.

41 Thornton, *Africa and Africans in the Making of the Atlantic World*, 235–71; Mullin, *Africa in America*, 174–212; Sobel, *Trabelin' On*, 3–135; Herskovits, *Myth of the Negro Past*, 207–60.

42 Frey and Wood, *Come Shouting to Zion*, 38.

43 Morgan, *Slave Counterpoint*, 641–42; Pierson, "White Cannibals, Black Martyrs," 152–53, 158; Gomez, *Exchanging Our Country Marks*, 116.

44 Ball, *Slavery in the United States*, 219.

CHAPTER TWO

1 Graves may have left the University of North Carolina to protest the university's reorganization under Republican-appointed Solomon Pool. See Snider, *Light on the Hill*, 74–84.

2 *Raleigh State Chronicle*, July 14, 1889.

3 Charles Spencer Scrapbook, North Carolina Collection, University of North Carolina at Chapel Hill.

4 Winston, "Sketch of the Life and Character of Prof. R. H. Graves." Ralph Graves is buried in a corner of what is now known as the Old Town Cemetery in Chapel Hill. His grave is under a large rock, and several of his family members are buried nearby.

5 *State Chronicle*, 14 July 1889.

59 *Greensboro Record*, 4 April 1904.

60 *Raleigh Christian Advocate*, 6 April 1904.

61 *Charlotte Observer*, 3 April 1904.

62 Charles B. Aycock to Alphonso C. Avery, 4 April 1904; B. F. Long to A. C. Avery, 3 April 1904, Alphonso Calhoun Avery Papers, SHC.

63 Avery, *Idle Comments*, vii, xii.

64 Ibid., 244–46.

65 For examples of black suicide, see *State Chronicle*, 1 April 1893; *People's Press*, 7 July 1881; and *State Chronicle*, 12 April 1889.

66 Botkin, *Lay My Burden Down*, 183.

67 Chesnutt, "Dave's Neckliss," 90–102; Andrews, *Literary Career of Charles W. Chesnutt*, 66; Stepto, "'Simple but Intensely Human Inner Life of Slavery,'" 29–55.

68 Simmons, *Men of Mark*, 366 (emphasis in original). On Whitaker's attempted suicide, see Shellum, *Black Cadet in a White Bastion*, 44–45.

69 On the role of religion as a protective factor against black suicide, see Early, *Religion and Suicide in the African-American Community*.

70 Rhodes, "Suicide"; Bigelow, "Aesthetics of Suicide"; Hamilton, "Suicide in Large Cities"; Bailey, "Suicide in the United States"; MacDonald, "Civilization and Suicide." Also see Kushner, "Suicide, Gender, and the Fear of Modernity."

71 The institution now known as Dorothea Dix Hospital underwent several name changes during the nineteenth century. For the sake of clarity, I have chosen to refer to it as the North Carolina Insane Asylum throughout this book. Both the Western North Carolina Asylum at Morganton and the Eastern (Colored) North Carolina Insane Asylum at Goldsboro were chartered in 1874, though Goldsboro did not admit its first patients until 1880 and Morganton until 1883. The institution at Morganton is now known as Broughton State Hospital. Goldsboro has been renamed Cherry State Hospital. A handful of small private asylums opened at the end of the nineteenth century. However, because they tended to treat only mild forms of mental illness, suicidal patients were uniformly sent to state-run institutions.

72 On the early history of insane asylums in the United States, see Grob, *Mental Institutions in America*. On the South Carolina Lunatic Asylum, see McCandless, *Moonlight, Magnolias, Madness*. On the Eastern Lunatic Asylum in Virginia, see Zwelling, *Quest for a Cure*.

73 Cahow, *People, Patients, and Politics*, 21–26.

74 Glob, *Mental Institutions in America*, 248–51; Zwelling, *Quest for a Cure*, 48.

75 *Report of the Board of Directors and Superintendent of the North Carolina Insane Asylum*, 1857.

76 *Report of the Board of Directors and Superintendent of the North Carolina Insane Asylum*, 1858.

77 *Report of the Board of Directors and Superintendent of the North Carolina Insane Asylum*, 1865.

78 *Report of the Board of Directors and Superintendent of the North Carolina Insane Asylum*, 1866.

79 Eugene Grissom Papers, DU; *Charlotte Observer*, 29 July 1902; *Oxford Public Ledger*, 31 July 1902.

80 Daniels, *Tar Heel Editor*, 417–18. For the details of the various coup attempts, see the scrapbooks in Eugene Grissom Papers, DU.

81 *Report of the Board of Directors and Superintendent of the North Carolina Insane Asylum*, 1871. Also see Alexander, *Reminiscences of the Past Sixty Years*, 207.

82 Murphy, "Care of the Insane and the Treatment and Prognosis of Insanity," 70.

83 "What Cases of Insanity Shall We Treat at Home?" 192.

84 *Report of the Board of Directors and Superintendent of the Western North Carolina Insane Asylum*, 1887.

85 Undated newspaper clipping, Patrick L. Murphy Papers, SHC. On Murphy's philosophy of treatment, see Getz, "'Strong Man of Large Human Sympathy.'"

86 Grissom, "Mechanical Protection for the Violent Insane," 30, 52–53. On the transatlantic aspects of the debate over the use of restraints on asylum patients, see Tomes, "Great Restraint Controversy."

87 Case Files, North Carolina Insane Asylum, NCDAH.

88 "Sketch of Michael Cosgrove," 15–18, North Carolina Collection, University of North Carolina at Chapel Hill; Register of Admissions, Eugene Grissom Papers, DU.

89 Grissom, "Leonard Medical School Commencement Address." The Shaw University Leonard Medical School opened in 1882, becoming the first professional medical school for African Americans in the South. See Savitt, "Education of Black Physicians at Shaw University."

90 "News and Items," *North Carolina Medical Journal* 43 (May 1899): 369.

91 McDuffie, "Few Thoughts on the Subdivisions of Insanity," 213.

92 McDuffie's account bears a strong resemblance to the theories proposed by French sociologist Émile Durkheim. See Durkheim, *Suicide*. For a modern assessment of Durkheim's work, see Lester, *Émile Durkheim*, and Pickering and Walford, *Durkheim's Suicide*.

93 Quotations in this paragraph and the next are from "Suicide in the United States," *North Carolina Medical Journal* 49 (December 1903): 615–17.

94 Roberts, "Insanity in the Colored Race," 258. Also see Alexander, *Reminiscences of the Past Sixty Years*, 134, 207, 229–33.

95 "Superintendent's Report for the Eastern North Carolina Insane Asylum", 1883, 12.

96 Admission Log Book, 22 November 1883, Eastern North Carolina Insane Asylum (Cherry Hospital), Cherry Hospital Museum, Goldsboro, North Carolina.

97 "Superintendent's Report for the Eastern North Carolina Insane Asylum",
   1884, 14–15.
98 Miller, "Effects of Emancipation," 287, 293.
99 Babcock, "Colored Insane," 168.
100 Hughes, "Labeling and Treating Black Mental Illness in Alabama," 447–48;
   Haller, "Physician versus the Negro," 164–65; Bannister and Hektoen, "Race
   and Insanity," 463.
101 Quoted in Miller, "Effects of the Emancipation," 286.
102 Babcock, "Colored Insane," 168.
103 Alexander, *Reminiscences of the Past Sixty Years*, 233.
104 Roberts, "Insanity in the Colored Race," 259.
105 Roberts's claim that African Americans' absence from mercantile life protected them from suicide parallels an argument made by Émile Durkheim.
   According to Durkheim, both financial losses and gains increased the likelihood of suicide. Durkheim, *Suicide*, 246.

CHAPTER THREE

1 Dean, *Shook over Hell*, 4.
2 Ibid., 42. The wide range of estimates depends on the criteria employed in different studies to define PTSD.
3 Farberow, "Combat Experience and Postservice Psychosocial Status"; Langone, "War that Has No Ending"; Dean, *Shook over Hell*, 17–18.
4 Pollack, "Estimating the Number of Suicides among Vietnam Veterans."
5 Boscarino, "Posttraumatic Stress Disorder and Mortality among U.S.
   Army Veterans."
6 Coleman, *Flashback*. For a recent survey of the literature on PTSD suicide
   among Vietnam War veterans, see Shay, *Odysseus in America*, 290–91.
7 Wiley, *Life of Johnny Reb*, 34–35; Sword, *Southern Invincibility*, 201–3. Also see
   Hess, *Union Soldier in Battle*, 110–17.
8 Foster, "Coming to Terms with Defeat," 20–22. On the Lost Cause, see Foster,
   Ghosts of the Confederacy, and Reagan, *Baptized in Blood*.
9 Howe, *Touched with Fire*, 149–50. Also see Hess, *Union Soldier in Battle*,
   68–72.
10 Dean, *Shook over Hell*, 100–114. Also see Brandt, *Pathway to Hell*.
11 Researchers quantified the degree of traumatic experience by employing several variables, including POW experience, being wounded, early age at enlistment, and the percentage of soldiers who died in a recruit's company (i.e.,
   percentage of company killed). Pizzaro, Silver, and Prouse, "Physical and
   Mental Costs of Traumatic War Experience among Civil War Veterans."
12 Manarin, *North Carolina Troops*, 5:20; Chapman, *More Terrible than Victory*,
   215.

13 Register of Artificial Limbs, 1866–1870, NCDAH; Wegner, *Phantom Pain*, 248–49.

14 *Charlotte Observer*, 14 June 1881; *Raleigh Farmer and Mechanic*, 16 June 1881.

15 Manarin, *North Carolina Troops*, 8:336.

16 Patient Records, North Carolina State Insane Asylum, NCDAH.

17 In addition to the nearly one hundred North Carolinians who fought for the Confederacy, at least three of those who killed themselves after 1865 in North Carolina fought for the Union. Of those who fought for the Confederacy, a significant number were members of the officer corps. Approximately one-third of these suicidal Confederate veterans were commissioned officers, including eight captains, two colonels, three sergeants, one major, one corporal, and one lieutenant.

18 Ready, *Tar Heel State*, 217.

19 Dean, *Shook over Hell*, 79–81; Sutker et al., "Person and Situation Correlates of Post Traumatic Stress Disorder among POW Survivors," 912–14; Tanielian and Jaycox, *Invisible Wounds of War*.

20 Manarin, *North Carolina Troops*, 11:332; *Winston-Salem People's Press*, 22 June 1870.

21 Manarin, *North Carolina Troops*, 1:326; *People's Press*, 4 November 1870.

22 Manarin, *North Carolina Troops*, 4:287; *Hillsborough Recorder*, 4 July 1877. On conditions at Fort Lookout, see Beitzell, *Point Lookout Prison Camp for Confederates*.

23 Tanielian and Jaycox, *Invisible Wounds of War*, 5–6; Mental Health Advisory Team (MHAT) V, Operation Iraqi Freedom, (2008), 38–47.

24 Reid, "USCT Veterans in Post–Civil War North Carolina," 409–10.

25 Glatthaar, *Forged in Battle*, 237–43.

26 *Raleigh Register*, 9 October 1861.

27 *Wilmington Daily Journal*, 18 May 1864.

28 *People's Press*, 21 April 1864; *Daily Journal*, 26 April 1864.

29 Gould, Wallenstein, and Davidson, "Suicide Clusters"; Wasserman, "Imitation and Suicide"; Coleman, *Suicide Clusters*; Phillips, "Influence of Suggestion on Suicide"; Durkheim, *Suicide*, 141.

30 White, *North Carolina Folklore*, 7:7.

31 Scott, *Ministerial Directory of the Presbyterian Church, US 1861-1941*, 771; Latta, *History of Little River Presbyterian Church*, 6–7; *People's Press*, 16 May 1872, 10 October 1873, 27 July 1876; *Hillsboro Recorder*, 14 August 1861, 26 May 1869, 21 June 1888; *Raleigh State Chronicle*, 29 July 1890; *Farmer and Mechanic*, 13 October 1881.

32 *People's Press*, 12 July 1883, 19 July 1883; *Farmer and Mechanic*, 1 August 1883. The passage from the *Winston Sentinel* was quoted in the *Farmer and Mechanic*.

33 *People's Press*, 13 May 1875.

34 *People's Press*, 14 October 1886.

35 *Farmer and Mechanic*, 23 June 1881.

36 *Hillsborough Recorder*, 24 September 1873; *People's Press*, 2 October 1873; *Farmer and Mechanic*, 13 October 1881.

37 Manarin, *North Carolina Troops*, 11:116; *People's Press*, 20 January 1871.

38 *People's Press*, 13 November 1890.

39 Fanny Whitaker was among North Carolina's most active clubwomen in the 1890s, particularly in the North Carolina Society of the Daughters of the Revolution. Her social activities and five young children probably account for her absence from the house during the Graves's residence. See Moffitt, "Biographical Sketch of Mrs. Spier Whitaker nee Hooper."

40 *News and Observer*, 2 July 1889; *Raleigh Observer*, 5 July 1889.

41 Daniels, *Tar Heel Editor*, 417.

42 Ibid., 420.

43 *News and Observer*, 27–30 June 1889.

44 Daniels, *Tar Heel Editor*, 420. Unbeknownst to Grissom, Daniels had long distrusted him and had been instrumental in convincing one of his accusers to bring the charges against him.

45 *News and Observer*, 9 July 1889.

46 Ibid., 11 July 1889.

47 Haywood, "Speech for the Defense," Pamphlet Collection, Special Collections, DU.

48 *News and Observer*, 16 July 1889.

49 *State Chronicle*, 26 July 1889.

50 *News and Observer*, 23 July 1889.

51 Ibid., 10 August 1889.

52 Ibid., 23 August 1889.

53 Daniels, *Tar Heel Editor*, 431.

54 Eugene Grissom to Albion W. Tourgée, undated (probably 1895), Albion Winegar Tourgée Papers (microfilm).

55 *Washington Post*, 28 July 1902.

56 Eugene Grissom to Albion W. Tourgée, undated (probably 1895), Albion Winegar Tourgée Papers (microfilm).

57 *News and Observer*, 29 July 1902; *Washington Post*, 28 July 1902.

58 *Raleigh Morning Post*, 29 July 1902.

59 *Charlotte Observer*, 29 July 1902.

PART II

1 *Adeline G. Dupree v. F. M. Dupree* (1885), Pitt County Divorce Records, NCDAH.

2 Earlier letter from Lorenzo to Addie, now lost, quoted in Addie to Lorenzo,

26 February 1896, Tabitha Marie DeVisconti Papers, ECU (emphasis in original).

3 Lorenzo to Addie, 26 May 1898, Tabitha Marie DeVisconti Papers, ECU (emphasis in original).

4 Ibid.

5 Addie to Lorenzo, 26 February 1896, Tabitha Marie DeVisconti Papers, ECU.

6 *Raleigh Morning Post*, 28 August 1901.

7 *Greenville Daily Reflector*, 29 August, 1901; *Morning Post*, 28 August 1901. Libbey was a popular author of dime store novels, most of which focused on the redeeming virtue of marriage for young women.

8 *Eastern Reflector*, 5 April 1901.

9 From the beginning, North Carolina law recognized two forms of divorce. The first, known as divorce a mensa et thoro ("bed and bath"), would today commonly be referred to as a legal separation. The second, known as divorce a vinculo matrimonii, severed the marital bonds entirely. The key distinction between the two forms of divorce was that remarriage was possible in the latter but not the former, and the standards for obtaining absolute divorce were consequentially more rigorous. Because the vast majority of the debate concerning divorce in North Carolina focused on absolute divorce (a vinculo matrimonii) and the issue of remarriage was fundamental to many of these debates, the term "divorce" in this study will refer to absolute divorce unless otherwise qualified. On abandonment during the late nineteenth century, see Schwartzberg, "'Lots of Them Did That.'"

CHAPTER FOUR

1 Censer, *North Carolina Planters and Their Children*, 72.

2 "Marriage and Divorce," *Southern Quarterly Review* 26 (1854): 332, 352–53.

3 *Raleigh Register*, 8 June 1809.

4 *Whittington v. Whittington*, 19 N.C. 65 (1836).

5 *Wood v.* Wood, 27 N.C. 553 (1845). On Ruffin, see Bardaglio, *Reconstructing the Household*, 17, 33–34; Bynum, *Unruly Women*, 68–70.

6 *Hansley v. Hansley*, 10 Ire. 509 (1849).

7 Bynum, *Unruly Women*, 60–62; Clinton, *Plantation Mistress*, 59–77.

8 *Joyner v. Joyner*, 59 N.C. 331 (1862).

9 Lebsock, *Free Women of Petersburg*, 54–86.

10 McCurry, *Masters of Small Worlds*, 86–91.

11 Censer, "'Smiling through Her Tears'"; Bynum, *Unruly Women*, 68–77; Clinton, *Plantation Mistress*, 79–82; Wyatt-Brown, *Southern Honor*, 242–47, 283–91, 300–307; Bardaglio, *Reconstructing the Household*, 33–34.

12 Laura Edwards persuasively argues that localized law, an embodiment of local knowledge, custom, and reputation, was often more important than state stat-

ues in determining the legality and permissibility of divorce. Edwards, *People and Their Peace*, 169–71, 213–14, 244–47.

13 Johnson, *Ante-Bellum North Carolina*, 217.

14 Schauinger, "William Gaston," 127–28. Also see Chused, *Private Acts in Public Spaces*, 9–11.

15 Basch, *Framing American Divorce*, 214 n. 4.

16 Extant records indicate that approximately 90 percent of antebellum Indiana divorces were granted for adultery or abandonment, which were also grounds for divorce in North Carolina. Wires, *The Divorce Issue and Reform in Nineteenth-Century Indiana*; Basch, "Relief in the Premises"; Riley, *Divorce*, 62–67; Cott, *Public Vows*, 50–55.

17 *Stacy Woodard v. William Woodard* (1845), *Polly Pearson v. Noah Pearson* (1835), Macon County Divorce Records, NCDAH; *John Wells v. Mary Ann Wells* (1843), Orange County Divorce Records, NCDAH.

18 This geographic profile is drawn mainly from Sharpe, *New Geography of North Carolina*.

19 *Lucetta McPherson v. George W. McPherson* (1898), Hyde County Divorce Records, NCDAH.

20 See, for instance, *Horne v. Horne*, 72 N.C. 530 (1875).

21 James L. Fleming to Prof. C. H. James, 1 February 1907, James L. Fleming Papers, ECU. North Carolina adopted no-fault divorce in 1965.

22 Adeline May to Lozenzo DeVisconti, 26 February 1896, Tabitha Marie DeVisconti Papers, ECU.

23 *Everton v. Everton*, 50 N.C. 202 (1857); *Everton v. Everton*, Perquimans County Divorce Records, NCDAH.

24 On the public spectacle aspects of court days, see Gross, *Double Character*, 22–46; Burton, *In My Father's House Are Many Mansions*, 28–29; Edwards, "Status without Rights," 378–81; and Roeber, "Authority, Law, and Custom."

25 Edwards, *People and Their Peace*, 169.

26 Rable, *Civil Wars*, 11–12.

27 *Prudence Briggs v. William G. Briggs* (1849), Wayne County Divorce Records, NCDAH.

28 *Martha Trice v. Zachariah Trice* (1843), Orange County Divorce Records, NCDAH.

29 *Amy Gilmore v. Stephen Gilmore* (1828), Orange County Divorce Records, NCDAH.

30 *Lemuel Ivey v. Harriett Ivey* (1837), Perquimans County Divorce Records, NCDAH.

31 *Green Partin v. Mary Partin* (1841), Orange County Divorce Records, NCDAH.

32 *Barnabas O'Fairhill v. Nancy O'Fairhill* (1831), Orange County Divorce Records, NCDAH.

33 *William Jackson v. Lucinda Jackson* (1842), Orange County Divorce Records, NCDAH.

34 *Willie Stagg v. Lucy Stagg* (1851), Orange County Divorce Records, NCDAH.

35 Smith, "Church Organization as an Agency of Social Control," 118; Lamb, *Historical Sketch of Hay St. Methodist Episcopal Church, South*, 14–15.

36 Paschal, *History of North Carolina Baptists* 2:228–29; Cove Creek Baptist Church, membership list, Southern Baptist Historical Library and Archives (microfilm).

37 Jean Friedman has argued that North Carolina churches punished women more severely for sexual offenses. However, her evidence focuses on adultery, abortion, and fornication rather than divorce. Friedman, *Enclosed Garden*, 13–18.

38 Because divorce records provide no identifying features of the litigants other than their name, identifying divorced individuals in census records can be challenging. To calculate this figure, I compared all divorced persons between 1820 and 1860 in the five counties under examination with the next census returns. However, I excluded those with very common names and those identified only by initials.

39 On the transfer of cultural practices concerning marriage from Africa to North Carolina, see Kay and Cary, *Slavery in North Carolina*, 155–60. They suggest that West African cultures displayed a variety of attitudes toward divorce. Also see Mullin, *Africa in America*, 159–73, and Roberts, "Yoruba Family, Gender, and Kinship Roles in New World Slavery," 248–59.

40 Fraser, *Courtship and Love among the Enslaved in North Carolina*, 32–51, 88–100; O'Neil, "Bosses and Broomsticks."

41 Gutman, *Black Family in Slavery and Freedom*, 18–21, 35–6, 145–59; Blassingame, *Slave Community*, 361; Stevenson, "Distress and Discord in Virginia Slave Families," 103–24.

42 Gutman, *Black Family in Slavery and Freedom*, 572 n. 17; Sitterson, "William J. Minor Plantations," 69; Blassingame, *Slave Community*, 152.

43 Gutman, *Black Family in Slavery and Freedom*, 159.

44 Ibid., 158.

45 Labinjoh, "Sexual Life of the Oppressed," 377.

46 Rawick, *American Slave*, 14(1): 360.

47 Raboteau, *Slave Religion*, 184.

48 Gutman, *The Black Family in Slavery and Freedom*, 287.

49 Logan, *Sketches, Historical and Biographical, of the Broad River and King's Mountain Baptist Associations*, 38.

50 Grandy, *Narrative of the Life*, 165.

51 West, *Chains of Love*, 62–65.

52 Redpath, *Roving Editor*, 117.

53 Gutman, *Black Family in Slavery and Freedom*, 270–73.

54 Ibid., 275.

55 Genovese, *Roll, Jordan, Roll*, 464, 472.

56 Durrill, "Slavery, Kinship, and Dominance," 11.

57 McDaniel, *Stagville*; Gutman, *Black Family in Slavery and Freedom*, 169–84.

58 Alexander, *Reminiscences of the Past Sixty Years*, 245.

59 Griffin, "'Goin' Back Over There to See That Girl'"; West, "Surviving Separation."

60 White, *Ar'n't I a Woman*, 156–57; Frankel, *Freedom's Women*, 12.

61 Rawick, *American Slave*, 15:435.

62 Redpath, *Roving Editor*, 27.

63 Regosin, *Freedom's Promise*, 89–92; Stevenson, "Distress and Discord in Virginia Slave Families," 118.

64 On the legal, political, and social questions involved in marriages between free blacks and slaves, see Uzzell, "Free Negro/Slave Marriages and Family Life in Ante-Bellum North Carolina."

65 Franklin, *Free Negro in North Carolina*, 185.

66 Lebsock, *Free Women of Petersburg*, 87–111.

67 Johnson and Roark, "Strategies of Survival," 92–93.

68 Franklin, *Free Negro in North Carolina*, 185.

CHAPTER FIVE

1 Quotations in this paragraph and the next two paragraphs are from *James M. Wells v. Nancy J. Wells* (1867), Orange County Divorce Records, NCDAH; Manarin, *North Carolina Troops*, 4:367.

2 Gutman, *Black Family in Slavery and Freedom*, 420–21; Evans, *Ballots and Fence Rails*, 92; White, *Somebody Knows My Name*, 2:775.

3 On the forced separation of slave families during the Civil War, see Mohr, *On the Threshold of Freedom*, 104–7.

4 Penningroth, *Claims of Kinfolk*, 163.

5 Berlin, Miller, and Rowland, "Afro-American Families in the Transition from Slavery to Freedom," 90.

6 Click, *Time Full of Trial*, 39; Mobley, *James City*, 9–10; Wiley, *Southern Negroes*, 203–9.

7 Conway, "Marrying on Roanoke Island."

8 Click, *Time Full of Trial*, 101.

9 Frankel, *Freedom's Women*, 93.

10 Rawick, *American Slave*, 14:221.

11 *New York Tribune*, 8 September 1865.

12 Rawick, *American Slave*, 15:188, 195.

13 Gutman, *Black Family in Slavery and Freedom*, 415.

14 J. E. Eldridge to Agt. Freedmen's Bureau, Wilmington, N.C., 29 July 1867, Let-

ters Received, ser. 2892, Wilmington, N.C. Records of the Assistant Commissioner for the State of North Carolina, Bureau of Refugees, Freedmen, and Abandoned Lands, 1865–1870 (microfilm).

15 Edwards, "'Marriage Covenant,'" 90–91.

16 Litwack, *Been in the Storm So Long*, 240.

17 *Report of the Joint Committee on Reconstruction*, 2:190.

18 Schwalm, *Hard Fight for We*, 242, 250; Crouch, "'Chords of Love,'" 334–51.

19 *Report of the Joint Committee on Reconstruction*, 2:170.

20 Dennett, *South As It Is*, 164.

21 This was the case in Alabama, Arkansas, Florida, Mississippi, Tennessee, Texas, and Virginia.

22 This doctrine held sway in Georgia and South Carolina.

23 Only Kentucky's marriage registration law bore any resemblance to the ordinance passed in North Carolina.

24 This figure reflects those in extant records. Given that the records from thirty-four counties are missing, the total number is undoubtedly much higher. White, *Somebody Knows My Name*, 1:xiv–xvii. Also see Gutman, *Black Family in Slavery and Freedom*, 415–16.

25 Gutman, *Black Family in Slavery and Freedom*, 412–18.

26 Edwards, *Gendered Strife and Confusion*, 54; Shaffer, "In the Shadow of the Old Constitution," 61.

27 Shaffer, "In the Shadow of the Old Constitution" 62. Comparing slave marriages mentioned in WPA ex-slave narratives with extant records of marriage registration indicates that many happily married couples did not register their union. See Rawick, *American Slave*, 1:220, 287–89, 2:32–33, 408. The registration of slave marriages is not mentioned in the vast majority of ex-slave narratives.

28 Litwack, *Been in the Storm So Long*, 242.

29 Shaffer, "In the Shadow of the Old Constitution," 64.

30 Litwack, *Been in the Storm So Long*, 241. Also see Rose, *Rehearsal for Reconstruction*, 236; Crouch, "'Chords of Love,'" 340.

31 Gutman, *Black Family in Slavery and Freedom*, 420.

32 Rawick, *American Slave*, 14:135–37.

33 On the stress to southern marriages caused by physical separation during the Civil War, see Whites, *Civil War as a Crisis in Gender*, 31–40. On how the Civil War caused white divorces outside the South, see Basch, *Framing American Divorce*, 80, 128–30.

34 Faust, *Mothers of Invention*, 139.

35 Ibid., 31.

36 Rable, *Civil Wars*, 51.

37 On antebellum white southern courting rituals, see Stowe, *Intimacy and Power in the Old South*, 50–121, and Clinton, *Plantation Mistress*, 59–69.

38 Rable, *Civil Wars*, 51–54; Faust, *Mothers of Invention*, 145–52.

39 Escott, "Poverty and Governmental Aid for the Poor in Confederate North Carolina"; Gross, "'And for the Widow and Orphan.'"

40 *John Bowling v. Elizabeth Bowling* (1867), Orange County Divorce Records, NCDAH; Manarin, *North Carolina Troops*, 2:171.

41 *Willie Couch v. Emma Couch* (1868), Orange County Divorce Records, NCDAH; Manarin, *North Carolina Troops*, 1:446, 587.

42 *Eli Patton v. Margaret Patton* (1866), Macon County Divorce Records, NCDAH.

43 *Joseph J. Shepard v. Charlotte Shepard* (1867), Macon County Divorce Records, NCDAH.

44 *Mary Herndon v. Chesley Herndon* (1867), Orange County Divorce Records, NCDAH; Manarin, *North Carolina Troops* 4:476.

45 Clinton, "'Public Women' and Sexual Politics during the American Civil War."

46 Hamilton, *Reconstruction in North Carolina*, 253–72; Zuber, *North Carolina during Reconstruction*, 15–19; Bernstein, "Participation of Negro Delegates in the Constitutional Convention of 1868 in North Carolina"; Zipf, "'Whites Shall Rule the Land or Die.'"

47 Powell, *Dictionary of North Carolina Biography*, 5:243–44.

48 *Journal of the Constitutional Convention of the State of North Carolina at Its Session 1868*, 119; *North Carolina Daily Standard*, 3 February 1868.

49 *Daily Standard*, 3 February 1868.

50 Ibid., 5 February 1868.

51 Petition of Martha Hopkins, 15 January 1868, Secretary of State Records, Papers of the Constitutional Convention of 1868, NCDAH; R. D. Hart to W. B. Rodman, 15 January 1868, William Blount Rodman Papers, ECU; Zipf, "No Longer under Cover(ture)," 193.

52 *Daily Standard*, 7 February 1868.

53 Ibid., 5 March 1868, Hamilton, *Reconstruction in North Carolina*, 271.

54 *Daily Standard*, 3 March 1868.

55 *Journal of the Constitutional Convention*, 446.

56 Letterpress books P: 232. Calvin J. Cowles Papers, NCDAH.

57 Petition, 26 February 1868, Secretary of State Records, Papers of the Constitutional Convention of 1868, NCDAH.

58 Undated petition, Secretary of State Records, Papers of the Constitutional Convention of 1868, NCDAH.

59 W. W. King to A. W. Tourgée, 2 March 1868, Albion Winegar Tourgée Papers (microfilm).

60 *Daily Standard*, 3 March 1868.

61 Zipf, "No Longer under Cover(ture)," 207–9.

62 *Daily Standard*, 7 February 1868. On Harris, see Powell, *Dictionary of North Carolina Biography*, 3:53.

63 *Journal of the Constitutional Convention*, 465, 467.

64 Undated petition, Secretary of State Records, Papers of the Constitutional Convention of 1868, NCDAH.

65 For instance, the Virginia legislature, which retained legislative divorce until 1851, granted divorces to only one in five petitions. Buckley, *Great Catastrophe of My Life*, 23.

66 *James C. Long v. Teresa H. Long*, 77 N.C. 304 (1877).

CHAPTER SIX

1 Willcox, *Divorce Problem*, 36.

2 Bynum, "Reshaping the Bonds of Womanhood," 320–33.

3 For examples, see *Rebecca Barbee v. November Barbee* (1872), *Nash Booth v. Peter Booth* (1875), *Martha Couch v. Alex Couch* (1892), *Susan Nichols v. Charles Nichols* (1871), in Orange Country Divorce Records, NCDAH.

4 Bureau of the Census, *Marriage and Divorce*, 1:277, 302, 323.

5 Men also initiated the majority of divorce cases in South Carolina during the brief period during which that state allowed divorce. However, the small number of divorce cases there pale in comparison with neighboring states.

6 Bureau of the Census, *Marriage and Divorce*, 1:86.

7 *Horne v. Horne*, 72 N.C. 489 (1875).

8 To a certain extent, this rhetorical shift may reflect a greater professionalization of the law during the nineteenth century and a dramatic increase in the number of lawyers practicing in North Carolina after the Civil War. However, there is no discernible way from the extant divorce records to determine whether the use of lawyers in divorce cases increased significantly after the Civil War. The fact that divorce petitions for those who did and those who did not employ lawyers after 1870 are largely indistinguishable in form or tone indicates that the effect of increased involvement of lawyers in the divorce process was negligible. Further, many antebellum divorce petitioners who did employ a lawyer's services still produced divorce petitions dripping with pathos. On the numerical increase of lawyers in North Carolina, see Hendricks, *Seeking Liberty and Justice*, 21–31, 39. On professionalization and use of lawyers see Edwards, "Status without Rights," 374–75.

9 *Raleigh News and Observer*, 10 March 1905.

10 Arrington, *Is Justice a Farce?* 2.

11 Beard, *My Own Life*, 1–2.

12 Arrington, *Is Justice a Farce?* 31.

13 J. Howard Jones to Mrs. March, 21 May 1881, J. Howard Jones Papers, DU.

14 Wright, *Report on Marriage and Divorce in the United States*, 132.

15 Bureau of the Census, *Marriage and Divorce*, 1:20–25.

16 Willcox, *Divorce Problem*, 29–32.

17 Bureau of the Census, *Marriage and Divorce*, 1:25.

18 Shaffer, "In the Shadow of the Old Constitution," 66; Rachleff, *Black Labor in the South*, 23.

19 Wheeler, *Uplifting the Race*. On the role of uplift for A.M.E. Zion ministers in North Carolina, especially with reference to temperance, see Harper, "Ballot or the Bottle." Also see Penningroth, *Claims of Kinfolk*, 182, and Edwards, *Gendered Strife and Confusion*, 56.

20 *Star of Zion*, 11 September 1885.

21 *A.M.E. Zion Quarterly Review* 2 (1892): 244.

22 Price, "Education and the Race Problem," 67.

23 Price, "Times Demand the Elevation of the Educational Standard of the Negro Ministry," 71.

24 Price, "Temperance Mission Work among the Colored People of the South," 288–89.

25 Yandle, "Joseph Charles Price and His 'Particular Work.'"

26 Price, "Times Demand the Elevation of the Educational Standard of the Negro Ministry," 72.

27 Hood, *One Hundred Years of the African Methodist Episcopal Zion Church*, 156–57.

28 Wills, *Democratic Religion*, 68–69, 81–82.

29 Whitted, *History of Negro Baptists in North Carolina*, 98–99.

30 Hood, *One Hundred Years of the African Methodist Episcopal Zion Church*, 157.

31 Clinton, *Christianity under the Searchlight*, 86–87.

32 "Minutes of Baptist Education and Missionary Convention," 1901, in *African-American Baptist Annual Reports, North Carolina*, 21.

33 *Star of Zion*, 5 February 1886.

34 Northrup, Gay, and Penn, *College of Life*, 115, 128.

35 *Star of Zion*, 11 September 1885.

36 Quoted in W. E. B. DuBois, *Negro Church*, 179.

37 Crummell, "Losses of the Race," 25–28.

38 Edwards, *Gendered Strife and Confusion*, 56–57; Edwards, "Marriage Covenant," 100, 108; Frankel, *Freedom's Women*, 79–108.

39 *Haywood Hargrove v. Harriett Hargrove* (1899), Orange County Divorce Records, NCDAH.

40 Edwards, *Gendered Strife and Confusion*, 57–58.

41 Edwards, "Marriage Covenant", 108.

42 Penningroth, "African American Divorce in Virginia and Washington, D.C.," 23–25.

43 On the topics addressed in white Protestant sermons in North Carolina during this period, see Jenkins, "Rhetorics of Discontent," 66–68, 123. Baptists in Georgia seemed to be more aware of divorce than their neighbors in North Carolina. See Spain, *At Ease in Zion*, 206.

44 Wills, *Democratic Religion*, 116–17; Shore "Church Discipline in Ten Baptist Churches"; Stroupe, "'Cite Them Both to Attend the Next Church Conference,'" 169.

45 *James C. Long v. Teresa H. Long*, 77 N.C. 304 (1877).

46 On the rise of the contractual conception of marriage and family in southern jurisprudence, see Bardaglio, *Reconstructing the Household*, 137–75.

47 *Cornelia A. R. Jackson v. Daniel Jackson*, 105 N.C. 433 (1890).

48 *James C. Long v. Teresa H. Long*, 77 N.C. 304 (1877).

49 *News and Observer*, 24 February 1889.

50 *Biblical Recorder*, 1 May 1889.

51 "The Law of Marriage and Divorce."

52 Foster, "Gentleman Prophet"; Powell, *Dictionary of North Carolina Biography*, 1:363–65.

53 Sermon #239/309, Joseph Blount Cheshire Papers, SHC.

54 On the origins of the Social Gospel among white North Carolina Baptists, see Starnes, "Is There a Balm in Gilead?"

55 Bode, *Protestantism and the New South*, 44–47.

56 Ibid., 125.

57 Charles W. Blanchard, "Divorcements," *Biblical Recorder*, 18 September 1901.

58 On Cheshire's racial attitudes and race relations within the Episcopal Church in North Carolina, see Foster, "Bishop Cheshire and Black Participation in the Episcopal Church."

59 *News and Observer*, 24 November 1904.

60 Sims, *Power of Femininity in the New South*, 21, 45, 65–66.

61 "Bishop Cheshire's Hostility to Easy Divorce," undated and unattributed newspaper clipping, Joseph Blount Cheshire Papers, SHC.

62 See, for instance, *News and Observer*, 12 March 1895, 14 March 1895, 1 February 1899.

63 Sermon #239/309, Joseph Blount Cheshire Papers, SHC.

64 "Bishop Cheshire's Hostility to Easy Divorce," undated and unattributed newspaper clipping, Joseph Blount Cheshire Papers, SHC.

65 *News and Observer*, 26 March 1904.

66 *Durham Daily Sun*, 25–26 March 1904; *News and Observer*, 26 March 1904, 23 November 1904.

67 *News and Observer*, 27 March 1904.

68 Ibid., 13–17, 24 November 1904, 2–3 December 1904.

69 Ibid., 13 November 1904.

70 Ibid., 17 November 1904.

71 Ibid., 13 November 1904.

72 Charles B. Aycock to J. B. Cheshire, 9 December 1904, Joseph Blount Cheshire Papers, NCDAH.

73 Connor, *Life and Speeches of Charles Brantley Aycock*, 186.

74 *News and Observer*, 6 January 1905.

75 Ibid., 7 January 1905.

76 Ibid., 12 January 1905.

77 Ibid., 17–18 January 1905.

78 Ibid., 7 February 1905.

79 Ibid., 12 February 1905.

80 *Presbyterian Standard*, 1 March 1905.

81 *News and Observer*, 7 March 1905.

82 Ibid., 10 March 1905.

83 J. B. Cheshire to C. B. Aycock, 5 February 1907, Joseph Blount Cheshire Papers, SHC.

84 *News and Observer*, 2 February 1907.

85 Foster, "Gentleman Prophet," 111.

86 *Marriage and Divorce, 1916*, 10.

87 Edwards, *Gendered Strife and Confusion*, 24–65.

PART III

1 North Carolina Bureau of Labor Statistics, *Annual Report*, 1887, 37, 41, 44, 76.

2 Genovese, *Political Economy of Slavery*, 19–24; Schweikart, "Southern Banks and Economic Growth in the Antebellum Period"; Govan, "Banking and the Credit System in Georgia"; Ransom and Sutch, *One Kind of Freedom*, 110–16; Blair, *Historical Sketch of Banking in North Carolina*.

3 Atherton, "Problem of Credit Rating in the Ante-Bellum South," 534.

4 Foner, *Nothing but Freedom*, 109. Dylan C. Penningroth has persuasively argued that slaves often held property. However, because household items and livestock formed the vast majority of slaves' property, slaves could not readily convert their property into credit. See Penningroth, *Claims of Kinfolk*.

CHAPTER SEVEN

1 For an assessment of the debt-slave metaphor, see Mann, *Republic of Debtors*, 131; Balleisen, *Navigating Failure*, 165–67; and Sandage, *Born Losers*, 193–94.

2 Kilbourne, *Debt, Investment, Slaves*, 3, 50–55. Kilbourne argues that although the majority of slave transactions were conducted on a cash basis, people interested in buying slaves often borrowed money to finance the purchase. Also see Gross, *Double Character*, 32.

3 Ransom, *Conflict and Compromise*, 75.

4 For the reproductive labor of slave women, see Morgan, *Laboring Women*.

5 Kilbourne, *Debt, Investment, Slaves*, 1–64. Also see Johnson, *Soul by Soul*; Breen, *Tobacco Culture*; and McCurry, *Masters of Small Worlds*.

6 For the gift economy in the antebellum South, see Greenberg, *Honor and*

Slavery, 51–86. The central works in anthropology on gift culture are Mauss, *The Gift*, and Hyde, *The Gift*.

7 Breen, *Tobacco Culture*, 93.

8 Edwards, *People and Their Peace*, 44.

9 Breen, *Tobacco Culture*, 94–95.

10 Many southern physicians were trained in Philadelphia. See Kilbride, "Southern Medical Students in Philadelphia."

11 A. D. Murphey to James Webb, 17 May 1817, James Webb Papers, SHC.

12 Wyatt-Brown, *Southern Honor*, 23, 73, 345; Greenberg, *Honor and Slavery*, 51–86.

13 A. D. Murphey to James Webb, 28 September 1817, James Webb Papers, SHC.

14 Wyatt-Brown, *Southern Honor*, 55.

15 Deed-in-Trust, 1 November 1842, James Webb Papers, SHC.

16 Population Schedules of the Sixth Census of the United States, 1840.

17 Membership list, Hillsborough Presbyterian Church, NCDAH.

18 Here I disagree with Jane Turner Censer, who argued that planters' primary motivation in loaning money was financial advancement. See Censer, *North Carolina Planters and Their Children*, 13.

19 Hoyt, *Papers of Archibald D. Murphey*, 1:173–75. Also see Edwards, *People and Their Peace*, 122–23.

20 Studies of local antebellum communities across the South reveal similar networks of credit and debt that bound white residents together. Vernon Burton's study of antebellum Edgefield, South Carolina, indicates that credit relations connected planters, slaveholding yeoman farmers, and slaveless freeholding whites. John T. Schlotterbeck notes that in the Upper Piedmont region of Virginia, "exchanges that bound people together by ties of mutual dependence transcended mere economic relations . . . these ties were social as well." These localized networks of credit facilitated economic growth in a region largely devoid of modern financial institutions. At the same time, they helped to build social bonds among members of the community. Burton, *In My Father's House Are Many Mansions*, 70; Schlotterbeck, "'Social Economy' of an Upper South Community," 18. Also see Lowe and Campbell, *Planters and Plain Folk*, and Hahn, *Roots of Southern Populism*.

21 Bolton, *Poor Whites of the Antebellum South*, 24.

22 Hahn, *Roots of Southern Populism*, 75. On the origins of homestead laws during the antebellum period, see Goodman, "Emergence of Homestead Exemption," and Morantz, "There's No Place Like Home."

23 Bolton, *Poor Whites of the Antebellum South*, 26.

24 The term "yeoman" is used to describe those white North Carolinians who owned their own land and owned very few or no slaves, occupying a significant position in white society between poor whites and planters. Historians have offered important distinctions between yeoman, plain folk, common

whites, poor whites, and nonslaveholding whites, though disentangling their conflicting definitions of these groups can prove difficult. See Hyde, "Plain Folk Yeomanry in the Antebellum South"; Cecil-Fronsman, *Common Whites*; and Hahn, *Roots of Southern Populism*.

25 Escott, *North Carolina Yeoman.*

26 Ibid., 229.

27 Ibid., 151, 176, 237. The biblical passage is from Proverbs 22:7.

28 Escott, *North Carolina Yeoman*, 56, 70.

29 Ibid., 151.

30 Escott, "Yeoman Independence and the Market"; Hahn, *Roots of Southern Populism*, 85; McCoy, *Elusive Republic.*

31 Cecil-Fronsman, *Common Whites*, 102; Escott, "Yeoman Independence and the Market," 282; Wright, *Political Economy of the Cotton South*, 63.

32 Escott, *North Carolina Yeoman*, 263.

33 Ibid., 176.

34 Forret, *Race Relations at the Margins*, 74–114; Lockley, "Trading Encounters between Non-Elite Whites and African-Americans in Savannah"; Reidy, "Obligation and Right"; Penningroth, *Claims of Kinfolk*, 45–78.

35 Franklin, *Free Negro in North Carolina*, 89–90, 162.

36 Some South Carolina and Louisiana planters facilitated a pseudo-credit system, serving as factors for their slaves' surplus production or offering credit at plantation stores. I have not been able to identify a similar practice among slave owners in North Carolina. Campbell, "As 'A Kind of Freeman'?" 265–70; McDonald, "Independent Economic Production by Slaves on Antebellum Louisiana Sugar Plantations," 295–99.

37 Ball, *Slavery in the United States*, 191–92; Penningroth, *Claims of Kinfolk*, 66; Hahn, *Nation under Our Feet*, 28.

38 Horton, *Poetical Works*, xiii–xiv; Sherman, *Black Bard of North Carolina.*

39 Horton, *Poetical Works*, 39.

40 Ibid., 68–69.

41 Grandy, *Narrative of the Life*, 162.

42 Ibid., 180.

43 Horton, "A Slave's Reflection the Eve before His Sale," in *Naked Genius*, 36–37.

44 Horton, "Division of an Estate," in *Poetical Works*, 87–89.

45 "Out of Debt out of Danger," *Biblical Recorder*, 30 September 1848.

46 Heyrman, *Southern Cross*, 87, 113, 115, 158.

47 Smith, "Church Organization as an Agency of Social Control," 14, 84, 86, 103, 121.

48 *Hillsborough Recorder*, 21 February 1855.

49 The best scholarship on the Bankruptcy Act of 1841 is Balleisen, *Navigating Failure*. Also see Mathews, "'Forgive Us Our Debts.'"

50 Webster, "A Uniform System of Bankruptcy," Senate Speech, 18 May 1840, in *The Great Speeches and Orations of Daniel Webster*, 472.

51 *Appendix to the Congressional Globe*, 27th Cong., 2nd sess. (1841), 29–32.

52 *New York Herald*, 14 December 1842.

53 The figure of thirty thousand bankruptcy filers in the North is derived from Senate Document 19, 27th Cong., 3rd sess., *Report of the Secretary of State* (Daniel Webster). The most complete account of the repeal of the Bankruptcy Act of 1841 can be found in Balleisen, *Navigating Failure*, 119–24.

54 Walker Anderson to Daniel Webster, in Senate Document 19, 27th Cong., 3rd sess., 153.

55 A moderately complete list of bankruptcy filers in 1842 from North Carolina can be reconstructed from two sources. The first is a scrapbook in the Edwin Robeson Papers, SHC. The scrapbook contains newspaper clippings listing bankruptcy filings from twenty-three (of sixty-eight) counties. The second is the extant but very incomplete bankruptcy records at the National Archives—Southeastern Branch. See Bennett, *Index of North Carolina Bankrupts*, 10–13.

56 *Congressional Globe*, House of Representatives, 27th Cong., 3rd sess., 156, 187.

CHAPTER EIGHT

1 The exact rate of inflation in the Confederacy depends in large measure on geographic location and the commodities used as indexes. The most complete study of inflation in the Confederacy is Lerner, "Money, Prices, and Wages in the Confederacy." Also see Thornton and Ekelund, *Tariffs, Blockades, and Inflation*, 59–80.

2 Inscoe and McKinney, *Heart of Confederate Appalachia*, 174–75.

3 Edmundston, *"Journal of a Secesh Lady,"* 376, 533, 545–46.

4 Schwab, *Confederate States of America*, 164; Godfrey, "Monetary Expansion in the Confederacy," 124.

5 Schwab, *Confederate States of America*, 152; Ball, *Financial Failure and Confederate Defeat*, 168.

6 Ball, *Financial Failure and Confederate Defeat*, 170.

7 Ibid., 169.

8 Godfrey, "Monetary Expansion in the Confederacy," 121.

9 Ibid., 124.

10 *Newbern Progress*, 1 November 1862.

11 Ibid., 6 January 1863.

12 Massey, *Ersatz in the Confederacy*, 37–38.

13 James Evans to James S. Evans, 2 October 1861, James Evans Papers, SHC. Massey, *Ersatz in the Confederacy*, 163.

14 Schwab, *Confederate States of America*, 295.

15 Lerner, "Money, Prices, and Wages in the Confederacy," 16–17.

16 Massey, *Ersatz in the Confederacy*, 44.

17 Thornton and Ekelund, *Tariffs, Blockades, and Inflation*, 38; Massey, *Ersatz in the Confederacy*, 74; Lerner, "Money, Prices, and Wages in the Confederacy," 60–69.

18 *Newbern Progress*, 1 October 1861.

19 Jonathan Worth to Alfred Brown, 1 August 1863, in Hamilton, *Correspondence of Jonathan Worth*, 1:248.

20 N. A. Waller to Zebulon B. Vance, 13 November 1862, in Watford, *The Civil War in North Carolina*, 1:81.

21 John H. Kinyoun to Zebulon B. Vance, 1 November 1862, in Johnston, *Papers of Zebulon Baird Vance*, 1:291.

22 Jonathan Worth to J. J. Jackson, 19 May 1862, in Hamilton, *Correspondence of Jonathan Worth*, 1:171.

23 Lerner, "Money, Prices, and Wages in the Confederacy," 101.

24 *Wilmington Journal*, 9 October 1862.

25 *Raleigh Standard*, 18 November 1862.

26 R. L. Abernathy to Z. B. Vance, 4 November 1862, in Johnston, *Papers of Zebulon Baird Vance*, 1:304–5.

27 Kilbourne, *Debt, Investment, Slaves*, 75.

28 *Raleigh Register*, 13 February 1861.

29 Ibid., 20 February 1861.

30 *Newbern Progress*, 19 February 1861.

31 Schwab, *Confederate States of America*, 109.

32 Jonathan Worth to A. G. Foster, 9 December 1861, in Hamilton, *Correspondence of Jonathan Worth*, 1:159.

33 B. F. Moore to Thomas Ruffin, 15 and 27 September 1861, in Hamilton, *Papers of Thomas Ruffin*, 3:187, 189; Escott, *Many Excellent People*, 40.

34 George Lacus to Robert G. Lindsay, 17 February 1863, Robert Goodloe Lindsay Papers, SHC.

35 Schwab, *Confederate States of America*, 109.

36 Alexander McBee to Vardy A. McBee, 10 March 1867, McBee Family Papers, SHC.

37 Richard Kilbourne calculates that slaves represented 45.8 percent of total wealth in the Cotton South. See Kilbourne, *Debt, Investment, Slaves*, 8, 75.

38 Edmundston, *"Journal of a Secesh Lady,"* 720.

39 Rawick, *American Slave*, Suppl. Series 1, 11:11.

40 Jonathan Worth to W. L. Springs, 22 September 1866, in Hamilton, *Correspondence of Jonathan Worth*, 2:791–92.

41 Clair, "Debtor Relief in North Carolina during Reconstruction"; *Raleigh Daily Sentinel*, 30 January 1866. For stay laws across the South in the aftermath of the Civil War, see Carter, *When the War Was Over*, 141–44.

42 Edwards, *Gendered Strife and Confusion*, 165–69.

43 Thompson, *Reconstruction of Southern Debtors*, 3–8. The bill's northern sponsors consciously linked the emancipation of debtor to the emancipation of slaves. See Balleisen, "Bankruptcy and Bondage."

44 *North Carolina Daily Standard*, 15 January 1868. Also see *Daily Sentinel*, 5 March 1868.

45 *Raleigh Standard*, 11 January 1868.

46 Thompson, *Reconstruction of Southern Debtors*, 52–58.

47 Ibid., 52–58, 105–20.

48 *North Carolina Daily Standard*, 20 January 1868.

49 J. H. Burnett to William Blount Rodman, 19 January 1868, William Blount Rodman Papers, ECU.

50 Edmund Moore to Rodman, 20 January 1868, William Blount Rodman Papers, ECU.

51 *North Carolina Daily Standard*, 21 January 1868.

52 Ibid., 15 January 1868.

53 Ibid., 15 January 1868.

54 Ibid., 4 February 1868.

55 *Raleigh Daily Standard*, 3 February, 6 March 1868. Also see Foner, *Reconstruction*, 325–27.

56 *North Carolina Daily Standard*, 4 February 1868.

57 Hahn et al., *Freedom*, 768, 772–73, 775–77, 794–95.

58 *North Carolina Daily Standard*, 7 February 1868. On the brief and extraordinary life of Abraham Galloway, see Cecelski, "Abraham H. Galloway."

59 Black delegates to the South Carolina Constitutional Convention in 1868 voiced similar sentiments about debt relief. See Holt, *Black over White*, 128–30.

60 *North Carolina Daily Standard*, 17 February 1868.

61 Ibid., 7 March 1868.

62 Ibid., 18 February 1868.

63 North Carolina Constitution of 1868, I:16.

64 Coleman, *Debtors and Creditors in* America, 223–24.

65 *Journal of the Constitutional Convention*, 32, 57, 83, 133–136; Hamilton, *Reconstruction in North Carolina*, 262–63.

66 North Carolina Constitution of 1868, X:1–2; Olsen, *Carpetbagger's Crusade*, 107–8, 135–36; Elliott, *Color-Blind Justice*, 131; St. Clair, "Debtor Relief in North Carolina during Reconstruction," 224–30.

67 *Congressional Record*, 45th Cong., 2nd sess., 1878, vol. 7, pt. 4, p. 3358 (emphasis added).

CHAPTER NINE

1 *Journal of Freedom*, 30 September 1865.

2 Woodward, *Origins of the New South*, 291–320; Ransom and Sutch, *One Kind*

of *Freedom*; Wiener, *Social Origins of the New South*; Wright, *Old South, New South*; Reidy, "Economic Consequences of the Civil War and Reconstruction."

3 Clark, *Pills, Petticoats, and Plows*.

4 Ayers, *Promise of the New South*, 83–86.

5 R. G. Dun and Company, *Mercantile Agency Reference Book: January 1870*; R. G. Dun and Company, *Mercantile Agency Reference Book: January 1875*; R. G. Dun and Company, *Mercantile Agency Reference Book: January 1890*. These findings match trends elsewhere in the South. See Kyriakoudes, "Lower-Order Urbanization and Territorial Monopoly in the Southern Furnishing Trade," and Random and Sutch, *One Kind of Freedom*, 141.

6 Ransom and Sutch, *One Kind of Freedom*, 151–52.

7 Stephanie McCurry's study of antebellum white yeoman farmers in the South Carolina low country indicates that they gave top priority to crops that contributed to self-sufficiency. They produced crops for market only after personal needs were met. Postbellum yeoman farmers inverted this pattern. See McCurry, *Masters of Small Worlds*.

8 Random and Sutch, *One Kind of Freedom*, 89–97.

9 Scholarly estimates of the percentage of general store trade conducted on the basis of credit range from 66 percent to more than 90 percent. See Clark, *Pills, Petticoats, and Plows*, 313, and Atherton, *Southern Country Store*, 53;

10 Ayers, *Promise of the New South*, 92; Ransom and Sutch, *One Kind of Freedom*, 142–46; Hahn, *Roots of Southern Populism*, 178–79.

11 Ransom and Sutch, *One Kind of Freedom*, 126–48.

12 W. A. Patterson Account Books, SHC.

13 Sharon Holt argues that African Americans generally required more collateral for loans than whites, though it is difficult to determine whether this difference is due to racial prejudice or differing financial conditions. See Holt, *Making Freedom Pay*, 26–27.

14 Ibid., 29–34.

15 Account Books, Henry Houston Patterson Papers, SHC.

16 The uniformity of the handwriting over the years in Henry Patterson's account books seems to indicate that Henry Patterson himself was responsible for recording the debts of his customers. At other general store account books, two or three different hands are in evidence, indicating that hired clerks were also responsible for this type of record keeping.

17 Woodman, *New South—New Law*, 64.

18 In particular see *Hudgins v. Wood*, 72 N.C. 256 (1875), and *Thigpen v. Leigh*, 93 N.C. 47 (1885). Also see Woodman, *New South—New Law*, 89.

19 U.S. Industrial Commission, *Report of the Industrial Commission on Agriculture*, 10:77.

20 Ayers, *Promise of the New South*, 92.

21 Testimony of George H. White, U.S. Industrial Commission, *Report of the Industrial Commission on Agriculture*, 10:4.19.

22 Hall et al., *Like a Family*, 129. For examples of workers who became hopelessly in debt to company stores, see the account of J. P. Revis in Gold Hill Mining Company Records, SHC, and the account of R. P. S. West in J. M. Odell Manufacturing Company Records, SHC.

23 North Carolina Bureau of Labor Statistics, *Annual Report*, 1887, 41. Also see Patrick Linehan Account Books, SHC.

24 Hall et al., *Like a Family*, 147; Herring, *Welfare Work in Mill Villages*, 188.

25 Noblin, *Leonidas LaFayette Polk*, 78; Beckel, "Roots of Reform," 184–94; Ayers, *Promise of the New South*, 223.

26 Blythe, *William Henry Belk*, 38–46; Ayers, *Promise of the New South*, 95–96.

27 Kenzer, *Enterprising Southerners*, 37–42, 59–60.

28 Litwack, *Trouble in Mind*, 80.

29 *A.M.E. Zion Quarterly Review* 8 (1898): 81.

30 "Debt," *Christian Recorder*, 6 February 1873.

31 W. E. B. DuBois, *Souls of Black Folk*, 154.

32 Harlan, *Booker T. Washington Papers*, 2:503. Also see Daniel, *Shadow of Slavery*, ix. On Washington's economic thought, see Coclanis, "What Made Booker Wash(ington)?" 81–106.

33 Woloson, "In Hock"; Hudson, *Pawnbroking*; Tebbutt, *Making Ends Meet*; Patterson, "Pawnbroking in Europe and the US."

34 Their absence may be attributed in part to census takers listing pawnbrokers as merchants or other alternative professions. Nevertheless, the total number of pawnshops was not significant.

35 *Wilmington, N.C. City Directory 1897*. Records from the 1900 census list Miller as a thirty-five-year-old African American peddler. His pawnshop may have closed as a consequence of the 1898 Wilmington riot. See Prather, "We Have Taken a City," 17–18, 30.

36 *Maloney's Raleigh City Directory* (1899); *Maloney's Raleigh City Directory* (1901).

37 Beard, *My Own Life*, 96.

38 Ibid., 98.

39 According to Harry Finkelstein's son, young Thomas Wolfe was a regular visitor to their pawnshop. Wolfe later based a character in one of his short stories on Harry Finkelstein. See Leo Finkelstein Papers, Special Collections, Appalachian State University; Thomas Wolfe, "Child by Tiger," *Saturday Evening Post*, 7 September 1937.

40 *Asheville Citizen*, 30 November 1929; Finkelstein, *Leo Finkelstein's Asheville and the Poor Man's Bank*, 1–6.

41 There is no consensus about the number of women who were widowed during the Civil War. The estimates presented here are based on the number of

fatalities during the Civil War, census records, and pension applications filed by Confederate widows. They should be treated as fairly crude estimates. Ann Firor Scott estimates that there were at least 25,000 widows in North Carolina. Scott, *Southern Lady*, 106. Robert Kenzer presents a more conservative estimate of 4,000–6,000 Civil War widows in Virginia. Kenzer, "Uncertainty of Life," 112–35.

42 Wood, *Masterful Women*, 60–65. Also see Edwards, *Gendered Strife and Confusion*, 134.

43 Censer, *Reconstruction of White Southern Womanhood*; Rable, *Civil Wars*, 274–88.

44 Fox-Genovese, *Within the Plantation Household*, 200–203; Wyatt-Brown, *Southern Honor*, 226–36.

45 Kennedy, *Braided Relations, Entwined Lives*, 16, 44, 121, 123, 138; Barber, "Depraved and Abandoned Women," 159–60; Gamber, *Boardinghouse in Nineteenth-Century America*, 102–4, 109–14, 127–30.

46 For the experience of women opening boardinghouses outside the South, see Gamber, "Away from Home"; Bradley, "Surviving as a Widow in Nineteenth-Century Montreal"; Goldin, "Economic Status of Women in the Early Republic"; Gambler, *Boardinghouse in Nineteenth Century America*.

47 Massey, *Refugee Life in the Confederacy*, 78–80, 100–104, 120–22; 25 May 1863, Calder Family Papers, SHC.

48 Nathans, "Quest for Progress," 388.

49 The terms "boardinghouse" and "hotel" were gendered in the nineteenth-century South. Although female-owned establishments tended to be referred to as boardinghouses and male-owned establishments as hotels, the functional differences between these two terms were minimal. Both hotels and boardinghouses accepted long-term and short-term residents, and the number of potential occupants in each did not differ significantly. Likewise, the cost and quality of accommodations were roughly equivalent for comparable hotels and boardinghouses. On rare occasions, however, one does find a male-owned establishment called a boardinghouse and a female-owned establishment called a hotel.

50 Alice Houston Diary, 4 February 1870, Alice Lee Larkins Houston Papers, SHC.

51 Ibid., 8 March 1870.

52 Ibid., 10 March 1870.

53 Ibid., 15 July 1870 (emphasis in original).

54 Ibid., 24 April 1871.

55 Ibid., 8 March 1870.

56 Censer, *Reconstruction of Southern White Womanhood*, 156–57.

57 Alice Houston Diary, 12 February 1870.

58 Ibid., 13 November, 17 November 1870.

59 Mrs. N. J. Howell Papers, NCDAH.

60 Alice Houston Diary, 1 March 1870.

61 Ibid., 1 January 1871.

62 Ibid., 15 January 1871.

63 Ibid., 26 April 1871.

64 Ibid., 23 October 1871.

65 New Hanover County index of deeds, NCDAH; *Sherriff's Wilmington Direc-tory*.

66 On Ralph Graves's suicide, see Chapters 2–3.

67 Thomas B. Venable to Julia Graves, 10 July 1889, Louis and Mildred Graves Papers, SHC.

68 Louis Graves, "My Memories of My Mother," *Chapel Hill Weekly*, 17 November 1944; Louis Graves, "Memories of Edwin A. Alderman," *Chapel Hill Weekly*, 8 May 1931; Cornelia Phillips Spencer to Julia Graves, 15 August 1889, Louis and Mildred Graves Papers, SHC.

69 Graves, "My Memories of My Mother."

70 Henry Houston Patterson Account Books, vols. 9–15: 1889–1902, SHC.

71 Graves, "My Memories of My Mother."

72 Beard, *My Own Life*, 5.

73 Ibid., 47.

74 Ibid., 75.

75 Ibid., 168.

76 Ibid., 169.

77 Ibid., 170.

78 Ibid.

79 Ibid., 123.

80 Ida Beard published two autobiographical volumes. The first, *My Own Life*, describes her troubled marriage to John Beard. A second, entitled *The Missis-sippi Lawyer*, describes a later failed relationship.

81 Graves, "Memories of My Mother." According to a letter from Cornelia Phillips Spencer to her daughter, Julia Graves purchased this separate set of tableware from a departing Chapel Hill family in early September 1890, one year after she opened her boardinghouse. Cornelia Phillips Spencer to Julia Spencer Love, 14 September 1890, Cornelia Phillips Spencer Papers, SHC. An example of another boardinghouse maintaining separate sets of tableware for the family and for boarders can be found in Peña and Denmon, "Social Orga-nization of a Boardinghouse."

82 Ransom and Sutch, *One Kind of Freedom*, 38. They also conclude that female government officials and cotton mill operators were more racially discrimi-natory, but the total number of women in these occupations was not large enough to be statistically significant.

83 Donald, *Look Homeward*, 6.

84 Wheaton, *Thomas Wolfe and His Family*, 31.

85 Starnes, "'Conspicuous Example of What Is Termed the New South,'" 62–63.

86 Donald, *Look Homeward*, 9.

87 Norwood, *Marble Man's Wife*, 40–44. According to Julia's daughter Mabel, the doctor diagnosed Leslie Wolfe with cholera infantum before she died. Wheaton, *Thomas Wolfe and His Family*, 31. A lack of proper plumbing probably also contributed to the child's death, as most homes in Asheville did not connect to a municipal sewer system until the 1920s. See Baroody, *1978 Excavation of Cistern at the Thomas Wolfe Memorial*.

88 Wolfe, *Look Homeward, Angel*, 127.

89 Ibid., 158.

90 Smith and Wilson, *North Carolina Women*, 206.

CHAPTER TEN

1 North Carolina Bureau of Labor Statistics, *Annual Report*, 1887, 130.

2 North Carolina Bureau of Labor Statistics, *Annual Report*, 1889, 266.

3 Friedman, "Crime of 1873."

4 For the purposes of this study, the term "agrarian" refers to those who advocated a reform program intended to remedy the significant economic dislocation experienced by farmers in the final decades of the nineteenth century. Most North Carolina agrarians had some affiliation, officially or unofficially, with the North Carolina Farmers' Alliance. Many, but by no means all, later joined the Populist Party. The term "agrarian" will be used, therefore, as an umbrella term to refer to those who held a particular political philosophy instead of limiting it to members of one particular organization or political party. Because this study focuses primarily on how North Carolina agrarians understood debt rather than the sometimes Byzantine history of agrarian politics, the following analysis of the agrarian movement in North Carolina will emphasize their public discourse on debt rather than the internecine battles that characterized the politics of the era. The author refers readers interested in the political maneuvering of North Carolina agrarians and their opponents to the substantial literature on this topic. The agrarian movement has a robust historiographical tradition. See, in particular, Hicks, *Populist Revolt*; Woodward, *Origins of the New South*; Hofstadter, *Age of Reform*; Goodwyn, *Democratic Promise*; Hahn, *Roots of Southern Populism*; McMath, *Populist Vanguard*; and Postel, *Populist Vision*.

5 Black Populism remains significantly understudied. My understanding of black Populism in North Carolina draws heavily from Ali, "Black Populism in the New South," 197–201.

6 Steelman, *North Carolina Farmers' Alliance*, 10; Edmonds, *Negro and Fusion Politics in North Carolina*, 23.

7   Steelman, *North Carolina Farmers' Alliance*, 9–17; Noblin, *Leonidas LaFayette Polk*, 150–207; McMath, *Populist Vanguard*, 38–40; Ayers, *Promise of the New South*, 223–24.

8   Logan, *Negro in North Carolina*, 84; Steelman, *North Carolina Farmers' Alliance*, 21.

9   *Progressive Farmer*, 8 December, 15 December 1891.

10 McMath, *Populist Vanguard*, 90–91; Goodwyn, *Democratic Promise*, 166–69; Ayers, *Promise of the New South*, 239.

11 *Progressive Farmer*, 17 September 1889.

12 Although Texan C. W. Macune usually gets credit for the originating the sub-treasury plan, John Hicks argued that he may have gotten the idea from an article written by North Carolinian Henry Skinner. Hicks, "Sub-Treasury Plan," 359.

13 Steelman, *North Carolina Farmers' Alliance*, 81.

14 Palmer, "*Man over Money*," 94.

15 *Caucasian*, 11 April 1895; Palmer, "*Man over Money*," 84.

16 North Carolina Bureau of Labor Statistics, *Annual Report*, 1895, 189.

17 North Carolina Bureau of Labor Statistics, *Annual Report*, 1887, 91.

18 North Carolina Bureau of Labor Statistics, *Annual Report*, 1893, 64.

19 *Carolina Watchman*, 20 August 1891.

20 *Progressive Farmer*, 23 June 1896.

21 *Caucasian*, 31 August 1893.

22 Palmer, "*Man over Money*," 89.

23 *Caucasian*, 16 November 1893.

24 Palmer, "*Man over Money*," 92–93.

25 *Progressive Farmer*, 8 December 1891.

26 *Tarboro Farmers Advocate*, 3 June 1891.

27 Hunt, *Marion Butler and American Populism*, 62.

28 North Carolina Bureau of Labor Statistics, *Annual Report*, 1887, 38.

29 Anderson, *Race and Politics in North Carolina*.

30 *Progressive Farmer*, 26 July 1892.

31 Thurtell, "Fusion Insurgency in North Carolina," 94.

32 Steelman, *North Carolina Farmers' Alliance*, 125.

33 Ibid., 162.

34 McMath, "Agrarian Protest at the Forks of the Creek." Although the vast majority of cooperative stores failed, a notable exception was the Farmers Alliance Store of Siler City, which, as of December 1999, remained open for business. See Baker, "Farmers Alliance Store of Siler City."

35 North Carolina Bureau of Labor Statistics, *Annual Report*, 1891, 68.

36 Lefler, *North Carolina History Told by Contemporaries*, 379.

37 Thurtell, "Fusion Insurgency in North Carolina", 109.

38 Bromberg, "'Worst Muddle Ever Seen in N.C. Politics,'" 28.

39 Vance evidently believed that the subtreasury plan was unconstitutional. Bromburg, "'Worst Muddle Ever Seen in N.C. Politics,'" 19–40; Steelman, *North Carolina Farmers' Alliance*, 66–81.

40 Beeby, *Revolt of the Tar Heels*, 59–84.

41 One significant exception to the Republican opposition to bimetallism was Republican (and former Greenbacker) governor Daniel Russell. See Crow and Durden, *Maverick Republican in the Old North State*.

42 Ali, "Black Populism in the New South," 196–201.

43 *Public Laws and Resolutions of the State of North Carolina* (1895), chap. 69. Trelease argues that white Republicans lukewarmly supported the measure, fearing that it would drive credit from the state. Trelease, "Fusion Legislatures of 1895 and 1897," 294. Also see Beeby, *Revolt of the Tar Heels*, 114–15, and Thurtell, "Fusion Insurgency in North Carolina," 256.

44 Trelease, "Fusion Legislatures of 1895 and 1897," 294–95.

45 Undated speech, Marion Butler Papers, SHC.

46 North Carolina Bureau of Labor Statistics, *Annual Report*, 1890, 35.

CONCLUSION

1 Alexander, *Reminiscences of the Past Sixty Years*, 9, 25, 134, 181.

2 Ibid., 159, 168–69, 172, 253–55.

3 Hood, *Negro in the Christian Pulpit*, 42–43.

4 *A.M.E. Zion Quarterly Review* 12 (1902): 53.

5 Wiebe, *Search for Order*.

6 Bender, *Community and Social Change in America*.

7 Faust, *This Republic of Suffering*, xv, 210.

8 Carter, *When the War Was Over*, 273–74.

APPENDIX

1 MacDonald and Murphy, *Sleepless Souls*; Anderson, *Suicide in Victorian and Edwardian England*; Watt, *Choosing Death*. Coroners' records, in conjunction with other official records, were similarly used to great success in Lane, *Violent Death in the City*. Other forms of official records are used to great effect in Morrissey, *Suicide and the Body Politic in Imperial Russia*; Merrick, "Suicide in Paris"; Goeschel, *Suicide in Nazi Germany*; Weaver, *Sadly Troubled History*; and Pérez, *To Die in Cuba*. Also see Snyder, "What Historians Talk about When They Talk about Suicide," 660.

2 Although North Carolina, like many British colonies, adopted the common-law prohibition on suicide, there is no evidence that it was ever enforced. See Burgess-Jackson, "Legal Status of Suicide in Early America."

3 *Raleigh News and Observer*, 30 July 1887.

4 "Coroners: Medical and Legal," 224. Ironically, the coroner's records from New Hanover County are among the best preserved in the state.

5 U.S. Census Bureau, *Tenth Census of the United States*, 365. Also see Thornton, *Politics and Power in a Slave Society*, 306. Based on census data, Thornton argues that the suicide rate in Alabama more than doubled between 1850 and 1860. However, he admits that the accuracy of mortality figures from census data is open to debate. Similarly, based on census data, Fogel and Engerman argue that suicide was more common among white southerners than slaves before the Civil War. See Fogel and Engerman, *Time on the Cross*, 1:124, 2:100.

6 Timmermans, "Suicide Determination and the Professional Authority of Medical Examiners"; Sainsbury, "Validity and Reliability of Trends in Suicide Statistics"; Jobes, "Medicolegal Certification of Suicide"; Fiala, "Medicolegal Officer and the Social Production of Public Health Statistics."

Bibliography

PRIMARY SOURCES

Manuscripts
Boone, North Carolina
  Special Collections, Appalachian State University
    Leo Finkelstein Papers
Chapel Hill, North Carolina
  North Carolina Collection, University of North Carolina
    "Sermons"
    "Sketch of Michael Cosgrove"
    Charles Spencer Scrapbook
  Southern Historical Collection, University of North Carolina
    Samuel E. Asbury Papers
    Alphonso Calhoun Avery Papers
    Avery Family Papers
    Badger Family Papers
    Hamilton Brown Papers
    Marion Butler Papers
    Calder Family Papers
    Joseph Blount Cheshire Papers
    Dialectic Society Records
    James Evans Papers
    Fisher Family Papers
    Glencoe Mills Records
    Gold Hill Mining Company Records
    Louis and Mildred Graves Papers
    John Wesley Halliburton Papers
    Alice Lee Larkin Houston Papers

Hubard Family Papers

Mary Susan Ker Papers

Robert Goodloe Lindsay Papers

Patrick Linehan Account Books

McBee Family Papers

Archibald Murphey Papers

Patrick L. Murphy Papers

Neal Family Papers

J. M. Odell Manufacturing Company Records

Henry Houston Patterson Account Books

Martha Virginia McNair Evans Patterson Papers

W. A. Patterson Account Books

Philanthropic Society Records

James Jones Philips Papers

Edwin Robeson Papers

John McKee Sharpe Papers

Cornelia Phillips Spencer Papers

James Webb Papers

Wyche and Otey Family Papers

Durham, North Carolina

Special Collections, Duke University

John Adolphus Bernard Dahlgren Papers

Enoch Faw Papers

Eugene Grissom Papers

David Bullock Harris Papers

A. W. Haywood, "Speech for the Defense"

J. Howard Jones Papers

Abraham Oettinger Papers

Henry Reid Papers

Goldsboro, North Carolina

Cherry Hospital Museum

Admission Log Book, Eastern North Carolina Insane Asylum, 1880–1900

Greenville, North Carolina

Special Collections, Joyner Library, East Carolina University

Kate Wheeler Cooper Papers

Tabitha Marie DeVisconti Papers

James L. Fleming Papers

J. Bryan Grimes Papers

William Blount Rodman Papers

Ephraigm H. Smith Collection

William H. and Araminta Guilford Tripp Papers

Whitehurst Family Papers

Raleigh, North Carolina
  North Carolina Department of Archives and History
    Joseph Blount Cheshire Papers
    Calvin J. Cowles Papers
    Guilford County Lunacy Records, 1826–95
    Hillsborough Presbyterian Church Records
    Mrs. N. J. Howell Papers
    Hyde County Divorce Records
    Macon County Divorce Records
    New Hanover County Coroner's Inquests, 1768–1880
    New Hanover County Index of Deeds
    Orange County Coroner's Reports, 1783–1911
    Orange County Divorce Records
    Patient Records, North Carolina Insane Asylum, 1887–93
    Perquimans County Divorce Records
    Pitt County Divorce Records
    Raleigh Register of Deaths
    Register of Artificial Limbs, 1866–70
    Secretary of State Records, Papers of the Constitutional Convention
      of 1868
    Wayne County Divorce Records
Salisbury, North Carolina
  Heritage Hall, Livingstone College
    A.M.E. Zion Quarterly Review

Microfilm Collections
Cove Creek Baptist Church Records, Southern Baptist Historical Library and
  Archives
Population Schedules of the Sixth Census of the United States, 1840
Records of the Assistant Commissioner for the State of North Carolina, Bureau of
  Refugees, Freedmen, and Abandoned Lands, 1865–1870
Albion Winegar Tourgée Papers

Newspapers

African Expositor (Raleigh)	*Christian Recorder* (Philadelphia)
Asheville Citizen	*Colored American* (New York)
Asheville News	*Durham Daily Sun*
Biblical Recorder (Raleigh)	*Eastern Reflector* (Greenville)
Carolina Watchman (Salisbury)	*Fayetteville Observer*
Caucasian	*Greensboro Recorder*
Chapel Hill Weekly	*Greenville Daily Reflector*
Charlotte Observer	*Highland Messenger* (Asheville)

Hillsboro Recorder

Hillsborough Recorder

Journal of Freedom (Raleigh)

National Era (Washington, D.C.)

Newbern Progress

New York Tribune

North Carolina Daily Standard
(Raleigh)

North Star (Boston)

Oxford Public Ledger

Presbyterian Standard (Charlotte)

Progressive Farmer

Raleigh Christian Advocate

Raleigh Daily Sentinel

Raleigh Farmer and Mechanic

Raleigh Morning Post

Raleigh News and Observer

Raleigh Observer

Raleigh Register

Raleigh State Chronicle

Richmond Daily Dispatch

Star of Zion (Charlotte)

Statesville Landmark

Tarboro Farmers Advocate

Washington (D.C.) Post

Washington (N.C.) Gazette

Wilmington Daily Herald

Wilmington Daily Journal

Wilmington Daily Record

Wilmington Journal

Winston-Salem People's Press

Published Primary Sources

African-American Baptist Annual Reports, North Carolina, 1865–1990. American Baptist–Samuel Colgate Historical Library, Rochester, N.Y., 1997.

Alexander, John Brevard. Reminiscences of the Past Sixty Years. Charlotte, N.C.: Ray Printing, 1908.

Arrington, Pattie D. B. Is Justice a Farce? A True Story of Love, Marriage, Separation, and Divorce. Raleigh: n.p., 1893.

Avery, Isaac Erwin. Idle Comments. Charlotte: Avery Publishing, 1905.

Babcock, J. W. "The Colored Insane." Proceedings of the National Conference of Charities and Correction 22 (1895): 164–186.

Bailey, William B. "Suicide in the United States, 1897–1901." Yale Review 12 (1903): 70–85.

Ball, Charles. Fifty Years in Chains. New York: H. Dayton, 1859.

———. Slavery in the United States. New York: John S. Taylor, 1837.

Bannister, Dr. H. M., and Dr. Ludwig Hektoen. "Race and Insanity." American Journal of Insanity 44 (1888): 455–70.

Battle, Kemp. History of the University of North Carolina. Vols. 1 and 2. Raleigh: Edwards and Broughton, 1907, 1912.

Beard, Ida. My Own Life: Or, A Deserted Wife. Winston-Salem: n.p., 1900.

Bertram, R. A. A Homiletic Encyclopedia. New York: Funk and Wagnalls, 1890.

Betts, Rev. A. D. Experiences of a Civil War Chaplain, 1861–1864. Greenville, S.C.: n.p., n.d.

Bigelow, L. J. "The Aesthetics of Suicide." Galaxy 2 (1866): 471–76.

Blair, William A. A Historical Sketch of Banking in North Carolina. New York: Bradford Rhodes, 1899.

Botkin, B. A., ed. *Lay My Burden Down: A Folk History of Slavery*. Chicago: University of Chicago Press, 1945.

Brame, Rev. John Todd. "The Folly and Danger of Making a Covenant with Death and an Agreement with Hell." *Southern Methodist Pulpit* 1, no. 9 (1849): 135–54.

Branson's North Carolina Business Directory. Raleigh: Branson and Jones, 1869.

Bureau of the Census. *Marriage and Divorce, 1867–1906*. 2 vols. Washington: GPO, 1909.

Chas. Emerson and Co.'s Raleigh Directory. Raleigh: Edwards, Broughton and Co, 1879.

Chataigne's Raleigh City Directory. Raleigh: J. H. Chataigne, 1875.

Chesnutt, Charles W. "Dave's Neckliss." In *Conjure Tales and Other Stories of the Color Line*, edited by William L. Andrews, 90–102. New York: Penguin, 2000.

Clinton, Bishop George W. *Christianity under the Searchlight*. Nashville: National Baptist Publishing Board, 1909.

Connor, R. D. W. *The Life and Speeches of Charles Brantley Aycock*. Garden City, N.Y.: Doubleday, Page, 1912.

Constitution of the State of North Carolina. Raleigh: Joseph W. Holden, 1868.

Convention of the Woman's Christian Temperance Union of the State of North Carolina. Greensboro, N.C.: n.p., 1883–1906.

Conway, T. W. "Marrying on Roanoke Island." *National Anti-Slavery Standard*, 25 October 1862.

"Coroners: Medical and Legal." *North Carolina Medical Journal* 29 (April 1892): 223–25.

Crummell, Alexander. "Losses of the Race." *A.M.E. Zion Quarterly Review* 10 (1900): 25–28.

Daniels, Josephus. *Tar Heel Editor*. Chapel Hill: University of North Carolina Press, 1939.

Dennett, John Richard. *The South As It Is, 1865–1866*. Baton Rouge: Louisiana State University Press, 1965.

Directory of the City of Raleigh. Raleigh: Observer Printing, 1888.

Directory of the City of Raleigh. Raleigh: Raleigh Stationary, 1896.

Directory of the City of Wilmington. Wilmington, N.C.: Julius Bonitz, 1889.

DuBois, W. E. B. *The Negro Church*. Atlanta: Atlanta University Press, 1903.

———. *The Souls of Black Folks*. New York: Modern Library, 2003.

DuBose, Rev. H. M. "Suicide—Causes and Cure." *Quarterly Review of the Methodist Episcopal Church, South* 21 (1884): 35–44.

Edmundston, Catherine. *"Journal of a Secesh Lady": The Diary of Catherine Ann Devereux Edmundston, 1860–1866*. Edited by Beth G. Crabtree and James W. Patton. Raleigh: Division of Archives and History, 1979.

Finkelstein, Leo. *Leo Finkelstein's Asheville and the Poor Man's Bank*. Boone, N.C.: Center for Appalachian Studies, Appalachian State University, 1998.

Grandy, Moses. *A Narrative of the Life of Moses Grandy*. Edited by Andreá N.

Williams. In *North Carolina Slave Narratives*, edited by William L. Andrews, 131–86. Chapel Hill: University of North Carolina Press, 2003.

Gray, Dr. John P. "Suicide." *American Journal of Insanity* 35 (1878): 37–73.

The Great Speeches and Orations of Daniel Webster. Boston: Little, Brown, 1879.

Grissom, Dr. Eugene. "Leonard Medical School Commencement Address." *African Expositor* 9 (April 1886): 1.

———. "Mechanical Protection for the Violent Insane." *American Journal of Insanity* 34 (1877): 27–58.

———. "True and False Experts." *American Journal of Insanity* 35 (1878): 1–36.

Hamilton, Dr. Allan McLane. "Suicide in Large Cities." *Popular Science Monthly* 8 (1875): 88–95.

Hamilton, J. G. de Roulhac, ed. *The Correspondence of Jonathan Worth*. Raleigh: North Carolina Historical Commission, 1909.

———, ed. *The Papers of Thomas Ruffin*. Raleigh: Edwards and Broughton, 1920.

Harlan, Louis R., ed. *Booker T. Washington Papers*. Urbana: University of Illinois Press, 1972.

Hood, James Walker. *The Negro in the Christian Pulpit*. Raleigh: Edwards and Broughton, 1884.

———. *One Hundred Years of the African Methodist Episcopal Zion Church*. New York: A.M.E. Zion Book Concern, 1895.

Horton, George Moses. *Naked Genius*. Raleigh: Wm. B. Smith and Co., 1865.

———. *The Poetical Works of George M. Horton, the Colored Bard of North Carolina, to Which Is Prefixed the Life of the Author, Written by Himself*. Hillsborough: Heartt, 1845.

Howe, Mark DeWolf, ed. *Touched with Fire: Civil War Letters and Diary of Oliver Wendell Holmes, Jr.* New York: Fordham University Press, 2000.

Hoyt, William Henry, ed. *The Papers of Archibald D. Murphey*. 2 vols. Raleigh: Publications of the North Carolina Historical Commission, 1914.

Jeter, Rev. Jeremiah Bell. *The Evils of Gaming: A Letter to a Friend in the Army*. Raleigh: n.p., 1861.

Johnston, Frontis W., ed. *The Papers of Zebulon Baird Vance*. Raleigh: State Department of Archives and History, 1963.

Journal of the Constitutional Convention of the State of North Carolina at Its Session 1868. Raleigh: Holden, 1868.

"The Law of Marriage and Divorce." *Baptist Quarterly Review* 11 (April 1889): 218–23.

Keckley, Elizabeth. *Behind the Scenes, or Thirty Years a Slave and Four Years in the White House*. New York: G. W. Carleton, 1868.

Kelley's City Directory. Wilmington, N.C.: George Kelley, 1860.

Logan, John R. *Sketches, Historical and Biographical, of the Broad River and King's Mountain Baptist Associations, 1800 to 1882*. Shelby, N.C.: Babington, Roberts, 1887.

MacDonald, N. "Civilization and Suicide." *Leslie's Illustrated Weekly*, 30 December 1897, 436.

———. "Prevalence of Suicide." *Leslie's Illustrated Weekly*, 18 November 1897, 331.

———. "Young Suicide." *Leslie's Illustrated Weekly*, 15 July 1897, 34.

Maloney's Raleigh City Directory. Atlanta: Maloney Directory Co., 1899.

Maloney's Raleigh City Directory. Atlanta: Maloney Directory Co., 1901.

"Marriage and Divorce." *Southern Quarterly Review* 26 (1854): 332–55.

Marriage and Divorce, 1916. Washington: GPO, 1919.

McDuffie, Dr. W. C. "A Few Thoughts on the Subdivisions of Insanity." *North Carolina Medical Journal* 5 (April 1880): 211–18.

Miller, Dr. J. F. "The Effects of Emancipation upon the Mental and Physical Health of the Negro in the South." *North Carolina Medical Journal* 38 (November 1896): 285–94.

Moffitt, Mrs. E. E. "Biographical Sketch of Mrs. Spier Whitaker nee Hooper." *North Carolina Booklet* 13 (1913): 234–49.

Murphy, Dr. Patrick L. "The Care of the Insane and the Treatment and Prognosis of Insanity." *North Carolina Medical Journal* 36 (August 1895): 68–80.

"News and Items." *North Carolina Medical Journal* 43 (May 1899): 368–69.

North Carolina Bureau of Labor Statistics. *Annual Reports*. Raleigh: Josephus Daniels, 1887–95.

Northrup, Davenport Henry, Joseph R. Gay, and I. Garland Penn. *The College of Life, or Practical Self-Educator: A Manual of Self-Improvement for the Colored Race*. Kansas City: Topeka Book Co., 1896.

Palmer, Hon. O. H. "Suicide Not Evidence of Insanity." *American Journal of Insanity* 34 (1878): 425–61.

Patterson, R. "Pawnbroking in Europe and the US." *Bulletin of the Department of Labor* 4 (1899): 273–79.

Pilgrim, Dr. Charles W. "A Study of Suicide." *Popular Science Monthly* 35 (1889): 303–13.

Price, Rev. Joseph C. "Education and the Race Problem." *A.M.E. Zion Quarterly Review* 1 (1890): 57–70.

———. "Temperance Mission Work among the Colored People of the South," *A.M.E. Zion Quarterly Review* 4 (1894): 288–96.

———. "The Times Demand the Elevation of the Educational Standard of the Negro Ministry." *A.M.E. Zion Quarterly Review* 3 (1893): 66–74.

"Proceedings of the Association." *American Journal of Insanity* 49 (1892): 251–52.

Public Laws and Resolutions of the State of North Carolina. Raleigh: E. M. Uzzell, 1895.

R. G. Dun and Company. *Mercantile Agency Reference Book: January 1870*. New York: Dun, Barlow and Co., 1870.

———. *Mercantile Agency Reference Book: January 1875*. New York: Dun, Barlow and Co., 1875.

————. *Mercantile Agency Reference Book: January 1890*. New York: Dun, Barlow and Co., 1890.

Raleigh, N.C. Directory. Richmond: Hill Directory Co, 1905.

Raleigh City Directory. Raleigh: Edwards and Broughton, 1883.

Raleigh City Directory. Raleigh: Edwards and Broughton, 1886.

Rawick, George P., ed. *The American Slave: A Composite Autobiography*. Westport, Conn.: Greenwood press, 1972–79.

Redfield, Horace V. *Homicide North and South*. Philadelphia: Lippincott, 1880.

Redpath, James. *Roving Editor*. New York: A. B. Burdick, 1859.

Reid, Rev. Frank L. "The Duty and Destiny of the Church." In *North Carolina Sermons*, edited by Rev. Levi Branson, 3:169–84. Raleigh: L. Branson, 1893.

Report of the Board of Directors and Superintendent of the Eastern North Carolina Insane Asylum. Raleigh: Josephus Daniels, 1883–1902.

Report of the Board of Directors and Superintendent of the North Carolina Insane Asylum. Raleigh: Josephus Daniels, 1851–1902.

Report of the Board of Directors and Superintendent of the Western North Carolina Insane Asylum. Raleigh: Josephus Daniels, 1883–1902.

Report of the Joint Committee on Reconstruction. Vol. 2. Washington: GPO, 1866.

Rhodes, Albert. "Suicide." *Galaxy* 21 (1876): 188–99.

Roberts, Dr. J. D. "Insanity in the Colored Race." *North Carolina Medical Journal* 12 (November 1883): 249–59.

Roper, Moses. A *Narrative of the Adventures and Escape of Moses Roper*. Edited by Ian Frederick Finseth. In *North Carolina Slave Narratives*, edited by William L. Andrews, 21–76. Chapel Hill: University of North Carolina Press, 2003.

Ruffin, Edmund. *Diary of Edmund Ruffin*. Edited by William K. Scarborough. Baton Rouge: Louisiana State University Press, 1972–89.

Scott, Rev. E. C. *Ministerial Directory of the Presbyterian Church, US 1861–1941*. Austin: Von Boeckmann-Jones, 1942.

Sherriff's Wilmington Directory. Wilmington, N.C.: Benjamin Sherriff, 1877.

Simmons, William J. *Men of Mark: Eminent, Progressive and Rising*. Cleveland: Rewell, 1887.

Smaw's Wilmington Directory. Wilmington, N.C.: Smaw 1867.

A Southern Physician. "Suicide." *American Whig Review* 6 (August 1847): 137–45.

"Suicide." *Methodist Review* 76 (1894): 621–29.

"Suicide in the United States." *North Carolina Medical Journal* 49 (December 1903): 615–17.

Sully, James. "Genius and Insanity." *Quarterly Review of the Methodist Episcopal Church, South* 22(1885): 611–35.

U.S. Census Bureau. *Tenth Census of the United States, 1880*. Vol. 11 (Mortality). Washington: GPO, 1884.

U.S. Industrial Commission. *Report of the Industrial Commission on Agriculture*. Washington: GPO, 1901.

Warren, Edward. *A Doctor's Experiences in Three Continents*. Baltimore: Cushing and Bailey, 1885.

Watford, Christopher M., ed. *The Civil War in North Carolina*. 2 vols. Jefferson, N.C.: McFarland, 2003.

Weaver, P. "A Legal Suicide, 1996." *Overland Monthly* 28 (December 1896): 680–90.

"What Cases of Insanity Shall We Treat at Home?" *North Carolina Medical Journal* 23 (March 1889): 192.

Wheaton, Mabel Wolfe. *Thomas Wolfe and His Family*. Garden City, N.J.: Doubleday and Co., 1961.

Whitted, Rev. J. A. *A History of Negro Baptists in North Carolina*. Raleigh: Edwards and Broughton, 1908.

Willcox, Walter F. *The Divorce Problem: A Study in Statistics*. New York: Columbia University Press, 1891.

Wilmington, N.C. City Directory 1897. Richmond: J. L. Hill, 1897.

Wilmington, N.C. Directory, 1905. Richmond: Hill Directory Co., 1905.

Wilmington Directory. Wilmington, N.C.: P. Heinsberger, 1865.

Winston, George. "A Sketch of the Life and Character of Prof. R. H. Graves." *University Magazine* 9, no. 1 (1889): 1–18.

Wright, Carroll D. *A Report on Marriage and Divorce in the United States, 1867–1886*. Washington: GPO, 1891.

SECONDARY SOURCES

Abstracts of Marriages and Deaths of Extant Washington, NC Newspapers. Washington, N.C.: Beaufort County Genealogical Society, 1991.

Ali, Omar. "Black Populism in the New South, 1886–1898." Ph.D. diss., Columbia University, 2003.

Allmendinger, David F., and William K. Scarborough. "The Days Ruffin Died." *Virginia Magazine of History and Biography* 97 (1989): 75–96.

Anderson, Eric. *Race and Politics in North Carolina, 1872–1901: The Black Second*. Baton Rouge: Louisiana State University Press, 1981.

Anderson, Olive. *Suicide in Victorian and Edwardian England*. Oxford: Clarendon Press, 1987.

Andrews, William L. *The Literary Career of Charles W. Chesnutt*. Baton Rouge: Louisiana State University Press, 1980.

Appell, Stephen Marc. "The Fight for the Constitutional Convention: The Development of the Political Parties in North Carolina during 1867." M.A. thesis, University of North Carolina, 1969.

Aptheker, Herbert. *American Negro Slave Revolts*. New York: International Publishers, 1993.

Atherton, Lewis. "The Problem of Credit Rating in the Ante-Bellum South." *Journal of Southern History* 12, no. 4 (1946): 534–56.

———. *The Southern Country Store*. Baton Rouge: Louisiana State University Press, 1949.

Ayers, Edward L. *The Promise of the New South: Life after Reconstruction*. New York: Oxford University Press, 1992.

———. *Vengeance and Justice: Crime and Punishment in the 19th-Century American South*. New York: Oxford University Press, 1984.

———. "Worrying about the Civil War." In *Moral Problems in American Life: New Perspectives in Cultural History*, edited by Karen Halttunen and Lewis Perry, 145–65. Ithaca, N.Y.: Cornell University Press, 1998.

Bailey, David Thomas. "A Divided Prism: Two Sources of Black Testimony on Slavery." *Journal of Southern History* 46 (1980): 381–404.

Baker, Bruce E. "The Farmers Alliance Store of Siler City, North Carolina, 1888–1999." Seminar paper, December 1999, in possession of the North Carolina Collection, University of North Carolina at Chapel Hill.

Ball, Douglas B. *Financial Failure and Confederate Defeat*. Urbana: University of Illinois Press, 1991.

Balleisen, Edward J. "Bankruptcy and Bondage: The Ambiguities of Economic Freedom in the Civil War Era." In *The Problem of Evil: Slavery, Freedom, and the Ambiguities of American Reform*, edited by Steven Mintz and John Stauffer, 276–86. Amherst: University of Massachusetts Press, 2007.

———. *Navigating Failure: Bankruptcy and Commercial Society in Antebellum America*. Chapel Hill: University of North Carolina Press, 2001.

Baptist, Edward. "'My Mind Is to Drown You and Leave You Behind': 'Omie Wise,' Intimate Violence, and Masculinity." In *Over the Threshold: Intimate Violence in Early America*, edited by Christine Daniels and Michael V. Kennedy, 94–110. New York: Routledge, 1999.

Barber, E. Susan. "Depraved and Abandoned Women: Prostitution in Richmond, Virginia across the Civil War." In *Neither Lady nor Slave*, edited by Susanna Delfino and Michele Gillespie, 155–73. Chapel Hill: University of North Carolina Press, 2002.

Bardaglio, Peter W. *Reconstructing the Household: Families, Sex, and the Law in the Nineteenth-Century South*. Chapel Hill: University of North Carolina Press, 1995.

Barney, William L. *The Passage of the Republic: An Interdisciplinary History of Nineteenth Century America*. New York: Heath, 1987.

Baroody, John C. *The 1978 Excavation of the Cistern at the Thomas Wolfe Memorial: A Report*. Raleigh: Division of Archives and History, 1978.

Basch, Norma. *Framing American Divorce: From the Founding Generation to the Victorians*. Berkeley: University of California Press, 1999.

————. "Relief in the Premises: Divorce as a Woman's Remedy in New York and Indiana." *Law and History Review* 8 (1990): 1–24.

Bassett, John Spencer. *Slavery in the State of North Carolina.* Baltimore: Johns Hopkins University Press, 1899.

Beckel, Deborah. "Roots of Reform: The Origins of Populism and Progressivism as Manifest in Relationships among Reformers in Raleigh, North Carolina, 1850–1905." Ph.D. diss., Emory University, 1998.

Beeby, James M. *Revolt of the Tar Heels: The North Carolina Populist Movement, 1892–1901.* Jackson: University Press of Mississippi, 2008.

Beitzell, Edwin W. *Point Lookout Prison Camp for Confederates.* Leonardtown, Md.: St. Mary's County Historical Society, 1983.

Bell, Richard J. "Do Not Despair: The Cultural Significance of Suicide in America, 1780–1840." Ph.D. diss., Harvard University, 2006.

Bender, Thomas. *Community and Social Change in America.* New Brunswick, N.J.: Rutgers University Press, 1978.

Bennett, William D. *Index of North Carolina Bankrupts: Acts of 1800, 1841, and 1867.* Raleigh: n.p., 1994.

Berlin, Ira, Steven F. Miller, and Leslie S. Rowland. "Afro-American Families in the Transition from Slavery to Freedom." *Radical History Review* 42 (1988): 89–121.

Bernstein, Leonard. "The Participation of Negro Delegates in the Constitutional Convention of 1868 in North Carolina." *Journal of Negro History* 34 (1949): 391–409.

Billings, Dwight B. *Planters and the Making of a "New South": Class, Politics, and Development in North Carolina, 1865–1900.* Chapel Hill: University of North Carolina Press, 1979.

Blassingame, John W. *The Slave Community: Plantation Life in the Antebellum South.* New York: Oxford University Press, 1972.

————. *Slave Testimony.* Baton Rouge: Louisiana State University Press, 1977.

Blythe, LeGette. *William Henry Belk: Merchant of the South.* Chapel Hill: University of North Carolina Press, 1958.

Bode, Frederick A. *Protestantism and the New South: North Carolina Baptists and Methodists in Political Crisis, 1894–1903.* Charlottesville: University of Virginia Press, 1975.

Bolton, Charles C. *Poor Whites of the Antebellum South: Tenants and Laborers in Central North Carolina and Northeast Mississippi.* Durham, N.C.: Duke University Press, 1994.

Boscarino, Joseph A. "Posttraumatic Stress Disorder and Mortality among U.S. Army Veterans 30 Years after Military Service." *Annals of Epidemiology* 16 (2006): 248–56.

Bradley, Bettina. "Surviving as a Widow in Nineteenth-Century Montreal." *Urban History Review* 17 (1989): 148–60.

Brandt, Dennis W. *Pathway to Hell: A Tragedy of the American Civil War.* Bethlehem, Pa.: Lehigh University Press, 2008.

Breen, T. H. *Tobacco Culture: The Mentality of the Great Tidewater Planters on the Eve of Revolution.* Princeton, N.J.: Princeton University Press, 1985.

Bromberg, Alan B. "'The Worst Muddle Ever Seen in N.C. Politics': The Farmers' Alliance, the Subtreasury, and Zeb Vance." *North Carolina Historical Review* 56 (1979): 19–40.

Broughton, Carrie. *Marriage and Death Notices in Raleigh Register and North Carolina State Gazette, 1856–1867.* Raleigh: State Library, 1950.

———. *Marriage and Death Notices in Raleigh Register, North Carolina State Gazette, Daily Sentinel, Raleigh Observer, and News and Observer, 1867–1887.* Raleigh: State Library, 1951.

———. *Marriage and Death Notices in Raleigh Register, North Carolina State Gazette, Daily Sentinel, Raleigh Observer, and News and Observer, 1888–1893.* Raleigh: State Library, 1952.

Brown, Vincent. "Spiritual Terror and Sacred Authority: The Power of Supernatural in Jamaican Slave Society." In *New Studies in the History of American Slavery,* edited by Edward E. Baptist and Stephanie M. H. Camp, 179–210. Athens: University of Georgia Press, 2006.

Bruce, Dickson D. "Sentimentalism and Honor in the Early American Republic: Revisiting the Kentucky Tragedy." *Mississippi Quarterly* 55 (2002): 185–208.

———. *Violence and Culture in the Antebellum South.* Austin: University of Texas Press, 1979.

Brundage, W. Fitzhugh. *Lynching in the New South: Georgia and Virginia, 1880–1930.* Urbana: University of Illinois Press, 1993.

Buckley, Thomas E. *The Great Catastrophe of My Life: Divorce in the Old Dominion.* Chapel Hill: University of North Carolina Press, 2002.

Burgess-Jackson, Keith. "The Legal Status of Suicide in Early America: A Comparison with the English Experience." *Wayne State Law Review* 29 (1982): 57–87.

Burton, Orville Vernon. *In My Father's House Are Many Mansions: Family and Community in Edgefield, South Carolina.* Chapel Hill: University of North Carolina Press, 1985.

Burton, Orville Vernon, and Robert McMath, eds. *Toward a New South? Studies in Post–Civil War Southern Communities.* Westport, Conn.: Greenwood Press, 1982.

Bynum, Victoria. "Reshaping the Bonds of Womanhood: Divorce in Reconstruction North Carolina." In *Divided Houses: Gender and the Civil War,* edited by Catherine Clinton and Nina Silber, 320–33. New York: Oxford University Press, 1992.

———. *Unruly Women: The Politics of Social and Sexual Control in the Old South.* Chapel Hill: University of North Carolina Press, 1992.

Cahow, Clark R. *People, Patients, and Politics: The History of the North Carolina Mental Hospitals, 1848–1960*. New York: Arno Press, 1980.

Campbell, John. "As 'A Kind of Freeman'?: Slaves' Market-Related Activities in the South Carolina Up Country." In *Cultivation and Culture: Labor and the Shape of Slave Life in the Americans*, edited by Ira Berlin and Philip D. Morgan, 243–74. Charlottesville: University of Virginia Press, 1993.

Camus, Albert. *The Myth of Sisyphus and Other Essays*. New York: Vintage, 1991.

Carter, Dan T. *When the War Was Over: The Failure of Self-Reconstruction in the South, 1865–1867*. Baton Rouge: Louisiana State University Press, 1985.

Cash, W. J. *The Mind of the South*. New York: Knopf, 1941.

Cecelski, David S. "Abraham H. Galloway: Wilmington's Lost Prophet and the Rise of Black Radicalism in the American South." In *Democracy Betrayed: The Wilmington Race Riot of 1898 and Its Legacy*, edited by David S. Cecelski and Timothy B. Tyson, 43–72. Chapel Hill: University of North Carolina Press, 1998.

Cecil-Fronsman, Bill. *Common Whites: Class and Culture in Antebellum North Carolina*. Lexington: University Press of Kentucky, 1992.

Censer, Jane Turner. *North Carolina Planters and Their Children, 1800–1860*. Baton Rouge: Louisiana State University Press, 1984.

———. *The Reconstruction of Southern Womanhood, 1865–1895*. Baton Rouge: Louisiana State University Press, 2003.

———. "'Smiling through Her Tears': Ante-Bellum Southern Women and Divorce." *Journal of American Legal History* 25 (1981): 24–47.

Chapman, Craig S. *More Terrible than Victory: North Carolina's Bloody Bethel Regiment, 1861–1865*. Washington, D.C.: Brassey's, 1998.

Chused, Richard H. *Private Acts in Public Spaces: A Social History of Divorce in the Formative Era of American Family Law*. Philadelphia: University of Pennsylvania Press, 1994.

Clark, Thomas D. *Pills, Petticoats, and Plows: The Southern Country Store*. Indianapolis: Bobbs-Merrill, 1944.

Click, Patricia C. *Time Full of Trial: The Roanoke Island Freedmen's Colony, 1862–1867*. Chapel Hill: University of North Carolina Press, 2001.

Clinton, Catherine. *The Plantation Mistress: Woman's World in the Old South*. New York: Pantheon Books, 1982.

———. "'Public Women' and Sexual Politics during the American Civil War." In *Battle Scars: Gender and Sexuality in the American Civil War*, edited by Catherine Clinton and Nina Silber, 61–77. New York: Oxford University Press, 2006.

Coclanis, Peter A. "What Made Booker Wash(ington)? The Wizard of Tuskegee in Economic Context." In *Booker T. Washington and Black Progress: Up From Slavery 100 Years Later*, edited by W. Fitzhugh Brundage, 81–106. Gainesville: University of Florida Press, 2003.

Coleman, Loren. *Suicide Clusters*. Boston: Faber and Faber, 1987.

Coleman, Penny. *Flashback: Posttraumatic Stress Disorder, Suicide, and the Lessons of War*. Boston: Beacon Press, 2006.

Coleman, Peter J. *Debtors and Creditors in America: Insolvency, Imprisonment for Debt, and Bankruptcy, 1607–1900*. Madison: State Historical Society of Wisconsin, 1974.

Coontz, Stephanie. *Marriage, a History*. New York: Viking, 2005.

Corbitt, David Leroy. *The Formation of North Carolina Counties, 1663–1943*. Raleigh: North Carolina Department of Archives, 1969.

Cott, Nancy F. *Public Vows: A History of Marriage and the Nation*. Cambridge, Mass.: Harvard University Press, 2000.

Courtwright, David. "The Hidden Epidemic: Opiate Addiction and Cocaine Use in the South, 1860–1920." *Journal of Southern History* 49 (1983): 57–72.

Crouch, Barry A. "The 'Chords of Love': Legalizing Black Marital and Family Right in Postwar Texas." *Journal of Negro History* 79 (1994): 334–51.

Crow, Jeffrey J., and Robert F. Durden. *Maverick Republican in the Old North State: A Political Biography of Daniel L. Russell*. Baton Rouge: Louisiana State University Press, 1977.

Daniel, Pete. *The Shadow of Slavery: Peonage in the South, 1901–1969*. Urbana: University of Illinois Press, 1972.

Dean, Eric T. *Shook over Hell: Post-Traumatic Stress, Vietnam, and the Civil War*. Cambridge, Mass.: Harvard University Press, 1997.

Donald, David Herbert. *Look Homeward: A Life of Thomas Wolfe*. Boston: Little, Brown, 1987.

Dublin, Louis I., and Bessie Bunzel. *To Be or Not to Be: A Study of Suicide*. New York: Harrison Smith, 1933.

Dunaway, Wilma A. *The African-American Family in Slavery and Emancipation*. Cambridge: Cambridge University Press, 2003.

Durkheim, Émile. *Rules of Sociological Method*. New York: Free Press, 1982.

———. *Suicide: A Study in Sociology*. Translated by John A. Spaulding and George Simpson. New York: Free Press, 1951.

Durrill, Wayne K. "Slavery, Kinship, and Dominance: The Black Community at Somerset Place Plantation, 1786–1860." *Slavery and Abolition* 13 (1992): 1–19.

Early, Kevin E. *Religion and Suicide in the African-American Community*. Westport, Conn.: Greenwood Press, 1992.

Edmonds, Helen G. *The Negro and Fusion Politics in North Carolina, 1894–1901*. Chapel Hill: University of North Carolina Press, 1951.

Edwards, Laura F. *Gendered Strife and Confusion: The Political Culture of Reconstruction*. Urbana: University of Illinois Press, 1997.

———. "Law, Domestic Violence, and the Limits of Patriarchal Authority in the Antebellum South." *Journal of Southern History* 65 (1999): 733–70.

———. "'The Marriage Covenant Is at the Foundation of All Our Rights': The

Politics of Slave Marriages in North Carolina after Emancipation." *Law and History Review* 14 (1996): 81–124.

———. *The People and Their Peace: Legal Culture and the Transformation of Inequality in the Post-Revolutionary South*. Chapel Hill: University of North Carolina Press, 2009.

———. "Status without Rights: African Americans and the Tangled History of Law and Governance in the Nineteenth-Century U.S. South." *American Historical Review* 112 (2007): 365–93.

Elliott, Mark. *Color-Blind Justice: Albion Tourgée and the Quest for Racial Equality from the Civil War to Plessy v. Ferguson*. New York: Oxford University Press, 2006.

Erikson, Kai. *Wayward Puritans: A Study of the Sociology of Deviance*. New York: Macmillan, 1966.

Escott, Paul D. *Many Excellent People: Power and Privilege in North Carolina, 1850–1900*. Chapel Hill: University of North Carolina Press, 1985.

———. *North Carolina Yeoman: The Diary of Basil Armstrong Thomasson, 1853–1862*. Athens: University of Georgia Press, 1996.

———. "Poverty and Governmental Aid for the Poor in Confederate North Carolina." *North Carolina Historical Review* 61 (1984): 462–80.

———. *Slavery Remembered: A Record of Twentieth-Century Slave Narratives*. Chapel Hill: University of North Carolina Press, 1979.

———. "Yeoman Independence and the Market: Social Status and Economic Development in Antebellum North Carolina." *North Carolina Historical Review* 61 (1989): 275–300.

Evans, Glen, and Norman L. Farberow, eds. *Encyclopedia of Suicide*. New York: Facts on File, 2003.

Evans, William M. *Ballots and Fence Rails: Reconstruction on the Lower Cape Fear*. Chapel Hill: University of North Carolina Press, 1967.

Farberow, Norman L., et al. "Combat Experience and Postservice Psychosocial Status as Predictors of Suicide in Vietnam Veterans." *Journal of Nervous and Mental Disease* 178 (1980): 32–37.

Faust, Drew Gilpin. *Mothers of Invention: Women of the Slaveholding South in the American Civil War*. Chapel Hill: University of North Carolina Press, 1996.

———. *This Republic of Suffering: Death and the American Civil War*. New York: Knopf, 2008.

Fiala, Irene Jung. "The Medicolegal Officer and the Social Production of Public Health Statistics." Ph.D. diss., Kent State University, 2003.

Fogel, Robert, and Stanley Engerman. *Time on the Cross: The Economics of American Negro Slavery*. Boston: Little, Brown, 1974.

Foner, Eric. *Nothing but Freedom: Emancipation and Its Legacy*. Baton Rouge: Louisiana State University, 1983.

———. *Reconstruction: American's Unfinished Revolution, 1863–1877*. New York: Harper and Row, 1988.

Forret, Jeff. "Conflict and the 'Slave Community': Violence among Slaves in Upcountry South Carolina." *Journal of Southern History* 74 (2008): 551–88.

———. *Race Relations at the Margins: Slaves and Poor Whites in the Antebellum Southern Countryside*. Baton Rouge: Louisiana State University Press, 2006.

Foster, Gaines M. "Bishop Cheshire and Black Participation in the Episcopal Church: Limitations of Religious Paternalism." *North Carolina Historical Review* 54 (1977): 49–65.

———. "Coming to Terms with Defeat: Post-Vietnam America and the Post–Civil War South." *Virginia Quarterly Review* 66 (1990): 17–35.

———. "Gentleman Prophet: Joseph Blount Cheshire, Jr." M.A. thesis, University of North Carolina, 1973.

———. *Ghosts of the Confederacy: Defeat, the Lost Cause, and the Emergence of the New South, 1865 to 1913*. New York: Oxford University Press, 1987.

Fox-Genovese, Elizabeth. *Within the Plantation Household: Black and White Women of the Old South*. Chapel Hill: University of North Carolina Press, 1988.

Frankel, Noralee. *Freedom's Women: Black Women and Families in Civil War Era Mississippi*. Bloomington: Indiana University Press, 1999.

Franklin, John Hope. *The Free Negro in North Carolina, 1790–1860*. Chapel Hill: University of North Carolina Press, 1943.

———. *The Militant South, 1800–1861*. Cambridge, Mass.: Harvard University Press, 1956.

Franklin, Vincent P. "Slavery, Personality, and Black Culture—Some Theoretical Issues." *Phylon* 35 (1974): 54–63.

Fraser, Rebecca J. *Courtship and Love among the Enslaved in North Carolina*. Jackson: University of Mississippi Press, 2007.

Frey, Sylvia R., and Betty Wood, *Come Shouting to Zion: African American Protestantism in the American South and British Caribbean to 1830*. Chapel Hill: University of North Carolina Press, 1998.

Friedman, Jean E. *The Enclosed Garden: Women and Community in the Evangelical South, 1830–1900*. Chapel Hill: University of North Carolina Press, 1985.

Friedman, Milton. "The Crime of 1873." *Journal of Political Economy* 98 (1990): 1159–94.

Gamber, Wendy. "Away from Home: Middle-Class Boarders in the Nineteenth-Century City." *Journal of Urban History* 31 (2005): 289–305.

———. *The Boardinghouse in Nineteenth-Century America*. Baltimore: Johns Hopkins University Press, 2007.

Genovese, Eugene. *From Rebellion to Revolution: Afro-American Slave Revolts in the Making of the Modern World*. Baton Rouge: Louisiana State University Press, 1979.

———. *The Political Economy of Slavery*. Middletown, Conn.: Wesleyan University Press, 1988.

———. *Roll, Jordan, Roll: The World the Slaves Made*. New York: Pantheon Books, 1974.

Getz, Lynne M. "'A Strong Man of Large Human Sympathy': Dr. Patrick L. Murphy and the Challenges of Nineteenth-Century Asylum Psychiatry in North Carolina." *North Carolina Historical Review* 86 (2009): 32–58.

Glatthaar, Joseph T. *Forged in Battle: The Civil War Alliance of Black Soldiers and White Officers*. New York: Free Press, 1990.

Godfrey, John Munro. "Monetary Expansion in the Confederacy." Ph.D. diss., University of Georgia, 1976.

Goeschel, Christian. *Suicide in Nazi Germany*. Oxford: Oxford University Press, 2009.

Goldin, Claudia. "The Economic Status of Women in the Early Republic: A Quantitative Evidence." *Journal of Interdisciplinary History* 16 (1986): 375–404.

Gomez, Michael A. *Exchanging Our Country Marks: The Transformation of African Identities in the Colonial and Antebellum South*. Chapel Hill: University of North Carolina Press, 1998.

Goodman, Paul. "The Emergence of Homestead Exemption in the United States: Accommodation and Resistance to the Market Revolution, 1840–1880." *Journal of American History* 80 (1993): 470–98.

Goodwyn, Lawrence. *Democratic Promise: The Populist Moment in America*. New York: Oxford University Press, 1976.

Gorn, Elliot. "'Gouge and Bite, Pull Hair and Scratch': The Social Significance of Fighting in the Southern Backcountry." *American Historical Review* 95 (1990): 57–74.

Gould, M. S., S. Wallenstein, and L. Davidson. "Suicide Clusters: A Critical Review." *Suicide and Life Threatening Behavior* 19 (1989): 17–29.

Govan, Thomas. "Banking and the Credit System in Georgia, 1810–1860." *Journal of Southern History* 4. no. 2 (1935): 164–84.

Grantham, Rose L., and Carol Haywood. *Marriage and Death Notices from the Mecklenburg Jeffersonian, 1841-1849*. Charlotte: Public Library of Charlotte and Mecklenburg County, 1966.

Greenberg, Kenneth S. *Honor and Slavery*. Princeton, N.J.: Princeton University Press, 1996.

Greene, A. Wilson. *Civil War Petersburg: Confederate City in the Crucible of War*. Charlottesville: University of Virginia Press, 2006.

Griffin, Rebecca J. "'Goin' Back Over There to See That Girl': Competing Social Spaces in the Lives of the Enslaved in Antebellum North Carolina." *Slavery and Abolition* 25 (2004): 94–113.

Grob, Gerald N. *Mental Institutions in America: Social Policy to 1875*. New York: Free Press, 1973.

Gross, Ariela J. *Double Character: Slavery and Mastery in the Antebellum Southern Courtroom*. Princeton, N.J.: Princeton University Press, 2000.

Gross, Jennifer Lynn. "'And for the Widow and Orphan': Confederate Widows, Poverty, and Public Assistance." In *Inside the Confederate Nation: Essays in Honor of Emory M. Thomas*, edited by Lesley J. Gordon and John C. Inscoe, 209–29. Baton Rouge: Louisiana State University Press, 2005.

Guice, John D. W., ed. *By His Own Hand? The Mysterious Death of Meriwether Lewis*. Norman: University of Oklahoma Press, 2007.

Gutman, Herbert G. *The Black Family in Slavery and Freedom, 1750–1925*. New York: Vintage Books, 1976.

Hackney, Sheldon. "Southern Violence." *American Historical Review* 74 (February 1969): 906–25.

Hahn, Steven. *A Nation under Our Feet: Black Political Struggles in the Rural South from Slavery to the Great Migration*. Cambridge, Mass.: Belknap Press, 2003.

———. *The Roots of Southern Populism: Yeoman Farmers and the Transformation of the Georgia Upcountry, 1850–1890*. New York: Oxford University Press, 1983.

Hahn, Steven, Steven F. Miller, Susan E. O'Donovan, John C. Rodrigue, and Leslie Rowland, eds. *Freedom: A Documentary History of Emancipation, 1861–1867*, ser. 3, vol. 1: *Land and Labor, 1865*. Chapel Hill: University of North Carolina Press, 2008.

Hall, Jacquelyn, James Leloudis, Robert Korstad, Mary Murphy, Christopher B. Daly, and Lu Ann Jones. *Like a Family: The Making of a Southern Cotton Mill World*. Chapel Hill: University of North Carolina Press, 1987.

Haller, John S. "The Physician versus the Negro: Medical and Anthropological Concepts of Race in the Late Nineteenth Century." *Bulletin of the History of Medicine* 44 (1970): 154–67.

Hamilton, J. G. de Roulhac. *Reconstruction in North Carolina*. New York: Columbia University Press, 1914.

Harper, Matthew J. "The Ballot or the Bottle: Temperance, Black Manliness, and the Struggle for Citizenship in North Carolina, 1881–1901." M.A. thesis, University of North Carolina at Chapel Hill, 2003.

Hendricks, J. Edwin. *Seeking Liberty and Justice: A History of the North Carolina Bar Association*. Raleigh: North Carolina Bar Association, 1999.

Herring, Harriet L. *Welfare Work in Mill Villages: The Story of Extra-Mill Activities in North Carolina*. Chapel Hill: University of North Carolina Press, 1929.

Herskovits, Melville J. *The Myth of the Negro Past*. Boston: Beacon Press, 1958.

Hess, Earl J. *The Union Soldier in Battle: Enduring the Ordeal of Combat*. Lawrence: University of Kansas Press, 1997.

Heyrman, Christine. *Southern Cross: The Beginnings of the Bible Belt*. Chapel Hill: University of North Carolina Press, 1998.

Hicks, John D. *The Populist Revolt: A History of the Farmers' Alliance and the People's Party*. Minneapolis: University of Minnesota Press, 1931.

———. "The Sub-Treasury Plan: A Forgotten Plan for the Relief of Agriculture." *Mississippi Valley Historical Review* 15 (1928): 355–73.

Hofstadter, Richard. *The Age of Reform, from Bryan to F.D.R.* New York: Random House, 1955.

Holt, Sharon A. *Making Freedom Pay: North Carolina Freedpeople Working for Themselves, 1865–1900*. Athens: University of Georgia Press, 2003.

Holt, Thomas. *Black over White: Negro Political Leadership in South Carolina during Reconstruction*. Urbana: University of Illinois Press, 1977.

Hudson, Kenneth. *Pawnbroking: An Aspect of British Social History*. London: Bodley Head, 1982.

Hudson, Larry E. *To Have and to Hold: Slave Work and Family Life in Antebellum South Carolina*. Athens: University of Georgia Press, 1997.

Hughes, John S. "Labeling and Treating Black Mental Illness in Alabama, 1861–1910." *Journal of Southern History* 58 (1992): 435–60.

Hunt, James L. *Marion Butler and American Populism*. Chapel Hill: University of North Carolina Press, 2003.

Hyde, Lewis. *The Gift*. New York: Random House, 1983.

Hyde, Samuel C. "Plain Folk Yeomanry in the Antebellum South." In *A Companion to the American South*, edited by John B. Boles, 139–55. Malden, Mass.: Blackwell, 2002.

Inscoe, John C., and Gordon B. McKinney. *The Heart of Confederate Appalachia: Western North Carolina in the Civil War*. Chapel Hill: University of North Carolina Press, 2000.

Jenkins, Richard Anthony. "Rhetorics of Discontent: A Comparison of Woman's Christian Temperance Union and Farmers' Movement Speeches with European American and African American Baptist and Methodist Sermons in North Carolina, 1880–1900." Ph.D. diss., Duke University, 1995.

Jobes, David Alan. "Medicolegal Certification of Suicide: An Investigation of Expert Determination Criteria and Construction of Empirical Criteria." Ph.D. diss., American University, 1988.

Johnson, Guion Griffis. *Ante-Bellum North Carolina: A Social History*. Chapel Hill: University of North Carolina Press, 1937.

Johnson, Michael P., and James L. Roark. "Strategies of Survival: Free Negro Families and the Problem of Slavery." In *In Joy and in Sorrow: Women, Family, and Marriage in the Victorian South, 1830–1900*, edited by Carol Bleser, 88–102. New York: Oxford University Press, 1991.

Johnson, Walter. *Soul by Soul: Inside an Antebellum Slave Market*. Cambridge, Mass.: Harvard University Press, 1999.

Kay, Marvin L. Michael, and Lorin Lee Cary. *Slavery in North Carolina, 1784–1775*. Chapel Hill: University of North Carolina Press, 1995.

Kennedy, Cynthia M. *Braided Relations, Entwined Lives: The Women of Charleston's Urban Slave Society*. Bloomington: Indiana University Press, 2005.

Kenzer, Robert C. *Enterprising Southerners: Black Economic Success in North Carolina, 1865–1915*. Charlottesville: University of Virginia Press, 1989.

———. *Kinship and Neighborhood in a Southern Community: Orange County, North Carolina, 1849–1881*. Knoxville: University of Tennessee Press, 1987.

———. "The Uncertainty of Life: A Profile of Virginia's Civil War Widows." In *The War Was You and Me*, edited by Joan Cashin, 112–35. Princeton, N.J.: Princeton University Press, 2002.

Kilbourne, Richard H. *Debt, Investment, Slaves: Credit Relations in East Feliciana Parish, Louisiana, 1825–1885*. Tuscaloosa: University of Alabama Press, 1995.

Kilbride, Daniel. "Southern Medical Students in Philadelphia, 1800–1861: Science and Sociability in the 'Republic of Medicine.'" *Journal of Southern History* 65 (1999): 697–732.

Klotter, James C. *Kentucky Justice, Southern Honor, and American Manhood: Understanding the Life and Death of Richard Reid*. Baton Rouge: Louisiana State University Press, 2003.

Kushner, Howard I. "American Psychiatry and the Cause of Suicide, 1844–1917." *Bulletin of the History of Medicine* 60 (1986): 36–57.

———. *Self-Destruction in the Promised Land: A Psychocultural Biology of American Suicide*. New Brunswick, N.J.: Rutgers University Press, 1989.

———. "Suicide, Gender, and the Fear of Modernity in Nineteenth Century Medical and Social Thought." *Journal of Social History* 26 (1993): 461–90.

Kyriakoudes, Louis M. "Lower-Order Urbanization and Territorial Monopoly in the Southern Furnishing Trade: Alabama, 1871–1890." *Social Science History* 26 (2002): 179–98.

Labinjoh, Justin. "The Sexual Life of the Oppressed: An Examination of the Family Life of Ante-Bellum Slave." *Phylon* 35 (1974): 375–97.

Lamb, Elizabeth. *Historical Sketch of Hay St. Methodist Episcopal Church, South*. Fayetteville, N.C.: n.p., 1934.

Lane, Ann J. *The Debate over Slavery: Stanley Elkins and His Critics*. Urbana: University of Illinois Press, 1971.

Lane, Roger. *Violent Death in the City: Suicide, Accident, and Murder in Nineteenth-Century Philadelphia*. Columbus: Ohio State University Press, 1999.

Langone, John. "The War That Has No Ending." *Discover* 6 (1985): 44–47.

Latta, Madeline Hall. History *of the Little River Presbyterian Church*. N.p.: n.p., 1942.

Lebsock, Suzanne. *The Free Women of Petersburg: Status and Culture in a Southern Town, 1784–1860*. New York: Norton, 1985.

Lefler, Hugh Talmage. *History of North Carolina*. New York: Lewis Publishing Co., 1956.

———. *North Carolina History Told by Contemporaries*. Chapel Hill: University of North Carolina Press, 1965.

Lefler, Hugh Talmage, and Albert Ray Newsome. *North Carolina: The History of a Southern State*. Chapel Hill: University of North Carolina Press, 1954.

Lerner, Eugene M. "Money, Prices, and Wages in the Confederacy, 1861–1865." In *The Economic Impact of the American Civil War*, edited by Ralph Andreano, 11–40. Cambridge, Mass.: Shenkman Publishing, 1962.

———. "Money, Prices, and Wages in the Confederacy, 1861–1865." Ph.D. diss., University of Chicago, 1954.

Lester, David, ed. *Émile Durkheim: Le Suicide, 100 Years Later*. Philadelphia: Charles Press, 1994.

Litwack, Leon. *Been in the Storm So Long: The Aftermath of Slavery*. New York: Knopf, 1979.

———. *Trouble in Mind: Black Southerners in the Age of Jim Crow*. New York: Vintage, 1998.

Lockley, Timothy J. "Trading Encounters between Non-Elite Whites and African-Americans in Savannah, 1790–1860." *Journal of Southern History* 66 (2000): 47–76.

Logan, Frenise A. *The Negro in North Carolina, 1876–1894*. Chapel Hill: University of North Carolina Press, 1964.

Lowe, Richard G., and Randolph B. Campbell. *Planters and Plain Folk: Agriculture in Antebellum Texas*. Dallas: Southern Methodist University Press, 1987.

MacDonald, Michael, and Terence R. Murphy. *Sleepless Souls: Suicide in Early Modern England*. Oxford: Clarendon Press, 1990.

Mallard, Shirley Jones. *Death and Marriage Notices of the Hillsborough Recorder, 1820–1879*. Chapel Hill: n.p., 1997.

Manarin, Louis H., comp. *North Carolina Troops, 1861–1865: A Roster*. 17 vols. Raleigh: State Department of Archives and History, 1966–2003.

Mann, Bruce. *Republic of Debtors: Bankruptcy in the Age of American Independence*. Cambridge, Mass.: Harvard University Press, 2002.

Marlowe, David H. *Psychological and Psychosocial Consequences of Combat and Deployment*. Santa Monica, Calif.: Rand, 2001.

Massengill, Stephen E., and Robert M. Tompkins. *Death Notices for the Raleigh Farmer and Mechanic: November 8, 1877–June 24, 1885*. Raleigh: n.p., 1990.

———. *Death Notices for the Raleigh State Chronicle: September 15, 1883–June 30, 1893*. Raleigh: n.p., 1992.

Massey, Mary Elizabeth. *Ersatz in the Confederacy*. Columbia: University of South Carolina Press, 1952.

———. *Refugee Life in the Confederacy*. Baton Rouge: Louisiana State University Press, 1964.

Mathews, Barbara Allen. "'Forgive Us Our Debts': Bankruptcy and Insolvency in America, 1763–1841." Ph.D. diss., Brown University, 1994.

Mauss, Marcel. *The Gift*. New York: Norton, 1990.

May, Elaine Tyler. *Great Expectations: Marriage and Divorce in Post-Victorian America*. Chicago: University of Chicago Press, 1980.

McCandless, Peter. *Moonlight, Magnolias, Madness: Insanity in South Carolina from the Colonial Period to the Progressive Era*. Chapel Hill: University of North Carolina Press, 1996.

McCoy, Drew R. *The Elusive Republic: Political Economy in Jeffersonian America*. Chapel Hill: University of North Carolina Press, 1980.

McCulloch, Margaret Callender. "Founding the North Carolina Asylum for the Insane." *North Carolina Historical Review* 13 (1936) 185–201.

McCurry, Stephanie. *Masters of Small Worlds: Yeoman Households, Gender Relations, and the Political Culture of the Antebellum South Carolina Low Country*. New York: Oxford University Press, 1995.

McDaniel, George. *Stagville: Kin and Community*. Raleigh: North Carolina Division of Archives and History, 1977.

McDonald, Roderick A. "Independent Economic Production by Slaves on Antebellum Louisiana Sugar Plantations." In *Cultivation and Culture: Labor and the Shape of Slave Life in the Americas*, edited by Ira Berlin and Philip D. Morgan, 275–99. Charlottesville: University of Virginia Press, 1993.

McMath, Robert C., Jr. "Agrarian Protest at the Forks of the Creek: Three Subordinate Farmers' Alliances in North Carolina." *North Carolina Historical Review* 51 (1974): 41–63.

———. *Populist Vanguard: A History of the Southern Farmers' Alliance*. Chapel Hill: University of North Carolina Press, 1976.

McPherson, James. *Battle Cry of Freedom: The Civil War Era*. New York: Ballantine Books, 1988.

Mental Health Advisory Team (MHAT) V, Operation Iraqi Freedom, 2008.

Merrick, Jeffrey "Suicide in Paris, 1775." In *From Sin to Insanity: Suicide in Early Modern Europe*, edited by Jeffrey R. Watt, 158–74. Ithaca, N.Y.: Cornell University Press, 2004.

Minois, George. *History of Suicide: Voluntary Death in Western Culture*. Baltimore: Johns Hopkins University Press, 1999.

Mobley, Joe A. *James City: A Black Community in North Carolina, 1863–1900*. Raleigh: North Carolina Department of Cultural Resources, Division of Archives and History, 1981.

Mohr, Clarence. *On the Threshold of Freedom: Masters and Slaves in Civil War Georgia*. Athens: University of Georgia Press, 1986.

Morantz, Alison D. "There's No Place Like Home: Homestead Exemption and Judicial Constructions of Family in Nineteenth-Century America." *Law and History Review* 24 (2006): 245–69.

Morgan, Jennifer L. *Laboring Women: Reproduction and Gender in New World Slavery*. Philadelphia: University of Pennsylvania Press, 2004.

Morgan, Philip D. *Slave Counterpoint: Black Culture in the Eighteenth-Century*

Chesapeake and Lowcountry. Chapel Hill: University of North Carolina Press, 1998.

Morrissey, Susan K. *Suicide and the Body Politic in Imperial Russia.* Cambridge: Cambridge University Press, 2006.

Mullin, Michael. *Africa in America: Slave Acculturation and Resistance in the American South and the British Caribbean, 1736-1831.* Urbana: University of Illinois Press, 1992.

Munson, Barry. *Afro-American Death Notices from Eastern North Carolina Newspapers, 1860-1948.* Greenville, N.C.: n.p., 2002.

Nathans, Sydney. "The Quest for Progress: North Carolina, 1870-1920." In *The Way We Lived in North Carolina*, edited by Joe A. Mobley, 353-465. Chapel Hill: University of North Carolina Press, 2003.

Noblin, Stuart. *Leonidas LaFayette Polk: Agrarian Crusader.* Chapel Hill: University of North Carolina Press, 1949.

Norris, David A. "'For the Benefit of Our Gallant Volunteers': North Carolina's State Medical Department and Civilian Volunteer Efforts, 1861-1862," *North Carolina Historical Review* 75 (1998): 297-326.

Norwood, Hayden. *The Marble Man's Wife.* New York: Scribner's, 1947.

Oakes, James. "A Failure of Vision: The Collapse of the Freedman's Bureau's Courts." *Civil War History* 25(1979): 66-76.

Olsen, Otto H. *Carpetbagger's Crusade: The Life of Albion Winegar Tourgée.* Baltimore: Johns Hopkins University Press, 1965.

O'Neil, Patrick W. "Bosses and Broomsticks: Ritual and Authority in Antebellum Slave Weddings." *Journal of Southern History* 75 (2009): 29-48.

Ownby, Ted. *Subduing Satan: Religion, Recreation, and Manhood in the Rural South, 1865-1920.* Chapel Hill: University of North Carolina Press, 1990.

Painter, Nell Irwin. *Southern History across the Color Line.* Chapel Hill: University of North Carolina Press, 2002.

Palmer, Bruce. *"Man over Money": The Southern Populist Critique of American Capitalism.* Chapel Hill: University of North Carolina Press, 1980.

Paschal, George Washington. *History of North Carolina Baptists.* 2 vols. Raleigh: Edwards and Broughton, 1955.

Peña, Elizabeth S., and Jacqueline Denmon. "The Social Organization of a Boardinghouse: Archaeological Evidence from the Buffalo Waterfront." *Historical Archaeology* 34 (2000): 79-96.

Penningroth, Dylan C. "African American Divorce in Virginia and Washington, D.C., 1865-1930." *Journal of Family History* 33 (2008): 21-35.

———. *The Claims of Kinfolk: African American Property and Community in the Nineteenth-Century South.* Chapel Hill: University of North Carolina Press, 2003.

Pérez, Louis A., Jr. *To Die in Cuba: Suicide and Society.* Chapel Hill: University of North Carolina Press, 2005.

Phillips, David. "The Influence of Suggestion on Suicide: Substantive and Theoretical Implications of the Werther Effect." *American Sociological Review* 39 (1974): 340–54.

Pickering, W. S. F., and Geoffrey Walford, eds. *Durkheim's Suicide: A Century of Research and Debate*. London: Routledge, 2000.

Pierson, William D. "White Cannibals, Black Martyrs: Fear, Depression, and Religious Faith as Causes of Suicide among New Slaves." *Journal of Negro History* 62 (1977): 147–59.

Pizzaro, Judith, Roxane Cohen Silver, and JoAnn Prouse. "Physical and Mental Costs of Traumatic War Experience among Civil War Veterans." *Archives of General Psychiatry* 63 (2006): 193–200.

Pollack, Daniel A., et al. "Estimating the Number of Suicides among Vietnam Veterans." *American Journal of Psychiatry* 147 (1990): 772–76.

Pope, Ida Waller. "Violence as a Political Force in the Reconstruction South." Ph.D. diss., University of Southwestern Louisiana, 1982.

Postel, Charles. *The Populist Vision*. New York: Oxford University Press, 2007.

Powell, William S. *Dictionary of North Carolina Biography*. Chapel Hill: University of North Carolina Press, 1979.

———. *North Carolina through Four Centuries*. Chapel Hill: University of North Carolina Press, 1989.

Prather, H. Leon, Sr. "We Have Taken a City: A Centennial Essay." In *Democracy Betrayed: The Wilmington Race Riot of 1898 and Its Legacy*, edited by David S. Cecelski and Timothy B. Tyson, 15–41. Chapel Hill: University of North Carolina Press, 1998.

Prioli, Carmine Andrew. "The Indian 'Princess' and the Architect: Origin of a North Carolina Legend." *North Carolina Historical Review* 60 (July 1983): 283–303.

Rable, George C. *But There Was No Peace: The Role of Violence in the Politics of Reconstruction*. Athens: University of Georgia Press, 1984.

———. *Civil Wars: Women and the Crisis of Southern Nationalism*. Urbana: University of Illinois Press, 1989.

Raboteau, Albert J. *Slave Religion: The "Invisible Institution" in the Antebellum South*. New York: Oxford University Press, 1978.

Rachleff, Peter J. *Black Labor in the South: Richmond, Virginia, 1865–1890*. Philadelphia: Temple University Press, 1984.

Ransom, Roger L. *Conflict and Compromise: The Political Economy of Slavery, Emancipation, and the Civil War*. Cambridge: Cambridge University Press, 1989.

Ransom, Roger, and Richard Sutch. *One Kind of Freedom: The Economic Consequences of Emancipation*. Cambridge: Cambridge University Press, 2001.

Ready, Milton. *The Tar Heel State: A History of North Carolina*. Columbia: University of South Carolina Press, 2005.

Reed, John Shelton. "To Live—and Die—in Dixie: A Contribution to the Study of Southern Violence." *Political Science Quarterly* 86 (September 1971): 429–43.

Regosin, Elizabeth. *Freedom's Promise: Ex-Slave Families and Citizenship in the Age of Emancipation*. Charlottesville: University of Virginia Press, 2002.

Reid, Richard. "USCT Veterans in Post–Civil War North Carolina." In *Black Soldiers in Blue: African American Troops in the Civil War Era*, edited by John David Smith, 391–421. Chapel Hill: University of North Carolina Press, 2002.

Reidy, Joseph P. "Economic Consequences of the Civil War and Reconstruction," In *A Companion to the American South*, edited by John B. Boles, 303–17. Malden, Mass.: Blackwell, 2002.

———. "Obligation and Right: Patterns of Labor, Subsistence, and Exchange in the Cotton Belt of Georgia, 1790–1860." In *Cultivation and Culture: Labor and the Shaping of Slave Life in the Americas*, edited by Ira Berlin and Philip D. Morgan, 138–54. Charlottesville: University of Virginia Press, 1993.

Riley, Glenda. *Divorce: An American Tradition*. New York: Oxford University Press, 1991.

Roark, James L. *Masters without Slaves: Southern Planters in the Civil War and Reconstruction*. New York: Norton, 1977.

Roberts, Kevin. "Yoruba Family, Gender, and Kinship Roles in New World Slavery." In *The Yoruba Diaspora in the Atlantic World*, edited by Toyin Falola and Matt D. Childs, 248–59. Bloomington: Indiana University Press, 2004.

Roeber, A. G. "Authority, Law, and Custom: The Rituals of Court Day in Tidewater Virginia, 1720–1750." *William and Mary Quarterly* 37 (1980): 29–52.

Rose, Willie Lee. *Rehearsal for Reconstruction: The Port Royal Experiment*. London: Oxford University Press, 1964.

Sainsbury, P. "Validity and Reliability of Trends in Suicide Statistics." *World Heath Statistics Quarterly* 36 (1983): 339–48.

Sammons, Helen Moore. *Marriage and Death Notices from Wilmington, North Carolina Newspapers: 1860–1865*. Wilmington, N.C.: New Hanover County Public Library, 1987.

Sandage, Scott. *Born Losers: A History of Failure in America*. Cambridge, Mass.: Harvard University Press, 2005.

Savitt, Todd L. "The Education of Black Physicians at Shaw University, 1882–1918." In *Black Americans in North Carolina and the South*, edited by Jeffrey J. Crow and Flora J. Hatley, 160–88. Chapel Hill: University of North Carolina Press, 1984.

Schantz, Mark S. *Awaiting the Heavenly Country: The Civil War and America's Culture of Death*. Ithaca, N.Y.: Cornell University Press, 2008.

Schauinger, Joseph H. "William Gaston: Southern Statesman." *North Carolina Historical Review* 18 (1941): 99–132.

Schlotterbeck, John T. "The 'Social Economy' of an Upper South Community: Orange and Greene Counties, Virginia, 1815–1860." In *Class, Conflict, and*

Consensus: Antebellum Southern Community Studies, edited by Orville Vernon
  Burton and Robert C. McMath, 3–28. Westport, Conn.: Greenwood Press, 1982.
Schwab, John Christopher. *The Confederate States of America, 1861–1865: A
  Financial and Industrial History of the South during the Civil War*. New York:
  Scribner's, 1901.
Schwalm, Leslie A. *A Hard Fight for We: Women's Transition from Slavery to
  Freedom in South Carolina*. Urbana: University of Illinois Press, 1997.
Schwartzberg, Beverly. "'Lots of Them Did That': Desertion, Bigamy, and Marital
  Fluidity in Late-Nineteenth-Century America." *Journal of Social History* 37,
  no. 3 (2004): 573–600.
Schweikart, Larry. "Southern Banks and Economic Growth in the Antebellum
  Period: A Reassessment." *Journal of Southern History* 53 (1986): 589–610.
Shaffer, Donald R. "In the Shadow of the Old Constitution: Black Civil
  War Veterans and the Persistence of Slave Marriage Customs." In *Southern
  Families at War: Loyalty and Conflict in the Civil War South*, edited by Catherine
  Clinton, 59–75. Oxford: Oxford University Press, 2000.
Sharpe, Bill. *A New Geography of North Carolina*. Vols. 1–4. Raleigh: Sharpe
  Publishing, 1954–65.
Shay, Jonathan. *Odysseus in America: Combat Trauma and the Trials of
  Homecoming*. New York: Scribner, 2002.
Shellum, Brian G. *Black Cadet in a White Bastion: Charles Young at West Point*.
  Lincoln: University of Nebraska Press, 2006.
Sherman, Joan R. *The Black Bard of North Carolina: George Moses Horton and His
  Poetry*. Chapel Hill: University of North Carolina Press, 1997.
Shore, George Edward. "Church Discipline in Ten Baptist Churches in Wake
  County, North Carolina, 1850–1915." M.A. thesis, Southeastern Baptist
  Theological Seminary, 1955.
Sims, Anastasia. *The Power of Femininity in the New South: Women's Organizations
  and Politics in North Carolina 1880–1930*. Columbia: University of South
  Carolina Press, 1997.
Sitterson, J. Carlyle. "The William J. Manor Plantations: A Study in Ante-Bellum
  Absentee Ownership." *Journal of Southern History* 9 (1943): 59–74.
Sloane, David Charles. *The Last Great Necessity: Cemeteries in American History*.
  Baltimore: Johns Hopkins University Press, 1991.
Smith, Cortland Victor. "Church Organization as an Agency of Social Control:
  Church Discipline in North Carolina, 1800–1860." Ph.D. diss., University of
  North Carolina at Chapel Hill, 1966.
Smith, Margaret Suplee, and Emily Herring Wilson. *North Carolina Women:
  Making History*. Chapel Hill: University of North Carolina Press, 1999.
Snider, William D. *Light on the Hill: A History of the University of North Carolina
  at Chapel Hill*. Chapel Hill: University of North Carolina Press, 1992.

Snyder, Terri L. "What Historians Talk about When They Talk about Suicide: The View from Early Modern British North America." *History Compass* 5 (2007): 658–74.

Sobel, Mechal. *Trabelin' On: The Slave Journey to an Afro-Baptist Faith*. Westport, Conn.: Greenwood Press, 1979.

Spain, Rufus B. *At Ease in Zion: Social History of Southern Baptists, 1865–1900*. Nashville: Vanderbilt University Press, 1967.

St. Clair, Kenneth Edson. "Debtor Relief in North Carolina during Reconstruction." *North Carolina Historical Review* 18 (1941): 215–35.

Starnes, Richard D. "'A Conspicuous Example of What Is Termed the New South': Tourism and Urban Development in Asheville, North Carolina, 1880–1925." *North Carolina Historical Review* 80 (2003): 52–80.

————. "Is There a Balm in Gilead? Baptists and Reform in North Carolina." In *History and Hope in the Heart of Dixie: Scholarship, Activism and Wayne Flint in the Modern South*, edited by Gordon E. Harvey, Richard D. Starnes, and Glenn Feldman, 66–85. Tuscaloosa: University of Alabama Press, 2006.

Steelman, Lala Carr. *The North Carolina Farmers' Alliance: A Political History, 1887–1893*. Greenville, N.C.: East Carolina University Publications, 1985.

Stepto, Robert B. "'The Simple but Intensely Human Inner Life of Slavery': Storytelling, Fiction and the Revision of History in Charles W. Chesnutt's 'Uncle Julius Stories.'" In *History and Tradition in Afro-American Culture*, edited by Günter H. Lenz, 29–55. Frankfurt: Campus Verlag, 1984.

Stevenson, Brenda E. "Distress and Discord in Virginia Slave Families, 1830–1860." In *In Joy and in Sorrow: Women, Family, and Marriage in the Victorian South, 1830–1900*, edited by Carol Bleser, 103–24. New York: Oxford University Press, 1991.

————. *Life in Black and White: Family and Community in the Slave South*. New York: Oxford University Press, 1996.

Stowe, Steven M. *Doctoring the South: Southern Physicians and Everyday Medicine in the Mid-Nineteenth Century*. Chapel Hill: University of North Carolina Press, 2004.

————. *Intimacy and Power in the Old South: Ritual in the Lives of the Planters*. Baltimore: Johns Hopkins University Press, 1987.

Stroupe, Henry S. "'Cite Them Both to Attend the Next Church Conference': Social Control by North Carolina Baptist Churches, 1772–1908." *North Carolina Historical Review* 52 (1975): 156–70.

Sutker, Patricia B., et al. "Person and Situation Correlates of Post Traumatic Stress Disorder among POW Survivors." *Psychological Report* 66 (1990): 912–14.

Sword, Wiley. *Southern Invincibility: A History of the Confederate Heart*. New York: St. Martins, 1999.

Tanielian, Terri, and Lisa H. Jaycox. *Invisible Wounds of War: Psychological and*

Cognitive Injuries, Their Consequences, and Services to Assist Recovery. Santa Monica, Calif.: Rand, 2008.

Taylor, John Swann. "North Carolina's Attack on the Mental Health Problem." M.A. thesis, University of North Carolina, 1957.

Tebbutt, Melanie. *Making Ends Meet: Pawnbroking and Working-Class Credit.* Leicester, England: Leicester University Press, 1983.

Thomas, Emory M. *The Confederate State of Richmond: A Biography of the Capital.* Baton Rouge: Louisiana State University Press, 1998.

Thompson, Elizabeth Lee. *The Reconstruction of Southern Debtors: Bankruptcy after the Civil War.* Athens: University of Georgia Press, 2004.

Thornton, J. Mills. *Politics and Power in a Slave Society: Alabama, 1800–1860.* Baton Rouge: Louisiana State University Press, 1978.

Thornton, John. *Africa and Africans in the Making of the Atlantic World, 1400–1680.* New York: Cambridge University Press, 1992.

Thornton, Mark, and Robert B. Ekelund. *Tariffs, Blockades, and Inflation: The Economics of the Civil War.* Wilmington, Del.: Scholarly Resources, 2004.

Thurtell, Craig Martin. "The Fusion Insurgency in North Carolina: Origins to Ascendancy, 1876–1896." Ph.D. diss., Columbia University, 1998.

Timmermans, Stefan. "Suicide Determination and the Professional Authority of Medical Examiners." *American Sociological Review* 70 (2005): 311–33.

Tomes, Nancy. "The Great Restraint Controversy: A Comparative Perspective on Anglo-American Psychiatry in the Nineteenth Century." In *The Anatomy of Madness: Essays in the History of Psychiatry*, edited by W. F. Bynum, Roy Porter, and Michael Shepherd, 190–225. London: Routledge, 1988.

Tompkins, Robert M. *Death Notices from the People's Press (Salem, North Carolina), 1851–1892.* Winston-Salem: Forsyth County Genealogical Society, 1997.

———. *Marriage and Death Notices from Extant Asheville, NC Newspapers, 1840–1870.* Raleigh: North Carolina Genealogical Society, 1977.

Trelease, Allen W. "The Fusion Legislatures of 1895 and 1897: A Roll-Call Analysis of the North Carolina House of Representatives." *North Carolina Historical Review* 57 (1980): 280–309.

Tyner, Bessie Hubbard. *Fayetteville Observer (NC) Marriage and Death Abstracts, 1841–1850.* Fuquay-Varina, N.C.: n.p., 1997.

Uzzell, Odell. "Free Negro/Slave Marriages and Family Life in Ante-Bellum North Carolina." *Western Journal of Black Studies* 18 (1994): 64–69.

Vandal, Gilles. *Rethinking Southern Violence: Homicides in Post–Civil War Louisiana, 1866–1884.* Columbus: Ohio State University Press, 2000.

Vinovskis, Maris A. "Have Social Historians Lost the Civil War? Some Preliminary Demographic Speculations." In *Toward a Social History of the American Civil War*, edited by Maris A. Vinovskis, 1–30. Cambridge: Cambridge University Press, 1990.

Wake Forest College. *North Carolina Obituary Records Taken from the Biblical Recorder, 1835–1877.* Salt Lake City: Genealogical Society of Utah, 1938.

———. *North Carolina Obituary Records Taken from the Biblical Recorder, 1877–1893.* Salt Lake City: Genealogical Society of Utah, 1940.

Waldrep, Christopher, and Donald G. Neiman, eds. *Local Matters: Race, Crime, and Justice in the Nineteenth Century South.* Athens: University of Georgia Press, 2001.

Warren, Robert Penn. *The Legacy of the Civil War: Meditations on the Centennial.* New York: Random House, 1961.

Wasserman, Ira M. "Imitation and Suicide: A Re-examination of the Werther Effect." *American Sociological Review* 49 (1984): 427–36.

Wasserman, Ira M., Steven Stack, and Jimmie L. Reeves. "Suicide and the Media: The *New York Times*'s Presentation of Front-Page Suicide Stories between 1910 and 1920." *Journal of Communication* 44 (1994): 64–83.

Watson, Alan D. "Women in Colonial North Carolina." *North Carolina History Review* 58 (1981): 1–22.

Watson, Harry L. *Jacksonian Politics and Community Conflict: The Emergence of the Second American Party System in Cumberland County, North Carolina.* Baton Rouge: Louisiana State University Press, 1981.

Watt, Jeffrey R. *Choosing Death: Suicide and Calvinism in Early Modern Geneva.* Kirksville, Mo.: Truman State University Press, 2001.

Weaver, John C. *A Sadly Troubled History: The Meanings of Suicide in the Modern Age.* Montreal: McGill-Queen's University Press, 2009.

Wegner, Ashley Herring. *Phantom Pain: North Carolina's Artificial-Limbs Program for Confederate Veterans.* Raleigh: Office of Archives and History, 2004.

West, Emily. *Chains of Love: Slave Couples in Antebellum South Carolina.* Urbana: University of Illinois Press, 2004.

———. "Surviving Separation: Cross-Plantation Marriages and the Slave Trade in Antebellum South Carolina." *Journal of Family History* 24 (1999): 212–31.

Wheeler, Edward Lorenzo. *Uplifting the Race: The Black Minister in the New South, 1865–1902.* Lanham, Md.: University Press of America, 1986.

White, Barnetta McGhee. *Somebody Knows My Name: Marriages of Freed People in North Carolina, County by County.* 3 vols. Athens, Ga.: Iberian Publishing, 1995.

White, Deborah Gray. *Ar'n't I a Woman: Female Slaves in the Plantation South.* New York: Norton, 1985.

White, Newman Ivey, ed. *North Carolina Folklore.* 7 vols. Durham, N.C.: Duke University Press, 1964.

Whites, LeeAnn. *The Civil War as a Crisis in Gender: Augusta, Georgia, 1860–1890.* Athens: University of Georgia, 1995.

Wiebe, Robert H. *The Search for Order, 1877–1920.* New York: Hill and Wang, 1967.

Wiener, Jonathan M. *Social Origins of the New South: Alabama, 1860–1885*. Baton Rouge: Louisiana State University Press, 1978.

Wiley, Bell Irvin. *The Life of Johnny Reb: The Common Soldier of the Confederacy*. Baton Rouge: Louisiana State University Press, 1943.

———. *Southern Negroes, 1861–1865*. Baton Rouge: Louisiana State University Press, 1974.

Wills, Gary A. *Democratic Religion: Freedom, Authority, and Church Discipline in the Baptist South, 1785–1900*. New York: Oxford University Press, 1997.

Wilson, Charles Reagan. *Baptized in Blood: The Religion of the Lost Cause, 1865–1920*. Athens: University of Georgia Press, 1983.

Wires, Richard. *The Divorce Issue and Reform in Nineteenth-Century Indiana*. Muncie, Ind.: Ball State University, 1967.

Woloson, Wendy A. "In Hock: Pawning in Early America." *Journal of the Early Republic* 27 (2007): 35–81.

Wood, Kristen E. *Masterful Women: Slaveholding Widows from the American Revolution through the Civil War*. Chapel Hill: University of North Carolina Press, 2004.

Wood, Peter H. *Black Majority: Negroes in Colonial South Carolina from 1670 through the Stono Rebellion*. New York: Norton, 1974.

Woodman, Harold D. *New South—New Law: The Legal Foundations of Credit and Labor Relations in the Postbellum Agricultural South*. Baton Rouge: Louisiana State University Press, 1995.

Woodward, C. Vann. *Origins of the New South: 1877–1913*. Baton Rouge: Louisiana State University Press, 1951.

Wright, Gavin. *Old South, New South: Revolutions in the Southern Economy since the Civil War*. Baton Rouge: Louisiana State University Press, 1996.

———. *Political Economy of the Cotton South*. New York: Norton, 1978.

Wright, Mike. *City under Siege: Richmond in the Civil War*. Lanham, Md.: Madison Books, 1995.

Wyatt-Brown, Bertram. *Hearts of Darkness: Wellsprings of a Southern Literary Tradition*. Baton Rouge: Louisiana State University Press, 2003.

———. *Shaping of Southern Culture: Honor, Grace, and War: 1760s–1890s*. Chapel Hill: University of North Carolina Press, 2001.

———. *Southern Honor: Ethics and Behavior in the Old South*. New York: Oxford University Press, 1982.

Yandle, Paul. "Joseph Charles Price and His 'Particular Work.'" *North Carolina Historical Review* 70 (1993): 40–56, 130–52.

Zipf, Karin L. "No Longer under Cover(ture): Marriage, Divorce, and Gender in the 1868 Constitutional Convention." In *North Carolinians in the Era of the Civil War and Reconstruction*, edited by Paul Escott, 193–219. Chapel Hill: University of North Carolina Press, 2008.

———. "'The Whites Shall Rule the Land or Die': Gender, Race, and Class in

North Carolina Reconstruction Politics." *Journal of Southern History* 65 (1999): 499–534.

Zuber, Richard. *North Carolina during Reconstruction*. Raleigh: State Department of Archives and History, 1969.

Zwelling, Shomer S. *Quest for a Cure: The Public Hospital in Williamsburg, 1773–1885*. Williamsburg: Colonial Williamsburg Foundation, 1985.

Index

Alderman, Edwin A., 196
Alexander, John Brevard, 51, 217–18
Alexander, Lizzie, 35
Alston, Tony, 100–101
AME Zion Church, 119–21
Anderson, Jeannie, 36
Arrington, Pattie, 117
Avera, David, 32
Avery, Alphonso, 125
Avery, Isaac Erwin, 38–39
Aycock, Charles, 39, 129, 132–34

Ball, Charles, 17–20, 151
Barnes, Mariah, 165
Beard, Ida, 117, 184–85, 189, 197–200
Belk, William Henry, 181–82
Bender, Thomas, 219
Bennehan, Thomas, 143, 145–46
Benton, Thomas Hart, 155–56
Berlin, Ira, 97
Bertram, R. A., 26
Blanchard, Charles W., 128–29
"Blanket marriages," 90
Bodenhamer, Elizabeth, 60
Bolling, J. T., 36–37
Boone, Andrew, 101
Boone, Billy, 101
Bowling, Elizabeth, 103–4

Bowling, John, 103–4
Brady, James, 109
Brady, Nancy, 109
Brame, John Todd, 13
Briggs, Prudence, 81–82
Broad River Baptist Association, 89
Brown, Alfred, 60
Brown, H. T., 12–13
Brown, M. S., 65
Bryan, John A. Q., 108
Bullock, E. B., 124
Bullock, Jane, 124
Butler, Marion, 209, 212
Bynum, Victoria, 114

Calder, Phila, 188
Cameron, Duncan, 143, 145
Camus, Albert, 2
Candler, Thomas J., 171
Carr, Elias, 208
Carroll, Ashby, 31
Censer, Jane Turner, 191
Chapel of the Cross (Chapel Hill), 127
Cherry Hospital. See Eastern North
    Carolina Insane Asylum
Cheshire, William Blount, 126–35
Chesnutt, Charles W., 40–41
Clinton, George W., 119, 122–23, 129

Constitutional Convention of 1865, 45, 99

Constitutional Convention of 1868, 105–11, 169–72

Conway, T. J., 97

Cooke, Charles, 62

Cosgrove, Michael, 47

Couch, Emma, 103–4

Couch, Willie, 103–4

Cove Creek Baptist Church (Sherwood), 86

Coverture, doctrine of, 76

Cowles, Calvin J., 108

Cowles, David, 33

Cowles, William H. H., 33

Crow, William, 25–26, 37

Crummell, Alexander, 123

Curtis, Mattie, 98

Daniels, Josephus, 24, 63–64, 66, 135

Davis, George, 86

Davis, Sary, 86

Dean, Eric T., 55

Debt: Bankruptcy Act of 1841 and, 155–58; Bankruptcy Act of 1867 and, 166–69, 172; black, antebellum, 151–53; black, postbellum, 168–74; boardinghouses and, 186; Civil War's effect upon, 159–65; debt-slave metaphor, 141, 149, 174; general stores and, 173–82; gift economy and, 142–43, 173; homestead legislation and, 148, 208; inflation, Civil War, 159–62; Insolvent Debtor Law, 148; pawnshops and, 184–86; stay laws, 163–66; white, antebellum, 141–58; white, postbellum, 165–74

DeVisconti, Lorenzo, 71–73, 80, 116

Divorce: black, antebellum, free, 93–94; black, antebellum, slave, 86–93; black, postbellum, 119–25; Catholic views of, 72; Civil War's impact on, 95–111; freedmen, 96–101; Indiana laws concerning, 78; judicial, 77–78; legislative, 77; N.C. Supreme Court decisions on, 80–81, 116, 125–26; reform, 126–35; religious sanction of, 86, 89–90, 119–23; slaveowners' views on slave, 87–89; trials, length of, 116; uncontested, 79–81; white, antebellum, 75–86; white, postbellum, 113–18, 125–35

Dix, Dorothea, 42–43

Dobbin, James C., 43

Domler, John, 11, 37

Dorothea Dix Hospital. *See* North Carolina Insane Asylum

Douglass, Frederick, 17

DuBois, W. E. B., 183

Duke, Brodie Leonidas, 130–32

Duke, George J., 55–56

Dupree, Francis, 71, 73

Durrill, Wayne, 91

Eastern North Carolina Insane Asylum, 42, 49–51

Eaton, Thomas, 33

Edmundston, Catherine Ann Devereux, 159–60, 165

Einstein, Sig, 28

Ellis, John W., 43

Eno Presbyterian Church, 59–60

Ensley, Newell, 41

Farmers' Alliance, 206–12

Faucette, Jana, 60

Faust, Drew, 219

Faw, Enoch, 12

Finkelstein, Harry, 185–86

Fisher, Edward, 43–44

Flat River Primitive Baptist Church, 89

Foster, Gaines M., 54–55

Franklin, John Hope, 151

Frapps, A. W., 35

Seven Days, battles of, 7–8
Seybold, Margarette, 25
Shepard, Charlotte, 104–5
Shepard, Joseph, 104
Sinclair, James, 99, 101
Sirls, Temperance, 59
Smith, J. D. L., 65
Somerset Place Plantation, 91
Southerland, Fendal, 32
Spencer, Cornelia Phillips, 23–24, 196
Stagville Plantation, 91
Subtreasury plan, 207–8
Suicide: African beliefs about, 20; attempted, 34–35; black, postbellum, 39–41, 49–51; burial practices and, 13–14, 24, 27–28; causes of, 35–38; clusters, 59–61; contagious, 59; coroner's reports, 221–22; gender and, 31, 33; group, 19; medical treatment of, 42–51; methodological problems, 221–23; newspaper coverage of, 28–31; Post-Traumatic Stress Disorder (PTSD) and, 53–59; slave, 14–21; "suicide mania," 9, 28–38, 42; "Werther effect" and, 59; white, antebellum, 11–14; white, postbellum, 23–39
Sullivan, A. V., 37
Sutch, Richard, 200

Taxation, Confederate, 161
Teague, Jane, 60
Thomasson, Basil Armstrong, 148–51
Thompson, Alfred, 62
Thompson, Elizabeth Lee, 168
Thompson, Irvin, 124
Tourgée, Albion, 66–67, 107–8, 171–72
Trelease, Allen, 213
Trice, Martha, 82

Underdue, Ann, 110
Underdue, Gilliam, 110

University of North Carolina, 11, 12, 13, 24, 57, 143, 151
Uplift, doctrine of, 62

Vance, Zebulon Baird, 33, 66, 102, 162–63, 212
Venable, Francis, 24, 133, 194

Waller, N. A., 162
Warren, Edward, 8
Warren, George, 86
Warren, Robert Penn, 5
Washington, Booker T., 183
Wayne County, 78–79, 102
Webb, James, 143–47, 150–51, 154–57, 164, 173
Webb, James, Jr., 173
Wells, James, 95–96, 103
Wells, Nancy, 95–96, 103
Western North Carolina Insane Asylum, 42, 46–48
Wheeler, Woodbury, 13, 26
Whitaker, Johnson C., 41
Whitaker, R. H., 134
Whitaker, Spier, 62–64, 66, 211
White, George H., 180
Whitted, J. A., 122, 129
Whittlesey, Eliphalet, 99
Widows, Civil War, 186
Wiebe, Robert, 218
Wilhelm, William, 60
Wilkerson, John C., 60
Willcox, Walter F., 118
Williams, Mittie, 102
Wilson, DeWitt, 105–6
Wilson, Joseph, 47
Wilson, Nancy, 105
Winston, George, 24
Withers, Benjamin A., 55–56
Wolfe, Julia, 185, 189, 200–203
Wolfe, Thomas, 200–203
Wolfe, W. O., 201

ML   2/11